# A Guide to Documentary Editing

Second Edition

## Mary-Jo Kline

Prepared for the Association for Documentary Editing
Linda Johanson, Project Director

THE JOHNS HOPKINS UNIVERSITY PRESS

BALTIMORE AND LONDON

The Johns Hopkins University Press
2715 North Charles Street
Baltimore, Maryland 21218-4319
The Johns Hopkins Press Ltd., London

Library of Congress Cataloging-in-Publication Data

Kline, Mary-Jo.
   A guide to documentary editing / Mary-Jo Kline. — 2nd ed.
      p.   cm.
   "Prepared for the Association for Documentary Editing."
   Includes bibliographical references and index.
   ISBN 0-8018-5686-8 (acid-free paper)
   1. Manuscripts—Editing.   2. Manuscripts, American—Editing.
3. Criticism, Textual.   4. American literature—Criticism, Textual.
I. Association for Documentary Editing.   II. Title.
Z113.3.K55   1998
808'.027—dc21                                           97-26927
                                                           CIP

A catalog record for this book is available from the British Library.

# CONTENTS

FOREWORD                                                    xiii

PREFACE                                                    xvii

CHAPTER ONE **Introduction**     1

    I.   *Early American Documentary Editing*   3

   II.   *Statesmen's Papers and "Historical" Editing*   5

  III.   *Editing the Nation's Literature:*
       *The Americanization of Copy-Text*   7

   IV.   *The Evolution of Distinctive Methodologies*   10

   V.   *The 1950s: The Critical Reception of*
       *Historical Editing*   11

   VI.   *The 1960s and 1970s: Editing and Relevance*   12

  VII.   *The MLA and Private Writings*   15

 VIII.   *Interdisciplinary Evaluations Begin*   17

   IX.   *A Period of Reexamination*   20

   X.   *Computer Technology and the Next Chapter*
       *in Editing*   24

   XI.   *The Organization of This Book*   26

  Suggested Readings   27

CHAPTER TWO **Initiating an Editorial Project**     33

    I.   *The Editor's Control File*   34

   II.   *A Historical Note on Computerized Control Files*   35

  III.   *Automated Databases and Documentary Editions*   37

   IV.   *Collection of Sources*   38

A. Defining the Scope of the Search 41
   1. Manuscripts 41
   2. Printed Documents 44
   3. Dealers and Collectors 46
B. Collecting Photocopies: The Mail Canvass 48
C. On-Site Searches 51
D. A Word on Research Etiquette 53

V. *Cataloging and Control* 56
A. Accessioning Materials 57
B. Labeling and Arranging Folders 58
C. The Functions of the Control Files 60
D. Arrangement and Sorting of Control File Data 61

VI. *The Blessings of Computers* 62
A. Subject Indexes of Control Files 63

VII. *Conclusion* 65

Suggested Readings 65

CHAPTER THREE **Defining and Organizing a Documentary Edition** 70

I. *Scope* 71
A. Comprehensive and Selective Editions 72
B. Facsimile Editions and Supplements 75
C. Other Supplementary Forms 79
D. Cautions on Selectivity 80

II. *Organization of the Printed Edition* 84
A. Topical Arrangement 84
B. Cautions on Topical Groupings 86
C. Some Conventions of Documentary Organization 87
D. Diaries and Journals 89

III. *Electronic Aids* 90

Suggested Readings 91

CHAPTER FOUR **Evaluating and Transcribing the Source Text** 93

I. *Authentication and Attribution* 94
II. *Choosing the Source Text* 96

|  |  | A. | Handwritten or Typewritten Materials | 96 |
|  |  | 1. | Letters | 97 |
|  |  | 2. | Papers | 100 |
|  |  | B. | Printed Works | 100 |
|  | III. |  | *Transcribing the Source Text: Methods of Inscription* | 102 |
|  |  | A. | Handwritten Source Texts | 104 |
|  |  | B. | Typewritten Documents | 105 |
|  |  | C. | Printed Source Texts | 107 |
|  |  | D. | Nonverbal Documents | 108 |
|  |  | 1. | Maps | 110 |
|  |  | E. | Transcriptions of Unlocated Originals | 111 |
|  | IV. |  | *Source Texts and Translations* | 111 |
|  |  | A. | Foreign-Language Sources | 112 |
|  |  | 1. | Translations for a Documentary Edition | 113 |
|  |  | B. | Authorial Shorthand | 116 |
|  |  | C. | Codes and Ciphers | 118 |
|  |  | D. | Telegrams | 120 |
|  | V. |  | *Transcribing the Source Text: Types of Documentary Records* | 122 |
|  |  | A. | Correspondence | 122 |
|  |  | 1. | Source or Provenance Note Information | 124 |
|  |  | B. | Business and Financial Records | 125 |
|  |  | C. | Professional and Technical Records | 125 |
|  |  | D. | Government Records | 126 |
|  |  | E. | An Author's Works | 127 |
|  |  | F. | Journals and Diaries | 127 |
|  |  | G. | Records of Oral Communications | 129 |
|  |  | 1. | Sound Recordings | 131 |
|  |  | H. | Electronic Records | 132 |
|  | VI. |  | *Conclusion* | 133 |
|  |  |  | Suggested Readings | 133 |
| CHAPTER FIVE |  |  | **The Conventions of Textual Treatment** | 136 |
|  | I. |  | *The Bases of Scholarly Editing: Standardizing, Recording, and Emending* | 139 |

II.  *Photographic and Typographic Facsimiles*                       141

III. *Editorial Texts Requiring Symbols or*
     *Textual Annotation*                                            144
     A.  Textual Symbols                                             144
         1.  Passages Deleted by the Author                          148
         2.  Unrecoverable Gaps in the Source Text                   148
         3.  Additions to the Original Inscription                   149
         4.  Underlining in the Source Text                          149
         5.  Authorial Symbols                                       149
         6.  Line Breaks in the Source Text                          151
         7.  Editorial Supply                                        151
         8.  Editorial Expansion of Abbreviations
             or Contractions                                         151
         9.  Editorial Omissions                                     151
         10. Alternative Readings                                    151
         11. Editorial Interpolations                                151
     B.  Some Rules for Using Editorial Symbols                      152
     C.  Descriptive Textual Notes                                   153

IV.  *Diplomatic Transcriptions*                                     155

V.   *The Middle Ground: Inclusive Texts and*
     *Expanded Transcriptions*                                       157
     A.  Inclusive Texts                                             158
     B.  Expanded Transcription                                      161
     C.  Textual Record                                              164

VI.  *Clear Text*                                                    166
     A.  Textual Records                                             169
         1.  Symbolic Method                                         169
         2.  Descriptive Method                                      170

VII. *Electronic Publication and Textual Methods*                    171

Suggested Readings                                                   172

CHAPTER SIX  **General Rules and Their Exceptions**                  174
I.   *Conservative Patterns of Emendation*                           174
     A.  Texts with Nonstandard English                              175
     B.  Other Special Cases                                         177
II.  *Documentary Problems with Textual Solutions*                   178
     A.  Genetic Elements in Source Texts                            178

|  | 1. | Synoptic Genetic Texts | 179 |
|  | 2. | Collaborative Source Texts | 180 |
|  | 3. | The Physical Presentation of Genetic Texts | 182 |
| B. | Multiple-Text Documents |  | 183 |
|  | 1. | "Second Thoughts": Authors Who Try to Rewrite History | 183 |
|  | 2. | Other Multiple-Text Documents | 185 |
|  | 3. | Nonauthorial Emendations and Additions | 186 |
| C. | Conflation |  | 188 |
|  | 1. | Fragmentary Source Texts | 188 |
|  | 2. | Reconciling Accounts of Independent Witnesses | 190 |

III. *Basic Rules for Documentary Editing* — 192

IV. *"Versioning" and Documentary Editing* — 192

V. *Conclusion* — 193

Suggested Readings — 194

CHAPTER SEVEN **The Mechanics of Establishing a Text and Text-Related Notes** — **195**

I. *Transcription Procedures* — 195
   A. Rules for Transcription — 197
   B. Special Transcription Methods — 199
   C. Transcription Forms and Control — 199
   D. Filing Transcriptions — 201

II. *Source or Provenance Notes* — 201

III. *Transcriptions as Working Copy* — 204
   A. Establishing the Editorial Texts — 204
   B. Back-of-Book Textual Notes — 207

IV. *Computers and Texts* — 209

Suggested Readings — 210

CHAPTER EIGHT **Nontextual Elements** *Informational Annotation and Its Supplements* — **211**

I. *Theories and Rationales of Annotation* — 212

II. *Special Sources, Special Needs* — 213

III. *The Needs of the Modern Audience* — 214

IV. *A Practical Framework for Informational*     215
*Commentary: What Editorial Apparatus*
*Should Explain*

    A.    Information Known to the Document's
        Author or Creator     215

    B.    Information Available to the Document's
        Original Audience     216

    C.    Modern Knowledge of the Document's
        Meaning and Significance     217

V. *Consistency and Clarity:*
*The Annotator's Watchwords*     218

VI. *Overannotation: The Editor's Nemesis*     219

VII. *Annotational Forms*     220

    A.    Source Notes     221

    B.    Footnotes     221

    C.    Back-of-Book Annotation     223

    D.    Introductory Editorial Notes     223

VIII. *Citation of Sources*     224

    A.    Implied Sources of Information     225

    B.    The Form of Citations in Editorial Notes     226

       1.    Bibliographical Economies     227

IX. *Preparation of Informational Notes*     228

X. *Supplements to Informational Annotation*     230

XI. *Conclusion*     232

Suggested Readings     232

CHAPTER NINE    **Publishing the Edition**    *Options for*    
*the Twenty-first Century*     **235**

I. *Book Editions: From Hot Type to No Type*     236
    A.    Desktop Publishing     239

II. *Microforms*     240

III. *Electronic Editions*     241
    A.    CD-ROM Editions     241

    B.    Internet Distribution of Electronic Texts     242

    C.    Standards for Electronic Editions     243

IV. *The Documentary Editor and the*
*Documentary Publisher*     243

V. *Front and Back Matter*     245

A. Statements of Editorial Policies 246

    1. The Statement of Textual Method 246

    2. The Statement of the Pattern
of Annotation 247

    3. Special Statements of Editorial Policy 247

B. Textual Symbols and Other
Source-Related Tables 247

C. Short Titles and Symbols for Repositories 248

D. Optional Editorial Apparatus 249

E. Permissions for Use and
Copyright Considerations 249

VI. *CSE Inspections* 250

VII. *Final Establishment of the Documentary Text* 251

A. Textual Notes and Apparatus 252

B. Nontextual Annotation 252

VIII. *The Index* 252

A. Designing the Index 254

IX. *After Publication* 258

Suggested Readings 259

APPENDIX ONE **Form Letters** 261

I. *A "Blind" Search Letter to Libraries* 261

II. *A Letter to Libraries Owning Pertinent Documents* 261

III. *Letters to Autograph Dealers and Auctioneers* 262

APPENDIX TWO **Sample Control File Database Records** 263

GLOSSARY 269

REFERENCES 275

INDEX 293

# FOREWORD

In the ten years since the first edition of this guide was published, the world of documentary editing has changed dramatically. Editors are using new methods to present documents, publishing new genres of documents, and seeking to reach different audiences. Moreover, distinctions between literary and historical editing that seemed so clear to some editors in the early 1980s have faded and become less useful over time. Thus, when the first edition was nearly sold out in 1994 and Barbara Oberg, then president of the Association for Documentary Editing (ADE), began exploring a revision of the *Guide*, it soon became apparent that the revision would be a drastic one.

The first edition's advice on the use of computers was seriously out of date. Editors not only use ever-more-powerful computers and software programs for every stage of a project, but they use computers to distribute their work in ways that were not even dreamed of a decade ago. Publication of documents on CD-ROMs and over the Internet has increased the range of documents that can be included, changed the methods of editing and preparing these documents, and broadened the audience that uses the resulting products. Editors producing printed volumes have also found themselves in new relationships with their publishers, as they have learned to prepare computer disks instead of hard copy. Some editors have taken on even greater responsibility, using desktop publishing programs to create exactly the volumes they want. Any revision of the *Guide* had to take these changes into account, and given how quickly computer technology and software goes out of date, the advice offered to documentary editors had to provide broader guidance on the many tasks editors can now do with computers.

A grant from the National Historical Publications and Records Commission in 1995 to the ADE, along with financial support from the association, enabled us to embark on this more ambitious revision. We received essential help and encouragement from members of the ADE and its officers, most notably Barbara Oberg, Richard Leffler, Charles Hobson, Thomas Mason, and Philander Chase. Mary-Jo Kline, the author of the first *Guide*, courageously agreed to revise her own work, knowing that she would have to rework her earlier text drastically as well as conduct additional research. A group of distinguished and diverse scholars agreed to serve on the Advisory Committee for the project. David Chesnutt, W. Speed Hill, Elizabeth Hughes, Thomas Mason, Beverly Wilson Palmer, and Michael Stevens provided valuable comments and ideas for improvements and read a draft of the revision in the fall of 1995, after which we met together and compiled a very much shorter list of needed changes. Throughout this process, Dr. Kline exhibited admirable graciousness and patience when faced with voluminous comments, and her wry sense of humor kept the rest of us laboring cheerfully. Meanwhile, she spent hours in the library updating the selected readings and bibliography, visited documentary editing projects to gather information on current practices, talked with editors and those who had used or taught from the first edition of the *Guide*, and wrote, revised, and rewrote the text.

This revision was possible only because the first edition of the *Guide* provided a solid foundation on which to build. Many people generously contributed their time and expertise in that work. Informal contributors to the first edition include John Blassingame, John Catanzariti, LeRoy Graf, Robert Hill, Donald Jackson, Sharon MacPherson, Richard B. Morris, Harold Moser, Gaspare Saladino, Harold and Patricia Syrett, and Eleanor Tilton. Representatives of university presses with wide experience in publishing documentary editions were especially generous in sharing their wisdom: Herbert Bailey and Gretchen Oberfranc of Princeton University Press, Gerard Mayers of Columbia University Press, Ann Louise McLaughlin of Harvard University Press, and Elizabeth Steinberg of the University of Wisconsin Press.

The colleagues who deserve the greatest thanks for their unstinting work on the first edition are the officers of the ADE and association members who served on the Committee on the Manual (Guide), some of whom also worked on proofreading and production of the volume: Charlene Bickford, Allida Black, John Morton Blum, Jo Ann Boydston, David Chesnutt, Don Cook, Charles Cullen, Thomas Jeffrey, John Kaminski, Glenn LaFantasie, George Hoemann, Arthur Link, Joel Myerson, David Nordlof, Barbara Oberg,

Carol Orr, Nathan Reingold, Richard Showman, John Simon, Paul Smith, Raymond Smock, G. Thomas Tanselle, and Helen Veit.

The support and expertise of staff memebers at the Johns Hopkins University Press also made the first edition possible, in particular, Henry Tom, Joanne Allen, and Nancy West. And it was in large part the press's enthusiastic support of a revision of this guide that brought it into being. Robert Brugger has provided much valued encouragement from the very beginning. Most heartfelt thanks go to Anne Whitmore, the copy editor of this volume, whose keen eye caught the infelicities and occasional lapses that revising a text engenders. Her exceptional editing skills have helped to make this revised volume a seamless whole.

The result of all this work is an updated and broad guide to the many choices available to documentary editors that includes what current practice and scholarship can offer to those seeking to produce various types of documentary editions in various media. Readers will find new aids to annotating and selecting documents, deciding how to handle translation problems, thinking about and planning for the ways to use computers, thinking about the needs of the audience for which a documentary edition is intended, and indexing the final product. We hope that this new edition of the *Guide* will serve all those who seek to learn about and do documentary editing or to teach it, so that ever-broader audiences can experience the immediacy of documents and the richness of their offerings.

Linda Johanson
Project Director
The Association for Documentary Editing

# PREFACE

My preface to the first edition of the *Guide* began with the complaint that my task had been made harder because documentary editors had apparently adopted as their professional motto: "Editing is more fun than *writing* about editing." In the decade that has passed, these scholars have taken better advantage of forums like *Documentary Editing* and *TEXT,* the proceedings of the Society for Textual Scholarship. Further, access to their writings has been eased immeasurably by Beth Luey's superb bibliography *Editing Documents and Texts* and by the modern luxury of electronic versions of reference tools like *America: History and Life* and the *MLA International Bibliography.*

Even with these aids, I remained heavily dependent on the good will of editors willing to answer the same question with which I nagged them in 1981 and 1982: "Why did you do that? . . . did you do that?" Members of the Council of the Association for Documentary Editing and of the association's Advisory Committee for the revised *Guide* carried the heaviest burden, and here I was well served by the balanced variety of editorial experience these scholars represented.

No fewer than four of the association's presidents, past and present, helped make the revised *Guide* a reality. Barbara Oberg of the Franklin Papers oversaw the thankless and time-consuming process of securing the grants that made the project possible. The Advisory Committee included her immediate successor, Richard Leffler, of the Documentary History of the Ratification of the Constitution, and the John Marshall Papers' Charles Hobson, president-elect during Leffler's term and himself president in 1995–96 when the *Guide* received its last editorial reviews. David Chesnutt, president in 1991–92, not only agreed to repeat his valiant service as a member of the committee that shepherded the original *Guide* to completion but brought to the committee for the revision the expanded experience in electronic technology and digital imaging he has gained as head of the new Model Editions Partnership.

Nonpresidential members of the committee were equally helpful and supportive. Elizabeth Hughes of the Eisenhower Papers reminded us of the special demands of twentieth-century records and of editors not yet deeply involved in modern technology. Michael Stevens of the State Historical Society of Wisconsin brought the lessons of years of administering formal workshops in documentary editing and ensured that the new *Guide* would better serve classroom needs. The City University of New York's W. Speed Hill, a founder of the Society for Textual Scholarship, was our eloquent and knowledgeable source for recent developments in textual editing and American literary scholarship. Beverly Wilson Palmer brought the practical wisdom earned through producing the streamlined Sumner and Stevens editions, where the papers of Civil War statesmen became available to scholars through the use of database-indexed microforms and selective annotated volumes. Thomas Mason of the Indiana Historical Society represented the association's publications program and proved to be the best proofreader that this editor has ever had reason to bless.

Linda Johanson, chair of the Advisory Committee and my fellow Daughter of the Burned-Over District of New York's Southern Tier, not only maintained peace and harmony among committee members and author but also drafted the book's section on foreign-language translations. These contributions pale, however, in comparison to her last and greatest labors on the book—acting as final copy-editor for the text chapters, suggested readings, and bits of front and back matter, as well as representing the association in coordinating production of the published volume with our publisher, the Johns Hopkins University Press.

These ADE officers and committee members were, of course, merely my most publicly acknowledged consultants. In person, in telephone conversations, and in long e-mail messages and Internet file transfers, dozens of others provided me with answers—and more than a few thought-provoking questions of their own that forced me to reevaluate my earlier work.

To the extensive roster of "informal contributors" listed in the first edition, I must now add Martha Benner, Philander Chase, Elaine Engst, Carl Fleishhauer, LeeEllen Friedland, Amy Friedlander, Louis Galambos, Robert Hirst, Susan Hockey, Thomas Jeffrey, Reese Jenkins, Martha King, Allen Renear, Robert Rosenberg, Richard Ryerson, Nancy Sahli, Kenneth Sanderson, Robert Schulmann, Dorothy Twohig, and Daun van Ee.

And sadly I must acknowledge the loss that I and other editors have suffered by the deaths of so many men and women whose good counsel was so essential to preparing the first *Guide*, among them Fredson Bowers, Lyman Butterfield, Marc Friedlaender, Donald Jackson, Richard Morris, Peter Shaw, Harold and Patricia Syrett, and Eleanor Tilton. Perhaps no absence was felt as sorely as that of Richard K. Showman, chairman of the Committee on the Manual," 1980-83, and a constant source of common sense and uncommon good humor and wisdom as he supervised creation of the first edition of the *Guide.*

I close this preface as I did that for the first edition of the *Guide* by taking responsibility for any errors of fact or proofreading in the pages that follow as well as for any passages that violate my mandate to prepare a "descriptive" rather than "prescriptive" or "proscriptive" treatise on documentary editing. The revised edition, like its predecessor, contains passages that describe certain methods and editorial decisions in less than laudatory terms. Unless such opinions are clearly attributed to others, they are my own. They should not, at all costs, be ascribed to the Association for Documentary Editing.

Now, as I did a decade past, I invite readers who are offended by my judgments to voice their objections—and, better still, to publish them. I have prepared the revision, as I did the original edition, with a conscious view to ending the tradition of editors who chose not to write about editing. With this in mind, I proudly continue to take my motto for the *Guide* from Sir Walter Greg: "My desire is rather to provoke discussion than to lay down the law."

*When the history of scholarship in the twentieth century comes to be written, a very good case should be made for calling it the age of editing.*

—Fredson Bowers, 1976

*[Documentary] editing is, in my opinion, the most important scholarly work being done in the United States, and, if well done, it will be the most enduring.*

—Arthur S. Link, 1979

# CHAPTER I

# Introduction

Great as the impact of modern American scholarly editing was in the third quarter of the twentieth century, the first edition of this *Guide* was made necessary by the puzzling fact that practitioners of the craft typically neglected to furnish the public with careful exposi- tions of the principles and practices by which they pursued their goals. The modern specialty of scholarly editing in America reached a critical point in both intellectual development and technological ad- vances during this period. Volumes of novels, letters, diaries, states- men's papers, political pamphlets, and philosophical and scientific treatises had been published in editions that claimed to be scholarly, with texts established and verified according to the standards of the academic community. Yet the field of scholarly editing grew so quickly that many of its principles were left implicit in the texts or annotation of the volumes themselves.

This lapse was most apparent in the area of noncritical, or docu- mentary editing, where editors seemed peculiarly reluctant to pub- lish discussions of their own goals and methods. This methodology emerged in the United States after World War II and was distinct from the more traditional textual, or critical, method of editing being applied to American literary texts during that period. Even though these methods often overlapped—with the text for one source in a series receiving noncritical treatment and that for another source re- flecting a critical approach—American scholars often neglected to define the occasions on which each technique should be used, much less spell out the different methods appropriate to each.

The very term *documentary editing* did not become current until the late 1970s, a quarter of a century after the publication of the first volumes that employed the methodology. A term was needed to dis- tinguish this technique from the more traditional approach of textual editors, who consciously applied critical judgment and scholarly experience to produce new, editorially emended texts for their audiences. Such textual editors were the heirs of classical scholarship, in which scholars were forced to rely on a variety of scribal copies instead of on original and authentic documents. To divest scribal texts of corrupt words and phrases introduced over centuries of copying and recopying, classicists devised complex methods to recover words, characters, and phrases of the lost archetype or original from which these copies had flowed. The invention of the printing press by no means halted such problems for scholars. Compositors corrupted the texts of the works that they set in type as surely and regularly as had the medieval scribes who distorted the writings of the authors of ancient Greece and Rome. To meet the challenge of this form of textual corruption, British scholars adapted the methods of classical and Biblical textual editing to meet the needs of the variants in early printings of Shakespearean dramas. This work culminated in Sir Walter Greg's exposition of the theory of copy-text.

Obviously, methods devised to serve the needs of scholars seeking an ideal, nonhistorical text did not serve those of political, intellectual, and social history. Here other editorial methods were required, and they emerged in a series of editions of American statesmen's papers published in the 1950s and 1960s. These documentary series were distinguished from critical editions in part by the sources on which their scholarly texts are based. Documentary editors must usually prepare modern editions from source materials that can themselves be described as documents—artifacts inscribed on paper or a similar medium or recorded by audiovisual means, whose unique physical characteristics and original nature give them special evidentiary value. The significance of such sources demands that their editors provide editorial texts that themselves will communicate as much of the sources' evidentiary value as possible. Generally, this means a far more limited level of editorial intervention than would occur were the same sources being edited critically, for the documentary editor's goal is not to supply the words or phrases of a vanished archetype but rather to preserve the nuances of a source that has survived the ravages of time. Documentary editing, although noncritical in terms of classical textual scholarship, is hardly an *un*critical endeavor. It demands as much intelligence, insight, and hard work as its critical counterpart, combined with a passionate determination to preserve for modern readers the nuances of evidence that exist in the sources on which the modern documentary editions are based.

The years since the preparation of the first edition of the *Guide* have seen extraordinary changes in the world of American scholarly editing. On the one hand, editorial specialists and the general public have been well served by the creation of a number of new resources for study and new forums for discussing the art and craft of editing. At the same time, American editors have been blessed with an embarrassment of technological riches from the information revolution that has reshaped the ways in which the world shares words and images. Further, the economic realities of American scholarship in the humanities have quietly changed the "typical" editorial project from a long-term undertaking with a good-sized permanent staff and reliable financial support from outside sources to one in which one or two scholars or enthusiastic laypeople try to apply the stringent standards of the editorial community to smaller bodies of texts, relying on their own skills and resources.

While all of these developments made revision of the *Guide* a necessity, the most forceful arguments for revision came from the first edition's discussion of computer methods, now hopelessly outmoded. Many of the results of the newest age of American scholarly editing have remained uncollected in a way convenient to the public at large, and editors busy with the daily tasks of upgrading old hardware or evaluating new software have had little spare time to share the wisdom of their experience of the past decade.

As the revised *Guide* must serve editors of the twenty-first century as well as the last years of the present one, I have made a conscious attempt to anticipate problems and suggest solutions. Whenever possible, the *Guide* will lead interested editors and would-be editors not only to published books and essays but also to ongoing informational sources (print and electronic) where they can find the newest standards in informational technology of special use and interest to this field.

Documentary editors, like any other mortals, have thought, worked, and written within the bounds and limitations of their own times and their own educational and professional backgrounds. Thus, a brief survey of the evolution of the craft of American scholarly editing must precede a survey of its present state and an assessment of its future.

## I. EARLY AMERICAN DOCUMENTARY EDITING

The very tradition of documentary publication in the United States is older than the nation itself. From the beginning, Americans were almost painfully aware of the historic role that their new republic would play, and both government and individual citizens showed this concern by publishing the records of the young society and its founders. As early as 1774, Ebenezer Hazard planned a series of volumes of "American State Papers" that would "lay the Foundation of a good American history." By the time Hazard published the first volume of *Historical Collections* in 1792, the cause of documentary publication had been joined by the Massachusetts Historical Society, which issued the first volume of its collections of New England records in that same year.

The major phase of American documentary editing began in the second quarter of the nineteenth century, when Jared Sparks of Harvard initiated his work. Sparks traveled widely to collect the manuscripts on which he based his *Diplomatic Correspondence of the American Revolution,* the *Writings of George Washington,* and the *Life and Correspondence of Gouverneur Morris.* In 1831 the federal government committed itself to the publication of its own records by inaugurating the *American State Papers* series. In the decades that followed, later generations of filiopietistic editors produced volumes of such varying quality as William Jay's *Life of John Jay: with Selections from His Correspondence and Miscellaneous Papers* and Charles Francis Adams' far superior edition of the papers of his grandfather, John Adams.

At the close of the nineteenth century there was a new burst of editorial activity. Earlier editors of American correspondence and public papers had considered themselves "men of letters," but as the division of academic disciplines developed, there was an increased sense of professionalism and adherence to standards. Some editions, like Henry Cabot Lodge's scissors-and-paste version of the *Works of Alexander Hamilton,* represented no improvement over earlier models. But others, like the editions prepared by the brothers Paul Leicester Ford and Worthington Chauncey Ford, showed considerable textual sophistication for the time.

As the twentieth century opened, the new professional historians were ready to make their voices felt in urging a systematic program of documentary publication. President Theodore Roosevelt, himself a historian and biographer, directed the creation of a committee to report on documentary publication. Worthington Ford chaired the committee, while J. Franklin Jameson, the great historian of the Carnegie Institution, acted as its secretary. The committee's report of 1908 urged the creation of a permanent federal commission on "national historical publications" as well as the revival of the *American State Papers* series, which had been discontinued in 1862. The American Historical Association urged adoption of the committee's recommendation, but nothing was done.

Piecemeal efforts were not wanting in those decades. In 1925 Congress authorized the project that led to the inception of *The Territorial Papers.* The Library of Congress continued to sponsor Worthington Ford's edition of the *Journals of the Continental Congress* and also began work on an edition of the *Writings of George Washington.* And at the Carnegie Institution, Jameson oversaw such major documentary series as *The Letters of Members of the Continental Congress* and *Documents Relative to the Slave Trade in America.*

In 1934 Congress created the National Historical Publications Commission (NHPC) as part of the National Archives Act. For practical purposes, this commission remained a fiction, and in the next sixteen years its members met only six times. It was not until 1950 that a new Federal Records Act gave the commission specific duties regarding documentary publication and, even more important, a permanent staff with which to discharge those responsibilities.

## II. Statesmen's Papers and "Historical" Editing

The transformation of the NHPC into an agency with real power and responsibility at this time reflected optimism about the efforts to reform and revolutionize American documentary editing begun by individual scholars during World War II. Even then, technological advances in microforms and photocopying offered an exciting prospect for the editors and publishers of documents. With these tools, photographic facsimiles of all the variant copies of a statesman's surviving letters, journals, and other writings could be assembled in one place for comparison and evaluation. For the first time, truly comprehensive editions became a practical possibility.

During the war years, two scholars began projects that produced the first fruits of what became known as historical editing. At Franklin and Marshall College, Lyman Butterfield undertook an edition of the correspondence of Benjamin Rush that drew on manuscript collections throughout the nation. At Princeton University, Julian P. Boyd won approval for an edition of the papers of Thomas Jefferson. Butterfield joined Boyd's staff at Princeton, and under Boyd's direction the framework of a historian's notion of a modern editorial project took shape. The availability of photocopies made possible a variorum edition, in which the locations of all extant copies of each document could be cited and variants among the versions could be noted. A systematic approach to cataloging manuscripts and photoreproductions allowed Boyd and Butterfield to create an archive that encompassed Jefferson's correspondence, his literary works, and his state papers. With these sources at hand, the editors could select the most authoritative version of a Jefferson document for print publication. A system of typographical symbols based on those used by textual scholars for works of earlier eras was devised to reproduce in print certain details of the original manuscript, such as authorial cancellations. For other details of the text, explanatory footnotes were provided.

The Boyd-Butterfield editorial tradition did not stop with supplying a reliable printed text for each document. These scholars felt an obligation to furnish their readers with explanatory footnotes that would allow them to understand the document in its historical context. These notes reflected scholarship as painstaking as any seen in major historical monographs of the time. The publication of the first volume of the *Jefferson Papers* in 1950 and of the two-volume edition of Rush's correspondence the following year established this combination of textual attention and explanatory annotation as the hallmark of American historical editing.

These examples of the promise and potential of documentary editing cleared the way for the revitalized NHPC to begin its work. The commission surveyed American historians to determine priorities for its program, and by the time that the final report on this survey was ready in 1954, the *Jefferson Papers* had been joined by three new "papers" projects: those of Henry Clay, John C. Calhoun, and Benjamin Franklin. Later that year, the Adams Papers project began its work, and in 1955 and 1956 projects for editions of the papers of Alexander Hamilton and James Madison were initiated. Each project focused on a figure whose papers were given priority in the 1954 NHPC report, and they soon received more practical encouragement in the form of grants from the Ford and Rockefeller foundations and from the *New York Times* and the Time-Life Corporation.

In the 1950s the NHPC offered guidance to editorial projects throughout the country and provided the services of its research facilities in Washington; after 1964 it offered money to these projects as well. The Ford Foundation granted $2 million to ensure the continuation of the five "priority" projects—the papers of Adams, Franklin, Hamilton, Jefferson, and Madison—and Congress increased the NHPC's authority, so that it not only administered the Ford Foundation monies but also could make grants from federal appropriations.

By the early 1970s the NHPC had provided money or official endorsement to more than sixty editorial projects throughout the country. Its responsibilities were expanded to include the preservation of historical records, as well as the microform and letterpress publication of documents, and in 1975 the agency's name was changed to the National Historical Publications and Records Commission (NHPRC). The NHPRC encouraged an increasing number of microform publication projects for the papers of lesser-known historical figures and for the records of organizations, which would make their records available to scholars without the expense of comprehensive print publication.

## III. Editing the Nation's Literature: The Americanization of Copy-Text

American literary scholars joined historians in organized editorial pursuits, but their course was an independent one, and they created a somewhat different editorial tradition. While America's concern for editing papers with historical significance is an old one, that of publishing authoritative texts of the works and correspondence of American literary figures is comparatively new. It was not until well into the twentieth century that America's role in the history of literature and world culture became recognized as a topic worthy of serious scholarly study. Such recognition was fully established only in the late 1930s, and World War II delayed a coordinated effort to provide American literary and cultural historians with edited resources for scholarship comparable to those available to the political historian. In 1947 the Modern Language Association (MLA) named its Committee on Definitive Editions, which first sought funds for a coordinated program to publish authoritative texts of American literary works. This attempt failed, and further efforts were not made until the early 1960s. By that time American literary critics had already shown their talent and ingenuity in applying textual criticism to seminal American works. Fredson Bowers' edition of Walt Whitman's *Leaves of Grass* and Harrison Hayford and Merton Sealts' "genetic" text of Herman Melville's *Billy Budd* demonstrated both that the American scholarly community had the skills and talent necessary to provide authoritative texts and that the raw materials of American literary documents required such critical attention.

The MLA revived its crusade on behalf of reliable editions of American literary works in 1963 by creating an executive committee to found the Center for Editions of American Authors (CEAA). By the time the CEAA was created, projects were either planned or under way to publish the writings of Ralph Waldo Emerson, Mark Twain, Herman Melville, Walt Whitman, and Nathaniel Hawthorne. Not long after the CEAA's committee was named, the federal government created the National Endowment for the Humanities (NEH), a grants-making agency receptive to the CEAA's aims.

In the spring of 1966 the NEH made its first grants to the CEAA. Once these funds were available, the CEAA published the list of

American writers whose editions would receive the first attention. The Emerson, Twain, Melville, Whitman, and Hawthorne projects were to be joined by ones for the works of Washington Irving, Henry David Thoreau, William Dean Howells, and Stephen Crane. Over the next decade the CEAA acted as a conduit for funds from the NEH to editorial projects that met the CEAA's standards. To make those standards explicit, the CEAA published the first edition of its *Statement of Editorial Principles* (1967), which set down guidelines for editors seeking the CEAA's endorsement. At the same time, it instituted an emblem, or seal, to be awarded to volumes that met its standards of editorial accuracy.

Those standards reflected a movement in scholarly editing whose effects on American literary studies would be as far-reaching as the NHPRC's program of edited papers was on historical research: the year 1950 marked not only the appearance of the first volume of the *Jefferson Papers* but also the publication of the issue of *Studies in Bibliography* that carried Sir Walter Greg's "The Rationale of Copytext." Greg's essay was an eminently clear and cogent summary of the experience of British scholars in editing the texts of Renaissance and early modern drama and literature. Greg described the false starts, intellectual detours, and careful experiments that had led him and his colleagues to codify and rationalize practical rules for the selection of the copy-text. He distinguished between those elements in a printed work that could be termed substantives, those that directly affected "the author's meaning or the essence of his expression," and those that could be regarded as "accidentals"—spelling, marks of punctuation, and other elements "affecting mainly its formal presentation." Greg assured his readers that he was well aware of the fragile line between substantives and accidentals. "The distinction I am trying to draw," he warned, "is practical, not philosophic."

The practical use to which Greg put the distinction was a simple one. In the absence of an author's manuscript, it was usually possible to identify one edition of a published work, usually the earliest, that drew most directly on that lost manuscript. Greg pointed out that the craftsmen responsible for later printings were likely to respect the words of earlier versions but were unlikely to feel themselves bound by what might seem old-fashioned or incorrect notions of spelling and punctuation in the edition that they reset and that writers who had a hand in revising their own works for later editions were likely to concern themselves more with changing inelegant substantive elements in the old edition than with standardizing punctuation or spelling. Thus, an appropriately chosen copy-text had authority for accidentals in establishing an edited reading text. When only one edition reflected the author's personal scrutiny, and later editions were merely "reprints," that early copy-text's authority extended to substantive readings as well. But Greg reminded his readers that "the choice of substantive readings belongs to the general theory of textual criticism and lies altogether beyond the narrow principle of the copy-text." He hoped that this explanation would end what he termed "the tyranny of copy-text"—the tendency of some editors to neglect the hard work and harder thought needed to establish the substantives of a text once they had identified the copy-text on which they could rely for the "accidental" patterns of punctuation and spelling.

It was no surprise that Greg's exposition of copy-text was published in an American periodical. Literary scholars in this country were as eager as historians to see a more systematic and scholarly publication of American materials, and Greg's essay on copy-text became part of the theoretical basis for the movement's claim that it possessed a scientific methodology that could ensure success in the quest for truly authoritative texts of American authors. The creation of the CEAA gave literary editors a chance to show the potential uses of this methodology.

Greg's techniques, translated for use with the writings of American authors, were implemented in the CEAA's standards for editions. For works written with the intent of publication, standards for the seal were clear. The CEAA demanded that such editions provide an edited "clear text," that is, a reading text uncluttered by textual or informational footnotes of any kind. Approved volumes were to provide a historical introduction tracing the work's creation and publication, as well as an essay on the modern editors' treatment of the author's text. The editors were to justify their choice of copy-text and present their analytical judgment of the author's intentions. An appendix in each volume provided the textual apparatus, which included textual notes, lists of editorial corrections (or emendations) of the text, a historical collation of the copy-text with other editions of a printed work, and lists of line-end hyphenations of possible compounds as they appeared in the copy-text as well as those line-end hyphenations to be retained when quoting from the critical text.

CEAA editions of an author's writings might also include private materials, such as letters and diaries or journals that had heretofore fallen into the realm of documentary editing. These private writings usually survived only in manuscript form, and the conventions of textual editing for works intended for publication could not be transferred automatically, so the CEAA's requirements for approved editions of correspondence and journals were less specific than those for published works. For instance, the editors of letters and diaries were not confined to clear-text versions of these manuscripts, although they were expected to list any editorial emendations that they might make.

## IV. The Evolution of Distinctive Methodologies

Thus, by the middle of the 1970s, two editorial establishments had developed in the United States, each focusing its attention on important American figures, each drawing on traditions of textual criticism and on modern technology. For the sake of convenience, they came to be known as historical and literary editing, a division many came to regard as unrealistic and unfortunate. Each editorial specialty had its own form of professional bureaucracy and oversight. Although the NHPRC, the NEH, and the CEAA all tried to avoid the charge of dictating to the editors who looked to them for funds and guidance, there were distinct patterns that marked an edition as historical or literary in its approach.

Historian-editors were expected to collect photocopies or originals of all the surviving papers of the individual or group being documented. Even if only a selective print edition of these papers was planned, the NHPRC increasingly insisted that the editors make the entire collection available to the scholarly public, usually through a microform supplement. In printed volumes, even those defined as selective, the editor was obliged to publish a sample of both incoming and outgoing correspondence, of writings intended for publication as well as those that a literary edition would define as private.

The literary edition of a figure's writings was far more exclusive. Edited volumes of an author's works, of course, were an expected part of the process; but when editors approached the writer's private documents, they often defined their task as editing the author's own writings, not all his or her papers. Consequently, literary editions of correspondence customarily printed only letters written *by* their central figure, not the letters that he or she received. Literary editors were not obliged to provide microform supplements of collected materials excluded from edited volumes or even to supply lists of the items they had omitted.

Historical and literary editors also took different approaches to the treatment of texts. Both groups recognized that the printed page could not reproduce all the details of inscription and physical appearance of the original documents. Historical editors customarily contented themselves with publishing a partially corrected reading text that reproduced only selected categories of such details, and most established general guidelines for the editorial emendation of archaic forms and punctuation in the originals. Such treatment was known as expanded transcription of the sources. Most literary editors were as ready as historical editors to emend the documentary text, but they were obligated to record most of these emendations at some point in the edited volumes, even if the emendations were in an appendix hundreds of pages away from the texts to which they referred.

There were differences, too, in the nature and amount of informational annotation supplied by the two groups. Historian-editors tended to supply more such annotation than did their literary counterparts, and many historical editors supplemented footnotes and headnotes with elaborate indexing systems that enabled readers to retrieve from their volumes almost any kind of information that might serve a scholarly purpose.

Some differences in technique and methodology can be traced to the respective editors' training. The models from which historical editors worked were nineteenth-century editions of historical documents. Those for literary editors were the textual apparatuses prepared for works in European literature, where it was often necessary to provide an eclectic text that combined, or conflated, elements from several sources. Still more differences arose from the editors' conceptions of the audience for their volumes. Historians assumed that readers would need a text closely tied to the original—a heavily emended clear text for a document would serve no useful purpose for the historian-reader who wished to use that text as evidence. Literary scholars assumed that readers would be concerned with evaluating the readability and literary merits of the letters and journals that they provided; for such a reader, clear text was a standard convenience. The historical editor dealt with papers of public importance that could not be understood without annotation that fixed their historical context. Literary editors assumed that the writings they were editing would be viewed as expressions of a person's private feelings and internal development.

Volumes of "papers" and "writings" began to crowd the shelves of American scholars and general readers, and their editors awaited the judgment of the reading public for which they had labored so long.

## V. The 1950s: The Critical Reception of Historical Editing

Scholars and laypeople welcomed the Jefferson and Rush volumes of 1950 and 1951 with open and grateful arms. Announcements of other series of this type brought cries of delight and, one suspects, of relief—relief at the prospect of authoritative printed texts that would spare scholars the trials of visiting inconveniently located manuscript repositories or of squinting at scratched microfilms. In 1981 Gordon Wood characterized this pattern of response as "effusively laudatory, but critically unhelpful" ("Historians and Documentary Editing," 877).

This is not to say that historians and historian-reviewers did not raise questions about the editions whose volumes began to crowd other books from their shelves by the early 1960s. The quality and quantity of annotation were discussed with increasing concern, and the effectiveness of indexes and other finding aids was analyzed, but reviewers largely ignored any questions raised by the editors' methods in establishing the printed texts that they offered as authoritative. (For a useful bibliography of such early criticism, see Fredrika J. Teute's "Views in Review.")

In 1951 Theodore Hornberger's review of the first volume of the *Jefferson Papers* pointed to the birth of a tradition of variorum editions of American documents, and Hornberger even raised constructive questions concerning Boyd's choices of source texts and his treatment of works printed during Jefferson's lifetime. But with rare exceptions, reviewers ignored such broad considerations. Isolated critics (usually editors themselves) compared specific printed texts with their sources for transcriptional accuracy, but for more than a quarter of a century after Hornberger, none posed even tentative questions about general textual standards for historical editions.

## VI. The 1960s and 1970s: Editing and Relevance

Editors in the new tradition being set by the Center for Editions of American Authors were less fortunate. The first volume to bear the CEAA emblem was published in 1963. Literary scholars and lay critics alike were more ready than observers of the historiographical scene to take issue with this new phenomenon. In one of the paradoxes common to the literature of American scholarly editing, the earliest and best-known public attack on CEAA methods in documentary editions concerned volumes that did not even bear the organization's emblem.

In January 1968 the *New York Review of Books* carried Lewis Mumford's scathing review of the first six volumes of the *Emerson Journals*, as well as his laudatory words for the first two volumes of *Emerson's Early Lectures*. The *Journals* recorded details of the original manuscripts with such a wealth of symbolic brackets and arrows in their texts that Mumford titled his essay "Emerson behind Barbed

Wire." The *Lectures* were in clear text, with omitted details of inscription recorded in back-of-book notes.

All eight volumes had been prepared before the CEAA began to inspect volumes and award its emblem. Still, Mumford used the *Emerson Journals* as a symbol of the evils he sensed in the CEAA program. He attacked the volumes on two scores. First, the editors had printed the journals in their entirety, "mingling the important with the inconsequential." Second, they had chosen "to magnify this original error by transcribing their notations to the very pages that the potential reader might wish to read freely, without stumbling over scholarly roadblocks and barricades."

As representatives of the Emerson edition and the CEAA quickly pointed out, Mumford had quite simply misunderstood the editors' aims and had not grasped the volumes' raison d'être. The only existing edition of the *Journals* comprised "selections" and rewritten snippets of the original source. There was no need for another such contribution. Instead of continuing in this tradition, William H. Gilman and his colleagues had given their readers the complete texts of these important records. They realized that their contents were not of consistent interest to every member of their audience, but they realized, too, that it was impossible for them to anticipate the needs of the thousands of scholars from a dozen fields who required access to the journal entries. As for the textual methods used in the *Journals*, the edition was an "inclusive" text that recorded specific inscriptional details, not a literal transcription, as Mumford seemed to believe. And there was good reason to make these texts more inclusive than the ones presented for the lectures, for the journal entries had no definable final form, as did drafts of the lectures that were delivered to an audience.

Mumford's review took on added significance when it became part of Edmund Wilson's broader attack on CEAA principles. In September 1968 the first of three essays by Wilson on the CEAA program appeared in the *New York Review of Books.* Wilson admitted that the award of NEH funds to the CEAA represented a personal defeat for him. His own proposal for a series of editions of American classics had been turned down by the NEH in favor of the MLA plan. While he did not challenge the authority or validity of the CEAA texts that he reviewed, he denounced both the expense involved in their preparation and what he considered their nonhumanistic tone and editorial procedures. He echoed Mumford's earlier complaints of "technological extravagance" and "automated editing" in the *Emerson Journals* along with Mumford's suspicions of the supposedly "scientific" methods of the CEAA approach. Mumford had even hinted at a parallel between editorial callousness and the Vietnam War when he cried, "The voice in which Emerson calls out to one is drowned by the whirring of the critical helicopter, hovering over the scene."

Wilson's essays were later published in pamphlet form as *The Fruits of the MLA*. MLA partisans, in turn, issued rebuttals to his and Mumford's attacks in *Professional Standards and American Editions*. Peter Shaw recalled the results of these articles at the MLA convention of December 1968: "The young antiwar professors who temporarily gained control of the organization . . . sold copies of Wilson's *Fruits of the MLA* and offered resolutions calling for both withdrawal from Vietnam and a cutoff of funds for the American editions" ("The American Heritage and Its Guardians," 735). Both the conflict in Southeast Asia and support for the CEAA survived these attacks, although neither escaped further critical scrutiny.

Historian-editors viewed the battles within the MLA with amusement. No one had yet examined their textual practices closely, and they quietly continued their work. In 1971, however, historical editions received their first broadside hit, from Jesse Lemisch, a member of the American Historical Association's Committee on the Commemoration of the American Revolution. Lemisch's "preliminary critique" of the NHPC's publications program appeared in the November 1971 AHA *Newsletter*, with a candid disclaimer that his report in any way represented "the committee's viewpoint or policy." In "The American Revolution Bicentennial and the Papers of Great White Men," Lemisch forced the historical community to reexamine the priorities established for documentary publication. On ideological and methodological grounds, he attacked the NHPC's focus on projects printing documents of "white male political leaders." This concentration of funds and public attention seemed to encourage the elitism that Lemisch and many of his generation decried. And by focusing on the collection and publication of the records of individuals who had distinguished themselves in politics and government, he said, the NHPC appeared to slight some of the most lively and fruitful areas of research in American history. Such a program did little to provide easily accessible source materials for quantitative analysts or for the social and economic historians whose focus was, of necessity, on groups rather than on single figures, no matter how distinguished they might be.

The NHPC responded quickly to Lemisch and his allies, and the 1970s saw an increased emphasis on creating projects with an organizational rather than an individual focus. Historians were encouraged to investigate new sources for documentary editions as well as new formats for presenting these materials, and the selection of appropriate topics for projects soon reflected the needs of a wide spectrum of interests. It was a mark of the success of early documentary editions that scholars with concerns in modern American history and in areas outside such traditional ones as politics and government demanded equal attention to records serving their scholarly needs. By 1982 the NHPRC had given support or endorsement to 386 published volumes whose subjects included not only individuals but institutions and organizations, women as well as men, and leaders of a variety of ethnic and racial groups whose significance lay in social and intellectual as well as political history.

In the best tradition of consumers of published historical papers, Lemisch raised no questions about the textual methods of existing editions, nor did he suggest that any new techniques might be required by the kind of historical editing he proposed, projects that focused on the records of groups, not merely on the documents left by the more literate men and women in America's past. But he had unwittingly contributed to a silent revolution in textual methodology among historian-editors. The editors of these new projects found that they could not confine their innovations to the collection and organizational arrangement of their sources. They had no choice but to ignore the patterns of emendation and standardization accepted by earlier editors of the writings of eighteenth-century statesmen and instead adopt far more literal methods of presenting editorial texts. Unfortunately, they did not publish their reservations about the efficacy of applying the older textual methods to more modern documents and ones by authors of different backgrounds. On the surface, at least, historical editing in the Boyd-Butterfield tradition continued unchallenged.

## VII. THE MLA AND PRIVATE WRITINGS

Had the CEAA and its successor, the Committee for Scholarly Editions (CSE), created in 1976, confined their activities to published works, their achievements and the debate surrounding their programs might have remained largely unnoticed by the editors of American historical documents. As William M. Gibson made clear in a 1969 statement about the Center for Editions of American Authors, the editor who adapted Greg's copy-text theory to American writings hoped to "achieve a text which matches no existing text exactly but which comes closer to the author's hand and his intent than any previously printed version," not to present a text that necessarily had documentary value.

Clearly, this goal could not be achieved easily when letters, diaries, and notebooks were published as part of each author's writings, so CEAA editors necessarily ventured into the realm of documentary publication. To complicate the discussion of editing further, CEAA and CSE rules demanded that editors transfer to these documentary materials the conventions devised for editions of printed works. While some of these conventions concerned an edition's format, others concerned textual method itself. Certain categories of emendation and suppression of detail (such as slips of the pen and details of inscription, like catchwords) in the source text of documents, like similar problems in editions of printed works chosen as copy-text, could be handled silently, that is, with no record in the edition, whether in the text, in footnotes, or in the editorial apparatus. These categories were identified explicitly in the edition's introductory "note on the text." Any editorial actions outside these categories, however, were to be reported somewhere in any volume that received a CEAA or CSE emblem. It was the application of such methods to what the CEAA called private writings, of course, that had been the focus of the controversy over the *Emerson Journals* in 1968. Although those volumes did not bear the CEAA emblem, critics had accurately assumed that their textual methods anticipated those that would be used in CEAA editions.

Paradoxically, once the CEAA adopted standards for editing private writings, those standards were criticized by William Gilman, editor of the *Emerson Journals* that Mumford had assailed. In his review essay, "How Should Journals Be Edited?" Gilman criticized what he saw as a slavish and ultimately futile attempt by the editors of the *Irving Journals* to meet the CEAA's demand that they "collate and report fully" any doubtful readings or peculiarities of inscription in the original manuscripts that they had translated to print. Despite the arrows and brackets of editorial "barbed wire" and the textual annotation in Gilman's edition of the *Emerson Journals,* there was no attempt to make a complete report of the original manuscript's details. The *Irving Journals,* on the other hand, aimed at providing the reader with a nearly literal, or "diplomatic" transcription, in which all details of inscription were recorded symbolically in the reading text or in adjacent descriptive footnotes.

Gilman's attack on the application of CEAA standards in the *Irving Journals* sparked no continuing public debate among editors of private writings. Certainly the problem was not ignored by editors at work on these series, but their discussions of the special challenges at hand were confined largely to notes contributed to the short-lived *CEAA Newsletter* (1968–71), which published a discussion of the degree to which private writings demand the same scrupulous reporting of emendations and inscriptional details found in editions of published works. In public, literary scholars confined themselves to arguing the merits of imposing copy-text theory and the standards of the CEAA on printed American works.

The special textual problems of documents in the history of American literature also received short shrift when the CEAA published its *Statement of Editorial Principles and Procedures* in 1972. Although described as a revised edition of the CEAA's original statement of 1967, it was in fact a new and far more explicit discussion of the CEAA's aims and requirements. It represented an attempt to report on the results of the first half-dozen years' experience of the CEAA and its editors, and the statement's appendix, "Relevant Textual Scholarship" (pp. 17–25) was the most complete bibliography to that date of writings pertinent to editing American literary works. But the 1972 statement paid scant attention to the variety of approaches that these editors had already brought to private writings. Its recommendations for inclusive textual treatment of such materials ignored the fact that the CEAA had given its emblem to volumes in the Mark Twain series that carried no textual record and to volumes in the *Hawthorne Notebooks* that approached clear text with an accompanying report of editorial emendations.

## VIII. INTERDISCIPLINARY EVALUATIONS BEGIN

The first observer to compare the work of literary and historical editors was Peter Shaw in his "American Heritage and Its Guardians." Shaw focused his attention on inconsistencies in quality and textual methods in CEAA editions of literary works rather than on the small but growing sample of edited private writings of American literary figures. Among historical editions, Shaw limited his discussion to those of "Founding Fathers" such as Jefferson, Adams, and Madison. Evaluating volumes in both traditions, Shaw concluded that historical editors had served their audience better than CEAA scholars, "not necessarily by common sense but by their fundamental respect for historical fact." Shaw later modified his judgment, suggesting that NHPRC-sponsored historical series were, indeed, no better than those of the CEAA and CSE mold. In large measure, Shaw was forced to revise his estimate because of an essay published two years after his own that changed irrevocably the literature of American documentary editing.

This essay was G. Thomas Tanselle's "Editing of Historical Documents," which appeared in January 1978 in volume 31 of *Studies in*

*Bibliography.* Tanselle surveyed the post–World War II tradition of historical editing of documents and took its practitioners to task on two scores. He pointed out that the statements of textual method in these volumes were often maddeningly vague and occasionally self-contradictory, and he argued that the application of heavily emended expanded transcription instead of more conservative methods of literal transcription was a disservice both to the documentary sources and to their readers. In 1981 historian John Y. Simon summarized the impact of Tanselle's article: "Some reacted as if the Japanese had again struck Pearl Harbor; more sought to repair their damaged vessels by altering, improving, or explaining transcription policies with a clearer understanding that inconsistent or silent alterations designed for 'the reader's convenience' more often represented the critic's opportunity. We may eventually come to regard Tanselle's article as the single most important step forward in American historical editing since the publication of the first volume of the Boyd *Jefferson*" ("Editors and Critics," 3).

Widespread and immediate as was the reaction to Tanselle's article, it did not take public form for several years. In private, many historical editors grumbled at an "outsider's" criticism of textual methods for materials that they felt he did not understand or appreciate. At projects where the textual methods of Boyd and Butterfield had been imposed on editors by advisory committees, there was a sigh of relief. Many heirs to such decisions offered private prayers of thanks to Tanselle for voicing their own reservations, and they either announced that their editions would henceforth abandon expanded methods for more literal treatment or they quietly adopted more conservative methods and prayed that their editorial advisers would not notice the difference.

When public debate came, it emerged, fittingly enough, in a forum that owed its existence to the private discussion of documentary editing sparked by Tanselle's essay. In September 1978 the NEH and NHPRC held a conference on literary and historical editing at the University of Kansas, the first occasion on which representatives of the two editorial traditions met en masse and exchanged views. At the annual meeting of the Southern Historical Association a few weeks later, the Association for Documentary Editing (ADE) was created to provide an institutional setting within which historical and literary editors could learn about and from each other.

The ADE meeting of October 1980 included a session, in which Tanselle participated, that saw the first formal debate of the issues that had made the association a necessity. Robert J. Taylor, Lyman Butterfield's successor as editor of the *Adams Papers,* presented his position in "Editorial Practices—An Historian's View." Taylor conceded the strength of Tanselle's criticism of statements of method in many historical editions. Paraphrasing Samuel Eliot Morison, Taylor confessed, "An historical editor's real sin is saying carefully and explicitly what he is going to do and then not sticking to it. And here Dr. Tanselle has indeed struck home." But Taylor challenged what seemed to him Tanselle's unbending standards for printed texts based on manuscript sources. Taylor argued that it was impractical to adhere to diplomatic methods, whereby every detail of the original manuscript would be recorded in the editorial text. As an aside, Taylor attacked the notion that printed documentary sources—unique pieces of historical evidence that existed in typeset, not handwritten form—should be presented as critically emended texts like those literary works bearing the CEAA emblem.

Unfortunately, the exchange between Taylor and Tanselle was unsatisfying. Tanselle did not address himself to Taylor's points at length, and his brief comments were never published. Their audience had to wait until 1981, when the MLA's *Introduction to Scholarship in Modern Languages and Literatures* carried Tanselle's essay, "Textual Scholarship." Here Tanselle made clear his complete agreement with Taylor on the special requirements of printed documents as source texts. He recognized the need for a "noncritical edition" of such works, one that would serve "essentially the function of making the text of a particular document (manuscript or printed) more widely available" (p. 34). But many parts of Tanselle's position remained unclear. He had not contented himself with pointing to the sins of historical editing; he had also suggested a path to salvation, and it seemed to be some single approach to the editing of documentary sources that would serve both literary and historical scholarship. Tanselle's long association with the CEAA led readers to assume that this single standard must be that of the CEAA.

The CEAA tradition had taken on added significance in 1976, when the CEAA, after awarding its seal to more than 140 volumes in a decade, was succeeded by the Committee on Scholarly Editions, another creation of the MLA. Although the CSE did not channel funds to editorial projects, it continued the CEAA's role of issuing a seal to approved editions and acting as a clearinghouse for information among editors. More significantly, the Committee on Scholarly Editions, as its name implied, hoped to spread the principles of textual scholarship and provide reliable editions "to encompass more than American literature." To be sure, the CEAA had already moved beyond purely literary works by awarding its seal to volumes in the *Works of John Dewey*, but it had been unable to give its aid and formal approval to editions that could not be described as American in origin. The CSE could expand its activities, and it not only continued to endorse the Dewey edition but encouraged approved editions of the writings of psychologist William James and editions of British authors.

The agency's change in name and purpose was accompanied by an official declaration of its new policies in 1977. Its broadened field of interest was reflected in the enumerative bibliography that accompanied this statement, a guide no longer confined to the problems of the Americanist. The statement offered no additional guidance in noncritical documentary editing, however, as it remained focused on the problems of the textual editor preparing an eclectic critical text rather than the challenges faced by documentary specialists concerned with presenting inscribed historical realities.

The debate over the application of textual methods to documentary sources and private writings had proceeded disjointedly. In November 1979 David Nordloh, textual editor of the *Howells Letters*, had presented "The 'Perfect Text': The Editor Speaks for the Author" at the annual meeting of the ADE. He suggested that an editor's goals were to "make" the text what its author had "wanted," and the practical results of his textual theory could be seen in the clear-text edition of the *Howells Letters*. Still, more than two years passed before a reaction to his remarks was published. Wayne Cutler, editor of the *Polk Correspondence*, in "The 'Authentic' Witness: The Editor Speaks for the Documents," took an exceptionally conservative position on the textual treatment of documentary materials. "The historical editor," he wrote, "speaks only for one document at a time." He decried Nordloh's suggestion that documents such as letters or private journals could be emended or conflated for the sake of "perfection." Neither party addressed the more basic question of whether a back-of-book textual record of emendations, provided by the *Howells Letters*, justified clear-text presentation of private writings.

## IX. A Period of Reexamination

As the 1980s progressed, scholarly editors of all schools found more opportunities for discussion and debate. The Society for Textual Studies, which held its first meeting in 1981, held a series of semiannual interdisciplinary conferences at which dozens of editors discussed the ways in which "text" might be presented and analyzed in historical documents, literary works, musical manuscripts, film, recorded sound, and artifacts of all periods. Selected papers presented at these meetings appeared regularly as volumes in the *TEXT* series. While the Association for Documentary Editing's annual meetings tended to focus more narrowly on the materials of "history" and conventional literature in the past four centuries, a distinctly interdisciplinary tone soon became apparent at those meetings and in the essays and reviews published in the quarterly *Newsletter of the Association for Documentary Editing,* rechristened *Documentary Editing* in 1984.

On a more practical level, the ADE became an active force in creating and disseminating reference materials for editors and would-be editors. First came the first edition of *A Guide to Documentary Editing,* in 1987, followed three years later by Beth Luey's *Editing Documents and Texts: An Annotated Bibliography.* To supplement these two more conventional resources, the ADE endorsed preparation at the State Historical Society of Wisconsin of the recently published *Editing Historical Documents: A Handbook of Practice.* The *Handbook,* designed for use in classrooms and workshops where documentary editors are trained, is an anthology of statements of editorial policy and examples of their execution.

Aside from these formally organized activities, continued academic debate has modified the tone and direction of much of the discussion of editorial principles and procedures and has called into question the binarism of "historical" versus "literary" editing. Most prominently, the debate over historicism forced literary scholars to reappraise their own assumptions and techniques as editors. As early as the late 1970s, the bibliographic scholar D. F. McKenzie called for increased sensitivity to the complicated social relationships among authors, publishers, editors, typesetters, and others who participate in the production of a printed book. (For an excellent summary of McKenzie's work in this area, see Tanselle, "Historicism and Critical Editing.") The American scholar Jerome J. McGann took this line of thought further in *A Critique of Modern Textual Criticism.* McGann openly attacked the Bowers-Greg emphasis on choice of a copy-text and the recovery of "authorial intentions." McGann called for a new approach that would liberate textual studies from what he saw as a narrow "psychological and biographical context" (pp. 119–20) by admitting that the production of printed literary works has long been "fundamentally social rather than personal." Authorial intention could no longer be used as a convenient anchor for editorial emendations, McGann and his supporters argued, and scholars must give equal weight to the variety of "texts" that reflect the contributions of different members of the social process of book publication.

Even editors outside the McGann camp of textual socialization were ready to question the search for a single text whose claims to authority or reliability overwhelmed all others. Hans Walter Gabler's discussions of his experience as editor of Joyce's *Ulysses* focused on the need to identify the evolutionary stages of an author's work and present these states in a "genetic" editorial text. Peter Shillingsburg's *Scholarly Editing in the Computer Age: Lectures in Theory and Practice* reconsidered the realities of the authorial process and urged an editorial pluralism, recognizing that a variety of methods were needed to preserve the various stages by which a literary work reached completion and to accommodate different readers' interests.

Both Gabler's and Shillingsburg's work implied a change in the apparatus of textual editing. Editors might still provide a clear text for the reader's convenience, but their record of variant readings would have to change. The textual notes would have to be organized so that they clearly traced patterns of emendation by one or another member of the group that had contributed to the text. And, in recognition of the importance of these variant texts, editors might be required to place their textual notes conveniently close to the passages to which they referred instead of providing a back-of-book record.

Keeping textual debate lively in the 1980s, Hershel Parker attacked accepted standards from another side, arguing that *original* authorial intention is so central to the determination of a work's text that the editor must sometimes deny an author's later revisions a place in the critical edition. As Tanselle pointed out, all of these commentators shared "a sense of urgency about the need for a renewed historical orientation in literary studies" ("Historicism and Critical Editing," 17).

This openness to a "historical orientation" led scholars in the tradition of American textual studies to show a greater willingness to experiment with new textual decisions. Gone were the days when an editor could win approval for speaking of final authorial intentions presented in a clear reading text. A variety of methods had to be weighed and tested against the needs of the source texts. Donald Reiman, editor of the *Shelley and His Circle* series, argued forcefully and effectively that manuscript private writings would be best served by publishing facsimiles of the originals opposite annotated, literal transcriptions of their contents as parallel texts. David Greetham has summarized this trend away from critical editions to those with evidentiary value as "documentalism." The poststructuralist historicist perspective has blurred the distinction between works of imaginative literature and the historical document as well as the distinction between public and private writing and between the political and the personal. The larger context of modern humanistic studies calls for similar methods, as does the emergence of interdisciplinary studies generally.

For their part, documentary historian-editors spent the 1980s and early 1990s focusing on nontextual issues, whose importance increased because of economic and political considerations. The age of generous government support to long-term editorial projects was over. In the first years of the Reagan administration, the very existence of the NHPRC was threatened by overzealous budget-cutters, and a dozen years later, the National Endowment for the Humanities and the National Endowment for the Arts faced extinction. Editorial projects that survived would have to operate more efficiently, and projects that began operations during this period often did so with smaller ambitions than their predecessors. The meetings of the ADE and the pages of *Documentary Editing* were often filled with discussions centering on the theory and practice of selective editions—criteria for selection and the role of annotation, calendars, or lists in recording omitted items. There was a renewed interest in economical facsimile publication, whether in microform or electronic format. University presses reminded editors that print editions, whether comprehensive or select, cost money; and editors reexamined their theories and practices in contextual annotation and such companion pieces of editorial apparatus as glossaries, biographical directories, and indexes.

Editors in the CEAA/CSE tradition soon demonstrated that they shared this concern. In 1985, David Nordloh, who had been a chairman of the CSE, warned that literary scholars could not ignore certain "documentary requirements" that had long been the concern of historian-editors: the special ethical problems of selective editions, provision of full "supporting information" about a text's source, and adequate indexing for both persons and topics ("Supplying What's Missing").

While American scholarly editors of the 1980s and 1990s might not have agreed on the need for back-of-book records of textual variants, they realized that they otherwise shared the same goal in dealing with documentary sources: how best to present cautiously emended texts that preserve as much as possible of the original's evidence, along with efficient textual and contextual apparatus that the reader might use to evaluate the editors' handiwork in both textual and historical terms. Those same editors found themselves bound even more strongly by a related problem: how to accomplish this task in the age of computer technology.

## X. Computer Technology and the Next Chapter in Editing

W. Speed Hill has described the basis of decision making in scholarly editing as a tripod constructed of three considerations: the source material for the edition, the projected audience the edition might engage, and the medium in which that edition might be issued ("Theory and Practice of Transcription," 25–32). Computer technology does not change these considerations, it merely alters and broadens the choices available to modern editors. When the first edition of this guide was prepared, it could offer only educated guesses about the form the computer revolution would take in reshaping scholarly editing. A substantial portion of this new edition is devoted to reporting new realities and offering a few more predictions.

In general, it is literary scholars who have contributed most handsomely to computer-assisted textual innovation in the last decades. With their early investigations of the opportunities of hypertext links between various versions of an author's work, they pointed the way for scholars in other fields. It was literary scholars, too, who broke ground in the mundane area of proofreading, recognizing the potential of computer collation as a substitute for grueling and unreliable human quality control.

Historically oriented documentary editors have proved more eager to use computer equipment for the physical and intellectual "control" of editorial collections and research data. Not coincidentally, it was a historian-editor, David Chesnutt, who devised CINDEX, a convenient mainframe-based indexing system for documentary editions; and another historian, Charles Cullen of the Newberry Library, was instrumental in securing funds to modify the program for use by desktop computers (see Chesnutt, "Optical Scanning for CINDEX").

While editors of all backgrounds now find that economic pressures make them, more and more, their own publishers, it has been editors funded by the NHPRC who have been most active in investigating the electronic transmission of facsimiles on a large scale. This merely reflects the NHRPC's longstanding preference for some form of comprehensive publication of all pertinent materials assembled by a project. Debate on such supplements once centered on the choice between microfilm and microfiche. Today the choice is more likely to be between issuing indexed digitally scanned images on CD-ROM or making them available on the Internet. (For a cogent discussion of a pioneering CD-ROM edition of statesmen's papers, see Benner, "The Abraham Lincoln Legal Papers.")

The most far-reaching aspect of the changes brought to editing by computers, however, may be the simple acceptance of desktop computers as standard office equipment for all modern scholars. This revised edition of the *Guide* assumes that anyone now beginning a documentary edition will employ a personal computer with word-processing software. Although I will refer to some older manual techniques still in use by many projects, such techniques owe their survival only to the trouble and expense of their replacement, not to their innate worth.

One legacy of those older traditions remains unchanged: a set of procedures to ensure the quality of work throughout the editing project. Even purists who still insist that "editing" is only the establishment of a text admit that the duties of a successful editor neither begin nor end with that process. The documents that merit critical attention must be assembled. Errors of fact or interpretation can be introduced into the documentary texts or their accompanying notes if there is no procedure for verifying and proofreading these materials. Publishers must be satisfied that an editor's design of any projected volumes, microforms, or electronic versions is thoughtful and useful. Increasingly, limited outside funding could force more and more editors to work alone or to accept expedients that result in products short of ideal goals.

Scholarly editors must be the most practical and hard-headed scholars in their disciplines. Such ruthless pragmatism may be unexpected in academic editors, who would appear to be the purest of modern scholars. They focus their attention on original sources, not on only the conclusions stated by others in secondary works. Theirs is a professional obsession with the best evidence that is to be had, and their goal is to communicate that evidence to others in a clear and accurate form. But every editor soon learns that all the scholarly dedication and critical insight in the world will not compensate for inattention to the practical considerations involved in preparing a documentary edition.

Any edition's success will be directly related to the degree to which the editors have planned and anticipated the problems that they meet, and that planning and organization must take into account what is both the delight and the curse of the trade—the appearance of the unanticipated problem or unexpected scholarly bonus. Beyond having an aptitude for careful planning, the editor must establish clear lines of responsibility for any project at its outset. It is not enough to outline an exhaustive search for source materials unless the editor ensures that each step in that process takes place. The most meticulous scheme for proofreading transcriptions of sources is useless unless the editor establishes pedestrian book-keeping procedures to record each step in such verification. Finally, editors must be prepared to expose the details of the planning and execution of their editorial decisions to public view. Printed volumes, electronic editions, or microform publications must provide an explanation of the edition's methods for establishing documentary texts, setting the scope of the search for materials, achieving standards for annotation, and proofreading and other quality control.

## XI. The Organization of This Book

This revised *Guide,* like its predecessor, will attempt to bring readers up to date on this changing field. I have used on-site visits to editorial projects, lengthy written correspondence, e-mail exchanges, and telephone conversations to supplement the information that American editors have offered in print. The volume is organized in terms of a rough chronology of the physical and intellectual tasks that confront any editor, beginning with the collection of sources and ending with the final review of materials as set in type for print publication or tagged and coded for electronic transmission. It is more accurate to say that this sequence is representative of the order in which editors *think* about projects they are going to undertake rather than the order in which they perform the tasks. As any editor knows, such organization is a polite fiction. The considerations of any edition must be regarded as a whole. A project's plan for collection (chapter 2) is inevitably influenced by the projected scope of the planned edition (chapter 3). Methods of transcription (chapter 4) must take into account the standards of the final editorial text (chapters 5 and 6). And editors of long-term editions will still discharge their responsibilities as collectors of sources (chapter 3) as they oversee publication of early sections of the edition (chapter 9). Error or miscalculation in one area can guarantee disaster in another, and the editor's failure to assign or to assume responsibility for discharging each aspect of the plan will delay or even doom the whole edition.

Finally, any advice or information offered in the *Guide* must be constantly supplemented by reference to current literature. Each chapter ends with a section entitled "Suggested Readings" that includes not only specific books and articles but the names of journals likely to contain studies of interest in a particular area and of agencies likely to furnish information on standards and practices in specific fields. Readers should bear in mind that the "Suggested Readings" sections that follow each chapter in this book were prepared at the end of 1995 and are only selections of studies in this area. Beth Luey's bibliography, *Editing Documents and Texts,* offers a convenient listing of pre-1990 publications not cited in this volume.

## Suggested Readings

To remain current in the literature of documentary editing, readers should regularly consult publications such as *American Archivist, TEXT, Documentary Editing, Analytical and Enumerative Bibliography* (with special attention to its "Recent Work in Bibliography" section), *Studies in Bibliography, Papers of the Bibliographical Society of America, Computers in the Humanities,* and *Scholarly Publishing,* as well as the CD-ROM or paper editions of *America: History and Life* and the *MLA International Bibliography* series.

Those with a taste for methodological pedagogy should consult the first edition of *A Guide to Documentary Editing* (Baltimore, 1987). Before the *Guide* was published the only attempt to present editing principles for student use had been Ross W. Beales, Jr., and Randall K. Burkett's *Historical Editing for Undergraduates* (Worcester, Mass., 1977), a brief pamphlet of limited scope. For thought-provoking discussions of the ways bibliography and critical and documentary texts can be a part of undergraduate and graduate curricula, see *Literary Research Newsletter* vol. 9, no. 4 (Fall 1984), a special issue devoted to bibliography and textual studies in a graduate curriculum, and vol. 12, nos. 2 and 3 (Spring–Summer 1987), "The Bibliography and Methods Course," another special issue.

There are several volumes of collected essays of interest to the student of documentary editing. While many of the older anthologies reflect a perceived distinction between "historical" and "literary" approaches, their usefulness survives. Among the older collections of "literary" studies are: Ronald Gottesman and Scott Bennett, eds., *Art and Error: Modern Textual Editing* (Bloomington, Ind., 1970); G. Thomas Tanselle's *Selected Studies in Bibliography* (Charlottesville, 1979); and Fredson Bowers' *Essays in Bibliography, Text, and Editing* (Charlottesville, 1977). More recent anthologies of Tanselle's essays are *Textual Criticism and Scholarly Editing* (1990) and *Textual Criticism since Greg* (1987), both also published by the University of Virginia Press. Documentary editors in the historical tradition were represented in Leslie W. Dunlap and Fred Shelley, eds., *The Publication of American Historical Manuscripts* (Iowa City, Ia., 1976), while George L. Vogt and John Bush Jones, eds., *Literary and Historical Editing* (Lawrence, Kans., 1981) presents the papers offered at the conference that began the move toward an interdisciplinary approach.

I. There are many entertaining essays on the beginnings of documentary editing in the United States. Some of the most valuable are: Lyman H. Butterfield, "Archival and Editorial Enterprise in 1850 and 1950: Some Comparisons and Contrasts," *Proceedings of the American Philosophical Society* 98 (1954): 159–70; Lester J. Cappon, "American Historical Editors before Jared Sparks: 'they will plant a forest . . . ,'" *William and Mary Quarterly* 30 (July 1973): 375–400; Philip M. Hamer, ". . . authentic Documents tending to elucidate our History," *American Archivist* 25 (1962): 3–13; Lee N. Newcomer, "Manasseh Cutler's Writings: A Note on Editorial Practice," *Mississippi Valley Historical Review* 47 (June 1960): 88–101; Newman F. McGirr, "The Adventures of Peter Force," *Records of the Columbia Historical Society* 42 (1942): 35–82; Richard N. Sheldon, "Editing a Historical Manuscript: Jared Sparks, Douglas Southall Freeman, and the Battle of Brandywine," *William and Mary Quarterly* 36 (April 1979): 255–63; Fred Shelley, "Ebenezer Hazard: America's First Historical Editor," ibid. 12 (January 1955): 44–73; and Conrad E. Wright, "Multiplying the Copies: New England Historical Societies and Documentary Publishing's Alternative Tradition," *Documentary Editing* 11 (June 1989): 32–36.

The history of efforts to organize a nationwide program of documentary publication in the early twentieth century is described in Theodore C. Blegen, "Our Widening Province," *Mississippi Valley Historical Review* 31 (June 1944): 3–20; Clarence E. Carter, "The United States and Documentary Historical Publication," ibid. 25 (June 1938): 3–24; Worthington C. Ford, "The Editorial Function in United States History," *American Historical Review* 23 (1917–18): 273–86; J. Franklin Jameson, "Gaps in the Published Records of United States History," ibid. 11 (1905–6): 817–31; Waldo Gifford Leland, "The Prehistory and Origins of the National Historical Publications Commission," *American Archivist* 27 (1964): 187–94; and Fred Shelley, "The Interest of J. Franklin Jameson in the National Archives: 1908–1934," ibid. 12 (1949): 99–130; Alexander Moore, "Present at the Creation: John Franklin Jameson and the Development of Humanistic Scholarship in America," *Documentary Editing* 16 (September 1994): 57–60.

The later claims and methods of documentary editing of the Boyd-Butterfield era should be contrasted with the discussion in Clarence E. Carter's comparatively modest *Historical Editing* (Washington, D.C., 1952), Number 7 in the National Archives *Bulletins* series.

II. Useful essays on the evolution of post–World War II historical editing include: Julian P. Boyd, "'God's Altar Needs Not Our Polishings,'" *New York History* 39 (January 1958): 3–21; and Lyman H. Butterfield's "The Scholar's One World," *American Archivist* 29 (1966): 343–61; Lester J. Cappon's three essays: "The Historian as Editor" (*In Support of Clio: Essays in Memory of Herbert A. Kellar,* William B. Hesseltine and Donald R. McNeil, eds. [Madison, Wisc., 1958], 173–93); "'The Historian's Day'—From Archives to

History" (*The Reinterpretation of Early American History: Essays in Honor of John Edwin Pomfret,* Ray Allen Billington, ed. [San Marino, Calif., 1966], 233–49); and "A Rationale for Historical Editing Past and Present" (*William and Mary Quarterly* 23 [January 1966]: 526–75). The bibliography in this area continues with Oliver W. Holmes, "Documentary Publication in the Western Hemisphere," *Archivum* 16 (1966): 79–96, and surveys of government-related documentary publication programs such as Richard B. Morris, "The Current Statesmen's Papers Publication Program: An Appraisal from the Point of View of the Legal Historian," *American Journal of Legal History* 11 (1967): 95–106; and Robert Rutland, "Recycling Early National History through the Papers of the Founding Fathers," *American Quarterly* 28 (Summer 1976): 250–61. Frank Burke, former director of the NHPRC, provides an excellent survey of the agency's work in "The Historian as Editor: Progress and Problems," *Public Historian* 4 (1982): 5–19, and "Automation and Documentary Editing," *British Journal for the History of Science* 20 (January 1987): 73–79.

In the late 1980s and early 1990s, several NHPRC-sponsored projects drew to a close and several editors of ongoing editions retired, events that inspired a useful array of reflections on the experiences of these editions: John C. Van Horne, "Drawing to a Close: The Papers of Benjamin Henry Latrobe," *Documentary Editing* 11 (September 1989): 63–69; the collection of essays on the history of the Woodrow Wilson project in the June 1993 (vol. 15) issue of *Documentary Editing;* Herbert S. Bailey, Jr., "Einstein's Collected Papers: Planning and Development," *Scholarly Publishing* 20 (July 1989): 202–17; *Prologue*'s issues of Fall 1986 and Spring 1989 carrying articles by editors of projects related to the Constitution and the creation of the federal government and the papers of American presidents; Donald Jackson, "What I Did for Love—of Editing," *Western Historical Quarterly* 13 (1982): 291–97; Tom Krattenmaker, "Reading Jefferson's Mail," *Princeton Alumni Weekly* (November 10, 1993), pp. 10–15; and Robert J. Taylor, "One Historian's Education," *William and Mary Quarterly* 41 (1984): 478–86.

III. Two entertaining accounts of editions of literary works before our own era are Donald H. Reiman, "Gentlemen Authors and Professional Writers: Notes on the History of Editing Texts of the 18th and 19th Centuries," *Editing and Editors: A Retrospect. Papers Given at the 21st Annual Conference on Editorial Problems. University of Toronto 1–2 November 1985* (New York, 1988), 99–136; and T. H. Howard-Hill, "Shakespeare Edited, Restored, Domesticated, Verbatim and Modernized," *Review* 15 (1993): 115–225, a jovial tour of editing Shakespeare from the beginning of the seventeenth century. Useful accounts of some of the first CEAA projects are Guy Cardwell, "Author, Intention, Text: The California Mark Twain," *Re-*

*view* 11 (1989): 255–88; and David Robinson, "The Legacy of Emerson's Journals," *Research for American Literary Study* 13 (1983): 1–9. David Nordloh provides an informative survey of the CEAA and CSE in "Theory, Funding, and Coincidence in the Editing of American Literature," *Editing and Editors: A Retrospect:* 137–55, and G. Thomas Tanselle's "Literary Editing," in Vogt and Jones, eds., *Literary and Historical Editing,* 35–56, remains worthwhile.

V and VI. Fredrika Teute's "Views in Review: A Historiographical Perspective on Historical Editing," in the *American Archivist,* provides a useful guide to patterns of reviewing American historical editing. Wayne Franklin's "The 'Library of America' and the Welter of American Books," *Iowa Review* 15 (Spring–Summer 1985): 176–94, is an excellent history of the Mumford-Wilson assault on the CEAA and its aftermath. Earlier records of that war of words are: Tanselle's articles in the 1975 and 1981 volumes of *Studies in Bibliography;* Michael Mancher's amusing "The Text of the Fruits of the MLA," *Papers of the Bibliographical Society of America* 68 (1974): 411–12; the less widely publicized but more serious challenges to the CEAA in the New York Public Library *Bulletin* 75 (1971), with informative contributions to the debate on pages 147–53 (March), 171–73 (April), 337–44 (October), 419–23 (November), and 504–5 (December); *Studies in the Novel* 7 (Fall 1975): 375–406, wherein Bruce Bebb, Hershel Parker, Vinton A. Dearing, Thomas L. McHaney, Morse Peckham, and G. Thomas Tanselle provide a "forum" on the CEAA in response to John Freehafer's "Greg's Theory of Copy-Text and the Textual Criticism in the CEAA Editions"; and Tom Davis, "The CEAA and Modern Textual Editing," *The Library* 32 (1977): 61–74. Other worthwhile contributions are Hershel Parker and Bruce Bebb, "The CEAA: An Interim Assessment," *Papers of the Bibliographical Society of America* 68 (1974): 129–48, and Peter L. Shillingsburg's down-to-earth "Critical Editing and the Center for Scholarly Editions," *Scholarly Publishing* 9 (October 1977): 31–40.

For discussions of critiques on NHPC and NHPRC programs, see Richard H. Kohn and George M. Curtis III, "The Government, the Historical Profession, and Historical Editing," *Reviews in American History* 9 (June 1981): 145–55; Simone Reagor, "Historical Editing: The Federal Role," *Newsletter of the Association for Documentary Editing* 4 (May 1982): 1–4; and John Simon's response, ibid. 5–6, and "Editors and Critics," ibid. 3 (December 1981): 1–4.

VII and VIII. Jo Ann Boydston's "The Collected Works of John Dewey," *Papers of the Bibliographical Society of America* 85 (1991): 119–44, is an excellent history of her thirty-year association with the Dewey project and the edition's role in CSE methodology. Followers of the impact of Tanselle's 1978 attack on historical editing will profit from Don Cook's useful summary of the issues in "The Short Happy Thesis of G. Thomas Tanselle," *Newsletter of the Association for Documentary Editing* 3 (February 1981): 1–4.

IX. Discussions of the implications of McGann's work include Barbara Oberg, "Documentary Editing as a Collaborative Enterprise: Theirs, Mine, or Ours?" *Documentary Editing* 17 (March 1995): 1–5; Peter L. Shillingsburg, "The Autonomous Author, the Sociology of Texts, and the Polemics of Textual Criticism," in Philip Cohen, ed., *Devils and Angels: Textual Editing and Literary Theory* (Charlottesville, 1991), 22–43, and "An Inquiry into the Social Status of Texts and Modes of Textual Criticism," *Studies in Bibliography* 42 (1989): 55–77; David J. Nordloh, "Socialization, Authority, and Evidence: Reflections on McGann's *A Critique of Modern Textual Criticism,*" *Analytical and Enumerative Bibliography* 1 (1987): 3–12; and Craig S. Abbott, "A Response to Nordloh's 'Socialization . . . ,'" ibid.: 13–16.

D. C. Greetham's "Textual and Literary Theory: Redrawing the Matrix," *Studies in Bibliography* 42 (1989): 1–24, points to broader areas of redefinition of textual scholarship. Other surveys of this nature are Stephen Mailloux, *Interpretive Conventions: The Reader in the Study of American Fiction*" (Ithaca, N.Y., 1991), especially chapter 4, "Textual Scholarship and 'Author's Final Intention,'" pp. 93–125; Joseph R. McElrath, Jr., "Tradition and Innovation: Recent Developments in Literary Editing," *Documentary Editing* 10 (December 1988): 5–10; and *Resources for American Literary Study* 20, no. 2 (1994), a special issue entitled "Textual Scholarship and American Literature," whose guest editor, Philip Cohen, offers a useful introduction in "Textual Instability, Literary Studies, and Recent Developments in Textual Scholarship" (pp. 133–48).

W. Speed Hill's "The Case for Standards in Scholarly Editing," *Literary Research* 13 (1988): 203–12, reviews attempts to set standards and regulate results in textual editions. Documentary editing in other nations is surveyed in Christopher Kitching, "The Status of Documentary Editing in the United Kingdom," *Documentary Editing* 11 (June 1989): 29–31; Johanna Roelevink and Augustus J. Veenendaal, Jr., "Undeleting the Dutch Past: The Netherlands Government Commission on National History," ibid. 12 (June 1990): 45–48; Mary Jane Edwards, "CEECT: Progress, Procedures, and Problems," *Papers of the Bibliographical Society of Canada* 26 (1987): 13–26.

X. Janice L. Reiff's *Structuring the Past: The Use of Computers in History* (Washington, D.C., 1991) is a useful survey of computer usage published by the American Historical Association. In "Historical Editions in the States," *Computers and the Humanities* 25 (1991): 377–80, David R. Chesnutt discusses computer use by documentary editors during the 1980s, while George P. Landow surveys the more adventurous use of computer tools by textual editors in "Hypertext in Literary Education, Criticism, and Scholarship," *Computers and the Humanities* 23 (1989): 173–98. Teresa M. Harrison and Timothy Stephen provide a broad introductory survey to the ways in which humanists learned to exploit computer technology during the early 1990s in "On-Line Disciplines: Computer-Mediated Scholarship in the Humanities and Social Sciences," *Computers and the Humanities* 26 (1992): 181–93.

# CHAPTER II

---

# Initiating an Editorial Project

When initiating a project, editors use skills demanded of any responsible scholar. They must anticipate problems and make decisions at an early stage of research, so that work can be completed as efficiently and thoroughly as possible. While some editors deal with an archival collection of sources (a discrete group of original documents in a single location) or a single document such as a diary or journal, most need to assemble the materials that will be the basis of their editions. And many of the most crucial editorial decisions concern this process of collection and the design of a system of physical and intellectual control over the collected materials that will ensure that none of the editor's work will be wasted or unnecessarily duplicated.

Documentary editors must exercise effective planning and organization more intensively than more conventional scholars, and they must often sustain careful scrutiny and meticulous planning for a longer period of time than writers of historical or literary monographs. For the documentary editor, planning can never begin too early, responsibility for implementing plans never ends, and discharging these responsibilities demands the assessment of a variety of constantly evolving technological aids. In earlier decades editors might fulfill such duties by weighing the costs and advantages of manual typewriters versus electrically powered office machines. Today, editors need not only master the mysteries and prices of computer hardware and software but also gauge the future of standards for digital scanning and weigh new methods of electronic publication.

Still, computer-related technology can make a modern editor's life easier at every stage of a project. New bibliographic tools discussed in this chapter expedite the search for sources, while database programs can organize those results. Word processing software has revolutionized the preparation of copy for publication as thoroughly as computer-assisted indexing has that arduous task. But these conveniences are available only to editors willing to take the time to investigate the hardware and software available, to ask embarrassing questions of those who sell these wares, and to be fearless in admitting their own ignorance in the face of technological advance and commercial jargon. Editors experienced in the field offer five pieces of advice: (1) Always explain clearly to an equipment vendor or computer technician just what tasks the project needs the computer to perform. (2) Make sure that the vendor or technician understands that explanation. (3) Never take at face value the word of a vendor who promises that a new toy can do everything that the project requires; demand a demonstration. (4) Whenever possible, consult an editor who has already worked with computer equipment—preferably the system being considered. (5) Never stop thinking of new ways in which computerized equipment can assist the editorial process.

## I. The Editor's Control File

Anyone who has written a book or an article or conducted a lengthy correspondence can imagine the ways in which a computer's word processing capabilities expedite the work of preparing edited materials for publication, but the value of informational technology becomes apparent as soon as the editor designs the control files that will assist the processes of collection and control. Databases, by any dictionary's definition, have always been part of a documentary editor's tool kit. Fifty years ago, when Julian Boyd launched the Jefferson project, his "collection of data organized especially for rapid search and retrieval" was an ingenious system of three-by-five-inch slips on which pertinent information about each known Jefferson document was typed in distinct, carefully arranged visual fields. Today, any editor who collects materials for an edition or catalogs a large archival collection is likely to use a computerized database that serves all the purposes met by Boyd's scheme and even permits some pleasant frills that a manual system could not provide. These databases, whether manual or computerized, must provide access not only to information *about* the materials that the editor may want to locate during the collecting phase of the project but also to information on the physical locations of the original documents or photocopies that form the collection amassed for the edition.

In general, control files have always had to give ready access to at least four types of information: (1) the specific location (name of owner-institution and collection) of the original of each photocopy

or the name of the collection that is the source of an original manuscript, (2) a record of the photocopied materials furnished by each
repository owning materials of interest to the project, (3) a chronological list of cataloged materials, and (4) some form of alphabetical
index to the documents' titles. (In addition, computerized databases
can make subject indexing an easy addition rather than a cumbersome luxury.)

In the earliest documentary projects, control files took the form of
multiple copies of index slips typed for each item in the project's collection. This process is described in Lyman Butterfield's "The Papers
of Thomas Jefferson: Progress and Procedures in the Enterprise at
Princeton." With manual methods, each photocopy or original was
first given its accession number and placed in a labeled folder before
a member of the staff prepared entries for the control files. Entries
were typed on self-carbon packs of slips or on a group of slips between which pre-cut sheets of carbon paper had been sandwiched. Information needed for sorting the slips for insertion into the various
files appeared near the top of the slip for easy visual reference and included such items as the date and place, document title, location
symbol and accession number, the name of the collection housing
the original, followed by description of the document's inscription.

Once these slips were typed and checked for accuracy, they were
separated and interfiled in their appropriate places in the project's
various control series. A minimum of three files was demanded: one
arranged chronologically, an alphabetical file arranged by authors or
recipients of letters or journals or titles of anonymous pieces, and
one arranged by order of accession number. Various methods were
used to record which items were provided by each contributor-
institution: some projects maintained separate notebooks for such
archives, while others produced still another faint carbon copy of the
typed record to be filed by institution.

## II. A Historical Note on Computerized Control Files

In the mid-1960s documentary editors began experimenting with using computers to create control files. One of the earliest experiments
was described fully in "Computer Applications for Historical Editing Projects: The Joseph Henry Papers Index of Documents," an unpublished report by James H. Hobbins and Kathleen Waldenfels.
The Henry editors had access to a mainframe computer at the Smithsonian Institution thirty years ago, and their staff entered data in

coded form on standardized sheets whose contents were later typed into the computer. Despite the pioneering work of the Henry editors and the new techniques that were becoming available, for the next twenty years comparatively few projects adopted automated databases. It was seldom wise to convert an existing manually prepared control file to computerized data: when thousands of documents had been recorded on typed slips, and the editorial collection was all but complete, it was impractical to incur the expense of conversion or to risk introducing error through retyping for the computer. Further, comparatively few new projects had access to the mainframe equipment then required for processing control files.

When staffs of new large-scale editions had mainframe privileges, however, they were eager to exploit automated control file methods. One such new edition was the Thomas A. Edison papers, a project remarkable for its size and complexity. The project was both an archival and a collecting endeavor, with more than three million original documents at the Edison laboratories in Orange, New Jersey, to be cataloged along with a projected additional mass of 100,000 photocopied documents from other sources. To complicate the problem, the Orange facility was not originally tied to the computer center of Rutgers University, which served the main offices of the Edison project. The project's unpublished reports, "Word Processing and Computer Support for the Edison Papers," are a fascinating chronicle of ingenuity and innovation. While the control file was being established, one group of Edison editors remained at Orange, entering data for the cataloged manuscripts on standardized coding sheets, which were periodically taken to the project's office on the Rutgers campus for data entry on the project's sophisticated word processor. Photocopied materials were cataloged on that word processor as they were received. From time to time, the records for both manuscripts and photocopies were communicated to the Rutgers computer center, where a comprehensive database of all Edison materials was created.

The advent of reliable stand-alone personal computers with word processing and database software made the automated processing of control data a realistic option for all editorial projects. One of the first editorial projects to exploit a system less elaborate than a full-scale mainframe unit was the Samuel Gompers Papers. These editors faced the challenge of processing the records of Gompers' decades as president of the AFL-CIO with word processing equipment and the promise of eventual telephone communication with the University of Maryland mainframe. For a while, the project's methods were an interesting combination of manual and automated methods: a word

processor's printer accommodated rolls of five-inch-wide paper per-
forated at three-inch intervals for separation into control slips that,
when sorted, provided a hard-copy version of the control file for
staff members. This makeshift arrangement was necessary because
the project's word processor was not powerful enough to manipulate
the massive amount of data generated by Gompers' career. Diskettes
from the word processor were periodically delivered to the university for entry into the mainframe system until the project's stand-
alone equipment could be linked to it, allowing more frequent updating of the database. Today a personal computer can perform these
database functions.

## III. AUTOMATED DATABASES AND DOCUMENTARY EDITIONS

Some small editing projects will be able to create a computerized
control file without recourse to a database program beyond that
contained in their word processing software, but many more will
need to investigate database software. Most commercially available
database programs have more than enough capacity to handle an editorial project's control files, but most database software was designed for the needs of businesses, not scholarly editing. Databases
to be used in documentary editing should offer these features:

1.  The database should have powerful "report capability," so that
    the data can be formatted and reformatted in printouts orga-
    nized in a variety of modes: reports of relevant documents
    arranged by location or authors, lists of repositories arranged
    by sources they hold, etc.
2.  The software should permit entry of a large number of subject
    terms and almost unlimited opportunities for entries recording
    names mentioned in the documents.
3.  The database's text fields should permit entries of substantial
    length, not limited by a database designer's assumptions that
    digits, not text and notes will be entered in these fields.
4.  The database should be compatible with the software already
    installed on the editorial office's computers (including word
    processing software), so that users will find the system as easy
    to learn as possible.
5.  If the database must generate encoded lists, catalogs, or for-
    matted indexes, the software package must allow the editor to
    write "scripts" or programs that will permit output of such
    encoded text.

6. Editors who must deal with the turn of a century in the documents being collected must find a database whose date fields can be modified to meet the needs of four-digit entries for years.

Editors must remember, as well, that databases can be either "flat-file" or "relational" systems. Flat-file databases are usually easier to use, because all of the information about a particular document is gathered in a single record and the database consists of a single file. If each record contains extensive information about the documents, flat-file databases can become unwieldy as the number of documents increases. The editor may then need to investigate the use of a relational database, which allows the user to link several different databases. Relational systems have been essential to large-scale, long-term projects like the Lincoln Legal Papers and the Thomas A. Edison Papers, which have exceptionally large amounts of data to be manipulated and very complex needs in terms of indexing and retrieval. The design of an effective relational database usually demands the assistance of an outside consultant, which may prove too expensive for a small, short-term edition.

Even though the control files' ultimate purpose is "control" of the materials identified as being appropriate to the edition's base of sources, editors will need to make prototypical entries in that database before sending out the first request to an owner-repository, so as to be prepared when materials arrive. And these prototypes can be entered only after the user has designed a screen for entering data. Modifying this screen by adding new fields once data have been entered can be extraordinarily difficult. Thus, the screen design must be carefully planned and thought out even before the editor can begin looking for the sources to be edited.

## IV. COLLECTION OF SOURCES

The mere need for a particular documentary edition may indicate that little is known about the source materials on which that edition will be based. If all the variant versions of the correspondence or papers of a given writer, group, or organization were in one convenient location, it would be unnecessary to fund a project to locate and catalog them. If an archival collection were already adequately arranged and described in a published finding aid, there would be no need to appoint an editor to assume the burden of creating one. No authoritative edition is possible without a thorough canvass of source materials that may deserve a place in it. No documentary edition is any better than the collection of materials on which it is based, and projects that misplace or lose documents or photocopies often waste more than time and money. Long before scholars begin to edit, they become tracers of lost documents and masters of archival management.

Thus, few editors can escape becoming experts in some aspects of the collection, care, retrieval, and cataloging of documentary materials. In all likelihood, they will be called upon to create an entirely new archive, which may include photocopies, original manuscripts, microfilm reels, and electronically transmitted facsimiles that together can be called "the Papers of X," "the Records of Y," or "the Writings of Z." It is the editor's responsibility to make sure that this archive is as complete as possible and that the project's staff, because of intelligent cataloging procedures, will be able to find what they need there. If they are truly diligent, they might receive a tribute like the one paid by Debra Newman to Robert Hill and his cadre of Marcus Garvey's editors: "While conducting research for a guide to records for black history among the civilian records in the National Archives, wherever I found Garvey records, there was evidence that Hill's staff had already seen them" (309).

Most editors must first identify the location of documents from a variety of sources. This phase of editing may be the most physically taxing, but the rewards of discovery and victory over the vagaries of time and chance, the accidents of war and natural disasters, and the carelessness of heirs are often the sweetest that editors taste. The work of collection begins with a survey of what is already known about the body of documents to be gathered. The editor will begin, then, as a conventional enumerative bibliographer for the individual, organization, or group that is the subject of his or her edition. The basic reference tools for the study of American history and literature will come into play: the appropriate sections of the monumental *Guide to Reference Works,* initiated under the editorship of Constance Winchell and continued by Eugene Sheehy and Robert Balay, and the *Harvard Guide to American History,* rev. ed. (1974). Modern editors now have access to such effort-saving tools as the cumulative electronic editions of abstracting and indexing services such as *America: History and Life* and the *MLA International Bibliography* for searching monographic literature since the early 1980s. Luckier still are editors who have access to on-line services, such as DIA-LOG, which provide access to dozens of bibliographic databases at once. Unfortunately, these electronic editions are not retrospective: the bound volumes of the printed equivalents of the series must be searched as well for publications of earlier decades. Once the background bibliography is completed and the works listed have been located, the editor combs footnotes for citations to original materials, noting the date, description, and location of every document that earlier scholars have unearthed. The editor should also enlist the co-operation of scholars who have shown an interest in the project's subject, for even if these men and women have published the findings of their earlier research, their notes on sources and their experience in canvassing the same repositories that the editor may visit will be of invaluable assistance.

The first use made of an edition's control file will be the creation of lists of the pertinent holdings of given repositories. Notes of likely sources can be entered in the control file without the accession number that indicates that a document actually exists as part of the office's collection. Entries into the field labeled "location" are usually based on the system of location symbols for American repositories devised for the Library of Congress's *National Union Catalog of Manuscript Collections (NUCMC)*. (The authoritative source for these location symbols is *Symbols of American Libraries*, 14th ed.) This standardized system avoids the possibility of duplication of symbols, which can occur when they are invented on the spot by the editor. The system is easily mastered by the editorial staff and expanded to its full form in an automated database. It consists of a code that contains two or three elements, each beginning with a capital letter. The first element stands for the state in which the repository is located, the second represents the city or town, and the third stands for the repository itself. If this is the official repository of records for a state or city, then not all elements are used. For example, "N" stands for the State Library of New York at Albany, "NBu" represents the archives of the City of Buffalo, and "NBuHi" stands for the Buffalo and Erie County Historical Society. Should the project need to devise symbols for libraries not listed in the *National Union Catalog,* the same principle can be used.

Editors should also check earlier editions of the correspondence, journals, or personal or organizational papers to be edited and index their contents for use in the collection phase of the new edition. Although such printed versions may be flawed, some may prove to be the only ones that survive. These citations, too, are entered in the edition's database, following the same pattern used for entries recording located documents. When earlier printed texts prove to be the only ones available for materials whose originals have been lost, these records remain part of that permanent file. When printed texts are matched to the originals that were their sources, the bibliographic information for the printed version is simply added to the "notes" field in the original's permanent record. Beyond their value as records of lost originals, these earlier editions also provide clues to patterns of correspondence: the identities of correspondents as well as geographical and chronological patterns of an individual's letter writing.

As back runs of periodicals often provide printed versions of documentary material, an editor should give special attention to those journals that customarily publish special sections of printed documents or routinely include portions of the collections of a historical society or other special library. Journals that consistently publish articles and documents related to the editor's subject are also excellent locations for notices of the inauguration of the editorial project. Unfortunately, editors of many scholarly journals have adopted strict policies on accepting such advertisements. Some may refuse to print such announcements, while others demand a fee. Still, editors should make every attempt to advertise the project as early as possible, in such journals and in newspapers like the *New York Times* and the *Washington Post,* which boast a nationwide audience, and in newspapers serving regions where the project's subject flourished.

## A. DEFINING THE SCOPE OF THE SEARCH

The editor's preliminary files will indicate the names of the individuals and organizations whose personal papers or institutional archives are likely to contain other materials useful for the project as well as those collections known to include specific sources of interest. Next comes the compiling of lists of certain and suspected repositories of documents for the new editorial archive that the project will create.

### *1. Manuscripts*

For American manuscript material, seven reference series offer the best guides for an outline of such a search for documents. Each has special limitations and individual virtues, and the editor may have to consult all of them.

a. The "Hamer Guide," Philip M. Hamer's *A Guide to Archives and Manuscripts in the United States,* appeared in 1961 as part of the NHPC program, of which Hamer was executive director. It lists 1,300 repositories. Descriptive entries for each source vary, depending on the information supplied by the repositories and on existing catalogs of their collections. The entries, however, are usually generous enough to make clear the major focus of each archive and to list its major collections by name. When printed catalogs for a repository or one of its collections exist, these are noted.

b. "NHPRC Directory" refers to the commission's *Directory of Archives and Manuscript Repositories in the United States* (2d ed., 1988). Although it covers thousands of repositories, its descriptions of individual collections are spare. The entry for each library or archive offers the institution's address and telephone number as well as information on policies for access and photocopying and a very general description of the focus of these collections. The Directory cites manuscript catalogs and calendars published since the appearance of the Hamer Guide, but it does not repeat information given in that earlier commission publication. The entries in the Directory, do, however, give generous cross-references to fuller descriptions of institutional holdings that may appear in the Hamer Guide, *NUCMC, American Literary Manuscripts,* and other printed sources.

c. The *National Union Catalog of Manuscript Collections* (*NUCMC*) began periodic publication by the Library of Congress in 1962. The volumes contain reduced photoreproductions of the cards prepared by the library for its union catalog of American manuscript collections. These cards were based on data furnished by each manuscript repository, and their thoroughness and accuracy vary greatly. The entries are arranged in the order of their accession by the library's staff, but the indexes to each volume and the periodic cumulative indexes to the series enable the determined reader to locate entries that contain information on specific persons, groups, or topics, as well as to pinpoint collections reported by a given repository. The development of the nationwide bibliographic utilities, Online Computer Library Center (OCLC) and the Research Libraries Information Network (RLIN), and the development of Machine-Readable Cataloging–Archives and Manuscripts Control (MARC-AMC), the standard machine-readable format for cataloging manuscript collections, demanded a modification of *NUCMC* and its scope. In the 1980s, it became clear that a substantial number of the records provided to the *National Union Catalog* merely duplicated MARC-AMC records that repositories were providing to the on-line OCLC and RLIN services. It was decided not only to end print publication of new *NUCMC* records with volume 29 but also to limit involvement of the Library of Congress staff to creating MARC records for manuscript cataloging data provided by repositories that were unable to enter their own manuscript cataloging into either of the computerized resources.

d. Because MARC format for manuscripts and archives did not become standard until 1984, researchers will also welcome the *Index to Personal Names in the National Union Catalog of Manuscript Collections, 1959–1984* (2 vols.).

e. RLIN and OCLC, then, will be the only nationally available sources for new NUCMC records in years to come, and these bibliographic databases should also be searched for entries submitted independently of NUCMC. These modern nationwide bibliographic utilities provide electronic union lists of the collections of many of America's major repositories of rare books and manuscript collections. While some major research libraries offer patrons access to links to RLIN and OCLC, most users will have to request that a "mediated search" be conducted on their behalf by a librarian trained in search techniques peculiar to these bibliographic utilities. Whether the search is direct or mediated, the editor should become familiar with the database's capacity for author and subject retrieval so that the search will be as efficient as possible. Because not every library and historical society has completed retrospective conversion of their catalogs to RLIN or OCLC records, searches of the converted records should be supplemented by consulting nonelectronic sources.

f. *American Literary Manuscripts* refers to J. Albert Robbins' *American Literary Manuscripts: A Checklist of Holdings in Academic, Historical, and Public Libraries, Museums, and Authors' Homes in the United States,* (2d ed., 1977). This guide reports the holdings of only six hundred repositories, but these are described in great detail. The entries are based on canvasses of the holdings of manuscripts written by 2,750 men and women deemed of special significance in the history of American literature. The entry for each individual includes Library of Congress codes for institutions holding his or her manuscripts, the size of these collections, and notes of any existing finding aids.

g. Researchers with access to a library owning Chadwyck-Healey's 1996 CD-ROM *Archives U.S.A.* will be spared much of this labor. This electronic source provides access to all pre-1984 *NUCMC* records, Chadwyck-Healey's own *Index to Personal Names in the National Union Catalog of Manuscript Collections, 1959–1984,* and the *NHPRC Directory* series.

Few significant American figures confined their correspondence or their professional activities to the United States, and their heirs did not limit the sale of family papers to American collectors. Editors should thus be equally cosmopolitan in searching for surviving papers. The best guide to published catalogs and other finding aids for materials in foreign repositories is the excellent section "Foreign Archives of Interest to American Historians" in the *Harvard Guide to American History*. It remains the most logical and comprehensive survey of such literature, although it is now twenty-five years old and has not been updated. To supplement the *Harvard Guide,* editors should consult recent issues of *American Archivist* and *America: History and Life: Writings in American History,* as well as pertinent sections in the Winchell-Sheehy-Balay *Guide to Reference Works.*

### 2. Printed Documents

Most individuals significant enough to warrant a documentary edition of their writings have written works for publication, which editors should also collect and evaluate. At this early stage, documentary editors can confine themselves to the basic methods and terminology of enumerative bibliography and the preparation of reliable and comprehensive listings of printed works and their various editions. Obviously, the editor of the papers of any public figure or organization should compile a bibliography of the printed works produced by that author or group. The editor's preliminary inventory of "known" writings will form a skeletal enumerative bibliography. To expand this list, the editor will probably need to consult a wide variety of reference works and published catalogs that apply to the period and the field in which the subject was prominent. For the eighteenth century, as an example, scholars routinely consult Charles Evans' *American Bibliography: A Chronological Dictionary of All Books, Pamphlets and Periodical Publications Printed in the United States of America from the Genesis of Printing in 1639 down to and Including the Year 1820* (13 vols.), which serves as a chronological dictionary of imprints through 1800, as well as Roger P. Bristol's *Supplement to Charles Evans' American Bibliography.* Students of American bibliography of the early nineteenth century consult the series familiarly called Shaw-Shoemaker, namely, *American Bibliography: A Preliminary Checklist for 1801–1819,* compiled by Ralph R. Shaw and Richard H. Shoemaker (19 vols.), which has been continued for the 1820s and 1830s as *A Checklist of American Imprints,* compiled by Shoemaker and other scholars. The most convenient source for guidance to such reference tools is G. Thomas Tanselle's *Guide to the Study of United States Imprints* (2 vols.). Holdings listed in these printed guides should be supplemented by reference to RLIN and OCLC.

Bibliography for the editor does not stop with an enumerative listing. Catalogs of rare books and pamphlets use the vocabulary of descriptive bibliography, which pinpoints the physical differences among various editions, impressions, states, or issues of the same work. Editors should master this terminology to determine whether they have located all the pertinent variants for such printed documents. The standard works in this field, such as Fredson Bowers, *Principles of Bibliographical Description*, and Philip Gaskell, *A New Introduction to Bibliography*, can intimidate novices, who may wish to introduce themselves to the field more gently by first reading Terry Belanger's helpful essay, "Descriptive Bibliography," in *Book Collecting*, edited by Jean Peters; the second edition of William Proctor Williams and Craig S. Abbott's *An Introduction to Bibliographical and Textual Studies*; Ronald B. McKerrow's classic, *An Introduction to Bibliography for Literary Students;* or chapters 3 and 4 of David C. Greetham's *Textual Scholarship: An Introduction*.

Planning a search of periodical literature is exceptionally challenging. While most magazines publish a cumulative index—or at least a table of contents—newspapers represent a greater problem. For an author's contributions to newspapers, earlier biographies and the writer's correspondence may offer clues for a search for pertinent issues. The editor whose study focuses on the pre-1820 period has the great advantage of access to Clarence Brigham's *History and Bibliography of American Newspapers, 1690–1820* (2 vols., 1947), plus his *Additions and Corrections,* published in 1961. For the later period, students can consult the work of the U.S. Newspaper Program, whose lists of volume-specific newspaper holdings for more than 77,000 libraries are now part of the OCLC database as well as being available on microfiche. The *Harvard Guide* and pertinent sections in Tanselle's *U.S. Imprints* offer the best discussions of finding aids of the pre-computer era. In some regions, surviving Works Progress Administration guides supplement these sources, and checklists of newspapers in microform will allow the editor to identify those periodicals that can be obtained in microfilm or microfiche on interlibrary loan. All of these sources should be supplemented by reference to the most current volumes of *A Guide to Reference Works* and its periodic supplements.

No two editors follow the same line of attack, but all will find it useful to consult colleagues who have completed a search similar to the one they project. The editors of the *Frederick Douglass Papers,* for instance, had to reconstruct the runs of antebellum newspapers that Douglass edited and published, and they first sent letters of inquiry to all American historical societies, to colleges founded before 1860, and to all public libraries founded before 1860 in the states in which most of the newspapers' subscribers lived. They also wrote to all libraries and historical societies in the United Kingdom and Jamaica. Appeals went to dealers as well. This mail canvass located 60 percent of the missing issues, and the editors then sent out a new mailing that covered all American libraries in states where subscribers resided. In the twenty years since the Douglass project began its work, progress on providing reliable, comprehensive union lists of American periodical literature have made such a search far less arduous, but the logical design of such canvasses should be as careful as ever.

Few editors will be able to afford the kind of search required of the Douglass editors, but their methods furnish good guidelines. In searching for printed documents, as for manuscripts, the law of diminishing returns applies. The editor should first make contact with the repositories most likely to have the needed materials. Only after these returns have come can the editor decide whether the first canvass was fruitful enough to justify a second and wider appeal.

### 3. Dealers and Collectors

Unless an edition's subject is a recently deceased and obscure figure, the editor will probably not be the first to have shown an interest in collecting relevant documents. Tracing the course of materials that have passed into the hands of dealers in rare books and manuscripts is one of the most time-consuming and frustrating tasks an editor must confront. Editors should gauge carefully the time allotted to searching for the records of such transactions and must accept the fact that they will never unravel every mystery concerning such sales. In the words of one experienced editor, "You do the best you can with the time and money available." Careful planning is essential if the editor is to make the best possible use of the weeks or months allotted to this aspect of the research.

Records of sales of documents fall into two categories: auction catalogs and dealers' listings. Catalogs list only items to be offered for sale to bidders at public auctions. Generally such catalogs receive a wider distribution than the periodic issues of listings prepared by individual dealers and circulated among special libraries and the dealers' longtime customers. The latter generally quote the prices asked for individual items, and sales are concluded by written or telephone contact between the purchaser and the dealer.

The wider circulation of auction catalogs ensures that they are more likely to survive. Consulting such catalogs is further simplified by the existence of the yearly volumes of *American Book-Prices Current (ABPC)*, which since 1895 has provided an indexed, comprehensive listing of manuscripts and rare books sold at auction in the United States. Volumes after 1956 also cover materials sold at London auction houses. Cumulative indexes to back issues of the *ABPC* simplify the editor's work in recovering listings of the sales of materials relevant to his or her project, and its records from 1975 to the present can be conveniently searched in a CD-ROM format as well.

The *ABPC* is only a starting point for the editor. Its descriptions of items cannot reproduce completely the information offered in the original auction catalogs, nor does it reproduce any photographic facsimiles that may have accompanied the original auction listing. Using its references, the editor should obtain the auction catalogs from which the *ABPC*'s notices were drawn. Here George L. McKay's *American Book Auction Catalogues, 1713–1934: A Union List* (New York, 1938) is an invaluable finding aid.

Although post-1956 *ABPC* listings include London auction sales, the editor whose subject maintained a considerable correspondence abroad or whose papers are popular among European collectors should weigh the need for a search of foreign dealers' records. Unfortunately, the autograph and rare book trades of the Continent have felt no need to create regular national listings comparable to the American *ABPC* or the analogous British series, *Book-Prices Current* and *Book Auction Prices*. (A notable exception is Germany's *Jahrbuch der Auktionpreise*.) Some American auction houses maintain in-house files of European catalogs, and the Grolier Club of New York City and the British Library in London boast generous holdings of these records. Before venturing outside the records of the American market, the editor should consult a dealer who specializes in manuscripts and books relating to the project's focus. Expert advice can save an editor months of wasted effort, particularly if the advice is, "Don't bother. It won't be worth your trouble."

Dealers' listings, because of their irregular publication and limited circulation, suffer a higher mortality rate than auction catalogs. Editors who can identify dealers who have consistently specialized in materials of interest to their work may obtain access to their back files of lists and offerings. Failing that, there are several other choices. Any repository with a large collection of the papers or writings of a prominent figure will be on the mailing lists of dealers who frequently offer these materials for sale and usually keep these circulars on file, available to scholars. Similarly, an individual collector with an interest in the editor's subject will share a place on those same mailing lists, and he or she may be able to provide access to such listings.

The editor whose manuscript materials fall in the period 1763–1815 can consult Helen Cripe and Diane Campbell's *American Manuscripts, 1763–1815: An Index to Documents Described in Auction Records and Dealers' Catalogs*. This monumental work indexes entries in auction catalogs before 1895 (the year of the *ABPC*'s inauguration) as well as dealers' listings through 1970. Entries are indexed by date, name of correspondent or author, and name of dealer. Even editors whose projects fall outside the 1763–1815 period should consult *American Manuscripts: Part 3*, which contains the only extant published inventory of dealers' listings (with repositories owning these items); its surveys of periodicals in the autograph- and book-collecting trades are invaluable. Like *ABPC, American Manuscripts* is only a starting point, providing nothing more than the dates and titles of manuscript materials. The bibliographical information offered in the volumes merely leads to the rare and scattered copies of dealers' lists and catalogs, where full descriptive entries appear.

In planning a search, the editor should enter the text of copies of notices from auction catalogs and dealers' listings in the project's database, just as was done with earlier printed versions of documents. These records, too, can reveal patterns of correspondence of which earlier researchers were completely unaware, and they will ensure that the editor pursues all fruitful leads in consulting guides to manuscript repositories and in making on-site searches of collections. Once the search is completed, the editor will often find that these listings are the only surviving evidence that X wrote to Y on a given day, and notices that offer précis, lengthy extracts, or photographic facsimiles of these "lost" documents will be an important addition to the edition's files.

## B. COLLECTING PHOTOCOPIES: THE MAIL CANVASS

When the results of these preliminary inventories of primary and secondary sources have been entered in a database, the data can be sorted into patterns that serve the editor's purposes. With manual methods, this will mean tedious ordering and reordering of slips. With automated equipment, it means a request for reports in appropriate formats. A report arranged by repository gives a convenient list of items that should be ordered from specific libraries or archives. A report arranged by correspondent can open a new range of searching if certain individuals appear frequently on this list. After consulting both budget and timetable, the editor can begin the process of locating the original materials and, where appropriate, of obtaining photocopies for the project's archives. Some institutions contain so much material that only a personal visit from editors or their deputies will ensure a complete search, but a good part of the search will probably be conducted by mail. When likely institutions have been identified, every effort should be made to learn whether finding aids to pertinent collections have been published or whether unpublished finding aids have been made available in electronic form.

The scope of the mail canvass will be dictated by several factors: the era in which the project's figure lived; the nature of the subject's prominence; and the history and geographical distribution of the personal or organizational records involved. At one end of the spectrum are the papers of men or women who (1) maintained meticulous files of their own papers, (2) spent a relatively obscure life unlikely to make their manuscripts attractive to autograph dealers, and (3) died within the previous decade, before their fame could spread and their papers could be dispersed. Here it can be assumed that such a figure's personal archive represents copies of all or nearly all the materials to be located and that there has not been time or reason for recipients' copies of letters to be scattered or destroyed. The search can be confined largely to the subject's correspondents (or their heirs) and to the files of the businesses, educational institutions, or government agencies in which that figure performed his or her professional work.

There is a correspondingly greater challenge for the editor of the papers of a more conventionally famous individual, whose personal papers are likely to have been dispersed during the decades or centuries after his or her death. Here the editor's contacts cannot be limited to repositories where there are known to be collections of papers likely to produce materials for the project. A blind search will be necessary, one that extends to institutions where there is no reason to suspect that such documents survive. Editors should again respect the law of diminishing returns in conducting such canvasses. Letters of inquiry should go first to libraries known to own materials pertinent to the project. Here the editor knows that photocopies should be made, bills should be paid, and questions should be answered. Obviously it makes sense to begin this chain of correspondence as soon as possible.

Editors of the records of formal groups or organizations must be even more resourceful. They will have to identify the officers and other leaders of such bodies, whose names frequently appeared as signatories on official correspondence. Many of the organizations' letters and other outgoing communications that have made their way to academic libraries or other repositories will have been indexed under the names of individual "authors," not the organization involved. And the editors must naturally pinpoint collections of the papers of such individuals as likely sources of materials for the organizational archive.

Whether an editor seeks the records of an individual or a group, the form letter used for the blind search will be the basis for the entire mail canvass. (A sample of such letters appears in the Appendix.) It should include (1) a description of the project's scope and an indication of its scholarly credentials in terms of sponsorship or endorsement, (2) a clear statement of the types of materials needed by the project, and (3) an indication of the editor's businesslike attitude toward library procedures, which may include enclosing a stamped self-addressed envelope for the addressee's convenience. When the form letter is modified for an institution where materials are known to exist, the editor should not only list the materials in question but also name the sources that indicate that these documents are part of the repository's collections. It is also wise to make clear that the editor's interest is not confined to the list offered, since additional acquisitions or improved cataloging may have enlarged the list of the repository's holdings.

The reasons for these elements in a project's appeals by mail are self-evident. A letter from an editorial project is only one of dozens of time-consuming inquiries a librarian or curator will receive each week. That letter should convince its recipients that the project is recognized as a worthwhile scholarly endeavor whose request merits the time and trouble it will demand. A specific description of the materials needed will spare curators unnecessary work and will ensure that the editor receives all the needed information and documents from an individual repository. A list of known materials will assist the librarian in locating items in the same collections that may not be cataloged. A statement of the editor's realistic attitude toward library procedures will reassure correspondents that the letter comes from an experienced professional, not an inexperienced or amateur researcher.

Word-processing equipment eases the burdens of a mail canvass, for much of this software was originally designed for business offices, where such form letters are routinely required. The preliminary control file's findings on institutions with pertinent holdings will provide the list of repositories that will become the basis for addresses for a word-processor's mail merge operations. For blind search letters, the word-processor can reproduce the body of the letter as many times as necessary, and most can import the appropriate inside addresses from a database. For those libraries known to have material for the project, the editor simply adds a paragraph listing specific items.

The mail canvass should establish early contact with institutions that may require more time to answer the editor's request, and the editor should first dispatch letters to institutions that are certain to possess materials essential to the edition. Letters to foreign repositories should be sent early in the process. Clearly it will take longer to obtain photocopies from abroad than from a neighboring state. It will also take longer for librarians at institutions that have a dozen manuscripts to locate and photocopy those items than for librarians whose collections contain no pertinent manuscripts to respond to a blind search letter with a polite note indicating that they can be of no help.

The scope of the blind search depends not only on the project's budget and schedule but also on the prominence of the figure or organization central to the project's work. For an exceptionally celebrated figure, that search may have to extend to every institution listed in the current editions of the *American Library Directory* and *Directory of Special Libraries and Information Centers* that admits to having a manuscript or special collections division, as well as to all historical societies in the United States. For lesser-known subjects, the blind search might be confined to institutions whose focus of collections or geographical location makes it likely that their holdings will include items of interest to the project. In general, it is better to cast the collecting net too widely than too narrowly. A veteran of a decades-long search remarked: "A vacuum cleaner is more efficient than a broom and a dustpan."

### C. ON-SITE SEARCHES

The editor's preliminary research usually produces a list of repositories whose holdings will require a personal search. Responses to the project's mail canvass will often reveal that the resources of an institution are so limited that its staff cannot even search for a half-dozen known items. The wise editor first turns for advice to other scholars who have visited the institution in question, learning from their personal experience of a given library's procedures.

Beyond this, no personal search should be undertaken without first confirming that a visit will be convenient for the institution and its staff. Budgetary considerations, local holidays, and even the opening of a new exhibition can force a library to modify its days or hours. Some of the collections to be consulted may be temporarily unavailable or housed in a separate facility with access limited to those who have made appointments in advance. Aside from such practical considerations, documentary editors must remember that their searches place far greater demands on a library than those of more conventional scholars. The editor who arrives unannounced at a historical society to canvass three dozen collections will receive a cold welcome. And any scholar who plans to bring special equipment such as a laptop computer, digital scanner, or personal photo-copier, must ask in advance whether a library's wiring or rules on the handling of rare materials permit their use.

The effective editor appears promptly and as well-prepared as possible. Upon arrival, the editor asks whether the library has un-published finding aids to the collections to be consulted. (Any pub-lished finding tools should be consulted in advance, and "publica-tion" now includes on-line availability over the Internet for many repositories.) Editors cannot assume that understanding the work-ings of one institution's catalog means that they have mastered the peculiarities of catalogs found elsewhere. Direct questions about any peculiarities in filing or access methods will help the editor find everything there is to find. The definition of a cataloged or an in-dexed manuscript collection, for instance, can differ from one repos-itory to another. Some archivists may consider a group of manu-scripts to be completely indexed if there is a file giving alphabetical access to the names of authors of pieces in the collection. In that case, the editor will need an alphabetically arranged enumeration of the subject's most constant correspondents. Working from this list, the editor can consult index files, alphabetically arranged "miscella-neous" folders, and collections of autographs for letters written by these men and women to or about the subject.

Since most editors conduct their searches with a view to placing orders for photocopies or microfilm, the editor should ask the cura-tor of a collection if there is a preferred method of marking or flag-ging items for photoreproduction before beginning work. If the ap-propriate marker, usually a piece of labeled acid-free paper, can be placed immediately with the appropriate document, the original ma-terials will be spared unnecessary handling, and the editor will not have to go back through the collections to insert these markers.

A running list of such materials should be kept whether or not markers are placed. This list should note each item's location and de-scription, record pertinent information about the document's physi-cal appearance, and indicate whether it is an original or a photocopy, a recipient's copy or an authorial draft of a letter, a fair copy or a pre-liminary authorial draft of a document. The list should also note the document's length and details such as address leaves or endorse-ments. This list will serve as the basis of the reproduction order it-self, and it will allow the editor to check the completed order. And since it may be necessary to consult the original manuscript or printed materials again, the detailed list will make it easy to retrieve the items a second or third time.

The editor with special requirements for document reproduction should explain these to the staff of the library or archive before placing an order. Some projects seek negative microfilms that can conveniently produce positive paper prints for their files, while many libraries prefer to keep the negative of any microfilm made from their collections as a security or record copy. In such a case, the library may be willing to furnish a direct-image duplicate negative. If the library's laboratory facilities do not permit such processing, the editor should be sure that the positive film provided will meet the requirements of the outside laboratory that will make the necessary conversion. When a project calls for a facsimile edition, whether of microform or scanned images, the degree of resolution and the reduction ratio in any films or digital images made for the project should meet appropriate, consistent standards. Most microfilm cameras and scanners can be adjusted, but instructions and resettings should be determined in advance. The editor with facsimile publication in mind should also attempt to obtain as many of the project's hard copy prints as possible in positive rather than negative form, since these will reproduce more clearly in the next generation of photoduplication.

The editor should accept as immutable law any special policies a library has for photoreproduction or scanning. Generally there are good and sufficient reasons for rules of this kind. Many libraries will not permit an editor—or any other patron—to use a personal copier or digital scanner to obtain images. This rule simply acknowledges the fact that rare materials require careful handling by a professional. If a library insists on retaining a negative of microfilms, it is only because of concern for security of the original materials. Libraries that demand the eventual return of any photocopies of their materials do so because some researchers have donated such photocopies to other research centers without the permission of the owner-institution. Restrictions on photocopying or scanning bound volumes and fragile manuscripts exist for the protection of these source materials. Curators of rare material are usually only too happy to explain the reasons for these and other rules.

## D.  A WORD ON RESEARCH ETIQUETTE

Curators and librarians respond favorably to kind and courteous treatment and intelligent questions. The librarian who answers a blind-search letter deserves a personal note of thanks. The curator who provides photocopies by mail or extends hospitality to on-site searches deserves even more praise and gratitude. Editors who make themselves memorable for good manners will be kept in mind when any institution acquires a new collection or catalogs an existing one and discovers unsuspected riches for their projects. A long-term project may have to conduct several canvasses, and the editor who needs to visit a repository more than once has special need for a warm welcome and the staff's full cooperation, not a cold shoulder and the brusque dismissal, "If it's not in the card catalog or the MARC records, we don't have it." Should the project need to hire searchers on a free-lance basis to canvass distant collections, these deputies should be drilled in the project's practical requirements and in the standards of proper scholarly behavior. If the editor is new to the area of scholarly research, John C. Larsen's edition of the *Researcher's Guide to Archives and Regional History Sources* provides a good introduction to professional vocabulary and procedural traditions.

Editors who hope to establish a working relationship with autograph dealers and collectors must exercise an even greater degree of diplomacy. Prudent editors exploit the results of their canvass of sale records for manuscripts and printed materials beyond planning the project's search and supplementing the document file. A review of the records of these transactions may reveal that a few dealers specialize in the project's subject. At the least, consideration shown to these dealers can ensure the editor a place on their mailing lists for future offerings. The lucky will find among such dealers a friend to offer advice and even introductions to private collectors and other dealers who will lead the editor to more original materials.

If the project's subject has been a popular one for collectors, it will pay the editor to pursue this tactic. A dealer or auction house may be willing to open its old records so that the editor can consult inventories of collections sold decades ago, for which there is no published listing of contents. Dealers will sometimes disclose the identities of institutional purchasers (though not of private buyers) of specific items. In some cases, the editor may find it worthwhile to consult books about patterns of collecting in his or her field. Working from published catalogs of auctions and from dealers' listings, an editor may be able to guess which collectors (or their agents) were likely to have purchased certain items; the editor can then begin discreet and tactful approaches to those collectors or their heirs.

Rare book and autograph collectors frequently choose not to advertise the existence, much less the extent or nature, of their collections because they have no wish to be troubled by the inquiries of scholars, and they are well aware that their collections can be the targets of theft. Dealers who wish to stay in business are conscious of their clients' concern for privacy. Dealers promise confidentiality to those individuals who purchase rare materials, and they will not and should not violate that promise to assist any editor. When an individual collector shares the contents of a collection with an editorial project, that individual's wishes concerning the use of these materials should be honored to the letter. When a collector directs that his or her name not be given as the owner of any documents used in the edition, then the source line for these texts should read "in a private collection." If there is public access to project files, correspondence with private collectors should be kept in a section of the office where security can be assured. Access to many private manuscript collections has been advanced by the creation of the Manuscript Society Database at Arizona State University, which provides access to hundreds of private collections owned by society members.

Some collectors and dealers voice concern that print publication of a manuscript's text will lessen its market value. The editor can often persuade them otherwise by pointing to what Katharine Kyes Leab calls the "imprimatur value" that original material receives by being chosen as the source for all or part of a definitive edition. Happily, there is one group of collectors unlikely to be concerned about devaluing their collections by authorizing publication: specialists in the collection of stamps and other materials relating to postal history. Frequently the items purchased because of their philatelic interest (envelopes and address leaves) are accompanied by the letter covered by that significantly franked or postmarked material. Not only are postal collectors more willing than autograph specialists to share their collections with editors, but they are also potentially valuable consultants, as their expertise in the mechanics of the transmittal of correspondence can save an editor countless errors in dating materials and in assessing the significance of details of postal markings.

Journals directed to collectors should be supplied with notices announcing a project's creation, but the editor need not wait for responses to these advertisements before establishing contact with dealers. During a project's life, its staff must continue to review current auction catalogs and dealers' listings. When such notices appear for an auction house in the vicinity of the edition's offices or in the neighborhood of a friendly editorial colleague, a member of the staff or other deputy can usually view the document while it is on public display before the auction. Although auction houses frown on the use of cameras during these viewing periods, few object to an editor's taking notes or even discreetly making a handwritten transcript of a letter.

Even the editor who obtains a transcript of a manuscript being offered for sale would prefer a photocopy of the original for the edition's files, and when it is impossible to have a transcription made, it is even more important that the editor make every effort to persuade the manuscript's purchaser to provide such a copy. No responsible dealer or auction house, however, will disclose a private purchaser's identity; and a pair of form letters must be prepared to meet this reality: one addressed to the dealer and the second directed to "To whom it may concern" and accompanied by a stamped, self-addressed envelope, to be forwarded to the item's purchaser. (Samples of such letters appear in the Appendix.)

When collectors fail to respond to such appeals, the editor should not curse them for insensitivity. Collectors of manuscripts of recent date are a sophisticated lot who understand the niceties of copyright law. Although they can claim physical ownership of the inscribed paper of interest to the editor, they hold no literary rights to the text embodied in that document. In these cases, a responsible collector cannot authorize further dissemination of the document without the permission of the author or the author's heirs or any others with copyright claims.

## V. Cataloging and Control

Even while the search continues, photocopied documents arrive on the doorstep of the collecting editor, who must master the art of cataloging and control of documents. The most comprehensive search is wasted if the editor or a project's staff are unable to retrieve individual items or groups of items that they have collected. The editorial staff should also guard against cataloging documents that do not fall within the project's scope or miscataloging pertinent items. The process of authenticating documents by handwriting, signatures, and literary style begins now. To these methods of identification the editor should add a sense of logic and historical context, assigning dates or authors to undated or unsigned materials. As Lester Cappon reminded editors, "authenticity of the document is the cardinal rule, axiomatic by the very nature of historical method" ("A Rationale for Historical Editing," p. 57).

In rare cases, the editor will be not only the publisher of printed texts of original source materials but also the curator of these documents during the project's life. Some large-scale documentary projects, such as the Adams Papers at the Massachusetts Historical Society, the Benjamin Franklin Papers at Yale, and the Thomas A. Edison Papers, have files that include both photocopies gathered throughout the world and original manuscript collections held at their sponsoring institutions. It is more usual, however, for editors to serve as manuscript or rare book curators when their editions are archival ones, limited to a specific group of manuscripts or printed works owned by the institution that sponsors the project.

Editors who are not archivists or rare book librarians by training must learn the rudiments of these professions so that the unique materials entrusted to their care do not suffer. Even editors who do not have this responsibility would be wise to learn the tricks of these trades, for the knowledge will assist them in understanding the methods of the repositories to be searched and in devising a system of cataloging the new editorial archives created by the edition's research.

Should an original collection be uncataloged before it is assigned to an editor, the curator of the institution's other holdings should be consulted, to make certain that the methods used to arrange the editorial collection will be compatible with those used for other materials at the repository. Editors who must plan the arrangement and description of these materials should consult the Society of American Archivists' *Basic Manual* series, which provides a continually updated group of pamphlets outlining approved methods for cataloging various kinds of manuscript, photographic, and artifactual sources in formats accepted by the professional archival community. Standard archival methods, however, may not meet all of the needs of a nonarchival editorial project. Editors who deal with variant versions of the same documents from several sources must often invent systems for identifying the source of each copy or original.

## A. ACCESSIONING MATERIALS

The first step in establishing physical control over an edition's documents file is to assign each document an identifying number (usually called the accession number) that indicates the order in which the document or its copy was added to the project's files. Projects that need to maintain separate files for discrete groups of materials can use two or more sequential series. One series may contain the numbers 01, 02, 03, and so on; the second can begin with 001, 002, 003; and the third, with 0001, 0002, 0003. For photocopies, these accession numbers can be stamped or written by hand on the back of the reproduction. If a document is represented by more than one page of photocopy, sequential page numbers are a convenience, and the leaves of the copy might be labeled 017.1, 017.2, and so on. Of course, no such stamps or written numbers should be imposed on original materials; identifying numbers on the documents' individual folders must suffice. Should the project's collection include such materials as letterbooks, notebooks, or ledgers containing dozens of items of varying dates and titles, the best initial method may be to assign the same accession number to the entire volume and to file the photocopied leaves together rather than to separate individual items. The chronological and alphabetical sections of the project's control file will furnish access to individual entries, and the integrity of the original will be preserved. Once editorial work begins, patterns that divide these volumes into distinct and independent sections often become apparent. The editor may then wish to add numerical extensions to the original accession number (10001.1, 10001.2. etc.) so that each discrete section can receive separate cataloging in terms of date, authorship, or topic.

The staff member responsible for accessioning materials must also check photocopies for completeness. If the copies result from an on-site search, the searcher's descriptive list is the basis for comparison. Should the copy arrive as the result of a mail canvass, the cataloger must check closely for possible omissions—margins cut off by careless photocopying or the absence of endorsement or address leaves whose existence can be deduced from show-through on another page of the copy. Any questions concerning such imperfections should be raised immediately in a letter to the curator of the original material.

### B. LABELING AND ARRANGING FOLDERS

With traditional manual control files, documents or their facsimiles were usually assigned control numbers before cataloging information was entered into the control file. Once an item had been assigned its identifying number, a file folder was prepared with a label containing the following information: accession number, date, and a brief version of the document's title. This label was placed where it could be seen easily when the editor flipped through the shelved folders. Arrangement of this information on the label in this manual system had to reflect the organizing principles of the project's archive: whatever element of information determined the document's location in the master section of the control file appeared at the top of the label. For collections focusing on correspondence, this was usually the date. For collections of technical material arranged topically, a key word in the document title might be the cue for filing. When several items existed for the same date or topic, a system of subclassification was necessary: for correspondence, the most convenient subheading would be the name of the correspondent who sent or received each letter; for subclassifications within a topic, either the document's date or the name of its author sufficed.

Computerized databases may modify the sequence of steps in

processing an accession to the edition's files. For instance, many projects find it more convenient to enter an item's cataloging information in the control database as a first step in accessioning. The database assigns the accession number and can generate an appropriate label to be printed out and attached to the folder that will contain the item, and even make additional labels to attach to the versos of photocopies in lieu of stamped numbers. While the notion of a "master" file is irrelevant with computerized methods, the database must be capable of generating a report that will serve as a shelf list, one in which the sequence of records matches the physical arrangement of the folders.

Computerized systems offer a special bonus to enterprising editors who plan a microform or other facsimile edition. These editors deliberately create an accession number field large enough to accommodate not merely the sequential identifying number that will be assigned each document but also the number of characters that will be needed to identify the item's final location in the microform. This allows the editor to substitute the microform-location information for the accession number in the document record, facilitating the final preparation of the index. Thus, if the editorial archive were expected to contain no more than 1,000 items, but the editor projected publication of 20 microfilm reels of 1,200 frames each, the accession number field would be set for seven characters, not the four needed to identify 1,000 pieces. When microfilming is completed, accession number "0000022" can be changed to "21/1002" to indicate that the document's image appears on frame 1002 of reel 21. The database can then be sorted alphabetically, topically, or chronologically to create index entries carrying accurate references to the new microform.

With both manual and automated methods, the document title on a file folder should be as brief as possible. It is usually wise to abbreviate the name of the project's subject in all records, and that process begins with the folder labels and entries in the control file. Thus, a letter from George Washington to Alexander Hamilton was labeled "George Washington to H" at the Hamilton Papers archive, but "GW to Alexander Hamilton" at the Washington Papers project. When a folder contains a copy of a printed pamphlet, government report, or other published writing with a long and complicated title, it is not necessary to reproduce the complete title on the folder so long as the full version is recorded in the control file.

Before the first document folder is filed, there must be guidelines for chronological arrangement of materials at the project. Most editors follow the principles of archivists and file undated material to which it is impossible to assign even a month or year at the very end of the collection's chronological series. There is less agreement, however, on the arrangement of partially dated material and documents that bear inclusive dates. Some projects file documents that bear only a fragmentary date, such as the year or the month of the year, at the end of the period recorded in that date. All materials dated simply 1771 would follow items dated 31 December 1771; all materials dated March 1771 would follow items dated 31 March 1771. Other projects adopt precisely the opposite course, placing partially dated materials at the beginning of the period into which they fall: here materials dated 1771 would precede those dated 1 January 1771. Whichever method the editor adopts, it must be followed scrupulously. The same general principle applies to documents with inclusive dates. Some projects file such items at the first date that appears: a ledger sheet with entries for 1 January 1771 through 2 March 1775 would be placed at the beginning of the year 1771. Conversely, others would file the item at the end of materials for 2 March 1775. The editor should choose the method that best serves the individual archive.

Even during the initial processing of materials, the editorial staff will be able to supply some details of authorship and dating that do not appear on the document itself. When the cataloger, by comparing handwriting, can identify as John Smith the correspondent who has signed himself "John," the full information should appear on the folder. And if the cataloger, through the use of a perpetual calendar or the application of common sense, can establish that a note dated "Wednesday, February 3," was written in 1808, then the full date should be placed on the folder. Information supplied by a member of the editorial staff usually appears within square brackets in these records, e.g., "John [Smith]" and "3 February [1808]."

## C. THE FUNCTIONS OF CONTROL FILES

The control file begins to grow while the editor plans the project's search, and it will shape the edition's form and be reshaped by the edition's progress. Almost every edition's control file demands fields for dates, authors, and repository locations, and a computerized database should prompt every editor to add subject headings to this list of control file essentials. But some projects will have special needs that dictate special fields. A project planning a comprehensive facsimile edition of its holdings, for instance, will probably need a separate field in which to indicate the number of pages each item represents. The editor then can give prospective publishers an accurate estimate of the number of images to be expected in the final product. Such facsimile publication projects might also demand special care in designing fields for subject entries, as the database will be the foundation of the finding aid that will accompany the facsimile edition, whether it be microform or digital images.

Control files undergo constant revision and improvement. An examination of newly accessioned manuscripts and photocopies allows an editor to assign dates to undated materials, to correct the dates on misdated items, and to determine the author of an unsigned letter or the intended recipient of one whose envelope or address leaf has been lost. For any date or title that is corrected or supplemented, the control file should contain duplicate records providing a cross reference from the date, author, or recipient once erroneously attributed to the item to a record with the accurate date or title. This prevents confusion over just which items from a given repository have been cataloged, so that two orders are not placed for the photocopy of a manuscript that has been cataloged under two dates or descriptions. When editorially supplied information is added to a control file, the corrected letters, words, or numerals should be enclosed in square brackets in the data entry as well as on the label attached to the document file folder. The folders will need to be rearranged to mirror their new cataloging.

## D. ARRANGEMENT AND SORTING OF CONTROL FILE DATA

Arrangement of data once posed a considerable physical and intellectual challenge to documentary editors, and many long-term projects created in the 1950s and 1960s still maintain manually created control files. While sorting is easier for the editor who maintains control through a computerized database, both manual and automated methods have the same goal: to provide intellectual and physical access to the materials collected. If letters of the same date were arranged alphabetically by the name of the sender or recipient, then the manually produced chronological slips were arranged in the same order; with a computerized database, a chronological report must be designed to list entries of the same date subclassified by that same alphabetical criterion. If letters of identical date are, instead, filed first by letters from the project's subject and then by letters to him or her, the control file should be able to produce file slips or reports arranged in the same fashion. And both manual and automated control files should be able to produce a shelf list that mirrors the physical arrangement of the original or photocopied materials that form the project archive, a process that extends to the creation of special rules for filing materials with partial dates or inclusive dates.

Using a single set of organizing principles for both folders and control file means that members of the staff need memorize only one set of rules, not two or three.

## VI. The Blessings of Computers

Computerized databases permit more flexibility in many areas of control file design and detail. For example, when editors were limited to manual methods, maintaining accurate lists of the documents contributed by various institutions was a cumbersome process. Some offices prepared a separate series of control slips to be filed by repository, while others recorded this information in separate notebooks. A computerized database with a separate field for owner-repository allows easy sorting by the name or symbol entered there.

Special location information in a control file is also handled more efficiently and accurately with such automated methods. Frequently, a project's limited funds or limited space rules out the creation of hard copy from microfilms. Here location information should carry not only the code for the owner-repository but also the full title and reel number of the film where the editorial staff can consult the text of the original. If the film's frames are numbered, references to the frames should also appear in the control file. The editor whose archive will include a substantial number of filmed reels should establish a separate system of control for these spools. Each can be assigned an identifying number reflecting the order of the film's acquisition by the project, and this can be included in the location information in the database control file. If this is cumbersome, the films themselves can be arranged in a rational and consistent order that will make their retrieval easy: this might involve shelving the reels in the order of the Library of Congress location symbols for the sources of the films' contents. All of these issues are far more easily addressed with automated methods, and the editor who anticipates these problems can include appropriate fields in the control file record in advance.

In manual control files, the location symbol was followed immediately by the accession number. Automated databases can either assign the number as each entry is processed (if photocopies or originals are conveniently at hand for numbering) or accept a number assigned by the cataloger (if processing is done in several stages). In manual systems, the space below the location-accession information was used for additional information on the specific location of the original. With database software, it is often wise to enter these data in a separate field for sorting by collection. In both manual and automated systems, it may sometimes be necessary to give more detail than the name of an individual collection. The automated database can assign the information to its logical field, not an area on a slip where appropriate space exists. Automated systems can be designed with specific fields for remarks concerning the physical appearance of the original, or such data can be entered in a catchall "notes" field analogous to the bottom half of the manual control slip, which traditionally held such comments.

Whatever the form of the control file, the same symbols ("ALS" for "autograph letter signed," and so on—for a discussion of these symbols, see "Source or Provenance Notes" in chapter 7) should be used in the control file as will be used in the printed or facsimile edition. Again, this reduces the number of abbreviations and codes that the staff must master. While computerized databases provide an editor with the flexibility to reconsider these codes as a project progresses and to make global changes in the file if second thoughts win out, any such modifications are cumbersome and may demand the services of a consultant. It is best to think these matters through carefully at the beginning and make decisions that can be lived with throughout the editorial project's career.

## A. SUBJECT INDEXES OF CONTROL FILES

In one area, automated control file databases give editors something more than better ways to perform traditional functions. Even a modest flat-file database will permit an editor the luxury of early subject indexing, simultaneous with establishing the control file itself. The editors of the Joseph Henry Papers sought to use a computerized system precisely because a subject index to their documentary collection was essential.

If a project will use subject indexing, still more planning is required. Not every topic or every proper name should be indexed; veterans in this field advise establishing a firm limit to the number of subject entries that will be made for a given document. The initial computerized index done at the time of cataloging will be only a rough one to guide the staff in later editorial work. In the words of the Henry editors, "the object is not to produce a definitive index at this pre-editorial stage. The purpose is to establish a rough content control, in addition to traditional controls." Although the number of entries that can be made for a given document will depend on the software being used, most editors find it prudent to place a limit, albeit a generous one, on the number of fields for subject entries at this initial stage. As the process of collection and analysis progresses, an editor can design a more comprehensive index and implement it electronically.

It is essential to anticipate the needs of an index rather than improvise in the process of cataloging. As most scholars come to editing with some knowledge of the subject of the edition, they are well qualified to identify, in advance, the subject headings most likely to be used in the index and to design a thesaurus or list of terms approved for use in the index. Thought should also be given to the forms in which proper names will be entered. Here a running authority list can easily be created. Editors should remember that they will not be the first to consider subject access to the information in their disciplines—librarians and archivists have anticipated them in most areas and created and published standard sources for thesaurus construction and name-authority lists. Examples of these are the *Library of Congress Subject Headings,* the fiche editions of the library's name-authority lists, and the *Art and Architecture Thesaurus.* For useful discussions of the advantage of using such standard lists and of exploiting the full array of the library and archival professions' work, see Ronald J. Zboray's "Computerized Document Control and Indexing at the Emma Goldman Papers" and Cathy Moran Hajo's "Computerizing Control over Authority Names at the Margaret Sanger Papers."

Once the index's design and authority lists have been established, the cataloger merely adds a step to the entry of basic information such as date, document title, and details of provenance. Some projects will find it necessary to investigate relational databases at this point. Editors of large collections that will receive intensive indexing, such as the Edison archive, need to design a system of codes for subject headings and personal names to expedite data entry. This system of codes may in turn demand a separate file that is linked to the control file. Once the limits of indexing have been established, the cataloger—or a senior staff member responsible for subject indexing —can enter codes for themes and individuals whose importance warrants a subject entry or can retrieve the full terms themselves from the project's thesaurus and authority files.

This subject-oriented content-control system can be initiated during the cataloging process itself or later in the project, prior to the selection of materials for publication. Early scheduling of an index provides an initial subject guide to the project's collection. Although implementing this system will slow the process of cataloging somewhat, an experienced cataloger working from a limited number of subject entries will probably need to spend only a few additional minutes when cataloging even the longest document. Even this small delay may be unacceptable, however, for a project that must catalog as quickly as possible. Such an occasion might arise when little is known about the patterns of an individual's correspondence, and it is imperative that materials be cataloged with the greatest haste so that planning of the search can progress. For most projects, however, a rough content-control file can be created simultaneously with cataloging control.

## VII. CONCLUSION

Even with automated methods, the processes of finding sources and maintaining control over the results of a search follow the same principles developed in the days of manual procedures: only the methods of entering and sorting the data and the form of the files themselves have changed, and the work of collecting materials and creating control files will remain anything but a neat linear progression. While editors may need to assure sponsors and funding agencies that their work moves along in a steady, easily defined fashion, they make no such pretense among themselves. While initiating a project, an editor periodically reviews the results of work to date before moving on to the next task, and the results of that "next" task may mean reevaluating steps in research or cataloging that seemed settled and done weeks or months earlier. As in other matters, the new editor's best source for both caution and encouragement in planning a search and creating control files may be the experience of editors who have survived the ordeal.

## SUGGESTED READINGS

I. On the subject of control files, the experience of other editors can be especially helpful. Useful guides to documentary editions already in existence are *Historical Editions, 1988: A List of Documentary Publications Supported by the National Historical Publications and Records Commission* (Washington, D.C., 1988), published by the NHPRC, and the more recent version, *Historical Documentary Editions* (1993). The index to Beth Luey's *Editing Documents and Texts*, under the names of those projects listed and the subject headings "control," "organization of projects," and "search," will be instructive.

Until the introduction of computerized methods, most American editors confined their writings on the technical problems of collection and control of sources to memoranda whose circulation was confined to the editorial office. The most exhaustive series of this kind was Lyman Butterfield's "Directives" for every aspect of the operations of the Adams Papers at the Massachusetts Historical Society. These are a model of the sort of planning and assignment of responsibility for which the editors of every project should aim. Less comprehensive descriptions of procedures have been prepared for many other projects, and these can be obtained by individual editors whose projects resemble the earlier undertaking in scope or focus. Helpful published materials are noted below. Published accounts of projects tend to be anecdotal rather than technical, but some essays are very helpful in describing the issues of collection and control. Among the best are Whitfield Bell, "Franklin's Papers and the Papers of Benjamin Franklin," *Pennsylvania History* 22 (1955): 1–17; Leonard W. Labaree, "In Search of 'B Franklin,'" *William and Mary Quarterly* 16 (April 1959): 188–97; Howard C. Rice, "Jefferson in Europe," *Princeton University Library Chronicle* 12 (Autumn 1950): 19–35; Albert E. Van Dusen, "In Quest of That 'Arch Rebel' Jonathan Trumbull, Sr.," in Leslie W. Dunlap and Fred Shelley, eds., *The Publication of American Historical Manuscripts* (Iowa City, Ia., 1976), 31–46; and Ralph L. Ketcham, "The Madison Family Papers: Case Study in a Search for Historical Manuscripts," *Manuscripts* 11 (Summer 1959): 49–55.

Special problems in provenance and bibliography that confront scholars at these projects are discussed in Paul G. Sifton, "The Provenance of the Thomas Jefferson Papers," *American Archivist* 40 (1977): 17–30; Kate Stewart, "James Madison as an Archivist," ibid. 21 (1958): 243–57; and Edwin Wolf II, "The Reconstruction of Benjamin Franklin's Library: An Unorthodox Jigsaw Puzzle," *Papers of the Bibliographical Society of America* 56 (1962): 1–16. Although it does not concern a modern editorial project, Thomas C. Reeve's "The Search for the Chester Alan Arthur Papers," *Manuscripts* 25 (Summer 1973): 171–85, is a valuable description of a related challenge.

The student who would keep abreast of writings on collection and control faces a considerable challenge. Editors who write brief histories of their projects, including summaries of their experience in searching out sources, are as likely to publish these reminiscences in journals issued by their collegiate alma mater or the library of their sponsor institution as in scholarly journals such as the *American Archivist, Documentary Editing,* or *Computers and the Humanities.*

II. An engaging memoir of a scholar's experience with early microcomputers (1979–1982) is William C. Creasy's "A Microcomputer Editorial Procedure," *Microcomputers and Literary Scholarship* (Los Angeles, 1986), 1–22.

III. Although documentary editors have been remiss in publishing detailed accounts of the design of control file databases, their experiences have been shared at several scholarly conferences. For summaries of papers, see "Using Databases in Editorial Projects: A Workshop," *Documentary Editing* 15 (March 1993): 15. Martha Benner of the Lincoln Legal Papers project has delivered a paper on that edition's experience with a relational database at the Conference on Computing and History, Montreal, August 1995; and the Lincoln Legal Papers project, like others with experience in computerized databases, is generous in sharing advice and samples of screen designs. Evaluation of the merits of hardware and software has become far easier because of the Association for Documentary Editing's *Computer User's Directory,* a publication updated every two years to provide access to information about the types of automated equipment and software packages currently in use by members of the association for specific purposes and phases in the editing process, such as indexing and document control.

IV. For an informative history of the NHPC/NHPRC *Directory,* see Richard A. Noble, "The NHPRC Data Base Project: Building the 'Interstate Highway System,'" *American Archivist* 51 (1988): 98–105. The most comprehensive source for the names of libraries that have made finding aids for special collections available electronically is the Society of American Archivists' World Wide Web site.

Recent and useful discussions of search experiences are William D. Beard's "American Justinian or Prairie Pettifogger? Lincoln's Legal Legacy: Documenting the Law Practice of Abraham Lincoln," *Documentary Editing* 14 (December 1992): 61–64; and Lois More Oberbeck's "Researching Literary Manuscripts: A Scholar's Perspective," *American Archivist* 56 (1993): 62–69, the graceful memoir of a literary scholar's introduction to archival research.

Of more antiquarian interest are these accounts by nineteenth-century editors of retrieving materials for their editions: Galen Broeker, "Jared Sparks, Robert Peel, and the State Papers Office," *American Quarterly* 13 (1961): 140–52; and William B. Hesseltine and Larry Gara, "The Archives of Pennsylvania: A Glimpse at an Editor's Problem," *Pennsylvania Magazine* 77 (1953): 328–31. Essays that give some notion of the challenges facing the collector of American historical materials are Francis L. Berkeley, Jr., "History and the Problem of the Control of Manuscripts in the United States," *Proceedings of the American Philosophical Society* 98 (June 1954): 171–78; and Leonard Rapport, "Dumped from a Wharf into Casco Bay: The Historical Records Survey Revisited," *American Archivist* 37 (1974): 201–10. James E. O'Neill's "Copies of French Manuscripts for American History in the Library of Congress," *Journal of American History* 51 (December 1965): 674–91, adds some useful information to older, more comprehensive listings of these materials.

The best description of the spirit and tenacity required of a searching editor in the twentieth century is found in the letters printed in Lyman H. Butterfield's *Butterfield in Holland: A Record of L. H. Butterfield's Pursuit of the Adamses Abroad in 1959* (Cambridge, England, 1961). Review essays that point to the unfortunate effects of an inadequate editorial search include George A. Billias's critique of the *Naval Documents* volumes in *American Historical Review* 73 (October 1967): 216–17, and T. Harry Williams' review of the *Collected Works of Abraham Lincoln* in the *Mississippi Valley Historical Review* 40 (June 1953): 89–106. Even in a favorable review, one now finds complaints that an editor has not described the search on which the edition is based; see Ronald W. Howard's review of *The Papers of Lewis Morris,* in *Documentary Editing* 17 (March 1995): 11–15.

Three useful articles dealing with the collection of materials for editions of the papers of British authors appear in J. A. Dainard, ed., *Editing Correspondence: Papers Given at the Fourteenth Annual Conference on Editorial Problems, University of Toronto, 3–4 November 1978* (New York, 1979): Alan Bell's "The Letters of Sir Walter Scott: Problems and Opportunities" (63–80), Wilmarth S. Lewis's "Editing Familiar Letters" (25–37), and John Matthews' "The Hunt for the Disraeli Letters" (81–92).

Editors who must master print bibliography may wish to investigate the University of Virginia's annual summer institute in rare books and special collections. For a useful introduction to the two forms of bibliography employed in the early stages of a project, read T. H. Howard-Hill's "Enumerative and Descriptive Bibliography," in Peter Davison, ed., *The Book Encompassed: Studies in Twentieth-Century Bibliography* (Cambridge, England, 1992), 122–29, with a brief but useful bibliography. Classics in this field include Fredson Bowers' two essays "The Function of Bibliography," *Library Trends* 7 (April 1959): 497–510, and "Four Faces of Bibliography," *Papers of the Bibliographical Society of Canada* 10 (1971): 33–45 (reprinted in his *Essays in Bibliography, Text, and Editing* [Charlottesville, 1975]). The special bibliographical problems in American government publications are dealt with in J. H. Powell's *The Books of a New Nation* (Philadelphia, 1957).

IV.A.3. Issues involved in working with manuscript and rare book dealers and collectors are addressed in B. Richard Burg, "The Autograph Trade and Documentary Editing," *Manuscripts* 22 (Fall 1970): 247–54; H. Bartholomew Cox, "Publication of Manuscripts: Devaluation or Enhancement?" *American Archivist* 32 (1969): 25–32; Leonard W. Labaree, "350 Were Approached, Only Three Said 'No,'" *Williams Alumni Review,* February 1967, pp. 11–12; and Claude M. Simpson, William Goetzmann, and Matthew J. Bruccoli, "The Interdependence of Rare Books and Manuscripts: The Scholar's View," *Serif* 9 (Spring 1972): 3–22. The June 1970 *CEAA Newsletter,* pp. 21–23, presents summaries of papers on the collection of manuscript information in both libraries and private collections. Herman Herst, Jr.'s "Philatelists Are the Luckiest People," *Manuscripts* 32 (Summer 1980): 187–90, is an informal introduction to the field of postal history.

For introductions to the world of American manuscript collecting, see Mary A. Benjamin, *Autographs: A Key to Collecting* (New York, 1963) and Charles Hamilton, *Collecting Autographs and Manuscripts* (Norman, Okla. 1961). The Arizona State database of private collections is described in Ira Brilliant, "The Manuscript Society Information Exchange Database Opens at Arizona State University," and Edward Oetting, "The Information Exchange Database: 'The Future is Now,'" both in *Manuscripts* 42 (1990): 5–12 and 13–17, respectively.

V. On the subject of control, editors have confined their wisdom almost completely to unpublished, in-house memoranda. Scholars may wish to improve their vocabulary in this area by consulting Frank B. Evans et al., "A Basic Glossary for Archivists, Manuscript Curators, and Records Managers," *American Archivist* 37 (July 1974): 415–31. A useful lesson in analyzing handwriting to date manuscripts appears in *The Letters of Charles Dickens*, Madeline House and Graham Storey, eds., vol. 1 (Oxford, 1965), xxiv–xxvi. And a classic demonstration of historical method and common sense in authenticating manuscripts is recounted in Arthur Pierce Middleton and Douglass Adair, "The Mystery of the Horn Papers," *William and Mary Quarterly* 4 (October 1947): 409–45. Suggestions on the need to coordinate training of archivists and editors can be found in Constance B. Schulz, "Do Archivists Need to Know How to be Editors? A Proposal for the Role of Documentary Editing in Graduate Archival Education," *Documentary Editing* 16 (March 1994): 5–9; Dennis D. Madden, "Historical Editing and the Practical Application of Archival Skills: Surveying Common Ground," ibid.: 10–12; and Philip B. Eppard, "The Archivist's Perspective: Implications for Documentary Editing," *Documentary Editing* 16 (June 1994): 47–50. An interesting discussion of the process by which, in the development of their specialties, archivists and scholarly editors took divergent paths appears in Richard A. Ryerson's "The Other Historians: Archivists, Editors, and Collective Biographers," *Pennsylvania History* 57 (1990): 3–12.

And an important overview of the function of manuscript materials for scholarly research is Donald H. Reiman's *The Study of Modern Manuscripts: Public, Confidential, and Private* (Baltimore, 1993).

# CHAPTER III

## Defining and Organizing a Documentary Edition

Sharing the resources collected or cataloged by a documentary editing project can be one of the greatest intellectual challenges a scholar faces. Most editors feel a moral obligation to communicate as much as possible of the data compiled in reconstructing the writings, works, or papers of their subjects; some are even under explicit directions from their sponsoring agencies to publicize their findings in a systematic way. Many of the issues an editor must ponder in this process are qualitative ones concerning what textual method will best preserve the character of the documents chosen for transcription and publication, but just as important are the questions concerning the process by which such documents are chosen and the order in which the editorial texts will appear in the edition. This chapter will discuss the ways in which an editor establishes an edition's scope (including the production of accompanying finding aids or supplements) and the options available for organizing the documentary texts to be published.

In few other areas will the reader see better examples of the non-linear nature of scholarly editing or of the constant interplay of the trio of basic considerations: the nature of the documentary sources, their expected audience, and the medium in which they will appear. Many editors are required to make some tentative, preliminary decisions about their editions' scope and organization when planning collection methods and cataloging procedures. Each editor's definition of the papers, writings, or records of his or her subject is reflected in the breadth or narrowness of the search. Cataloging and control methods of projects whose printed volumes or facsimile editions will have a chronological framework often differ from those in which the elements will be arranged topically. Yet editors can make no final decisions concerning an edition's size and organization, much less initiate transcription of the source texts that meet these criteria, until collection is well under way and the control files have revealed the editorial archive's patterns. Inevitably, the patterns that emerge will modify and refine the notion of the audience the edition may serve, and they may even influence the choice of the medium of publication.

The Indiana scholars who began a search for surviving papers of William Henry Harrison, for instance, expected that they would publish an annotated book edition based on the results. Their success in reconstructing the records of Harrison's career exceeded their wildest dreams, and they quickly changed their goal to a comprehensive microform. Some qualitative results of the search, in turn, influenced the very nature of that microform. Many of the manuscripts reproduced so badly that they had to be transcribed for legibility, and some repositories denied permission to reproduce the images of the manuscripts in their collections. Thus, the editors chose to transcribe all materials, so that the film's frames would give readers a consistent level of textual reliability.

## I. SCOPE

Considerations even more prosaic than the audience's optical requirements may dictate whether an edition is comprehensive—inclusive of all the materials defined in the project's rubric—or selective, representing some portion of the materials uncovered by the search. It may be prudent to clarify the distinctions between this pair of terms and that equally common pair, *definitive* and *authoritative*. *Comprehensive* and *selective* have quantitative meanings only; they refer to an editor's decision to publish all or only some of the documents that could be considered appropriate to the project in question. *Definitive* and *authoritative*, by contrast, have qualitative meanings. Modern editors are too realistic to speak any longer of producing a definitive edition of an individual's writings, one that is not only all-inclusive in scope but also so rigorous in its textual methods that the reader would never have reason to consult the original materials on which those transcribed or photoreproduced texts are based. Scholars now realize that, where manuscript or typescript sources are concerned, definitive printed texts are a practical impossibility. At best, editors can offer readers an "authoritative" or "scholarly" edition, a collection of accurate and reliable transcribed versions of those elements of the sources that can be either translated into printed symbols or adequately described in editorial notes. Some details of inscription, some nuances in the sources, will resist the most ingenious editor. Scholars whose interests demand access to these details will need to consult the original materials or their accurate photoreproductions. Few editions will ever include complete versions of every text related to its subject. Instead, they will usually be a selection of documents relating to some rational and clearly stated criteria.

Editors normally provide a statement of the limits of their textual methods so that readers can judge when the printed texts may not serve their purposes, and the quantitative process of choosing materials for a selective edition requires an equally straightforward explanation. When the NHPRC sponsored a nationwide survey of users of documentary editions, Ann Gordon, the survey's director reported: "The strongest reservations about reliance on editions from the users contacted in this study all came from users of the same edition. Their cautions spoke not to the quality of the editorial work but to the relationship between the edition and a massive, modern political archive from which it derived" (p. 9). Reviewers now recognize that the process of selection can be an interpretive tool, and any bias inherent in the criteria for inclusion in a set of edited printed volumes or facsimiles must be addressed openly in an edition's introduction.

## A. COMPREHENSIVE AND SELECTIVE EDITIONS

Few editors claim that theirs is a truly comprehensive edition. The editor of the published works of a well-known literary figure may achieve this goal, and so may the editor of a small archival edition of documents, but most editors frankly state their standards of selection and devise methods that will give readers clues to both the nature and the location of the materials that do not appear in print. In his remarks in "The Canons of Selection," John Y. Simon identified three methods of selective publication: the comprehensive publication of a series of letters chosen from some larger group (such as all letters exchanged by Thomas Jefferson and John Adams); comprehensive coverage of some narrowly defined topic; and, last, truly selective publication, in which editorial judgment, not some predetermined factual criterion, is responsible for every choice.

One plan for comprehensive publication was outlined by Julian Boyd in the initial volume of the *Jefferson Papers.* Boyd set out to print both letters and other documents addressed to Jefferson as well as those written by him. Certain categories of routine materials that the editors did not believe warranted full print reproduction were to be noted in a calendar summarizing the documents' contents and indicating their owner-repositories. In addition, the volumes carried entries for letters not found, now-vanished items of specific dates mentioned in surviving Jefferson documents for which the full texts have vanished or in entries from Jefferson's own register of his personal and official correspondence. The documentary texts, the calendar entries, and the notes of letters not found appear in a single chronological sequence. Thus, though Boyd never promised the complete texts of all the known materials that Jefferson's papers once comprised, he did work to provide a comprehensive *record* of those papers.

A similar combination of the full texts of significant documents with letters-not-found entries for missing items and calendar entries for routine administrative papers became the rule for editions of America's Founding Fathers: Washington, Hamilton, Franklin, Madison, John Marshall, and the Adamses. A more highly selective variation on this technique was seen in the papers of political leaders of somewhat lesser significance, such as Henry Clay and John C. Calhoun: these volumes contain full printed texts of comparatively few documents of the greatest significance, with brief calendar entries and other forms of lists for all others.

Volumes in the tradition of literary scholarship adopted somewhat different methods. Until recently, such editions seldom provided descriptive calendar entries for letters of secondary interest or records of letters not found, although it was not uncommon to furnish lists of surviving letters collected for the projects but excluded from the modern print editions. David Nordloh, a former chairman of the Committee on Scholarly Editions, has argued persuasively that editors of authors' papers should imitate the example of "historical" editions by sharing all the results of an editorial project's archive— whether through a calendar or a facsimile supplement ("Supplying What's Missing"). His own experience as an editor and reader of edited letters had led him to "call on the editor to identify for the reader what isn't there."

Still, while publication of comprehensive records of authors' correspondence and papers is becoming more common, there remain some differences between the way these records are treated. Editors of an author's papers generally impose a parallel chronological order on the edited texts and any supplementary guides to unlocated or unpublished items. Thus, lists or more detailed calendars usually appear in appendixes to edited volumes or as separate, independent publications that precede an annotated print edition. The editor with a historical background is more likely to integrate calendar entries, notices of letters not found, and so on, into the same chronological sequence in which the complete documentary texts appear. The *Jefferson Davis* edition, which originally had consigned calendar listings for routine documents to an appendix, later integrated these entries with the full documentary texts, and one reviewer commented that the change allowed "students to trace the exchange of correspondence over time without having to refer to calendared letters in an appendix" (Hattaway, p. 1178).

The editors of the correspondence of a literary figure sometimes assume that readers will use these volumes as much for their aesthetic value as for biographical or broader historical research: in a design assuming such use, calendar entries and the like might seem intrusive. Historical editors, however, assume that readers will approach the volumes with a historian's bias toward chronology: such readers will be best served by a format that allows easy access to all documents written on a given date.

Editors who launch a new enterprise should be prepared to revise their policies of selection or even their methods of publication when faced with changes in the nature of the records that they plan to publish or the funds available to support such publication. The editors of the *Laurens Papers* followed a near-comprehensive policy for the first nine volumes of the series, but with volume 10, which brought Laurens to the forefront of the Revolution in South Carolina, the choice of texts became highly selective. A future supplement will offer complete transcriptions of the documents omitted from the volumes. The editors of the *Franklin Papers* had to devise a new system for calendar entries and samples of certain types of routine materials, to meet the explosion of documents created by Franklin's 1776 appointment as American commissioner to France. On more than one occasion, the demands of funding agencies forced the editors of the *Papers of Robert Morris* to modify their criteria of selection in the name of economy and efficiency.

Other editors eschew any attempt at a comprehensive chronological record of the editorial archive in the printed volumes but, instead, attempt in their annotation to the documents selected for full publication to offer a guide to the broader collection. In editions confined to letters written *by* a given author, editors normally supply complete data on the location and contents of the incoming letters to which the outgoing correspondence is a reply. Excellent examples of this technique can be found in the *Papers of Ulysses S. Grant* and *Mark Twain's Letters*. Footnotes in selective editions of both sides of a correspondence can also be used to indicate the location of surviving related materials not printed in full. Similarly, when a covering letter is printed without its enclosure, editorial notes usually identify that unpublished document and sometimes summarize it in detail. All of these methods try to make the selective edition, in the words of Wayne Cutler, a "window to the larger collection" from which its printed texts are drawn.

Still, there are times when a printed format cannot provide adequate and convenient access of this sort. The comprehensive-record technique led the reviewer of one volume of statesmen's papers to remark despairingly that the calendar had become the text. If the printed edition draws on only one chronological period in its subject's life, or if it focuses on but a single area of concern in his or her correspondence and papers, the published volumes and the footnotes to the items chosen for print publication cannot serve as the clear "windows" for which editors like Cutler strive. When confronted with such problems, the editor may want to consider the publication of separate finding aids or facsimile supplements to the printed volumes.

## B. FACSIMILE EDITIONS AND SUPPLEMENTS

For most of the last fifty years, microforms of the editorial archive have been the most common supplement to a selective print edition or alternative form of publication for materials that did not warrant an annotated book edition. Although electronic publication of images is likely to replace microforms for some editions, the older techniques will remain the methods of choice for many facsimile editions for some time to come, and the value of facsimiles as part of the editorial arsenal only becomes greater with the advent of the newer technology.

The advantages of some form of facsimile supplement to transcribed, annotated texts in a selective edition are obvious. When a facsimile series precedes the book edition, the need for a calendar of unpublished documents vanishes, as scholars already have access to an indexed edition of complete imaged versions of these sources. Publication of microform facsimiles of the documents or their transcriptions after completion of the book edition is the choice of other editors. While this method ensures that all the project's collected materials are available in the supplement, it can delay publication of the microform for a decade or more, and in the interim scholars may harbor the lingering suspicion that editorial enthusiasm for compiling a microform will vanish after the last printed volume appears. An electronic companion edition of digitally scanned images may precede, follow, or accompany the edited, annotated texts it supplements. As it is far easier to update an electronic edition than one in microform, documentary editors of the future may issue a preliminary electronic facsimile series in advance of their annotated series and then provide a final facsimile version when editorial work is completed.

Questions of format and technical quality are always factors in determining the format of a facsimile edition. Traditionally, editors have published micrographic supplements on 35-millimeter film meeting the standards of the NHPRC for such editions. In the 1970s the editors of the *Latrobe Papers* successfully experimented with a microfiche edition—a format with special advantages for the reproduction of the graphic records of Latrobe's career as an engineer and architect. Editors of the *Charles Willson Peale Papers* selected this format for the same reasons, and the editors of the *Lydia Maria Child Papers* successfully used microfiche for more conventional documentary materials. The editors of the *Documentary History of the Ratification of the Constitution* continue to use fiche supplements to their selective printed volumes for excluded items.

Microforms may remain the media of choice for large-scale facsimile editions into the twenty-first century. Electronic facsimiles can be issued as a self-contained CD-ROM edition or can be offered, on demand, through an Internet facility. But, while a CD-ROM may hold more images than a dozen reels of microfilm, the costs of publishing such a disk may be correspondingly higher. A CD-ROM edition is presently practical only when the number of images is great, not when it could easily be accommodated by ten reels of microfilm or its equivalent. An edition of images can be offered over the Internet at lower cost, but not every project will find an institution willing to provide a permanent Internet site to a facsimile edition. Only projects deemed to be of exceptional significance will warrant this kind of virtual hospitality. Further caution in the use of "electronic microfilm" is dictated by the fact that at present there are no standards for digitally scanned images as an *archival* medium, that is, one that can provide safe storage of the data they contain for a substantial length of time. Thus, an electronic facsimile edition requires both periodic "refreshment" of the images to ensure quality and the presence of a nonelectronic version of the facsimiles for archival purposes. As an electronic edition's backup version is likely to be a microform, editors must be familiar with the older technology as well as the new.

Microfilm and microfiche each have special advantages and disadvantages. Microfilm allows a wider range of reduction ratios and density values that can better reproduce legible versions of mutilated or faded originals or less than perfect photocopies. Microfiche cards provide less opportunity for such camera adjustments, because the apertures on such cards are of standard size. Oversized documents can be legibly reproduced on fiche only by a complicated and expensive paste-up process or by transcribing the documents to produce typed sheets that the fixed fiche aperture can accommodate.

In general, microfilm is preferable for documents that antedate the late nineteenth century. Originals or photocopies from that earlier period assume widely varying dimensions and even shapes. The longer passage of time since the inscription of the originals will have produced greater ranges of discoloration or fading, problems better solved with the more flexible microfilm camera. Materials of the modern era, however, tend to be inscribed or printed on paper whose size can be accommodated easily by the fiche format without any distorting reduction, and original materials that were generated recently have been subjected to less wear and tear of the years and often display a consistent level of legibility. Fiche is also the microform of choice for collections of comparatively short printed documents, such as pamphlets and published short stories and essays (see, for instance, the microfiche edition of the materials listed in Charles Evans' *Early American Imprints*). Standards do exist for converting existing microfilms to digitized form, and facsimile editions done as microfilms can easily be converted to electronic form.

But if electronic technology's impact on the medium of image publication may not be felt fully for several years, its effect on access to such facsimiles is already apparent. Modern microfilm and -fiche editions provide convenient formats for indexing, but early microform indexes, like those for the Library of Congress's Presidential Papers series, were forbidding and cumbersome: index entries offered references only to the dates of letters and papers, not to their locations in the film. In later years, automatic frame-numbering attachments for microfilm cameras ensured that each image on a reel was numbered in sequence, thus providing convenient location references in the finding aids. For microfiche, the Latrobe editors' alphanumeric reference system of location of items on a fiche card was an easy and practical solution to this reference problem. Other microfiche editors assigned identifying sequential numbers to each document in the fiche, and index entries refer the user to these document numbers. Whether on microfilm or microfiche, such editions provided "targets" for each item—editorially supplied labels for each item reproduced. In early years, these targets were simply one of the multiple copies of the control file slips; today they are computer-generated.

With any or all of these techniques, microform indexes could be as compact and readable as those to a printed volume. Entries for a correspondence series might offer each item's full date as well as its location in the film or fiche. A "letters" entry for a correspondent could be broken down into "letters to" and "letters from," with only the year given for each letter or group of letters. Rough subject indexes became common for microforms when the mass of material likely to appear on fiche or film made some sort of topical control essential. Microform editors using manually created control files displayed considerable ingenuity in creating efficient finding aids to accompany their facsimile editions. The index to the *Papers of Aaron Burr*, for instance, furnished a correspondents index to letters, a plaintiff-defendant index to legal papers, a subject index to the records of Burr's professional career, and a personal-name index to Burr's journals in 100 printed pages covering 27 reels of microfilm. The guide to the Latrobe fiche edition, using a different format, provided similar depth of indexing for 315 fiche cards in 94 printed pages.

The ready availability of electronic indexing programs now enables documentary editors to create superior indexes at a fraction of the cost in time and effort. A new edition's control file now routinely includes subject entries for each item as well as traditional data on date, author, and source location; and a desktop computer can generate indexes in a variety of formats, allowing the editor to choose the one best suited to the edition at hand. In fact, the editors of the Thomas A. Edison microfilm edition learned that they had generated more indexing information than a microform publisher could absorb. The Edison edition features parallel publication of a selective print edition and reels of microfilmed facsimiles whose chronological sequence keeps step with the printed volumes. Each Edison document receives careful subject indexing along with more conventional cataloging, and even though no more than three subject entries were assigned to any item, inclusion of these references in the printed guide and index that accompanies the microfilm reels would have created a volume of unmanageable dimensions. Instead, the Edison editors have made the subject index available in electronic form over the Internet.

It is easy to see how the methods of traditional microform facsimiles can be translated into digital technology. Scanned images of original materials or their photoreproductions will provide the facsimile reproductions, while the automated database can generate the electronic equivalent of targets, or editorially supplied labels reproducing control file information for individual items, to precede each item's images and provide the base for the edition's indexing system.

When editing for microform, editors could not begin the work of photographing images until collecting had been completed and the physical results of that process had been put into the order in which they would appear in the microform. The editor of a series of scanned images has an enormous advantage here: digital images can be entered into the electronic files as they are collected—to be re-ordered by the user's commands, not by the editor's decisions.

The John Paul Jones Papers microfilm introduced a new technique that may have considerable influence in the newer technology of electronically transmitted facsimiles. Following traditional methods, the Jones Papers microfilm reproduced images of original Jones manuscripts introduced by targets. But the Jones editors also pre-pared transcriptions for these materials, and these typescripts fol-lowed the images of manuscripts. The implications of this technique for an electronic edition are obvious. When the edition includes not only digitally scanned images of the originals but machine-readable transcriptions of these texts, users of the electronic edition can sup-plement the access capabilities of the index with full-text searching.

The first example of electronic publication in documentary editing is the *Legal Papers of Abraham Lincoln,* to be published in 1998. Anyone who compares the ease of using this CD-ROM, with its easy links between case files and subject indexes, with the labor of consulting a traditional multiple-reel microfilm edition like the legal papers section of the Aaron Burr Papers will see immediately the new technology's advantages.

Editors considering some form of facsimile edition or supplement should be aware that modern documentary editing has irrevocably raised the standards of expectation among members of their audi-ence. The periodic "Microform Reviews" column in the *Journal of American History* shows a consistent demand by reviewers for good indexing and a statement of principles for selection for the micro-form and even of the scope of the search that produced the archive of images.

C. OTHER SUPPLEMENTARY FORMS

Some editorial projects do not pretend to produce a comprehensive publication in the form of records, calendar entries, or microform supplements. Editors of the correspondence of literary figures, for instance, customarily confine their editions to the letters written by their subjects. The editorial office's control files are usually available to scholars who can travel to the project site, but the printed volumes themselves seldom carry a calendar of unpublished materials, and no project with the CEAA or CSE emblem has published a comparable facsimile supplement to a selective book edition.

Projects outside the tradition of historical editing, however, are increasingly aware of their responsibility to provide students with an independent, interim published record of their collections during the years that the preparation of annotated volumes takes place. The Mark Twain Papers project, for instance, published a printed *Union Catalog of Clemens Correspondence* before issuing the first volume of the modern edition of *Mark Twain's Letters* in 1988, and the editors of *Selected Letters of Louisa May Alcott* (1987) issued "A Calendar of the Letters of Louisa May Alcott" in *Studies in the American Renaissance* in 1988. Thus, Twain scholars who would otherwise have waited decades for the completion of the edition of Clemens letters can now pursue their own research interests while the Twain editors publish the printed, annotated texts, and Alcott buffs have easy access to the locations of the nearly 600 Alcott letters that did not appear in the book edition.

Automated methods have removed the creation of such finding aids from the luxury category for documentary editors. The Mark Twain Papers' *Union Catalog* would have been impossible had the project not converted its files to a computerized database. More modest projects with word processors can produce equally sophisticated supplementary finding aids, whether they be indexes of a facsimile edition or the catalog of unpublished documents. Editors who know that they must issue such facsimiles or catalogs are obliged to adopt automated database methods.

Some supplements are separately printed volumes of documents excluded from the standard edition's annotated volumes by overall selection criteria but judged to be of special merit. One example of this type is *Advice after Appomattox: Letters to Andrew Johnson, 1865–1866*. This paperback volume contains letters from agents sent by Johnson to report on conditions in the former Confederacy, dispatches given summary treatment in volume 8 of the *Johnson* edition proper and printed separately here with minimal editorial annotation.

### D. CAUTIONS ON SELECTIVITY

Even with facsimile editions, electronic publication, microform technology, computer-generated checklists, or other finding aids to the editorial collection as a whole, the editor is responsible for making an intelligent and fair selection of materials for print. Indexed bound volumes will be used more often and more thoroughly than the supplements, and even the editor whose annotation carries generous quotations from unpublished materials or pointed references to documents in a supplementary facsimile must remember this fact. Scholars are as lazy as other mortals. Most are accustomed to the convenience of a book format, and many will avoid reference to unprinted materials at all costs. The editor's standards for selection in any printed volumes remain crucial.

Pressured to streamline their volumes, conscious of publishers' pleas for interesting and lively series, editors may risk distorting the documentary record in the process of selection. One of the most common methods of selection is that of printing only one side of a subject's correspondence and public papers. This produces an edition of the "writings of" a subject, not one including all of his or her papers. The sheer bulk of the surviving records of the careers of modern political and military leaders like Eisenhower and George Marshall, for example, dictated highly selective editions of materials written by their central figures. This criterion for selection has several merits. It is easily understood by both editors and readers, and it is especially appropriate to a collection of writings by someone who, like Eisenhower and Marshall, is likely to be of greater interest than that writer's correspondents. The interpretive bias that may result from this policy is discussed in James B. Stewart's review of the Garrison Letters. While this source of unintentional interpretation through selection is easily recognized, other causes are more subtle. Another reviewer pointed out that "different editorial frameworks and the decisions made within them affect the reader's picture of the subject to a far greater degree than [the reader] probably imagines" (Kraditor, p. 519).

As an example, consider the decision of the editors of the papers of political leaders or other public figures to provide calendar entries for materials that appear "routine." This can produce a misleading picture of the overall collection, for correspondence of a routine or administrative nature occurs with varying frequency during a public figure's life. Calendaring such documents creates inconsistent degrees of selectivity from one volume to another in an edition. Paradoxically, it may result in publishing the complete texts of all or nearly all the correspondence and papers for years when a public figure was in private life, while printing only a percentage of such materials in their entirety for periods when the same person held an important public office. (Examples of such fluctuation are evident in the *Clay* and *Calhoun* editions.) In addition, a decision to give preference to the records of a figure's public or professional life may slight the needs of scholars interested in the wide varieties of social history and intimate human experience recorded in that same figure's private correspondence.

Editors should remember the needs of an edition's audience in weighing the virtues of these alternatives to comprehensive publication. Jean Berlin has suggested, for instance, that calendars of letters omitted and letters not found are better suited to the interests of a scholarly audience, while explanatory introductory notes may better communicate similar information to a more general audience (p. 29).

There is, obviously, bias inherent in the choice to omit potentially important materials from an edition, but editors can also weaken the appeal and utility of their work by including trivial or inappropriate materials. Even the most restrained editors can be guilty of an occasional lapse. With the advantage of hindsight, the editors of the *Woodrow Wilson Papers* suggested that they erred in printing the complete texts of reviews of Wilson's published writings in their early volumes; they realized later that their readers would have been satisfied with a simple checklist.

Perhaps the greatest temptation in setting selection standards is that of giving readers what they *expect* to find in the edition. The discovery of the unexpected is the basic justification for appropriating time and money to a systematic search for materials, and editors should beware of establishing the final organizational plan for an edition too early. A plan based on the findings of earlier scholars may presuppose that a given chronological period in a subject's career will be too dull or insignificant to warrant extensive attention. The documents gathered in a project's search can put the lie to such an easy assumption, for letters scattered in two dozen repositories may show that an apparently minor correspondent was, in fact, a constant and regular part of the letter-writing life of the project's subject.

An editor should ensure that the new, authoritative edition reflects the most current knowledge of the documentary record the editorial process has reconstructed, and one of the editor's many roles is that of an honest and accurate reporter of the results of the expensive and time-consuming search on which any edition is based. The limitations of earlier scholarship and outmoded assumptions about what is significant underlie the justification for new editions (see "The Editor's Craft: Looking Back to Look Ahead," *Documentary Editing* 17 [March 1995]: 22–24, for a summary of papers discussing just such shortcomings and erroneous assumptions). In a review in the *Journal of American History,* William Gilmore roundly criticized the new Harvard University Press edition of *The Letters of John Greenleaf Whittier* for adopting as its primary selection criterion the assumption that the years before 1861 were "the most crucial ones in his development as man and writer." Thus, the edition published all 961 extant pre-1861 Whittier letters and only 527 of the more than 4,500 letters of later date. By slighting the decades of Whittier's life assumed to be less important, the editors made it impossible for scholars to study the very years in the poet's career that have been most neglected in the past. And Jean Berlin faulted the selection criteria of the *Webster Papers* edition with this comment: "After a careful reading of their general statements on selection, one might conclude that they chose documents which tended to reflect the prevailing historical interpretation of Webster" ("Selecting the Essential Webster").

The knowledge gained in searching for materials for a modern scholarly edition is usually the best basis for determining how selective that edition should be and identifying the most useful criteria for the selection process. By the time most editors complete the bibliographic research, personal visits to repositories, and physical processing of the records discovered in this process, they have a knowledge of the papers, writings, or records of their subject that no other scholar can match. One of their most challenging tasks is putting that knowledge to work in analyzing what the users of their editions will consider significant or balanced and in explaining how they have come to these conclusions.

While each editor must make decisions about selection based on the source materials at hand, John Simon has suggested a useful canon of considerations for all editors who must devise a scheme of selection. He begins with the observation that "selection of documents is at best a necessary evil," reminding readers that "editors forced to select still struggle to achieve a degree of comprehensive coverage," by using any or all of the supplements and aids suggested in this chapter. Standards of selection must be "set forth as explicitly as possible," he says, and warns that "selection should not be tendentious," as "rigorous selection involves a realistic prediction of the audience.... When an audience cannot be predicted, it can at least be respected." A cumbersome, inefficient editorial apparatus has few attractions in a selective edition, Simon admonishes, because, quite simply, "documents are more important than apparatus." This exposition of his canon closes with a plea that editors who have established standards then follow their own guidelines and always remember that "editors serve the best interests of scholarship by decisions to include documents" ("Canons of Selection").

## II. Organization of the Printed Edition

Selectivity versus comprehensiveness is not the only choice editors face in determining the formats of their printed volumes or facsimile editions. Nor is that the only preliminary editorial decision with interpretive effects on an edition: the arrangement of the documents selected for print can be equally important.

One intellectual ancestor of modern American papers editions, the *Correspondence of Horace Walpole,* grouped Walpole's letters by his major correspondents. Thus, Walpole's exchanges with the Reverend William Cole are contained in volumes 1 and 2, his exchanges with Madame du Deffand and her circle appear in volumes 3–8, and so forth. This feature of the Walpole edition is one that American editors—of all traditions—have generally chosen not to imitate. While two early volumes in the Mark Twain edition, *Mark Twain's Letters to his Publishers* and *Mark Twain's Letters to Henry Huddleston Rogers,* segregated the author's letters by their recipient, this practice was discarded long before work began on the comprehensive and more authoritative edition of *Mark Twain's Letters.* For almost every other modern scholarly edition of correspondence, all items selected for full publication are usually printed in a single chronological sequence.

### A. TOPICAL ARRANGEMENT

When it comes to documents recording a subject's professional life—whether as an author or a lawyer or a diplomat—documentary editors are more likely to create special groupings of related materials for their editions. Legal papers generated by American statesmen have traditionally appeared in separate series in both the microform and book editions of those statesmen's papers. Obviously, the editors of an author's literary works have little choice but to group together the draft versions of a specific novel, essay, or poem if they are to give their readers any sense of the evolution of an author's thoughts, but editors in other fields have used topical organization as well. Julian Boyd inaugurated a similar practice of grouping documents relating to specific foreign policy issues in the *Jefferson Papers* (see, especially, volumes 16–20) into special topical sections. The editors of *The Papers of Daniel Webster* provided their edition with separate subseries for Webster's career as secretary of state and for his law practice. Within both these subseries, documents are also grouped topically.

Some groups of documents defy a unifying chronological organization. The records of a lawyer's practice, for instance, would be unintelligible were the editor to print all legal documents in one time sequence. Pleas, depositions, subpoenas, and affidavits that relate to a given case must be grouped together if their contents are to make sense. The principle of organization by case has been adopted consistently by most modern editors of legal materials in both print and facsimile editions (Adams, Burr, Hamilton, Lincoln, and Webster). Editors whose subject is the record of a movement or agency may also find topical organization attractive.

Often the degree of selectivity and topical organization is so high that the resulting publication is titled a "documentary history" rather than the "papers" or "records" of a group. Perhaps the best known example of this method is *Freedom: A Documentary History of Emancipation,* which combines topical and chronological arrangement to enable its readers to sift through a vast bureaucratic archive to uncover a wealth of social history. (For a chronicle of the *Freedom* project and analysis of its organization, see Ira Berlin et al., "Writing 'Freedom's History.'") One reviewer aptly termed the series "a history . . . based upon documents" (Brook D. Simpson, 7). Similar considerations shaped the *Documentary History of the Ratification of the Constitution,* the *Documentary History of the First Federal Congress,* and the *Documentary History of the First Federal Elections.* Here, as in any editorial decision, intelligibility and utility were overriding considerations. The needs of an audience for a documentary history are just as exacting as those for near-comprehensive, chronologically ordered series. A perceptive discussion of this problem appears in Randall M. Miller's "Documentary Editing and Black History: A Few Observations and Suggestions."

Departure from conventional chronological organization, like departures from any other general editing principle, should be taken only after serious thought. And this rule is even more important when an editor considers changing the rules of organization or selection *within* an edition. The necessity for such a deviation was recognized in the *John Marshall Papers.* Selected records of cases that Marshall tried as a practicing attorney appear in volume 5, *Selected Law Cases,* with papers for each case grouped together and records for related cases in separate sections. Marshall's opinions as Chief Justice of the Supreme Court, however, appear in their appropriate places in the chronological sequence of the *Marshall Papers,* interspersed with personal and professional correspondence, business papers, and other documents. Records of a given legal case only make sense together; the earliest papers relating to an action may precede the suit by a hundred years, and the final settlement may come decades after the death of the parties in the original action. A judge's decision, however, can be logically and honestly tied to a narrow period of time, to the days, weeks, or months in which the jurist considered the matter in question. The John Marshall edition, then, follows in the honored tradition of documentary editing by allowing individual documents and groups of documents and the needs of the reading audience to dictate organization.

### B. CAUTIONS ON TOPICAL GROUPINGS

All editors realize that haphazard topical arrangement can make it more difficult for the reader to reconstruct the patterns that will meet his or her needs. Electronic publishing will make such personal reorganization of an archive far simpler, but print editions and microforms do not give users this luxury. Many traditional forms of editorial apparatus, such as name and subject indexes, exist to allow scholars to make their own arrangement of related materials for personal research purposes. Still, the casual destruction of the general organizational pattern can make the volumes less, not more, useful.

The demands of dealing simultaneously with the impatience of sponsoring institutions, the challenge of varied groups of documents, and the expectations of several audiences for the same edition can create organizational systems that challenge the reader. The Daniel Webster edition's annotated printed volumes of selected documents appeared in four distinct series: *Correspondence, Legal Papers, Diplomatic Papers,* and *Speeches and Formal Writings.* Two of the series included comprehensive calendars while the other two (*Diplomatic* and *Legal*) did not. Comprehensive microfilm supplements for three of the four series preceded publication of the first volumes, while the microform of Webster's legal papers came much later. One reviewer complained wearily: "The lack of any lengthy introduction to editorial techniques and choices, particularly in describing the relationship of the various letterpress series to the microfilm, is confusing; some reviewers of various volumes have written inaccurate accounts of this connection. Will the student or layman understand it better?" (Jean V. Berlin, 26).

Just as important, editorial arrangement can distort the documents as effectively as a biased choice of documents, a fact discussed at length by American editors in the history of science. The Joseph Henry, Thomas Edison, and Albert Einstein editions consciously broke with the European tradition of publishing scientific documents in topical groupings. Modern intellectual historians, whether their interest be science, philosophy, or the arts, realize that such a prepackaging of source materials makes it virtually impossible for the reader to understand the context within which each step of the intellectual process occurred. History, of whatever subject, places a premium on time as an organizing principle.

A peculiar set of circumstances led the John Dewey edition to embark on a chronologically arranged series. When the project began its work, Dewey's widow still lived, and she proved reluctant to cooperate. Thus, despite suggestions from some Dewey scholars that his writings appear in some sort of "logical" series, the editors had no choice but to begin publication with Dewey's earliest published writings, materials for which copyright protection had expired. Even when Mrs. Dewey had died and more cooperative executors took control, the Dewey edition remained true to the chronological organization, which proved more helpful to their goals (Boydston, "The Press and the Project").

## C. SOME CONVENTIONS OF DOCUMENTARY ORGANIZATION

Modern documentary editors have adopted certain conventions for the subdivisions of the papers or writings of their subjects. All CEAA and CSE editions, for instance, publish works composed for publication separately from private writings such as letters and journals, a method employed in the Albert Einstein edition. One chronological series of materials appears in the *Early Years* series, but for Einstein's mature life, surviving records of correspondence, laboratory notes, and other papers are segregated from the series of *Writings*, works of Einstein that actually saw print publication. No one quarrels with this division in the case of authors whose works were designed for a wide audience quite distinct from the one to which the letters and journals were addressed. Each group of documents must be studied separately. But further subdivision should be undertaken only for compelling reasons, and any editor who publishes documents in separate series or subseries must be prepared to devise different, though equally clear and cogent, standards of selection for each group.

The problem of grouping documents is addressed at length in the introductions to the *Adams Family Correspondence* and *The Papers of John Adams*. When editorial work began, some advisers suggested that all the correspondence and papers of three generations of the Adams Family be published in one chronological series, with even diary entries broken up and interspersed among letters, state papers, legal records, and literary works. This plan was quickly vetoed: the

Adamses' diaries were major autobiographical writings that deserved to have their integrity preserved in discrete volumes. Aside from this consideration, the editors believed that having a single chronological series of Adams family papers, public and private, would be less useful than having an edition with carefully designated divisions. They assumed that comparatively few readers would approach the volumes with the intention of studying the Adamses as a family; rather, readers would have an interest either in personal interrelationships among family members or in some individual family member's professional activities in law, literature, or public service. Thus, the Adams edition appears in three series: *Diaries and Autobiographical Writings*, *Family Correspondence*, and *Papers,* the last including letters and other writings bearing on the Adamses' professional and public careers.

As the Adams project has progressed, its editors have identified varying patterns of selectivity among the series. Richard Ryerson analyzed these shifts in "Editing a Family Legacy: The Adamses and Their Papers." With successive volumes, the *Papers of John Adams* volumes became more selective, falling from a record of 99 percent of available documents in volumes 1 and 2 to 75 percent in volumes 5 and 6. Meanwhile, the *Adams Family Correspondence* volumes continue to include 80 to 90 percent of qualifying letters.

Although volumes of the Adams Papers now routinely carry lists of excluded Adams materials and their editors scrupulously disclose statistics on selection, recent reviewers have challenged some of the basic organizational assumptions the editors have made. As print publication takes John Adams into public life and diplomatic service, some have become uneasy with the distinction between "public" and "family" letters. Adams discussed his career as a statesman in letters to family and personal friends, and division of his correspondence into two series creates problems for some users. An even more fundamental objection is raised by historians of culture and the family, who argue that modern scholarship has created a large body of readers who are, indeed, interested in the papers of all the Adamses, male and female, public and private, and these readers are ill served by the edition's divisions.

Practical considerations of staff expertise have led other editions to publish a number of separate chronological series. The George Washington papers, for instance, are divided among colonial, revolutionary, confederation, and presidential series. Work on later series began even before the final volume of colonial papers went to the printer, and three editorial teams now work simultaneously on the remaining trio of series. Documents within each are arranged chronologically, and when all the series are completed, one chronological run will exist. A similar method was adopted by the James Madison edition, with teams of editors working ahead on series for Madison's career as secretary of state and president while another group completed work on the records of his last years as congressman.

## D. DIARIES AND JOURNALS

The common practice of publishing diaries and journals separately from other papers was criticized by Arthur S. Link, who felt that diary entries should be printed in the same sequence with the rest of a figure's papers unless overriding considerations demanded a discrete series (Link, "Where We Stand"). This was seconded by Lyman Butterfield, editor of the four-volume *Diary and Autobiography* of John Adams. A separate series for diaries presupposes that their contents are so full and interesting that readers will need to study them as an independent work: the Adamses' diaries fall within this category, while Woodrow Wilson's do not.

Before creating a special series for a group of diaries, the editor must weigh the relationship between the contents of the diaries and those of the diarist's other papers. Some diaries are little more than appointment books that do not stand alone; their only purpose is to illuminate the fuller exposition of the diarist's life as represented in his or her correspondence and other papers. If only scattered leaves of a diarist's memoirs survive, it would also be foolish to allot them a separate series. Thus, the editions of James Fenimore Cooper's *Letters* and Robert Morris's records of the Revolutionary Finance Office integrate surviving scattered journal entries into the chronological series of correspondence for the same period. Whenever the writer is an intermittent record keeper, making entries only during extended trips, such travel journals may also benefit from incorporation into the general series of his or her writings.

For some diarists, a personal journal represents a life quite distinct from that reflected in correspondence and other records. Many professional authors use journals less as a record of daily events than as a literary daybook in which they jot down ideas for stories or essays and even use some pages to draft their skeletal inspirations into fully developed literary passages. Were daily entries from such journals interspersed with authors' correspondence for the same period, the editors would destroy the sources' intellectual integrity to no useful purpose. Readers would have to reconstruct the sequence of journal entries. There is no question about the ability of such journals to stand alone in terms of literary quality, length, and subject matter, and their editors need not hesitate to publish them as separate series. Modern typesetting and photoreproduction technology allows editors to find creative solutions to special problems created by journals of this kind. An appendix to volume 3 of the *Albert Einstein Papers* includes parallel publication of the pages of Einstein's scribbled "Scratch" notebook with editorial transcriptions of the notebooks' contents.

There may be other considerations behind a decision to publish journals or diaries separately. The repository owning the originals may withhold permission for publication unless the new edition preserves the originals' integrity. Editors under pressure to begin publication early may look to a series of easily located journals and diaries that can be prepared for publication while the project completes its search for more elusive correspondence and other papers. And there may be, quite simply, some overwhelming public expectation of separate publication of a set of diaries.

## III. Electronic Aids

Modern electronic techniques offer more choices in the area of scope and organization, but they do not obviate the need for careful consideration of the nature of the text and of its expected audience. Computers enable the editor to plan more accurately both in terms of subject and organization. A control file database that includes a field for the number of pages in each source text will allow preliminary calculation of the collection's physical bulk and likely length in print or photofacsimile form, providing the editor and sponsoring agencies with some sense of the degree of selectivity that will be required in the published text. Subject indexing during the stage of collecting and creating the control files can expedite many decisions for selection and organization. Although manual control files gave editors a rough idea of the wealth or poverty of materials for specific chronological years, they were limited in pinpointing topics and their occurrences. An automated indexing system with subject entries can produce reports showing patterns of discussion of topics in terms of periods of greatest activity and the identity of correspondents. Materials identified in this way can then be reviewed for evaluation as "representative" or "routine" material for the edition. The editors of the Edison papers invested time and money in a sophisticated relational database for their project precisely because they knew that theirs would be a highly selective edition. Only computerized methods enabled them to analyze accurately the intellectual themes and technological problems in given periods of Edison's long life so that these could be reflected in their published volumes.

Here, as in other areas of scholarly editing, the use of computer equipment does not change the rules—it merely makes playing the game a bit easier. Whatever electronic aids are available, whatever external or internal pressures determine the organizational format and scope of a series, the editor must remember that the scope of an edition and the arrangement of its contents may determine how widely the edition is used—or whether it can be used at all.

## Suggested Readings

The body of literature in the field of selection and organization of materials in documentary editions is generous, though scattered. The introductions to selective and topically organized editions cited in this chapter should be supplemented by the entries indexed under "selection" and "organization" in Luey, *Editing Documents.* Also helpful would be *Editorial Specifications: The Papers of George Catlett Marshall,* an internal publication of the Marshall Papers project.

I. Reviewers of specific editions often raise helpful issues regarding the scope of a project, and references to individual editions in Luey's index will produce useful results. More recent literature in the area includes Thornton Miller's review of *John Marshall Papers,* vol. 6 in *Virginia Magazine* 101 (1993): 172–73, and Judith Giblin James, "'I Know my Worth': Lillian Smith's Letters from the Modern South," *Documentary Editing* 16 (December 1994): 85–87. Jack D. Warren's "The Counter-Revolutionary Career of Peter Porcupine," ibid., 88–93, is a useful discussion of all the problems in using printed source texts, from selection through organization and annotation.

Luey's index references under "microforms" ably cover writings on the subject before 1989. For an independent microform supplement to a "literary" edition see the Bruccoli-Clark edition of the facsimile of Stephen Crane's *The Red Badge of Courage (A Facsimile Edition of the Manuscript),* edited with an introduction and apparatus by Fredson Bowers, 2 vols. (Washington, D.C., 1972–73).

More recent discussions of microforms include Sherry Byrne, "Guidelines for Contracting Microfilming Services," *Microform Review* 15 (Fall 1986); 253–64, which even includes a sample contract for microfilming; and Marc Rothenberg, "Documenting Technology: The Selective Microfilm Edition of the Thomas A. Edison Papers," *Documentary Editing* 12 (September 1990): 53–55. The *Journal of American History* publishes occasional "microform reviews," which provide useful and often harshly critical consumer response to these products.

Editors needing guidance in the preparation of a large-scale facsimile edition, whether microform or digital images, can turn to the NHPRC and the NEH. These agencies can refer them to projects that have anticipated some of their problems as well as provide up-to-date technical standards for such publications.

The use of nonmicroform supplements to selective editions has not been examined closely, and Luey's index entries for "calendaring" provide access to this literature, which the student should supplement by reading James P. McClure's "The Neglected Calendar," *Documentary Editing* 10 (September 1988): 18–21; and James H. Hutson's discussion of contrasting calendaring policies in the Adams and Franklin series in *Pennsylvania Magazine* 114 (1990): 295–96.

II. The reader who wishes models of varying organizational formats has many choices. For examples of the organization of legal papers in documentary editions, see the appropriate volumes in the Adams, Hamilton, John Marshall, and Webster series. The best example of a series format with a fully realized system of cross-references is that described in the introduction to volume 1 of the *Papers of John Adams.* And the techniques of the new *Freedom* edition are models for topical organization.

The editor of a diary or journal will profit by consulting Laura Arksey et al., eds., *American Diaries: An Annotated Bibliography of Published American Diaries and Journals*, 2 vols. (Detroit, 1982 and 1987), a guide to examples of editorial treatment of any kind of diary or journal over the past three centuries. The editions of journals and notebooks in the Emerson, Thoreau, Hawthorne, and Mark Twain series present examples of editorial treatment of literary daybooks.

III. For a summary of the role of databases in selecting and organizing documents, see "Using Databases in Editorial Projects: A Workshop," *Documentary Editing* 15 (March 1993): 15.

# CHAPTER IV

---

# Evaluating and Transcribing the Source Text

Documentary editing is most clearly distinguished from traditional critical textual editing by its customary reliance on a single hand-written, typed, printed, or otherwise recorded document (the source text) for each editorial text. Although documentary editors occasionally use such tools of textual editing as conflation to establish an ideal text of some kind (see chapter 6), their general rule is that one source text, whether an original document or its reproduction, will be the basis of one editorial text. Even though variants between the source text and other versions of the same document will be recorded in editorial notes, it is the words, phrases, and punctuation of a single source that should be readily and conveniently available to the reading audience. Even in an electronic edition in which the reader can use links to move back and forth from transcriptions of one stage of a document's evolution to another, the editor must choose one of the versions as the basic text from which the links will radiate. Thus, the selection of that source text and its accurate transcription, into typescript or machine-readable form, are crucial matters for any editorial project.

Only after collecting and cataloging are complete can an editor begin to assess the special problems that these sources will present. The individual documents or groups of documents themselves dictate the best textual approach. Before an editor can put that textual treatment into effect, however, there must be reliable transcriptions of the carefully selected source texts as working copy. For some editions, that initial transcription may be almost identical with the editorial text that readers will see; for others, the transcription will be expanded and become the foundation on which the editorial text, editorial apparatus, and annotation are erected.

Early-nineteenth-century American documentary editors like

Jared Sparks did not concern themselves with the labor of transcribing the texts they wished to publish; instead, they simply used those original manuscripts as printer's copy. The autograph letters of Gouverneur Morris and George Washington bear mute witness to the method, their pages filled with Sparks' penciled "corrections" of the author's style and punctuation. Even though photocopies of some printed documents can serve as the editor's copy or the basis of a facsimile edition, most items must be transcribed to produce working copy for the editor and for print publication.

The problems of transcribing an edition's source texts fall into two obvious categories: what to transcribe and how to transcribe it. Almost every editor will sometimes have to choose from among several candidates for a document's source text. Once the source texts for an edition are identified, they must be transcribed so as to expedite rather than impede later editorial work. Even modern technology will not shield the editor from this labor. Although word processing software now enables editors to make extensive changes in the initial transcription without the need for complete retyping, it is vastly more efficient—and more reliable—to choose the correct source texts and transcription methods at the outset.

## I. Authentication and Attribution

The most important criterion to be met by any document published in a scholarly edition is that it is indeed the intellectual product of the person or organization purported to be its author. Editors must rule out forgeries and misattributions while they simultaneously make every effort to identify documents not previously recognized as the work of the subject.

The editors of the papers of well-known individuals are at greatest risk of falling victim to forged materials. The commercial market for letters and other manuscripts penned by heads of state, military and naval leaders, famed scientists and inventors, and literary lights is centuries old in the Western world, and forgery is almost as old as that trade. Joe Nickell's *Pen, Ink, and Evidence: A Study of Writing and Writing Materials for the Penman, Collector, and Document Detective* (1990) and its bibliography provide a useful introduction to the history of documentary forgeries, and experienced dealers or auction house experts familiar with the subject of the editorial project can also offer hard-earned knowledge of such fakes.

Almost as common is the problem of ruling out published or unpublished works that, while historically genuine, have been erroneously credited to the subject of an edition. Perhaps the best-known discovery by the editors of the two-volume *Political Corre-spondence and Public Papers of Aaron Burr* (1983) is the fact that the cipher letter from Burr to James Wilkinson that led to Burr's denunciation as a traitor was not, in fact, written by Burr but by his associate Jonathan Dayton. Less well publicized but more historically significant was the editors' decision to omit from volume 17 of the modern *Madison Papers* edition the 1799 Virginia Resolutions and Address of the General Assembly once they became convinced that Madison was not, in fact, the author of these statements.

Traditionally, scholars have shown more concern for the attribution of works to famous authors than to renowned politicians or generals. Novelists and poets are more likely to be the subjects of exhaustive investigations of the claims of anonymous and pseudonymous literature credited to them. A notable exception is Benjamin Franklin, whose newspaper contributions were the subject of J. A. Leo Lemay's monumental *Canon of Benjamin Franklin, 1722–1776: New Attributions and Reconsiderations.* For any published author, computer analysis of usage may help corroborate or disprove attributions. (See Merriam, "An Experiment with the Federalist Papers.) In most cases, the editor will not be the first scholar to examine this issue for his or her subject, and questions of attribution will be addressed throughout the editorial project, from the time of collection until the point when informational footnotes are added to the editorial text. The editors of the *Papers of John Adams,* for instance, were able to credit Adams with drafting a March 1773 message of the Massachusetts House of Representatives only after they had reviewed all of Adams' correspondence concerning the incident (1:312–13).

It is not only published works that may raise questions of attribution. Scholars who deal with the papers of any figure who commanded a large civilian or military staff must establish guidelines that define when a document may be considered that figure's work and when it will be credited to the junior associate who drafted the document, which may have been dispatched without a moment's review by the person whose signature it bears. The editors of the papers of Dwight D. Eisenhower and George C. Marshall admit that their task in this regard has been made easier by the clear chain of command demanded by both Eisenhower and Marshall. These generals were sticklers not only for clearly established office procedures but also for putting those procedures on the record. This meticulousness has enabled scholars to understand these patterns of documentation and identify which set of initials or stamps identify documents that were, indeed, the work of Marshall and Eisenhower.

Even these editors, however, faced a decision requiring Solomon-like judgment when they confronted a radio message to Douglas MacArthur of 7 February 1942. As a member of Marshall's staff, Eisenhower drafted the dispatch, and a typescript copy of that draft was submitted to Marshall, who then covered the margins and inter-linear spaces with his additions and changes. So extensive were Marshall's revisions that a complete retyping was necessary before the message could be coded and dispatched. Here two sets of editors saw two documents with two authors: the Eisenhower edition (1:101–3) printed the typescript portions of the draft, noting Marshall's revisions in footnotes. The text in the Marshall edition (3:100–102) was based on the typescript that incorporated those changes, the version that reflected Marshall's authorship.

## II. Choosing the Source Text

The rules for selection of the source texts, like all editorial procedures, should be stated clearly in the edition's introduction. For modern and Anglo-American documents, the criteria used to establish these rules generally involve little more than common sense. The following guidelines apply to the major categories of documentary materials for the modern period.

### A. HANDWRITTEN OR TYPEWRITTEN MATERIALS

1. The manuscript or a reliable photocopy is to be preferred over any later scribal copies or transcriptions as the source text.
2. If the original has been lost or destroyed, contemporary copies are preferred over later ones unless evidence survives to demonstrate that later copyists both had access to the original and were more accurate than the earlier scribes.
3. In general, the most nearly final version of a document is the preferred source text. Editors can take comfort in the thought that variants can and should be noted in the editorial apparatus. By choosing one version as source text, editors do not deny readers access to significant differences between versions of a document. That source text is simply the version that serves as the best working basis for the edition and most closely meets the needs of the edition's audience.

Other criteria for establishing priorities among versions are listed below.

## *1. Letters*

The first order of preference is given to a version of the original letter (preferably signed to denote authorial approval) known to have been received by its addressee. The best evidence for identifying a recipient's copy of a letter can be an attached address leaf, the recipient's endorsement, the presence of a mailing envelope, or the location of the letter in the addressee's papers. Even when no attached address or envelope survives to prove the receipt of a particular copy of a letter, fold patterns and other physical evidence often mark a particular document as the recipient's copy, and the editor familiar with the subject's letter-writing habits generally will be able to identify "finished" versions with little trouble.

A special problem may arise with the correspondence of statesmen who were assigned to foreign posts in times of national emergency. At such periods, diplomats frequently sent duplicate or even triplicate or quadruplicate signed copies of their dispatches to their home government. When two or more such multiple addressee's copies survive, the editor may have to decide which version to use as source text. The basis for such a judgment can include the completeness of the variant copies and the care that the letter's author or his or her secretary used in copying the dispatch. A triplicate letter in which words are carelessly omitted or in which the handwriting reflects haste would be a less desirable source text than the quadruplicate of the same letter in which the text is complete and the manuscript shows that it was copied more accurately than the triplicate. Nontextual considerations may be decisive in such cases. For example, a carelessly copied duplicate copy that reached the Department of State in June and became the basis for a foreign-policy decision would be a better source text than an elegantly inscribed quadruplicate that arrived several weeks later.

A second order of preference is given to copies of the letter in the hand of the author or someone under his or her direction that were not received by the addressee. Such versions fall into four categories: drafts, letterbook copies, copies that present fairly exact facsimiles of the recipient's version, such as letterpress and carbon copies (see below), and independently prepared loose file copies.

Preliminary draft versions on separately inscribed sheets are easily identified, but some of the other categories are not mutually exclusive. In the eighteenth century, bound blank volumes were used to record outgoing correspondence. Many authors used such letterbooks as a convenient place in which to draft their correspondence, recopying the final version on a separate sheet for mailing, while others copied texts into their letterbooks from the final version of the letter. Thus, some letterbooks represent bound volumes of drafts while others are assemblages of file copies of the recipients' correspondence. Worse still were public figures who did not leave well enough alone. George Washington, for instance, could not resist tinkering with youthful letterbooks once he achieved middle age, correcting spelling and awkward usage and then directing a clerk to recopy the emended results, thus creating a textual nightmare for his twentieth-century editors (Abbot, "An Uncommon Wareness of Self").

Documents that represent contemporary facsimile versions include letterpress copies, carbon copies, and, in our own time, photocopies and computer files. The efforts of American letter writers to provide themselves with files of their outgoing correspondence without retranscribing such materials are a tribute to Yankee ingenuity. In the late eighteenth century such American statesmen as Thomas Jefferson enthusiastically experimented with every invention that could ease their burden. Stylographic pens and pencils, which produced duplicate images of holograph materials, were employed. Correspondents purchased devices that made two pens move simultaneously to produce two copies of each letter, one for transmittal and one for filing. And last, but not least, there was the letterpress. In the earliest letterpresses, a thin, nearly transparent sheet of paper was moistened and pressed against the inscribed surface of handwritten material. Ideally, enough ink was transferred from the original to the back of the blank sheet that the handwritten words could be read from the front. In practice, most such letterpress copies were fragile, smudged horrors, until the mid-nineteenth century, when more sophisticated letterpresses produced more satisfactory copies. (For a history of one man's experimentation with such devices, see Bedini, *Thomas Jefferson and His Copying Machines*.)

The invention of the typewriter and the use of carbon paper added still another form of simultaneously created facsimile copy. Despite the fact that the carbon copy of typed materials has been part of American life and language for more than seventy-five years, editors have seldom written on the problems of rendering intelligible versions from uncorrected carbon copies, much less on those created by photocopying techniques that generate files of retained copies. A notable exception is Fredson Bowers' "Multiple Authority: New Problems and Concepts of Copy-Text." Until more such literature appears, editors who confront these issues can only use common sense, and the experience of their own and other editions will often be their guides.

A third order of preference is given to transcriptions and printed copies. Editors commonly designate as "transcriptions" copies made substantially later than a document's composition and executed by someone acting without the authority or assistance of the author. As source texts, such typed or handwritten transcriptions and printed versions of letters rank far below a contemporary copy, if one exists.

Editors must often choose among several transcribed copies of the same document to determine which is the best source text, the one closest to the original. For modern materials, nontextual evidence may identify the best transcription: patterns of handwriting, results of chemical tests of paper, and a comparison of typefaces in printed sources. When nothing useful can be learned from such historical evidence, editors should use more advanced methods of classical textual filiation to determine which offers the soundest source text. In filiation, the editor determines the families, or groups, to which the copies belong, creating a textual family tree reflecting the relationships among the surviving manuscripts, thus identifying the copy closest to the original. The editor of modern documents seldom needs to employ the more complicated techniques by which the classicist uses filiation, but its common-sense rules apply to modern as well as ancient materials. These rules require that the editor (a) attempt to learn something about the copyist for each scribal version and (b) identify patterns of common and unique errors in the copies, to determine the sequence in which the variant transcripts came into existence. Transcripts that contain the same errors are likely to be part of the same family, one descended from the other in order of transcription.

Like handwritten transcriptions, previously printed versions of a letter can reflect the interpretation and even the style of a later copyist, not the author's intentions. The problem addressed here is not that of establishing the preferred text of a work written for publication and printed during an author's lifetime but of letters or other private materials for which the original has disappeared and only the version printed in some earlier edition survives. When more than one such printed text survives, the editor must decide which has the greatest claim to authenticity and accuracy. Some of the techniques of choosing among several handwritten or typewritten transcriptions should be applied here. Obviously the editor has an advantage in establishing chronological patterns among printed texts, which usually bear a date of publication. But even this is not always a determining factor, for earlier editors may have prepared their printed versions of the same original source by independent reference to an archetype. The eye of the editor who published a text in 1830 need not have been more reliable than that of the editor who prepared a new text in 1880. When the evidence indicates that two printed versions or two transcripts of original materials were both based on the same archetype, then the editor relies on such internal evidence as faithfulness to known patterns of the author's spelling, punctuation, and capitalization, as well as the accuracy of the copyists' readings of proper nouns. Many printed versions dating from the nineteenth and early twentieth centuries appear in editions that carry no statements of editorial policy, and modern editors must often resort to their own critical judgment in selecting a source text.

### 2. Papers

In general, the rules that apply to an individual's correspondence also apply to selecting source texts from variant versions of his or her papers, records of professional activities or public life that cannot be defined as any form of letter or diary. This category includes the legislative reports of a lawmaker, the technical notes of a scientist, the general orders of a military commander, or the lecture notes of an educator.

Special considerations sometimes arise that make the best source text something other than the most nearly final version that survives. These considerations are very practical ones that relate to the availability of reliable printed editions of these final versions and the absence of such printed sources for preliminary versions that might have displayed significant variants. This problem arises frequently in the papers of men and women who held public office. Official government publications often contain adequate versions of the texts of legislative committee reports and formally adopted statutes; given their limited resources in terms of time and money, modern documentary editors may hesitate to republish an already available printed version of the same materials. But if the search for the edition project uncovers manuscript or typewritten draft versions of such reports or preliminary versions of legislative bills, then these little-known documents might better serve readers as source texts, with their notes directing scholars to the location of the printed "final" versions, which can be used to create parallel texts of the stages in the evolution of the same document.

### B. PRINTED WORKS

The literary works of any writer—prose and poetry composed for publication and issued in print more or less as intended by the author—present special problems to the documentary editor. Of these, the first is the choice of that version of the published work that will be used as the basis of the text to appear in the new edition. The editor who aspires to the CSE emblem will naturally refer to the guidelines of that organization before choosing a version for transcription. The choice may be the most appropriate copy-text, not a source text, and the criteria for its selection lie outside the boundaries of this volume. The copy-text may be the foundation of an emended critical text, whose aim is to represent the author's final intentions, intentions that may or may not appear in all respects in any one surviving copy of the work in question. The critical edition will itself be a new document, recording the best judgment of the editor, not the words or punctuation of any single version of the work published in the author's lifetime or available to any earlier reader. A documentary edition of a work, however, is normally a noncritical one based on a single version that was actually read by the audience for which it was intended.

The differences between the goals of a textual and a documentary editor, then, are not confined to varying textual treatments. They also extend to the choice of the version of the work that will be transcribed. Traditionally, textual editors of literary works preferred the printed version that reflected the author's most fully expressed intentions. They assumed that most readers of such materials were concerned with the development of the author's literary craftsmanship, which is often reflected by his or her correction of earlier printed errors. Modern textual scholarship has questioned these assumptions, but a focus on authorial intention is still an overriding consideration for many editors of literary works. Documentary editors, on the other hand, have always had to weigh other factors, such as the historical impact of different editions of the same book or essay, not merely an edition's reflection of the author's most clearly refined literary art. Many considerations can make something other than the final version in a set of printed variants far more important than the later, more polished edition.

As an example, textual and documentary editors might make very different decisions were they faced with the problem of choosing between two versions of a pamphlet originally published in Boston in 1773 and then revised by its author for a new edition a year later. An editor concerned with the author's literary intentions might conflate elements of the two into a critical edition, but the documentary editor would weigh the influence of each edition. If the 1773 printing was an important factor in rousing public opinion in Boston during the Tea Party crisis and the 1774 revision languished unread in a limited edition, the documentary editor would choose the earlier version. The pamphlet's significance for an audience of political historians is its impact in 1773. The author's later improvements would be recorded as variants in footnotes, but it would be nonsensical to use the 1774 edition as a source text, because it would force the reader to reconstruct laboriously the more significant 1773 version through reference to footnotes or tables of emendations.

For printed material, as for any source text, both the source and the projected audience will dictate textual treatment and transcription methods. Whether literary or historical values are the primary reason for republishing a printed document, the choice of a source text or copy-text demands a thorough knowledge of the document and its author and the needs of those likely to consult the new edition. An editor must assume the role of historical bibliographer to master the story of a work's composition and publication before deciding on the appropriate basis for a new edition. Knowledge of the technology of publication methods must be a part of this skill.

Newspapers present a special editorial challenge, for pieces published in this medium are peculiarly affected by changes in the mechanics of dissemination. Until the mid-nineteenth century, the newspaper that first printed an author's essay or articles was usually the one to which the writer had submitted the manuscript version, and its columns were most likely to carry a version that received some authorial proofreading. Later newspaper printings customarily drew on the first, and the variations that appear are more likely to be typographical errors that can be noted, if significant, in the editorial apparatus. Tracing authorial contributions to the press in this era can be challenging, but textual problems are comparatively straightforward. (See, for instance, John M. Robson, "Practice, Not Theory: Editing J. S. Mill's Newspaper Writings.) This situation changed, however, with the development of newspaper syndication in the late nineteenth century. If an author's article or story was published in syndicated form, the editor's research to determine which newspaper version has special claims to notice should expand to the methods used by the news syndicate in question. Here the methods of classical filiation may be useful, for the original can often be reconstructed by analyzing the variants in second- and third-generation copies.

III. Transcribing the Source Text:
    Methods of Inscription

The same factors that determine the choice of source texts will dictate the appropriate method of their transcription. The means used to record documentary evidence are often the primary factor that an editor considers in determining standards of transcription and in settling on the final textual method. Certainly it is always the first factor to be weighed. Only after editors have mastered the intricacies of all the methods used to inscribe the sources in their editorial collections can they begin to rule out textual practices that would distort the details of those sources. The form of documentary evidence represented by each source text—letter, diary, state paper, scientific treatise—will raise another set of questions. The editor should consider the method of communication that each embodies before reaching a final decision on its treatment in the new edition. Whether the editor is his or her own transcriber or delegates this task to a staff, work will move more smoothly if transcription follows carefully thought-out decisions that can be applied consistently rather than beginning so early that its rules must be changed over and over again.

Editors stress the need to master the inscriptional history of unprinted documentary sources, as well as the history of printed materials that will be the basis of a documentary edition. While choosing among competing source texts, the editor should learn as much as possible about the methods by which these variants were produced. The knowledge may run the gamut from the practices of a group of clerks in the same office to the peculiarities of a particular eighteenth-century letterpress or the details of book production or newspaper composition. For comparable discussions of the inscriptional and organizational history of nonprint sources, see the *Eisenhower Papers,* "Essay on Primary Sources" (9:2259–73) and "Notes on Primary Sources" (11:1521–23 and 13:1507–11).

Unfortunately, there are few secondary studies of modern methods of non-typeset inscription to which an editor can refer. In European medieval studies, there is the recognized academic discipline of "diplomatics," which offers systematic studies of record-keeping methods of particular groups of clerks and administrators. There are no such formal courses from which to learn how the secretary of the American Continental Congress maintained his records in 1785 or how elementary students were taught to standardize the forms of personal correspondence in 1830. Each editor must learn these methods for him- or herself. Often the best introductions appear in edited volumes, and the novice should consult an edition that drew on sources similar to the one he or she hopes to publish. Documentary editors who have survived the agonies of learning the intricacies of American inscriptional history frequently share this wisdom in their own edited series. The general rules to be drawn from those experiences are incorporated throughout this text.

## A. HANDWRITTEN SOURCE TEXTS

Anyone who has transcribed handwritten materials or proofread the resulting copy knows that no typewriter or typeface can reproduce all the subtle distinctions in such originals. Any typed or printed transcription of such a source is a critical one, because it silently incorporates dozens of editorial judgments and decisions. The editor cannot indicate every instance in which experience allows her or him to recognize a scrawled mark as a period instead of a comma nor every occasion when skill and training enable the editor to recognize a slightly inflected line as an *n* instead of an *m*. Often the experienced editor exercises such judgment quite unconsciously. Knowing this, the editor should choose a textual policy whose conventions do not conceal additional subtleties in a source that is already being transformed from script to type.

Only a careful analysis of the sources at hand enables the editor to decide which conventions will least distort the source. Some writers may employ one method of punctuation in correspondence with close friends and another, more formal system in letters to strangers and professional colleagues. Obviously the standardization of such marks would conceal important evidence of the author's relationship with each correspondent. Still other writers vary the length of a standard mark of punctuation such as the hyphen for different functions. If the editor deems such differences important, he or she can mark or code the keyboarded transcription to reproduce the author's consistent, if idiosyncratic, patterns. Individual patterns of capitalization, the use of contractions, and care or carelessness in spelling often provide unexpected insights into an author's state of mind. The editor cannot responsibly ignore such slips of the pen until certain that they do not represent significant patterns in the writer's orthography.

It is difficult enough to discover such patterns in the handwriting of a single individual: they can change with a writer's progressive education or with advancing age. The possibility of distinguishing and analyzing such patterns in a group of documents representing a number of authors is far more challenging. Editors who are tempted to impose arbitrary, often modern notions of punctuation or spelling to normalize the two sides of a handwritten correspondence, journals that may have been kept by a dozen scribes, or reports and papers from a hundred contributors should consider the consequences of such a practice. Such standardization can mean the loss of information about their subjects that readers of the edition might have found informative.

The process of translating handwritten text to print has sometimes necessitated standardization. Such alterations to details of inscription as lowering superscript letters might be necessary to reduce the costs of producing the print edition. Adding editorial emendations beyond those dictated by printing practices, however, can fundamentally undermine a documentary edition and even invalidate the undertaking's justification. Fortunately, modern computer-assisted technology makes faithful transcription and publication of handwritten sources in a print edition more affordable. Commercial word-processing software enables users to reproduce superscripts and subscripts, dashes of various lengths, and other details. Computer composition of printed pages makes retention of such details a practical possibility and traditional emendations like expanding the "tailed p" no longer an economic necessity. Thanks to these technological blessings, source texts can be transcribed as literally as their legibility allows.

The age and condition of the manuscripts that bear the author's script may make even a rough transcription of their contents difficult. In such cases, editors should verify transcriptions against the originals before even beginning an assessment of the importance of each detail of inscription. And they may have to refer to those originals again and again during the period in which they labor to establish their texts for the edition, sometimes resorting to ultraviolet light to pick up faded ink.

B. TYPEWRITTEN DOCUMENTS

Only in recent years have documentary editors confronted the textual problems created by modern office machines. A recipient's copy of a signed typewritten letter or other communication presents few problems: no matter what its flaws, it may be considered to represent the author's final intentions. If the typescript carries handwritten corrections or revisions by the author, those can be indicated by textual symbols, special typefaces, or annotation. Often the same methods that the edition adopts to meet the needs of handwritten sources can be modified for typed sources. In the absence of such symbols, the editor may choose a special typeface to be reserved for handwritten additions to typed pages, and if such authorial revisions are rare, footnotes can explain these occasional details of inscription. Whatever the final decisions may be, the initial transcription should indicate all these details, so that they can be recorded as the formal textual apparatus dictates.

An uncorrected carbon copy creates new problems. Faced with file drawers full of such uncorrected copies of outgoing correspondence, the editors of the *Woodrow Wilson Papers* compared surviving carbon and ribbon copies of the same letters and found that Wilson himself had corrected the originals. They concluded that the ribbon copies of these letters had been corrected before dispatch, and the texts were emended accordingly. The *Eisenhower* edition takes a similar approach. After analyzing Eisenhower's patterns in proofreading outgoing typed correspondence, the editors adopted a twofold policy of emending errors in typed letters for which only the retained carbon copy survived. Mere typographical errors and errors of spelling, which Eisenhower routinely corrected, are emended silently, but editorial corrections of misspellings of proper nouns are accompanied by a footnote recording this emendation.

Editors of late-nineteenth-century typescripts should exercise special caution. Any assumptions about "typographical" errors here must take into consideration the specific keyboard of the machine employed. Decades passed before these keyboards were standardized, and emendations can occur only with full knowledge of the particular instrument involved. Contemporary photographs of the subject's office, bills, or correspondence ordering office equipment may enable the editor to identify the machine employed. If the machine's manufacturer is no longer in business under the same name, the editor may have to embark on a new career as corporate historian to find a source for an image of the typewriter's keyboard and determine patterns of likely typographic error. If no such records survive, the editor may have to abandon plans to correct such errors wholesale, for the identification of their patterns may be well nigh impossible.

Transcriptional and textual policies for typed sources should reflect not only that medium of inscription but also the basic nature of each source. A typed draft letter with handwritten or typed revisions has requirements quite different from a nonauthorial typed transcription of a handwritten source. Editors who ignore this rule and lump together typed letters, retained carbon copies, typed transcriptions, and printed transcriptions of lost sources into one textual category compromise their product before the process of transcription even begins. Typewriting is merely an exceptionally legible form of inscription, and the appearance of a typed document should not mislead one into ignoring other factors that may dictate editorial treatment.

C. PRINTED SOURCE TEXTS

The editor who establishes the text of a published work for the purposes of a critical edition may sometimes legitimately depart from the substantives and accidentals of any single surviving printed copy of that writing. But the documentary editor views print as merely another way to inscribe a document, and the surviving copies of a given source must be evaluated to determine which is the best document, the one that is a unique, authoritative source with evidentiary value. Once that source has been identified, it should be printed without being subject to emendation, conflation, or the other heavy artillery of textual editing.

Noncritical editors of printed sources should not, however, be *uncritical* in their methods by ignoring methods of textual scholarship or other disciplines that can helpfully be adopted. Many printed items can be viewed as documents: official government publications, pamphlets, essays, books. Within each category, the editor may need to become familiar with all the tools of bibliography and textual criticism, even though the editorial product itself will not be a critical one. To edit printed sources as documents, one must investigate their printing history with all the care employed by an editor hoping for a CSE emblem. Various—and variant—printings of the document will need to be collated as rigorously as for any MLA series. And the results of that historical research and the mechanical collation should be analyzed scrupulously.

Neglecting the tools of sophisticated bibliography for documentary editions can have embarrassing results. The editors of the *Laurens Papers* admit openly, if not happily, to having committed such a blunder in the fifth volume of their series, wherein they present a scrupulously printed facsimile of Laurens' 1767 pamphlet *A Representation of Facts*. Variant readings from all surviving copies of the pamphlet are recorded in textual notes, but the introduction to the document states that the editors were unable to discover the precise order in which the last two versions of the pamphlet were issued. Had the editors used the tools of modern bibliography to compare the variants for such clues as broken type, they might have determined the sequence in which the versions of the pamphlet were run.

In documentary editing, the compositor's type font should be regarded as an element of inscription as important as a scribe's copying practices, the configuration of the keyboard of an 1882 typewriter, or Woodrow Wilson's use of Graham shorthand. Editors of printed documents cannot assume that their task is easier because their sources already exist in typeset form. Instead, they must make themselves experts in this method of documentary inscription. Fredson Bowers' *Principles of Bibliographical Description* will disabuse such editors of the notion that editing printed sources is simple, and the members of the CSE are ready to offer advice and encouragement to novices in their fields of specialization.

For a sharp reminder of the ways in which a disregard for bibliography and printing history can invalidate an edition of printed documents, see Jack Warren's "The Counter-Revolutionary Career of Peter Porcupine." In speaking of the failures of modern reprintings of pamphlet literature that pretend to scholarly quality, Warren remarks: "A pamphlet edition ought to present complete and authoritative versions of clearly defined source texts, sufficient to make it unnecessary for scholars pursuing most lines of inquiry to refer to the originals; the edition as a whole should be based on well-defined selection criteria relevant to the contemporary importance of the writings involved; the notes should provide as much information as possible about the publishing history of the texts and should point out any significant variations between contemporary editions. Such basic standards may seem obvious to most documentary editors, but they are often neglected by those editing pamphlets" (p. 93).

### D. NONVERBAL DOCUMENTS

The editing of completely nonverbal documents has been addressed only recently by editors in the NHPRC and CSE traditions. Earlier, many editors had to solve the problem of how to present scattered authorial illustrations and even doodles that were part of a more conventionally inscribed source. When these elements have recognized equivalents in type, the transcriber can enter such ready-made symbols from the printer's font in good conscience. The editors of the *Hawthorne Notebooks* translated the author's hand-drawn marginal "fists" into the existing standardized type unit for this symbol (called a "fist graphic"); the editors of the *Emerson Journals* employed the conventional typeset caret ($_\wedge$) for Emerson's mark for interlineation; and Mark Twain's editors translated Clemens' autograph proofreading symbols in his *Notebooks* and *Letters* into the equivalent printer's symbols.

Unfortunately, writers seldom confine themselves to such easily translated marks. Some authors, like William Blake, were artists as well, and neither critical nor documentary editions of their works would be complete without reproduction of the images that are an integral part of their texts (Bentley, "Blake's Works as Performances"). With modern print publication techniques, the photoreproduction of sketches, drawings, doodles, or maps in a printed volume of documents is less dauntingly expensive than it once was, but the method is still limited to occasions when the literal presentation of such elements seems essential to understanding the documents. (See, for instance, the facsimile of a Jefferson diagram in *Jefferson Papers,* 22:74.) In the September 1984 issue of *Documentary Editing,* Reese Jenkins and Thomas Jeffrey pointed out that most editors have actually retreated from these challenges. Julian Boyd, they note, relegated Jefferson's nonverbal documents such as architectural sketches to a separate series—one that has not even been started as the Jefferson project moves into the second half of its first century. The *Franklin Papers* excluded nonverbal materials altogether except as illustrations. And although the Emerson editors reproduced Emerson's easily translatable symbol for an insertion, they excluded all of his pen and pencil sketches from the *Journals and Miscellaneous Notebooks* (Jenkins and Jeffrey, 7–9).

As Jenkins and Jeffrey also noted, editors of papers in the arts and sciences have a better record for the treatment of nonverbal documents than editors of the papers of a statesman or a novelist. The graphic records of great artists and illustrators introduce a new dimension to the problem of editorial transcription. Reproduction of such records for author-artists must meet technical standards that are higher than the ones adequate for the comparatively simple line drawings of a scientist or the doodles of an author in a notebook. More sophisticated and costly reproduction techniques are necessary in editions of the papers of figures like Benjamin Henry Latrobe and Charles Willson Peale. In these two examples, the costs of reproducing all sketches as a physical part of printed pages would have been prohibitively expensive, so separate microfiche supplements were published to provide students with a comprehensive reproduction of graphic materials, while the book editions reproduced selected drawings and sketches on plates inserted as illustrations to the printed text.

The nature of a sketch or drawing may be essential to the reader's understanding of a document's verbal elements even when literal photoreproduction of the sketch is not required. In such cases, the transcriber should note the drawing's existence so that the editor can describe it in a note adjacent to the text. If such graphic materials are common to the group of documents being edited, the editor may need to imitate the Latrobe and Peale editions by issuing facsimile supplements where the reader can consult the unprinted and even unprintable elements of the documents.

The diagrams and schematic drawings of great figures of science obviously fall into this category. Joseph Henry's sketches and diagrams are conscientiously reproduced in the *Henry Papers,* as are such elements in laboratory notebooks and other technical sources in the Papers of Thomas A. Edison and Albert Einstein. Here the "transcription" of the source text is a photoreproduction, as much a translation of the original as a typescript is of a manuscript letter. The nature of the original (an artist's oil painting or an inventor's line drawing) and the needs of the audience (art historians or students of the history of technology) dictate whether that translation needs to reproduce the original's colors or subtle shadings or whether a photocopy will suffice. When the "transcription" is a photograph of a three-dimensional artifact, the gap between source and editorial text is even more obvious, and edited nonverbal texts can present problems analogous to verbal sources at almost every stage. For instance, an editor may have to *emend* a photographic transcription by retouching it for photoreproduction in a print or facsimile edition or create a critical clear text by creating a new schematic redrawing of an original technical sketch so crude that it fails to convey its creator's obvious intent.

The most useful literature on this subject thus far has come from the editors of the Edison edition. Reese Jenkins' "Words, Images, Artifacts and Sound: Documents for the History of Technology" and Robert Rosenberg's "Technological Artifacts as Historical Documents" extend the discussion beyond images to artifactual documents and recorded sound. Jenkins concedes that this is a special concern for historians of technology: "To 'read' the nonverbal artifactual record is to read what the inventive enterprise was all about. In the case of the Edison papers, to have a documentary edition without the artifacts would be equivalent to having a marriage without the bride" (45). But Jenkins and his colleague Jeffrey also argue persuasively that all editors must now confront the challenges of nonverbal documents: "While acknowledging that our Western historical tradition was rooted from the beginning in words, we must also realize that the documents of the past, and, increasingly, of the present and future beckon for recognition and challenge us with diverse languages expressed in symbols other than words" (Jenkins and Jeffrey, 8).

## 1. Maps

While most documentary editors use maps only as helpful illustrative adjuncts to their texts, some have had to confront the question of editing maps themselves as historical documents. Stephen E. Wiberley, Jr., offers a detailed discussion on the cartographic equivalents of facsimile publication, emended transcriptions, and "clear text" in "Editing Maps: A Method for Historical Cartography." Wiberley's discussion centers on his experience with the *Atlas of Early American History*. A more strictly documentary approach to maps as evidentiary sources was pursued in the *Atlas* volume of *The Journals of the Lewis and Clark Expedition*.

## E. TRANSCRIPTIONS OF UNLOCATED ORIGINALS

Whether handwritten, typed, or printed, transcriptions of unlocated original documents are to be regarded as scribal copies—or copies of copies—of the documents that they represent. They should be transcribed literally for the modern edition, and any later emendations should be as sparing and carefully considered as possible. Frequently, the editor will be able to second-guess the earlier transcriber, recognizing that the scribe has consistently read the author's *a* for *o* or *r* for *n*. Such systematic mistranscription by a specific copyist can and should be emended, but only when the editor's notes provide readers with adequate warnings that both explain the reasons for these decisions and pinpoint the areas where emendation has occurred. Similarly, typographical errors in printed transcriptions (whether based on manuscript, typed transcriptions, or on the lost originals) can be corrected sparingly if such emendation is needed to make the transcriptions intelligible. Here, too, notes should explain editorial decisions in the case of any substantive emendations.

The transcriptions' punctuation and other accidentals usually should stand without any attempt to make them conform to conventions established for original source texts in the new edition. Second-guessing an earlier transcriber does not extend to mind reading.

## IV. SOURCE TEXTS AND TRANSLATIONS

Traditional textual methods of transcription and emendation cannot convert some source texts into editorial texts intelligible to their intended modern audience. Even though transcribed accurately and published in special typefaces, these materials would be printed sources of bafflement and not enlightenment. Much foreign-language material, as well as material written in authorial shorthand or cryptography, will remain of little use to most readers unless it is translated.

## A. FOREIGN-LANGUAGE SOURCES

Editorial policy concerning source texts in a foreign language may depend both on the amount of foreign-language material that will appear in the edition and on the intended audience for the newly edited volumes. Some editors choose to present all documents in their original languages: a single volume for Woodrow Wilson's presidential years may include materials in French, German, Spanish, and Japanese as well as English. In such cases, the sources are transcribed literally. The foreign-language materials that qualify for inclusion in the Wilson edition form but a small percentage of the whole, and the editors have assumed that diplomatic historians interested in specific documents are already masters of the languages in which these letters and state papers are inscribed.

The Lafayette editors followed another course. Lafayette's papers for the Revolutionary era included so many documents in French that only bilingual readers could have used the series had all documents appeared in their original tongues. The editors chose to translate the materials into English, the language of the audience to whom the edition was primarily addressed. These translations were clearly labeled as such, and they appeared in the annotated, chronological series of editorial texts in the Lafayette volumes. An appendix to each volume printed transcriptions of the French originals.

The editors of Albert Einstein's papers based their decisions on a different body of sources whose audience would be substantially different from any the Lafayette edition might reach. In an article in *Scholarly Publishing* ("Einstein's Collected Papers"), Herbert S. Bailey, Jr., director of the Princeton University Press at the inauguration of the Einstein project, described the process by which the editors and their publisher found a viable method. There was never a question of presenting English translations of Einstein's writings in German as editorial texts. Unlike Lafayette, who learned English as a young man and who maintained a substantial correspondence with English-speaking friends throughout his long life, Einstein thought and wrote in German—only rarely did he compose in English or French. Many argued for parallel texts of non-English documents and their facing-page translations in the printed volumes, but Einstein's life and intellectual contributions made him a figure of world interest. Americans might have been well served by English translations in the annotated volumes, but the books would then have been of little use for the cosmopolitan audience they deserved. It was finally determined to publish all documents in German, English, and French in their original languages; translations would appear for the small number of sources inscribed in other tongues. A simultaneous microform of unannotated English translations for German and French texts appeared with the first printed volume, but interest in these first translations was so great that a paperback edition was issued as well, and this format continues throughout the series. John Stachel, the Einstein edition's first director, explained his rationale: "Placing the translations in a separate and clearly subsidiary position has an additional advantage: it reminds readers that German was Einstein's language, which he habitually used when he wanted to express himself precisely; hence, a struggle with the German text, using the translation as a pony if need be, is highly preferable to assuming that any translation has adequately conveyed the full import and all the nuances of Einstein's deceptively simple German" (64).

## 1. Translations for a Documentary Edition

Realistically, few editors will be completely fluent in every language used to create the materials relevant to their editions. The editor working on the Papers of Jacob Leisler, for instance, must deal with documents in German, French, Dutch, and pidgin English-Dutch. In such cases, the preparation of these documents for publication will be a cooperative and iterative process among editors and translators.

This collaboration begins before the first word is translated. Even when foreign-language documents will be published only in English translation, unless they are extremely legible, they should still be transcribed first rather than handed to the translator in their original or photocopied form. It is easy to miss a word or a phrase when translating untranscribed documents, especially if they are handwritten. If possible, the transcriber should have some knowledge of the language in which the document is written, so that diacritical markings will be read accurately. The translator will then subject the transcription to what is, in effect, a rigorous proofreading, finding errors and inconsistencies that require access to the original documentary sources or their photocopies for purposes of comparison.

While the transcription can be prepared by someone with only a basic knowledge of the foreign language in question, any translations for a documentary edition should be prepared, or at least revised, by people not only fully fluent in that language but familiar with the usage of the era in which the documents were inscribed. Although an expert in twentieth-century Spanish literature might not be able to translate adequately the records of an early eighteenth-century New Mexican mission, he or she could probably produce a draft of a literal translation that editors knowledgeable in the period could revise for eventual publication. This was the course adopted by the editors of the Lafayette Papers, who did their own translations until they began working on a volume with a large number of French documents. To speed the translation process, they used a freelance translator whose translations they then revised using their knowledge of the period.

Because of the collaborative nature of preparing translations for a documentary series, the translator who is not a native English speaker must have exceptionally high English-language skills. The translator, like the editors, must be able to understand not only the editors' questions voiced in modern English but be able to grasp appropriate patterns of English usage for the period in which the documents were created.

Translating into English for a documentary edition raises many questions that cannot be ignored. While some editors might be tempted to retain the punctuation, capitalization, or sentence structure of the foreign-language source in the translation, this may create a less-than-readable document in English. A more reasonable course is creating in the translation a document that parallels the original through its style and tone. A formal document can be translated into formal English, an informal one into more colloquial English. If translations will be published side by side with documents of the same period inscribed in English, translators can use the English-language documents as a guide in translating nouns, forms of address, or other diction that appears in both languages. The translation cannot replace the original foreign-language document, but it can give the English-speaking reader the original's substance and a sense of the language in which that meaning was conveyed.

Editors intending to publish translations will have to decide how to treat irregular spellings of proper nouns—whether to give them spellings that are correct and consistent in English usage or to retain unusual spellings from the foreign-language document. The choice may be easy for geographical place names: it would, for example, be disconcerting to retain the Spanish "Londres" for "London" in an English translation of a document, but other nouns will raise more difficult questions. Editors have made different choices in this matter, basing their decisions on the nature of their documents and their audience. Some use the correct English spellings of proper nouns in translation (when these can be determined), providing in a footnote variant spellings used in the original, while others retain the author's usage from the original, untranslated document. Editors should explain these and any other translation policies in their introductory

statements or in source notes to the specific translations so that readers can judge the translation's relationship to the original.

Some of the texture of the original can easily be conveyed in a
translation: formal elements such as underlining and block letters
can easily be retained in the English translation. But if the editor's
goal is a readable text in English, other features may have to be ignored or relegated to notes. Authorial methods of rewriting or correcting the text can create especially difficult problems. Interlineations or insertions may have to be recorded in footnotes when
significant. An attempt to reproduce them in the translated text itself
may defeat the purpose of providing a convenient, readable English
version, for words or groups of words in one language seldom translate into exactly the same number of words or phrases in another
tongue. One word in English may be the perfect equivalent of a
several-word phrase in a foreign language, or it may take half a line
of English words to convey the meaning of a single word in Greek.
It may be impossible to find an appropriate place to insert translations of interlineations or substitutions when they differ in length
from the original. For example, the common French term "il y a"
(literally, "it there is") is rendered in English as "there is" or "there
are," depending on what follows. If a French author carelessly omitted the "y" in drafting the phrase and then inserted it into the text
with a carat, there would be no way to show this insertion in the
translated phrase "there is" or there are"; an editorial note could dis-
pose of the matter clearly and concisely.

A final issue that some editors need to consider is the treatment of
documents that intermingle languages. Again, the goal should be a
readable text for the intended audience. In *Family Letters of Victor
and Meta Berger,* for example, letters that Victor Berger wrote entirely in German are printed entirely in English translation, but
when Berger wrote in English and dropped in an occasional German
phrase, the German words remain in the text, with a translation in a
footnote. For more complex language problems in a collection of
documents, an editor may need to experiment with several of the
most difficult documents, trying out a number of different solutions,
and then settle on the conventions for translation that will produce
the most usable texts for the audience likely to consult the edition.

In rare instances, editors enjoy access to the foreign-language
translations actually used by their subjects to read letters or other
documents written in an unfamiliar tongue. Here the appropriate
source text is obviously that contemporary translation, whatever its
shortcomings as an accurate rendering of the original. The George
Washington Papers editors had this luxury for documents in French

sent to Washington during the Confederation and his presidency. In the first four volumes of the edition's *Presidential Series,* the editorial reading texts for such foreign-language materials were transcriptions of the translations read by Washington, with the French texts transcribed in the last footnote to the document. In later volumes of the *Presidential Series* and in the edition's *Confederation Series,* the French texts have been omitted, as these will be made available as part of a CD-ROM supplement.

## B. AUTHORIAL SHORTHAND

The writer who employs either a personal or a standardized form of shorthand leaves later editors with a very special problem. Moreover, the editor who deals with this challenge risks letting the method chosen to solve the specific puzzle at hand distort the edition's overall textual policy. The ease with which this warning can be ignored was demonstrated by no less an editor than Julian Boyd. In expounding the merits of expanded methods of transcription (see chapter 5) in volume 1 of the *Jefferson Papers,* Boyd explained,

> If presented literally, what Jefferson wrote as he took down hasty notes in a congressional investigating committee in the busy summer of 1776 would read as follows: "Carleton havg hrd yt we were returning with considble reinfmt, so terrifd, yt wd hve retird immedly hd h. nt ben infmd by spies of deplorble condn to wch sm pox had redd us." Such a passage, by the conventionalization to be followed in these volumes will read: "Carleton having heard that we were returning with considerable reinforcement, [was] so terrified, that [he] would have retired immediately had he not been informed by spies of [the] deplorable conditions to which small pox had reduced us. (xxxi)

In using this extract from Jefferson's notes in the Continental Congress to justify expanded method, Boyd loaded the argument in his own favor. The extract given reflects accurately Jefferson's methods of informal note taking, but Jefferson did not employ the same system of idiosyncratic shorthand in making fair copies of letters dispatched to correspondents, in writing legislative reports, or even in making entries in his famed "Anas." There were good reasons to emend Jefferson's shorthand notes, but the same considerations did not apply to his other writings, public or private. Editors since Boyd have come to recognize this distinction.

Most of the source texts that serve the *Woodrow Wilson Papers,* for instance, are printed in a very conservatively emended form, but Wilson's editors would have served no purpose by publishing handset printed facsimiles of the notes and drafts that Wilson made in Graham shorthand. Instead, such source texts were translated, and they appear in the Wilson volumes in English, not in Graham symbols. Since Wilson usually indicated his preferred marks of punctuation and paragraph breaks in his shorthand materials, these could be honored in the editorial texts. Still, the editors never pretended that they could guess all of the author's intentions for translation from Graham, and their standard for the treatment of shorthand materials differs from that given to materials drafted by Wilson in clear English. A statement of these special methods appears in editorial notes in volume 1, pages 8–19 and 128–31, and notes to individual documents alert the reader to the use of translated shorthand source texts.

Even writers without Wilson's stenographic skills lapse into unusual abbreviated forms when taking notes or drafting letters or other documents. The editor will have the opportunity to compare and analyze a wide selection of such idiosyncratic forms, while scholars without access to the project's editorial archives are denied this luxury. This imposes a special duty on the editor to determine the meaning of such forms and to represent them verbally in the editorial text for the reader's convenience and enlightenment. For material such as Wilson's formal shorthand, the editor will often have to present a more heavily emended editorial text than is usual in the series. If the nature of the shorthand allows the expansion of alphabetic contractions within square brackets, the editor's responsibility is fulfilled. If the symbols make such expansion and explication within brackets impractical, the document may be presented in something approaching clear text. In either case, the notes accompanying the document must indicate that a departure from the usual editorial practice has occurred, and the edition should include an editorial statement of the techniques used to translate the shorthand symbols or abbreviations into readable English.

When the duties of transcriber and editor are divided, responsibility for such emendations belongs to the editor, not to the initial transcriber. Even editors who are their own transcribers would do well to follow the general principles of the practices discussed above. The process of transcription itself is instructive, and any editor responsible for his or her own transcribing should concentrate on translating the originals as conservatively as possible instead of assuming, in advance, that he or she knows what textual methods will finally be applied to the initial transcription.

## C. CODES AND CIPHERS

Coded and enciphered communications present textual problems analogous to those of standardized shorthand. In both cases the editor should make every effort to translate symbols into verbal equivalents that the modern reader can understand. With codes, as with shorthand records, the editor is obliged to share with the reader the details of the method that established the clear reading text.

Systematic codes and ciphers are customarily used to ensure confidentiality in a writer's communications with a second party. Such cryptic passages usually appear in communications of considerable historical significance, such as diplomatic dispatches or private correspondence between political leaders. These documents are in the form of communications between two parties. Not only should the translated clear text of coded documents enable the reader to see just which sections were entered in code and cipher, but the text or the accompanying notes should also record what the editor has been able to determine about the recipient's success in mastering the ciphered passages. Indicating which words, phrases, or sentences were significant enough to deserve encoding allows the reader to see exactly which information in the letter was judged confidential and which facts the writer felt free to leave open to prying eyes. Noting both the author's skill in encoding his or her own words and the correspondent's accuracy in using the key to the same code is critical in showing the effectiveness of the transmission of the ciphered information.

Diplomatic records of the nineteenth and twentieth centuries usually contain exhaustive files of every version of an encoded message, and their editors are seldom left in doubt as to what message could be read by whom, but modern editors of the writings of statesmen of the American Revolution frequently confront greater challenges. Many of these leaders established personal codes or ciphers for use in private correspondence during their public service in wartime, and the same men often received diplomatic appointments that required them to use official government ciphers for their correspondence.

Such source texts may survive in several forms. In a draft letter, symbols for passages that the author entered in cipher may have been entered above their verbal equivalents. The author's file copy may carry interlined cipher equivalents, or it may be copied directly from the final recipient's version, with only numerical symbols or hieroglyphics for the coded passages. Among the recipient's papers, the editor may find a virgin copy, with or without an accompanying sheet of the deciphered lines. Sometimes recipients translated cipher passages interlinearly on the pages of the letters they received.

The textual treatment of such documents often depends on the survival of the keys to the codes and ciphers employed. When ciphered materials survive only in encoded form and no key exists, the editor must admit defeat and offer readers what little there is to provide. With brief and scattered coded passages, it may be simplest to print the numerical or alphabetical symbols within the unencoded portion of the text, warning the reader of the existence of untranslatable codes. If the coded sections are lengthy, editors often omit them, indicating an ellipsis followed by a superscript number keyed to an explanatory footnote or by a bracketed editorial interpolation in the reading text (e.g., "[ten lines in cipher are omitted here]"). This may prove unnecessary in electronic hypertext editions, where the lengthy undeciphered passages can be linked to the reading text. When surviving copies of the document carry the author's or recipient's decoded version of cryptic passages, the editor must decide how to represent these sections in the reading text. Modern documentary editors generally eschew the use of brackets to enclose such passages, instead using either footnotes or special typefaces to indicate the encrypted writing.

In his introduction to volume 6 of the *Jefferson Papers,* Julian Boyd objected to any "fixed method" for indicating coded passages. Instead, he used italicized characters for isolated words or short phrases that had been in code while using numbered textual footnotes to indicate longer passages that had been encoded. Unfortunately, Boyd sometimes combined these two methods within the same document, and the reading text of these cipher letters might require the reader to flip back and forth to numbered footnotes that designate some coded passages while remembering that other cipher sections in the same letter appear in italic type. Later editors of eighteenth-century diplomatic cipher materials discarded this dual system, finally settling on the sensible device of printing ciphered passages in small capital letters or some other typeface that does not appear elsewhere in the editorial texts of handwritten sources. This method eliminates the need for additional footnotes and ensures that the reader cannot confuse it with any other textual device.

Editors with access to the key to a cipher or code have a concern beyond the choice of typeface for encoded passages: the author's accuracy in enciphering the passages and the recipient's skill in decoding them. Madison's editors found that a recipient's errors in deciphering the coded text had led earlier, less conscientious editors to publish inaccurate versions of significant political correspondence (see *Madison Papers,* 6:177–79). John Jay's editors discovered that the inventor of one code misused his own system so badly that his correspondent was unable to decipher his letters (*Papers of John Jay,* 2:117–18). The editor should indicate instances in which a significant difference exists between what the author intended and what the second party was, in fact, able to comprehend. The simplest solution to this problem consists in offering an editorial text that approximates the author's intentions, no matter how badly fulfilled or how poorly the recipient or other readers managed to grasp the writer's meaning. Numbered footnotes can describe discrepancies between intentions and perceptions. (A detailed analysis of a cipher document representing the full array of such problems of communication can be seen in the *Madison Papers,* 6:177–79.)

With ciphers, as with shorthand, it may be impossible to guess the author's intentions as to capitalization and punctuation. Writers in cipher and code often deliberately omit marks of punctuation or paragraph breaks to avoid assisting the efforts of enemy cryptologists. Many editors have decided against supplying any of these omissions: since the coded message's recipient had to guess at punctuation, it may be more accurate to print the newly decoded text in the same ambivalent fashion.

Whatever policy is adopted, the initial transcription and deciphered version should reflect the peculiarities of the original, and the editor can decide on any necessary emendations at a later stage. The reader must be warned that all such emendations have been supplied by the editor, and in the substance of deciphered texts, as in those based on a clear source text, the editor must note when editorial guesswork or imagination has been employed.

The editors of modern political and military records seldom need to decode enciphered materials. Unlike eighteenth-century diplomats, who were responsible for encoding and decoding their own official correspondence, twentieth-century statesmen and generals seldom saw the ciphered version of confidential dispatches. Instead, aides or technicians unraveled the mysteries of increasingly sophisticated systems of encryption. The messages' addressees customarily saw only deciphered texts or summaries of them prepared by these aides. The challenge for editors of this category of ciphered documents is identifying the deciphered version read and acted on by the recipient. This one, of course, is the appropriate choice for the source text.

D. TELEGRAMS

With the text of received telegraphic messages, editors deal with a ready-made translation of Morse code signals based, in turn, on a text given to a distant telegrapher. For editors of nineteenth- and twentieth-century sources, telegraphic communications present a variety of problems in transcription and final textual treatment. The words of any telegram existed at one time or another in at least three different versions: the text the sender submitted at the telegraph office, the Morse code signals transmitted by the telegrapher while looking at the sender's text, and the translation of those signals as inscribed on the telegraph form finally delivered to the addressee. While it is rare, a record of the second coded form may survive, and the tripartite nature of telegraphic transmission must be remembered while dealing with cabled communications.

The editor generally has at hand either the sender's manuscript *or* the recipient's translation of Morse code. While the first represents an author's final intentions, the second is evidence of what was actually communicated to the recipient. The puzzle is compounded in coded telegraph transmissions, where the possibilities for corruption reach extraordinary levels. The files of World War II military leaders' headquarters are filled with requests for retransmission of garbled coded materials. The George Marshall and Dwight Eisenhower editions generally contain the paraphrased texts of such messages as they reached the recipient's office, because these, at least, are evidence of what each commander learned from the cables. Similarly, most editors' choice of text reflects the standpoint of the subject of their editions. When draft or final versions of outgoing cables survive in the hand of the edition's subject, they will be chosen as source texts. For incoming cables, the editor will choose as a source text the decoded copy of the telegram that reached the subject's hands, because this represents the information that influenced that person.

Editors of nineteenth-century archives that contain a substantial body of telegraphic material follow a conservative policy in emending received telegraph texts. In this era, the decoded message was written out by hand in the receiving telegraph office, and the words and phrases are usually copied in conventional form, using upper- and lowercase letters and marks of punctuation. The twentieth century, however, brought automated printing of decoded telegraph messages in uppercase characters only, with the additional convention of writing out the names of marks of punctuation (e.g., "stop") instead of translating the words back into the symbols themselves. Editors of cables received in the modern era, then, face new decisions in rendering a cable's text. The editors of World War II leaders like Marshall and Eisenhower have chosen readability over documentary fidelity, translating "stop" to a period and supplying appropriate patterns of uppercase and lowercase letters. This method has added justification, as these generals customarily saw these incoming messages as summaries neatly retyped by their aides, not in their original form as telegrams.

## V. TRANSCRIBING THE SOURCE TEXT: TYPES OF DOCUMENTARY RECORDS

The editor's method of transcription should also reflect the type of documentary record that each source represents. The traditional literary distinction between a writer's public and private writings is of little use to the documentary editor. Unpublished letters have influenced the course of history. State papers not set in type in their author's lifetime have shaped the thinking of legislators and executives. Confidential technical reports have radically affected the history of science. Each of these is private under the literary scholar's definition, but all were composed for an audience, and all derive their historical importance from the influence they exerted on those contemporary readers. Documentary editors long ago abandoned any methodological division between public and private writings and, instead, examine how these source texts functioned as agents of communication. Any edition of such sources should strive to preserve the communicative intention and/or effect of the original. Recent scholarship in the humanities as a whole, of course, seconds this decision.

With documents, the editor may also have to modify notions of what constitutes the appropriate contents of an edited text. Elements in the source that could safely be ignored by the editor of an author's published works may be an integral part of a source's documentary contents. Such accidentals as capitalization, indention, and spacing may perform important functions in the design of certain modes of communication. And for some documents, even nonauthorial contributions must be considered part of the source's evidentiary contents.

### A. CORRESPONDENCE

Until recently, the small body of literature on editing correspondence focused on the need to make the letters of an earlier age "readable"—even "enjoyable"—for a modern audience (see, for instance, Halsband, "Editing the Letters of Letter-Writers"). Today, discussions of the textual needs of correspondence are considerably more sophisticated, even if agreement on methods remains distant (see Robert Stephen Becker's report on his survey of editions of nineteenth- and twentieth-century letters in "Challenges in Editing Modern Literary Correspondence").

The move toward clear text in CSE-approved editions of correspondence was justified, in part, by the claim that the literary critics who form a large part of these volumes' audience would not wish to be distracted by textual symbols or numbered footnotes pointing out details of the original. Yet even exponents of silently emended expanded transcription concede that readers soon become used to archaic and idiosyncratic usage in a documentary edition, and Ernest W. Sullivan has pointed out that literary critics were ill-served by the practice of standardizing texts in editions of personal correspondence ("The Problem of Text in Familiar Letters"). Steven Meats lectured the editors of the correspondence of literary figures: "As a general rule, the less editing (that is, the less editorial emending and altering) done to the text of letters, the better the job of editing. A letter is, after all, a primary historical document; one might even call it a 'fact.' . . . In any case, silent emendation in the editing of letters should be severely restricted" (p. 38). As the editor's compulsion to conventionalize, normalize, or otherwise emend the text of letters came under serious attack, editors of the private writings of American literary figures moved further and further away from the aim of a clear text.

When letters survive in some preliminary form that reflects revision by the author, they may require the application of textual methods appropriate to genetic elements (see chapter 6) that reflect the evolution of a text, not merely its final form. But when a letter survives in the form in which its author dispatched it to its addressee, it should be transcribed literally. Literal transcription of hastily scrawled and ill-proofread recipients' copies of letters may be untrue to the author's final intentions, but such transcription is true to the documents. Equally important in documentary terms, it represents the form of the letter that influenced its recipient. Unnecessary emendations will make the editorial text of any letter useless as evidence either of what its author wrote or of what its addressee read. It is not the business of documentary editors to introduce new readings into a documentary text for the sake of historically unrealized clarity. Even editors who are their own transcribers should make initial transcriptions of such sources as literal as possible. Any policy of emendation for letters adopted later should be as conservative as their method of inscription allows. A detailed back-of-book textual record grants no license to violate this rule. If any corrections are to be imposed on the author's prose, they will come after the editor has established the edition's final textual policies.

Still, transcribers are generally authorized to incorporate certain conventions for standardizing formal elements of letters. Such standardization most commonly concerns the location of datelines, greetings, and closings. Even this degree of intervention may prove short-sighted if the letter writer employs individual formats for different types of correspondence. David Knight, editor of Sir Humphry Davy's correspondence, pointed out that there was much to be learned from the openings and closings of these letters: "[W]e can trace, for example, through the tops and tails of his letters, his relationship with Faraday as he progressed from amanuensis/valet to what in modern terms might be 'research student,' to 'research assistant,' and on to colleague" (10). Should these variations show a significant pattern, the original format should be maintained. When the writer used stationery with an imprinted letterhead, there is no reason to repeat this form at the beginning of the transcription of every letter inscribed on such paper. The editor may reproduce the letterhead's text verbatim at some point in the edition and design an easily recognized contracted form that can be used in the printed edition.

### 1. Source or Provenance Note Information

The letter's transcriber is also responsible for recording information that may eventually find its way into the document's source note or provenance note rather than into the editorial text. If the letter's envelope or address leaf survives, all authorial inscriptions should be transcribed verbatim. At the very least, the transcriber should note postal markings. When they represent the basis for assigning a date to an undated letter, they should be described in detail. Any notations by postal officials or others involved in forwarding a letter to its intended recipient should also be noted. Once these elements have been transcribed, the editor can review them and decide on their treatment in the edition. They can be handled at the foot of a letter's printed text or in the source note (see chapter 7).

The transcriber should also indicate the existence of any "endorsement," that is, a notation made on the letter, its envelope, or its address leaf after its receipt. Whenever such an endorsement indicates the date of the letter's arrival, summarizes the reader's reaction, or otherwise supplies important documentary evidence, it should be transcribed verbatim. Correspondence with governments or their agents often carry endorsements made after the letter's receipt by someone other than its addressee and other important documentary notations. The transcriber should record these in full.

These suggested practices apply only to sources that are truly letters, not essays or other short works written in letter form with the intention of print publication. The problem of distinguishing between the two is discussed in John A. Walker's "Editing Zola's Correspondence: When Is a Letter Not a Letter?", John M. Robson's "Practice, Not Theory: Editing J. S. Mill's Newspaper Writings," and E. Grace Sherrill's "'The Daily Crucifixion of the Post': Editing and Theorizing the Lowry Letters."

As Herman Saatkamp points out in "Private Rights vs. Public Needs," editors also need to consider how to treat letters that were intended to be private but were published nonetheless. He gives a hypothetical example of an unknown author whose letter became a rallying point for political revolution and was published and republished, with significant variants. The documentary editor's decision whether to publish the earliest or the last version is a choice between authorial intention and the letter's context and significance. While the author's intention would be represented best in the earliest published version, the political movement's use of the letter would be more evident in the last-published version. A volume of the individual's writings might well include the earliest published version of the letter, while an edition of the records of the political movement would demand use of the last published form. Here, the "context is not the letters of an individual, but the letters of the revolution" (92).

## B. BUSINESS AND FINANCIAL RECORDS

Documentary editors generally agree that such documents as business records, accounts, and all others recorded in a tabular manner should be printed in the most literally transcribed format possible. The reasons are twofold. First, such documents make sense in visual terms only if the original arrangement of columns and indentions is preserved. Within such a format, it is usually impossible to expand contracted or abbreviated forms devised by the author to make headings or entries fit into the spaces available. Second, there is no theoretical justification for emending such records in the name of recovering the author's literary intentions. Such sources have only evidentiary, documentary value, and there is no reason to emend them to achieve easily appreciated literary value.

## C. PROFESSIONAL AND TECHNICAL RECORDS

Editors who publish professional and technical records should not only master the technical terms in the document's verbal text but also become familiar with the special formats peculiar to such professions as law, medicine, physics, or mathematics. They can assume that a large proportion of their readers will themselves be specialists in the history of these fields. Such readers will be best served by a faithfully printed facsimile of the source's format, preserving the styled brackets of the attorney and the indentions and spacing of scientific formulas. These elements need not be standardized in the name of readability, for they will already be familiar to the edition's audience, and their normalization would destroy important aspects of the source as it was communicated to its original audience of judges, court clerks, or fellow scholars.

Yet with scientists and businessmen, just as with statesmen and authors, the line between public and private writing will blur again and again to make the editor's life more difficult. M. J. S. Hodge's instructive review essay discussing Charles Darwin's *Notebooks* and *Correspondence* comments on this phenomenon: "[I]t would be a mistake to see Darwin as addressing himself in the notebooks, addressing single, known correspondents in his letters, and only going openly to an indefinitely broader public in the books. For, even when Darwin wrote in his notebooks or his letters, he was articulating thoughts that were formulated and refined in his mind as potential contributions to the intrinsically public activity that natural history and science were explicitly committed to being" (179).

## D. GOVERNMENT RECORDS

Official records of any government or its agents cannot bear emendations in the name of clarity, readability, or enjoyability. They are what they are what they are. Government financial records, of course, are subject to the rules for tabular documents, but special respect is also due the formats and accidentals of nonfiscal records. Legislative journals, like financial records, are often intelligible only when their original patterns of spacing and indention are retained. Some editors have found it convenient to use contemporary print editions of similar sources as a model for their own treatment. This was the case in the *State Records of South Carolina* series begun by the South Carolina Archives in 1960. The editors had generous samples of the methods of American printers of the period in printing official texts of colonial and early state legislative and executive journals, and the modern edition mirrors these patterns. Greater respect is also usually shown the original formats of state papers outside the definition of journals, for these visual and inscriptional patterns were familiar to the lawyer-legislators and lawyer-clerks who inscribed them.

The nonauthorial labels and notations on government records should also be noted, described, or printed verbatim. Because such documents are remarkably long-lived in terms of their documentary significance, an unprinted legislative report or treasurer's account from the 1790s may well have been consulted by congressional committees two decades later, and this may be indicated by the notations of the clerk responsible for filing and refiling the manuscript. Unless such dockets are transcribed or noted fully in the edition (either as part of the text or in a note), the source's documentary elements have been only partially reproduced.

## E. AN AUTHOR'S WORKS

An author's works—essays, stories, plays, books, or other forms written with the intention of print publication—used to receive different treatments from the textual editor and the documentary editor. Textual editors who hoped to recover an author's intended meaning would sometimes emend one source text or conflate authorial portions of two or more sources into one new text. Textual scholars are now looking with more favor on the approach of documentary editors, who focus on a single source for their new edition, with the new noncritical editorial text reflecting the characteristics of that one source. If the source is a draft version, it should be transcribed according to the edition's general rules for sources with genetic elements (see chapter 6). If it is a fair copy or a printed version, the transcription should be a verbatim rendering of that single source, with later emendations indicated clearly by the editor and with variants recorded later in adjacent notes rather than incorporated into the new editorial text.

## F. JOURNALS AND DIARIES

The nature of a source's original intended audience may influence transcriptional policies and textual method for literary works, public papers, and even letters, but this is not the case for an author's journals or diaries. Here the intended audience is the author (although one wag remarked that in the case of the Adams family, the diarists' audience was posterity). These intimate records, revealing so much of the inner life of a public figure, demand the most literal textual treatment their method of inscription permits.

Informal in nature and private in intent, diaries lose rather than gain by any attempt to impose excessive conventions of print publication. If a writer's punctuation or spelling is less regular and correct in diaries than in correspondence, so be it. The very fact that an author allows himself or herself such lapses may be significant. If the author employs any form of shorthand, then, as noted above, more liberal editorial intervention is not only permissible but necessary.

The format of a diary or journal may also require special treatment. Diary entries inscribed in books whose pages carry no preprinted dates will demand additional editorial intervention in standardizing or expanding the dates of entry furnished by the author. The editor's annotational format may play a part in this decision. When numbered informational notes follow each daily entry, an arbitrarily formalized heading, free of brackets or other typographical barbed wire, may be less distracting; with footnotes, the daily headings are less striking visually. Some standardization is often necessary even during transcription, and the most common method consists in placing each date flush to the left-hand margin. The editor will decide later whether to set the date in boldface or italic type or in full and small capital letters to give the reader easy reference. With such a run-on text of diary entries, it may be necessary to normalize the substantive elements of the date as well as its form. Expanding abbreviated forms in the dateline or even standardizing the author's arrangement of day, month, and year may be necessary to give the reader consistently useful reference points.

Bound diaries and journals often require a more complete description of the original source than letters and other shorter manuscript sources. If the author has paginated the journal, or if the journal carries preprinted numbers on its pages, these should be noted by the transcriber for reproduction, in brackets, in the new print edition. If the diary's pages are unnumbered, the editor may need to assign numbers for easy reference (see the explanation of such a plan in the introduction to the *Irving Journals*, vol. 1).

Editions in the CSE mode tend to carry more detailed descriptions of the physical appearance of bound journals and diaries, but even historical editors recognize the need to offer more descriptive information for this category of source text (see introductory notes for the John Adams, John Quincy Adams, and Charles Francis Adams diaries). The reason for such explicit description is practical. The reader must be able to locate the original entry for comparison with the editorial text, and this is clearly a greater challenge within a bound volume of diary entries than in a separately cataloged one- or two-page letter. Thus, the transcriptions themselves should indicate breaks between volumes, as well as note any special problems in arrangement of entries in the original.

Some diaries, like some letterbooks or pocket notebooks, have been subject to subsequent revision and improvement by their authors and/or later editors. When the resulting earlier printed versions have achieved wide circulation and popularity, a new edition of the source, restoring its value as documentary evidence, can be one of the greatest challenges in documentary or textual editing. C. Vann Woodward recounts his efforts to deal with this problem in "Mary Chesnutt in Search of her Genre," and Joel Myerson and Daniel Shealy discuss their more conservative methods of dealing with another nineteenth-century woman's journals in "Editing Louisa May Alcott's Journals."

## G. RECORDS OF ORAL COMMUNICATIONS

Editors transcribe records of the spoken word with special care, for any printed or even handwritten versions will be far removed from their originals. (While future multimedia electronic editions offering access to both the audio record of spoken words and their machine-readable transcription can address this problem, readers who can compare recorded words with their editorial transcriptions will be even more impatient with inaccuracy.) These inscribed sources present a visual record of words and thoughts intended to be communicated orally. Only with the greatest skill can such a text aspire to be even second-best in documentary terms. The pauses, tonal inflections, and accompanying physical gestures that once gave these words their authors' full intended meaning are lost, and editors are often faced with conflicting inscribed versions of the same spoken words. Here, documentary editors often resort, again, to the critical methods of textual editing to reconcile transcriptions of variant versions (see chapter 6). The editors of the *Frederick Douglass Papers* have furnished a convenient list of the forms in which such records are likely to survive.

The first is a "pretext," which may be the author's draft, outline, or notes for a speech. In the absence of any other record, it is impossible to determine whether the pretext bears any relationship to the lecture or oration actually delivered. Whenever a pretext is the sole source, it is transcribed and edited as conservatively as its method of inscription allows. The question of audience here is a delicate one, for the pretext itself was intended for its author in visual form, an *aide memoir* to the words and phrases that he or she intended to utter. When a pretext was scribbled hastily or inscribed in some authorial shorthand, editors should consider the expanding idiosyncratic contractions and translating shorthand symbols. The editor should be exceptionally restrained in emending or standardizing such formal elements as spacing, punctuation, and the like, for each device may have served the author as stage directions in speaking, and no useful purpose is served by destroying the clues that format provides. The modern edition of Jonathan Edwards' *History of the Works of Redemption*, for instance, retains all of Edwards' unique marks of punctuation to indicate pauses for emphasis in these sermons.

Of course, the author is not the only person likely to leave records of sermons or lectures. The editors of the Douglass Papers group the records left by witnesses to his speeches in the following categories: "mention," "summary," "narrative," "extract," and "stenographic text." The first three are usually brief paraphrases of the words actually spoken, and the distinctions among them refer to the completeness of the paraphrased record left behind. When one of these forms is the only record of an oral text, it is transcribed and reproduced in a documentary edition as literally as possible. Editorial notes can explain the nature of the source, and readers can judge for themselves how accurately the reporter has mentioned, narrated, or summarized the speech or conversation involved.

Fragmentary paraphrases can also occur in other documents, like a newspaper article on a matter irrelevant to the edition. In such cases, there is no need to transcribe the larger document. The editor customarily omits those portions that do not concern the oral text in question, always indicating omissions with ellipses or some other device reserved for that editorial intervention. (See, for instance, the treatment of "third party" documents discussed in the introduction to volume 1 of the *Lafayette* edition.)

Through the early nineteenth century, various mentions, narrations, and summaries of the same speech or conversation often survived in textually irreconcilable versions. In the absence of systematic shorthand, no two reporters left accounts of the same spoken words that could be viewed as variants of the original. They are usually so dissimilar that there is no question of conflating or combining them into one master record of the spoken words. Instead, each should be transcribed literally, for any normalization of format or punctuation could obscure the meaning of the original that the reporter tried to convey. The editor may be unable to identify one source text here, choosing instead to give readers access to *all* conflicting reports. Should one record of the speech be a ten-page narration, while the others are paragraph-long summaries of the same words, editors usually transcribe and print the longest record as the editorial text, reporting transcriptions of the shorter versions in notes or as separate documents.

Lectures and political speeches are only one variety of orally transmitted texts to have received attention from modern documentary editors. Sermons have received considerable attention, and many American divines have left modern editors both manuscripts used as reading texts in the pulpit and manuscript or printed versions modified later for the reading public. For a valuable discussion of the differences between such sermons as oral events and as literary documents, see Wilson Kimnach's "Realities of the Sermon: Some Considerations for Editors." Other difficulties in editing oral communication were faced by a group of editors of conversations with well-known writers that were published in the Victorian era. In any series of published interviews, the personality of the interrogator may be as important to the reading public as the words of the person being interviewed. When more than one version of an interview survives, the expected audience of the modern edition may dictate the choice of source text: an earlier, uncorrected version would best serve those interested in a biography of the interviewee; the published, final versions serve the study of that same figure's public reception or reputation (Scott and Thesing, "Conversations with Victorian Writers").

Verbatim extracts and stenographic reports of speeches are more common in documents inscribed after the mid-nineteenth century, when systematized methods of shorthand became increasingly common. If one verbatim extract or a single stenographic report of a speech or conversation survives, it should be transcribed literally; however, if more than one verbatim report, partial or complete, survives, the editor should consider the more sophisticated, classically textual methods discussed below in chapter 6.

## 1. Sound Recordings

Scholarly editors have just begun to address the textual problems of the newest documentary records, those created by the perfection of sound-recording equipment. When tapes or phonograph discs for actual speech or conversation survive, editors have at hand something close to the archetype for the document—their transcriptions will be the first imperfect witnesses in a long series. The skill or awkwardness with which documentary editors meet this challenge will take the measure of their scholarly specialty. At the moment, the edition giving closest attention to these problems is the Martin Luther King project. Here, the editors have as source texts audio recordings of the sermons King delivered at various African-American churches. The "text" of these recorded sermons includes not only the words King uttered but also the words of the congregation's responses. The methods used to translate these elements for print publication are described by Peter Holloran in "Rediscovering Lost Values: Transcribing an African-American Sermon."

An even more complicated issue arises as a result of the oral history movement initiated more than thirty years ago by Allan Nevins. Practitioners of oral history interview historically significant figures and then create an archive of transcriptions of these conversations. The very setting of the oral history interview introduces an intellectual challenge. As Ronald Grele has pointed out, unlike written diaries and letters, "oral history interviews are constructed, for better or worse, by the active intervention of the historian" ("Movement Without Aim: Methodological and Theoretical Problems in Oral History"). For a discussion of the range of problems created by oral history methodologies, see J. A. Prögler, "Choices in Editing Oral History."

The editor of oral history interviews should learn as much as possible about the peculiar inscriptional history of this form of document, for the practices of American oral history archives can camouflage pertinent facts. Customarily, both the interviewer and the subject review the typed transcriptions of such memoirs, the first correcting errors of transcription and the second making emendations for style and indicating passages that he or she wishes omitted from the final archival version of the transcript. Some oral history projects even destroy the original tapes, thus eliminating any chance for comparing the typed witness against its archetype.

Most oral history projects now use word-processing equipment to emend transcriptions after review. This use of computer technology may ensure that only the final version of such interviews survives in the word processor's storage, with earlier and fuller versions lost forever. As American documentary editors catch up with the products of phonographic technology, this form of source text will become a focus of lively debate.

## H. ELECTRONIC RECORDS

Because this volume is confined to the experience of American scholarly editors, and this group of scholars has not yet addressed the special problems created by electronic documentary records, I offer no advice or guidelines here beyond the commonsense words of G. Thomas Tanselle in "Textual Criticism and Literary Sociology": "Computerization is simply the latest chapter in the long story of facilitating the reproduction and alteration of texts; what remains is the inseparability of recorded language from the technology that produced it and makes it accessible" (*Studies in Bibliography*, 88). Readers interested in anticipating these challenges should read Ronald W. Zweig's "Electronically Generated Records and Twentieth-

Century History," and A. J. Meadows, "Changing Records and Changing Realities."

## VI. Conclusion

Even these general rules for transcription of source texts raise the questions central to scholarly editing—the considerations that make possible the establishment of printed texts that reflect the editor's experience and knowledge. A series of literal, verbatim transcriptions is usually the most appropriate base for any documentary edition, but the edition's textual standards as well as its organizational format may require a modification of this rule. The conventions by which American editors have presented documentary texts are analyzed in the next chapter. Even before they begin transcribing source texts, editors need to familiarize themselves with these modern textual conventions, lest their working transcriptions make the business of editing a greater challenge than necessary.

## Suggested Readings

II. The proper selection of the source text has largely been ignored in monographic literature by editors, although reviewers of documentary editions have not been so negligent. See, for instance, the reviews by Ira D. Gruber and George A. Billias of the *Naval Documents of the American Revolution* series in *William and Mary Quarterly* 22 (October 1965): 660–63, and *American Historical Review* 77 (June 1972): 831, respectively. For useful discussions of the techniques of classical scholars in applying filiation to ancient texts, see Paul Maas, *Textual Criticism,* trans. Barbara Flower (Oxford, 1958), and Paul Oskar Kristeller, "The Lachmann Method: Merits and Limitations," *TEXT* 1 (1984): 11–20.

III. Special problems of handwritten inscription that confront American editors are discussed in Maygene Daniels, "The Ingenious Pen: American Writing Implements from the Eighteenth Century to the Twentieth Century," *American Archivist* 43 (1980): 312–24; P. W. Filby, *Calligraphy and Handwriting in America, 1710–1967* (New York, 1963); Thomas H. Johnson, "Establishing a Text: The Emily Dickinson Papers," *Studies in Bibliography* 5 (1952–53): 21–32; E. Kay Kirkham, *How to Read the Handwriting and Records of Early America* (Salt Lake City, 1964); Leonard Rapport, "Fakes and Facsimiles: Problems of Identification," *American Archivist* 42 (1979): 13–58; and Laetitia Yeandle, "The Evolution of Handwriting in the English-Speaking Colonies of America," ibid. 43 (1980): 294–311.

Useful essays on the relationship between bibliography and editorial problems appear regularly in *Studies in Bibliography.* Volume 3 (1950–51) includes Fredson Bowers' "Some Relations of Bibliography to Editorial Procedures." The same scholar's "The Function of Bibliography," *Library Trends* 7 (April 1959): 497–510, remains an able introduction to the topic. G. Thomas Tanselle provides a good discussion of the bibliographical problems raised by nineteenth-century authors in "Bibliographical Problems in Melville," *Studies in American Fiction* 2 (Spring 1974): 57–74. Jennifer Tebbe's "Print and American Culture," *American Quarterly* 32 (1980): 259–79, is a good introduction for novices. A more sophisticated treatment of a bibliographical problem with significance for documentary editors who must use periodicals as source texts is found in Bowers' "Multiple Authority: New Problems and Concepts of Copy-Text," *Library* 27 (June 1972): 81–95, and Tanselle's "Editorial Apparatus for Radiating Texts," ibid. 29 (September 1974): 330–37.

IV. Eugene A. Nida offers general reflections on the problems of foreign-language translation and editing in "Editing Translated Texts," *TEXT* 4 (1988): 13–27. In the realm of practical examples, the quinquicentennial of Columbus's voyage inspired a spurt of translations of significant works from Spanish with editorial apparatus that borrows from traditions of documentary and textual editing. See, for example, Charles Hudson and Paul Hoffman's edition of *The Juan Pardo Expeditions* and the review of this work by David Henige in *Documentary Editing* 13 (June 1991): 30–34.

Ralph E. Weber surveys important elements of cryptography in *United States Diplomatic Codes and Ciphers, 1775–1938* (Chicago, 1979). Editorial notes in *Adams Family Correspondence* (4: viii–ix, 393–99) comment on the specific editorial problems raised by the cryptographs employed by one group of correspondents.

V. Some of the essays in Dainard, *Editing Correspondence,* touch on the special problems of transcribing letters. Good examples of editorial treatments of business and financial records can be found in the Hamilton Papers and the Morris Papers. The editions of the legal papers of Hamilton, Adams, John Marshall, and Webster provide examples of skillful editing of this form of professional record, while the editions of Edison's, Einstein's, and Joseph Henry's papers offer generous examples of the treatment of a variety of scientific materials spanning a century.

Although much of American historical editing has been devoted to government records, editors have contributed little to the literature in this field. Students who wish to introduce themselves to this form of diplomatics should consult Christopher N. L. Brooke, "The Teaching of Diplomatics," *Journal of the Society of Archivists* 4 (April 1970): 1–9, and Buford Rowland, "Recordkeeping Practices of the House of Representatives," *National*

*Archives Accessions* 53 (Washington, D.C., 1957). The state of the art of print bibliography for government records is discussed in review essays by Ted Samore and Stewart P. Schneider in *Government Publications Review* 7A (1980) and 8A (1981), respectively, and in Martin Claussen's review essay in *American Archivist* 36 (1973): 523–36. The most pointed critique is Edwin Wolf's "Evidence Indicating the Need for Some Bibliographical Analysis of American Printed Historical Works," *Papers of the Bibliographical Society of America* 63 (1969): 261–77. For analysis of modern editions of government records in the United Kingdom, see Christopher Kitching, "Record Publication in England and Wales, 1957–1982," *Archives* 17 (April 1985): 38–46.

The reading lists and handbooks of the CEAA and CSE, of course, should be consulted for any edition that presents the text of a published work.

On a theoretical level, read Leonard N. Neufeldt, "Neopragmatism and Convention in Textual Editing, with Examples from the Editing of Thoreau's Autograph Journal," *Analytical and Enumerative Bibliography,* n.s. 1(1987): 227–36, Klaus Hurlebusch, "'Relic' and 'Tradition': Some Aspects of Editing Diaries," *TEXT* 3 (1987): 143–53. For a rare account of one well-known diarist's explanation of his diary-keeping methods, see Tony Benn, "The Diary as Historical Source," *Archives* 20 (April 1993): 4–17 and the summary of a British conference on "Editing Political Diaries,' *Contemporary Record* 7 (1993): 103–31.

Additional discussions of orally communicated texts include: T. K. Ryjes, "Keynes's Lectures, 1932–1935: Notes of a Representative Student. Problems in Construction of a Synthesis," in D. E. Moggridge, ed., *Editing Modern Economists: Papers Given at the Twenty-Second Annual Conference on Editorial Problems, University of Toronto, 7–8 November 1989* (New York, 1988): 91–127; and Mary Kupiec Cayton's review of *The Complete Sermons of Ralph Waldo Emerson,* "A Transcendentalist in Transition: Emerson and His Sermons, from Sacred to Secular," *Documentary Editing* 13 (March 1991): 9–12. In addition to the series cited in the chapter, the *Documentary History of the Ratification of the Constitution* series, vol. 2, *Pennsylvania,* provides interesting parallel texts for accounts of speeches too discordant to be reconciled in one single emended editorial text.

Morris Fishbein offers useful general reflections in "The Evidential Value of Nontextual Records: An Early Precedent," *American Archivist* 45 (Spring 1982): 189–90.

# CHAPTER V

---

# The Conventions of
# Textual Treatment

This chapter is, in part, that least loved of creatures, a reference book's glossary. It presents not only summaries of technical methods of confronting textual and nontextual problems but also tables of symbols and repetitive examples of the different results that can be obtained by applying varying methods to the same source. The problems and solutions discussed here are the most basic an editor will address. In documentary editions, the patterns of characters, words, phrases, and paragraphs offered to the reader are seldom the only ones that the edition's source could produce. Instead, they form but one text that the editor might have extrapolated from the hand-written, typed, spoken, or printed material that is the edition's base.

It is difficult to make the choices necessary to establish an author-itative documentary edition without being familiar with earlier edi-torial traditions and gaining the knowledge necessary to invent new methods for novel materials created by new technologies. The editor of modern documents often has problems and goals different from those of analysts of classical texts or canonical literary works. The classicist's aim is usually to recover a lost archetype, usually by care-fully comparing the surviving witnesses to that archetype—copies made directly from it or even later transcriptions based on earlier scribal versions. Since it is impossible to hazard guesses about the formal accidentals (spelling, punctuation, or format) of that missing archetype, modern editors often standardize such elements of the text. Editors of literary works published in an author's lifetime may have something more complicated than recovery of the author's original manuscript as their goal. Instead of trying to reconstruct a lost archetype, they may seek to determine the author's final inten-tions in an idealized form that combines elements of an incomplete authorial manuscript and subsequent printed editions of the work based on that manuscript. Frequently, such editors cannot point to a single source that represents all of the author's careful proofreading or stylistic revisions. Instead, they must painstakingly collate, or compare, manuscripts and printed editions for their variants. They must familiarize themselves with the work's publishing history so that they can evaluate responsibility for such changes, to determine authorial patterns in the accidentals of punctuation and spelling as well as in the substantive elements of patterns of words. Thus, the editions prepared by the classicist or the literary critic can themselves be new works. Critical judgment and scholarly insight can give the reader the text of an archetype that no longer exists in a physical sense or of something that never existed, such as a critical edition of a novel that is more intellectually consistent and textually reliable than any published during the author's lifetime.

Documentary editors of American historical materials have certain advantages over classical analysts and editors of literary works. In most cases, their source texts are themselves archetypes, and if they survive in transcribed form, such copies were usually made within decades, not centuries, of the original inscription. Thus, textual recovery is a comparatively rare concern. Unlike the editor of published literary works, the documentary editor seldom has to compare dozens of variant versions hundreds of pages in length. There are seldom more than two or three copies with any claim to such consideration, and most such source texts are unarguably the final intention of the author—copies of letters dispatched to and received by their addressees or public papers that the author signed and submitted to government bodies or other agencies.

This is not to say that the documentary editor's task is easier than other scholarly editors', merely different. He or she may, for instance, have at hand a sufficiently wide selection of holograph materials left by the subject to justify conclusions about that writer's customary use in such accidentals as paragraph indention, punctuation, and spelling; but the documentary editor does not have license to exploit this knowledge by emending the literal transcription of the source text to standardize its accidentals.

The printed versions of materials that have been edited as documents rather than reconstituted as idealized texts should themselves be usable as documents—as evidence for factual research. The aim of such editorial texts is to present what was written or spoken, not what might have been inscribed had the author had the luxury of revising the materials for publication. It is the responsibility of documentary editors to translate handwritten, typescript, or printed source texts into a form that their readers can trust as an accurate representation of the specific original materials they represent. Even when they use traditional techniques of textual scholarship such as emendation and conflation, documentary editors stop short of making their texts too smooth, too finished in appearance. Their readers usually need to know when words or phrases in the reading text are the result of editorial judgment, not the clear evidence of the source text.

If every author of documentary material obliged posterity by inscribing his or her letters, journals, and other papers in a regular, immaculate hand (or, better still, by leaving behind impeccably proofread typescripts), documentary editors could discharge their duties by serving as little more than faithful scribes. But historical figures are seldom so considerate. Their records are filled with inconsistent and confusing usages, with symbols for which no equivalent exists in any printer's font. Water, fire, insects, the ravages of time, and the scissors of autograph collectors may have defaced pages that were scarcely legible in the beginning. The array of physical details of the source texts ranges from authorial idiosyncrasies that are clearly pertinent to marks such as a cataloguer's notations, whose value to the edition's readers may not be immediately apparent.

Thus, after collecting and cataloging materials, documentary editors must survey these source texts and their initial transcriptions to inventory their peculiarities. Next, they must devise ways to present an edited version of this collection that will serve the majority of users almost as well as would the archive itself. And they must remember that each stage in establishing an edited text of these documents may take both editors and readers a step further from the source's full meaning.

If the source collection consists of printed source texts, the editor's task is comparatively easy. Textual decisions are limited to choosing a typeface that will accommodate any archaic characters in the old printing and determining the degree to which original formatting should be retained in terms of page and line breaks, line spacing, and paragraph indention. The editor may need to do nothing more than devise a method of indicating corrections of obvious typographical errors.

But the editor of unprinted sources must make one agonizing decision after another while considering how to standardize details of inscription whose nuances might serve the purpose of some researcher. The very act of printing such source texts suppresses some of their details, for the informational content of an unprinted document can extend far beyond textual elements. The character of the handwriting or typewriting can offer clues to the author's alertness or health.

Careless penmanship in one recipient's copy of a letter and painstaking inscription of a letter addressed to another can indicate different degrees of formality between the author and the two correspondents. The nature of the paper, ink, or pencil or typewriter ribbon can provide important clues to the time and place of the preparation of an undated letter or journal entry. Many of these important factors in the source's documentary contents cannot be reproduced; they can only be described.

Even elements of the document added by persons other than the author must be considered part of the source text's documentary contents. The recipient's endorsement of a letter can be an exposition of his or her reaction to that communication, making the endorsement, in its turn, a separate document that is physically a part of the first. Notations by third parties can also be significant: postal markings indicating a letter's date of receipt; words, numbers, and codes entered by a clerk in the docket of a public document; similar notations made by a compositor on a manuscript that was printer's copy for a published essay or poem. These can be important parts of a source's documentary evidence.

In short, the special problem of the modern documentary editor is more often an embarrassment of textual riches than the absence of an archetype or of some single manuscript that represents final authorial intentions. The question that faces the documentary editor is how to share as much of this wealth as possible without making the printed pages of the new edition an incomprehensible mass.

## I. THE BASES OF SCHOLARLY EDITING: STANDARDIZING, RECORDING, AND EMENDING

Documentary editors generally agree that standardization should be limited to certain formal elements of the texts, that the recording or describing of physical details of the source should be limited to those that cannot readily be reproduced in print, and that emendation of the source's transcriptions should meet a few clearly defined standards. The boundaries between these categories of editorial intervention are not well defined, and one editor's standardization may be another's emendation.

In general, standardization concerns elements in the source's physical format. An edition of correspondence may arbitrarily place all datelines for letters at the beginning of their texts, no matter where the date appears in the source text. Similarly, it is customary to standardize an author's paragraph indention in handwritten source texts so that all paragraphs in the print edition follow a consistent visual pattern.

Many of the details of inscription in a handwritten source text are not readily translated into printed symbols and so defy standardization. A writer may use different forms of capital letters or vary the length of dashes. In revising a draft, the author may employ a variety of methods to cancel rejected versions, sometimes using a line to cross out an earlier thought and sometimes simply writing over the preliminary version. The editor faced with such patterns must not only decide which patterns are worth recording in the editorial text or its accompanying notes but also find a system of symbols or abbreviations that will most conveniently communicate the detail in the source.

Beyond standardizing formats and recording significant patterns of inscription, editors must decide how lightly or heavily to emend, or correct, the transcriptions of the source texts and must choose the method of emendation most appropriate to the sources and the edition's likely users. The term *silent emendation* describes changes made in a text that are not enumerated individually. Silent emendation is the method traditionally used in critical editions of literary works and transferred by CEAA/CSE editors to documentary series: the editorial reading text itself contains no hint that emendations or alterations have occurred, but such emendations are reported in a back-of-book textual record. *Overt emendation* refers to changes indicated within the editorial text (usually enclosed in some form of bracket) or in notes immediately adjacent to the text.

In choosing methods for standardizing documentary formats, recording details of inscription, and emending an author's spelling or punctuation, the editor should bear in mind the discouraging fact that the printed version of an unprinted source text—or even of a printed source with unique characteristics—will always be an inexact copy. One can hope to do nothing more than choose those conventions of print publication that best communicate the significant patterns of the source text at hand.

What is more, the editor must be aware that any documentary edition that encompasses more than one source text may have to use more than one textual method. Even different passages within a single lengthy source text may require varying approaches. The editor's wisest course is to choose a textual method that will serve the bulk of the material being edited. When exceptional circumstances require a departure from the general rule, a note to the reader can explain the reasons for this variation, as well as the implications that the new method may have for the source text at hand.

Modern editors of American documents usually perform their tasks within five general methodological frameworks, and an infinite variety of results is possible within each general approach. This chapter examines the theoretical principles and practical results of these methods: facsimiles, diplomatic transcriptions, inclusive texts, expanded texts, and clear texts. Of these, facsimiles produce editorial texts closest to the source in physical appearance. At the other extreme, eclectically constructed clear texts of documents can suppress a great many elements of inscription, making recovery of the details of the original extraordinarily difficult. Diplomatic transcriptions, inclusive texts, and expanded texts fall between these two poles, and they are described in the order in which they may move away from the literal presentation of a facsimile toward the systematic emendations sanctioned in a clear text.

A theoretical and historical discussion of each method will be followed by a demonstration of the results of applying that approach to the same source text, the handwritten draft of a note from the author of this book to Richard K. Showman, chairman of the committee that supervised her work on the first edition of the *Guide.* The advantages and failings of each method are apparent.

## II. Photographic and Typographic Facsimiles

Facsimiles of documentary texts in an authoritative edition may be photoreproductions or typographic facsimiles. Traditionally, examples of photofacsimile editions have been limited to companion or supplementary microform series, particularly for NHPRC series in which select print editions were paired with comprehensive microforms. For editors of historical documents, the use of photofacsimiles in published volumes remains generally limited to reproductions of printed sources. A recent exception was Marvin E. Gettleman's five-volume edition of *The Johns Hopkins University Seminar of History and Politics: The Records of an American Educational Institution, 1877–1912,* presenting facsimile reproductions of the manuscript records of the seminar with accompanying editorial notes. More typical is the Albert Einstein edition's *Works* series, which reproduces facsimiles of the print pages bearing Einstein's published essays and reports rather than having them reset in modern typeface, and the modern edition of Thomas Jefferson's *Extracts from the Gospels,* which provides a volume with facsimile reproductions of the clipped Bible verses in Jefferson's compilations.

Both theory and technology now make such editions more common and more intellectually demanding. Among literary scholars, the call for a document-based approach to sources customarily served by highly emended, printed editorial texts has created a demand for convenient access to images of source materials. Increasingly common are print editions in which a photofacsimile appears as part of a parallel text accompanied by a printed editorial transcription. Digital scanning creates wider options for editors who wish to offer such photoreproduced images conveniently linked to machine-searchable transcriptions, accessed through automated indexes. The technical processes of creating such facsimile editions are described in chapter 9.

The typographic facsimile demands more discussion here, for its rationale and methods play a significant role in textual and documentary editions. This form attempts to duplicate exactly the appearance of the original source text insofar as this is possible within the limits of modern typesetting technology. Naturally, a typographic facsimile reproduces the author's spelling and punctuation without any correction. No contractions or abbreviations are expanded. An author's additions above the line are printed interlinearly. Marginal material is set in the margins. Passages crossed out by a line are rendered in canceled type (~~canceled type~~). The author's format and spacing are followed exactly. Headings, titles, datelines, greetings, and salutations are set line for line so that the line breaks in the printed version mirror those in the original.

Modern typographic facsimiles of handwritten material customarily do not present pages whose breaks correspond to changes in the original's pagination, but those page breaks are recorded within the editorial text, usually by an editorial interpolation within some form of bracket. Such editorial interpolations as "[2]" or "[new page]" can appear in the body of the text (when the author begins a new page in the middle of a sentence) or in the margin (when the new page represents a new section of the document).

Examples of a pure typographic facsimile, without the use of any textual symbols or other editorial conventions, are rare in modern editions. An approximation of facsimile technique can be found in Julian Boyd's "literal presentation" of Jefferson's drafts of the Declaration of Independence (*Jefferson Papers* 1:417–27), in the texts of letters in *Shelley and His Circle,* and in the Cornell *Wordsworth* edition.

Because typographic facsimiles can be more time-consuming and costly to produce than other formats, they generally are used for nonprinted source texts only when textual symbols will not adequately communicate the nuances and complexities of the original. The users of a series of colonial laws, for instance, would be more concerned with the final versions of statutes—the words or phrases that were promulgated by the provincial government—than with a clerk's corrections of his copy of that law; for them, a typographic facsimile would be a needless luxury. By contrast, the editor of documents relating to the legislative history of a colonial assembly would have good reason to consider a typographic facsimile of a draft of an important legislative report, a document in which the placement of interlineations and marginal additions would indicate the evolution of the final version of laws, arguably essential to understanding their history.

Some elements of typographic facsimile techniques may be used for individual documents in editions that otherwise modify this editorial technique. One legal historian has remarked, for instance, that the reproduction of the format of Hamilton's draft legal papers in the *Hamilton Law Practice* volumes "allows the reader to see Hamilton's mind at work." This edition uses conservative expansion of some archaic abbreviations and contractions and thus cannot be described as a true typographic facsimile, but its editors recognized those special documents whose full meaning could be conveyed only by retaining Hamilton's format.

Some form of typographic facsimile is, of course, the method of choice for reproducing printed documentary source texts. Even within editions where editors take substantial liberties with manuscript source texts, they do their best to reproduce as exactly as possible the appearance of such printed sources as pamphlets and newspapers (see, for example, the treatment of "A Representation of Facts" in volume 5 of the *Laurens Papers*). This rule for the treatment of printed source texts is consistent among editions of eighteenth-century materials, but editors of more modern documents have departed from it. In the *Woodrow Wilson Papers,* for example, the same rules for emending spelling and punctuation are applied to both manuscript source texts and Wilson's published works. The editors of the *Harold Frederic Correspondence* allowed themselves far greater latitude in emending printed and even typewritten source texts of letters than in treating handwritten sources.

The economies offered by modern technology have made this textual approach economically practical for many more editions. The first volume of the *Documentary History of the Supreme Court,* published in 1985, offers its readers page after page of documents in which superscript letters, marginal additions, interlineations, and archaic symbols are reproduced literally in type. The project's editors put encoded editorial copy for both documents and notes into computer files, which were then translated into print by Columbia University Press. The press estimated that the cost of producing each page of the Supreme Court volumes in printed facsimiles in 1985 was a bit less in real terms than the per-page cost at which they had produced the more standardized texts of a final volume of the *Hamilton Papers* in 1978.

Although philosophy and technology have now combined to make facsimile editions more popular, the most important theoretical consideration in publishing facsimiles remains the same: their editors and their audiences alike must remember that the facsimiles themselves are edited forms or versions of their sources, with cameras or scanning equipment performing the editorial function.

Figures 1 and 2 display the results of imposing facsimile treatment on the chapter's sample document. Figure 1 shows a photographic facsimile, which can be compared against the typographic facsimile in figure 2. In a scholarly edition, readers would be informed that the letter was written in April 1982, when the author was engaged in arranging the date for a meeting in Bloomington, Indiana, where she was to discuss the final details of the *Guide* with an executive subcommittee composed of David Chesnutt of the University of South Carolina, David Nordloh of Indiana University, and Paul Smith of the Library of Congress. It was expected that another person might attend these meetings—Don Cook, then president of the ADE and a member of the Indiana University Department of English.

## III. EDITORIAL TEXTS REQUIRING SYMBOLS OR TEXTUAL ANNOTATION

Only editors who prepare facsimiles are spared the use of editorial devices that communicate original inscriptional details that cannot be readily duplicated in a typeset version. And in putting general theories of textual method into practice, American editors have used a broad, sometimes bewildering variety of mechanical devices and techniques. In a diplomatic transcription, symbols or abbreviations appear in the documentary text itself. In inclusive or expanded texts, the symbols may appear both in the text and in supplementary notes. In clear text, symbols and notes appear in the back-of-book records of editorial emendations and details of inscription.

### A. TEXTUAL SYMBOLS

The use of textual symbols goes back to the work of classical scholars in their editions of ancient works. The first systematic use of textual symbols for more recent materials appeared in the early 1920s in

Figure 1.   Photofacsimile

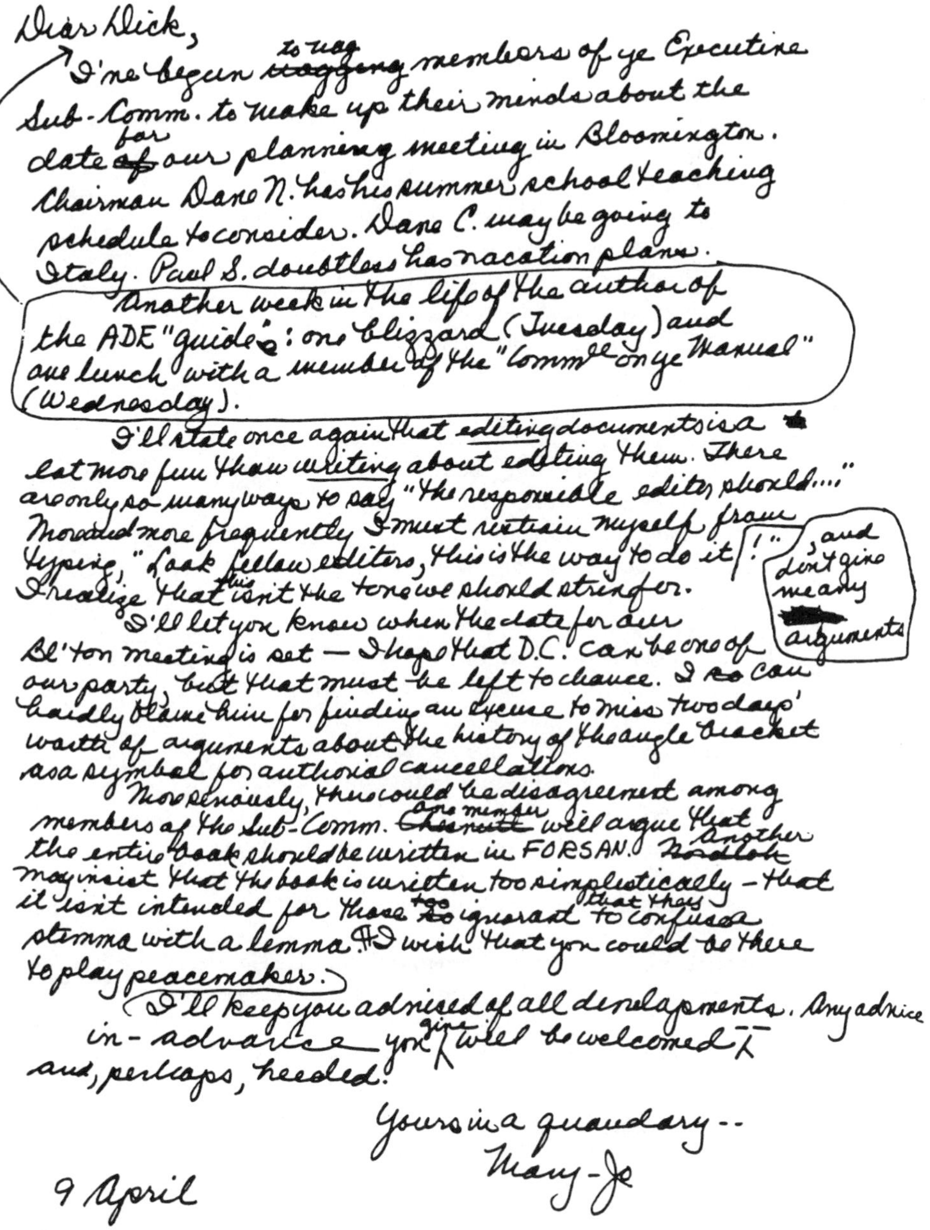

Dear Dick,

I've begun ~~tagging~~ to nag members of ye Executive Sub-Comm. to make up their minds about the date ~~of~~ for our planning meeting in Bloomington. Chairman Dave N. has his summer school teaching schedule to consider. Dave C. may be going to Italy. Paul S. doubtless has vacation plans.

Another week in the life of the author of the ADE "guide's: one blizzard (Tuesday) and one lunch with a member of the "Comm'e on ye Manual" (Wednesday).

I'll state once again that editing documents is a lot more fun than writing about editing them. There are only so many ways to say "the responsible editor should ..." Mounted more frequently I must restrain myself from typing, "Look fellow editors, this is the way to do it!", and don't give me any arguments. I realize that this isn't the tone we should strive for.

I'll let you know when the date for our Bl'ton meeting is set — I hope that D.C. can be one of our party, but that must be left to chance. I so can hardly blame him for finding an excuse to miss two days' worth of arguments about the history of the angle bracket as a symbol for authorial cancellations.

More seriously, there could be disagreement among members of the Sub-Comm. ~~Theorist~~ One member will argue that the entire book should be written in FORSAN. Another may insist that the book is written too simplistically — that it isn't intended for those too ignorant that they to confuse a stemma with a lemma. I wish that you could be there to play peacemaker.

I'll keep you advised of all developments. Any advice in-advance you ~~will~~ give be welcomed, and, perhaps, heeded!

Yours in a quandary --
Mary-Jo

9 April

Figure 2.  Typographic Facsimile

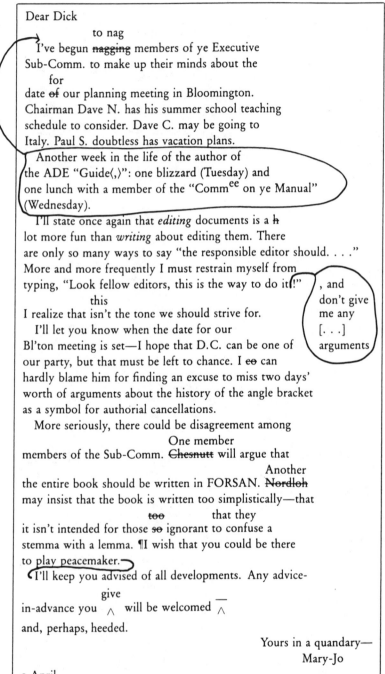

Dear Dick

      to nag
I've begun ~~nagging~~ members of ye Executive
Sub-Comm. to make up their minds about the
    for
date ~~of~~ our planning meeting in Bloomington.
Chairman Dave N. has his summer school teaching
schedule to consider. Dave C. may be going to
Italy. Paul S. doubtless has vacation plans.
 Another week in the life of the author of
the ADE "Guide⟨,⟩": one blizzard (Tuesday) and
one lunch with a member of the "Comm^ee on ye Manual"
(Wednesday).
 I'll state once again that *editing* documents is a h
lot more fun than *writing* about editing them. There
are only so many ways to say "the responsible editor should. . . ."
More and more frequently I must restrain myself from
typing, "Look fellow editors, this is the way to do it!" , and
     this            don't give
I realize that isn't the tone we should strive for. me any
 I'll let you know when the date for our  [. . .]
Bl'ton meeting is set—I hope that D.C. can be one of arguments
our party, but that must be left to chance. I ~~eo~~ can
hardly blame him for finding an excuse to miss two days'
worth of arguments about the history of the angle bracket
as a symbol for authorial cancellations.
 More seriously, there could be disagreement among
         One member
members of the Sub-Comm. ~~Chesnutt~~ will argue that
            Another
the entire book should be written in FORSAN. ~~Nordloh~~
may insist that the book is written too simplistically—that
       too    that they
it isn't intended for those ~~so~~ ignorant to confuse a
stemma with a lemma. ¶I wish that you could be there
to play peacemaker.
 I'll keep you advised of all developments. Any advice-
      give
in-advance you ∧ will be welcomed ‾∧
and, perhaps, heeded.

            Yours in a quandary—
              Mary-Jo

9 April

the Malone Society's *Reprints* series, edited by W. W. Greg. The society's editions of British literary works of the Renaissance and the early modern period employed two sets of characters to indicate details in manuscript sources: angle brackets (⟨ ⟩) to enclose passages lost through mutilation or other damage and restored by the editors, and square brackets ([ ]) to enclose passages deleted in the original manuscript.

After World War II, these and other symbols were applied to American documents and literary works. The first system of textual symbols for American materials was devised by Julian Boyd and Lyman Butterfield for their Jefferson and Rush editions. They confined themselves to the same two pairs of symbols used by the Malone Society, but they modified the meaning of each set of brackets. Because common American usage had already assigned to square brackets the function of setting off interpolated material, these symbols were given a related meaning in the text of American documentary editions. Instead of denoting authorial deletions, square brackets in the Jefferson and Rush volumes were used to indicate some form of editorial intrusion into the text—the insertion of characters or words not physically a part of the original, whether these were added to restore mutilated passages or interjected to explain some aspect of the text. Angle brackets, which had no generally accepted function in American usage of the time, were a "neutral" symbol to the eyes of readers of the Jefferson and Rush editions. They bore no preexisting connotations, and the editors arbitrarily assigned them to enclose restored canceled material in their source texts.

During the thirty years following publication of the first volume of the *Jefferson Papers,* scholarly editors here and abroad devised symbols and abbreviations for almost every detail of inscription of which the human mind, hand, and pen could be guilty. The use of symbolic description of textual detail won popularity so quickly that many of its adopters were unaware of the novelty of their methods. In the statement of textual method for the first volume of the *Emerson Journals,* published in 1961, the use of angle brackets to enclose restored authorial deletions was described as traditional, although that tradition was only a decade old. The symbol has become so widely used that some editors no longer bother to define its meaning in prefaces to their volumes of documentary texts.

Other conventions have won less universal acceptance and acclaim. The list that follows records only some of the devices that modern editors have devised to represent textual details—what Lewis Mumford dubbed the "barbed wire" of modern American scholarly texts:

## I. PASSAGES DELETED BY THE AUTHOR

| | |
|---|---|
| ⟨*italic*⟩ | *Jefferson Papers* |
| ⟨roman⟩ | Emerson, Howells, Irving, and Frederic editions; most historical editions |
| ⟨⟨*italic* or roman⟩⟩ | A deletion within a deletion in an edition that employs single angle (or "broken") brackets for a primary deletion |
| ~~canceled type~~ | Grant and Hamilton papers; most editions of literary works |
| ⟨ | A crossed-out deletion, *Billy Budd* |
| ⟨ | An erasure, *Billy Budd* |

## 2. UNRECOVERABLE GAPS IN THE SOURCE TEXT

| | |
|---|---|
| [ . . . ] | The number of suspension points within the square brackets usually offers a clue to the length of the lacuna, or unrecoverable material. In the Jefferson and Adams papers, "[ . . . ], [ . . . . ]" indicates one or two missing words; if a footnote number follows the brackets, the lacuna is longer, and a note estimates the number of missing words. The Cooper edition employs a similar technique. In the *Grant Papers,* the number of points represents the approximate number of missing letters, not words. |
| [ ] | A missing portion of a number, *Jefferson Papers* |
| ‖ . . . ‖ | The number of suspension points approximates the number of missing words in the *Emerson Journals,* with three dots representing one to five words; four dots, six to ten words; and five dots, sixteen to thirty words. The abbreviation *msm* within the vertical lines stands for "manuscript accidentally mutilated." |
| xxx | Missing letters in the *Emerson Journals,* with the number of *x*'s approximating the number of lost characters |
| [ - - - ] | Missing words in the Grant and Wilson papers, with the spaced hyphens indicating the number of words lost. The editors of the *Ratification* series employ the same symbol, but three |

|  | hyphens are used regardless of the length of the lacuna. |
|---|---|
| . . . | Lacunae in the *Hamilton Papers,* with the suspension points representing the approximate number of unrecoverable characters |
| // . . . // | Illegible words in *Mark Twain's Satires* |
| [ *** ] | Unrecoverable shorthand characters, *Wilson Papers* |

Countless variations upon this theme are possible. The Irving edition, which employs angle brackets (⟨ ⟩) to enclose deleted passages, combines that symbol with italicized descriptive words or phrases to indicate unrecoverable canceled passages, as with "⟨*illegible*⟩" for a hopelessly obliterated section.

### 3. ADDITIONS TO THE ORIGINAL INSCRIPTION

| ⟩ | An insertion with Melville's caret, *Billy Budd* |
|---|---|
| ⋏ | An interlinear insertion without a caret, *Billy Budd* |
| ∧ roman ∧ | All insertions (interlinear and marginal), *Mark Twain's Satires*; interlineations only, *Frederic Correspondence*; interlineations made with author's symbol for an interlined addition, *Emerson Journals* |
| ↑ roman ↓ | "Substitutions for a deletion," *Mark Twain's Satires*; interlineations in *Emerson Journals,* Irving edition, and most other "literary" series |
| / roman / | *Marcus Garvey Papers* |
| I roman I | Marginal additions, *Emerson Journals* |
| *w.o.* | Superimposed addition ("written over"), *Billy Budd* |

### 4. UNDERLINING IN THE SOURCE TEXT

| *italic* | Single underlining (universal) |
|---|---|
| small capitals | Double underlining (universal) |

### 5. AUTHORIAL SYMBOLS

| thorn | The handwritten thorn, which had been formalized to *y* by the mid-eighteenth-century, |
|---|---|

is customarily printed as a *y* or as *th* for materials in American history and literature.

~ Many eighteenth- and early nineteenth-century authors employ the curved tilde or a simple straight line at the point in a word where characters have been omitted to form a contraction. The tilde is reproduced in type by the Laurens, *Ratification,* and Burr editors. Many editions, following the lead of the *Jefferson Papers,* ignore the tilde and silently expand the resulting contraction where it is employed.

ꝑ The "tailed *p*" is either rendered by the character for this symbol in print ( *Jefferson Papers*) or expanded to the intended form of *per, pre,* or *pro* (*Hamilton Papers, Letters of Delegates*). If the meaning of the symbol is unclear, an edition that ordinarily expands it must indicate an ambiguous usage by "p[er?]" or some other method reserved by the edition for conjectural readings. Changes in modern day typesetting are rapidly eliminating the option of using the symbol.

\* The asterisk is the most commonly employed rendition of an idiosyncratic symbol used by authors to indicate their own footnote numbers (*Emerson Journals*). However, when the author uses a standardized (even if rather archaic) form of citation, it is preferable to retain those forms that have equivalents in modern type fonts, such as a dagger (†).

☞ A "fist" or "index" drawn by the author in the margin to call attention to a passage in his or her text can be translated to the printed "fist" that survives in many typefaces.

{ } Bracket used in the *Emerson Journals* to enclose page numbers supplied by Emerson himself

¶ Author's marking for a new paragraph

no ¶ Author's marking for the consolidation of paragraphs

6. LINE BREAKS IN THE SOURCE TEXT

| | |
|---|---|
| / | Most historical editions; *Howells Letters* |
| \| | Hawthorne, Whitman, and James editions |

7. EDITORIAL SUPPLY

| | |
|---|---|
| [roman] | The most common device for both literary and historical series; if doubt exists concerning the supplied material, a question mark precedes the closing bracket ("[reading?]"). |
| ⟨roman⟩ | *Hamilton Papers* |
| ‖ roman ‖ | *Emerson Journals* |
| \| roman \| | *Howells Letters* |
| {roman} | *Frederic Correspondence* |
| ⊦roman⊦ | *Wilson Papers* device for "word or words in the original text which Wilson omitted in copying" |

8. EDITORIAL EXPANSION OF ABBREVIATIONS OR
   CONTRACTIONS

| | |
|---|---|
| [roman] | Universally accepted symbol in those editions that expand such forms within the text |

9. EDITORIAL OMISSIONS

| | |
|---|---|
| [ … ] | *Emerson Journals* |
| . . . . | *Booker T. Washington Papers* |

10. ALTERNATIVE READINGS

| | |
|---|---|
| / | Introduces alternative readings in *Mark Twain's Satires* |
| /roman/ | The virgules enclose alternative readings in the *Emerson Journals* |

When variant copies provide alternative readings in documentary materials, it is far more common to describe the variations in notes than to represent them symbolically within the text.

11. EDITORIAL INTERPOLATIONS

| | |
|---|---|
| [*italic*] | This is the most comonly used device, although both the *Emerson* and *Ratification* volumes |

employ "[roman]." If the documents in the
edition contain a substantial amount of material
that must be represented within square brackets
for other reasons (lacunae in the text; expanded
abbreviations; supplies of mutilated passages),
then the editorial apparatus must distinguish
clearly between bracketed material that can at
least be inferred from the source text and
bracketed contributions that do not stem
from the source (corrections of outrageously
misspelled words; catchwords such as *illegible*,
and so on). The reader must not be left to
wonder to which category the bracketed
material belongs. If brackets are used sparingly
in the text, and there is no possibility of
confusion, then all bracketed letters, words,
and phrases can be in roman type.

*italic*          *Frederic Correspondence*


## B. SOME RULES FOR USING EDITORIAL SYMBOLS

The variety of symbols used by different editions to represent the
same textual detail is so great that it is hard to escape the conclusion
that some symbols were adopted because editors were unaware of the
conventions already in place. Others may have tried to prove their in-
ventiveness by adopting a new form of bracket or a new arrangement
of virgules (slashes) instead of imitating another edition's practices.
Nothing short of an editorial Council of Trent could impose order
on the symbolic chaos in existing documentary editions.

A careless choice of symbols can make the reader's task more difficult. If two symbols are to represent related details in the manuscript, then the symbols themselves should have a visual relationship.
The reader's memory will be burdened sufficiently without the addition of sets of characters that contradict each other in appearance and
meaning. Following this rule, the editors of Melville's *Billy Budd*
used variations on the opening half of a pair of angle brackets (⟨ ) to
indicate different kinds of authorial cancellation and employed variants on the closing angle bracket ( ⟩) to represent two methods of interlineation in the source text. If the edition requires a lengthy series
of textual symbols, the editor should use as many devices as possible
that mirror the physical appearance of the original. If an author can-
cels material both by lining out phrases and by erasing them, the

lined-out deletions should appear in canceled type, whose meaning is easily grasped, with symbolic designation reserved for the erasures.

Fortunately, computerized publishing technology makes it possible to eliminate a good many symbols altogether. Those symbols were frequently adopted because of the expense of producing a typeset facsimile of the source text's details. Today many of those details can be reproduced with no more trouble to the editor nor expense to the publisher than inserting codes for symbols. Arbitrary symbols can be reserved for problems that cannot be so easily translated, and the list of symbols the reader is required to memorize will be reduced correspondingly.

## C. DESCRIPTIVE TEXTUAL NOTES

Despite the thicket of editorial symbols cultivated by modern scholars, many details of inscription stubbornly defy symbolic representation, and some editors simply prefer to avoid the use of textual symbols altogether. Instead of symbols, their textual notes use verbal descriptions of textual problems whenever possible. Such textual descriptions can be provided in three ways: (1) in the documentary text within square brackets (as in the *Calhoun Papers*); (2) in footnotes whose numbers are keyed to the location of the cancellation, interlineation, marginal addition, or other detail in the edited text of the document (*Franklin Papers*); and (3) in a back-of-book textual record. The reasons for choosing each variation on the method are instructive.

The format of the *Calhoun Papers* allows for no footnotes of any kind. All editorially supplied historical notes as well as textual explanations are presented within square brackets in the text. This design does not lend itself easily to arrows and other symbols within the initial brackets. In the *Franklin Papers*, William Willcox explained that he found the use of symbols within the texts of printed documents to be "disfiguring," and his choice of descriptive methods rested on this aesthetic preference.

Traditionally, editions of the writings of American literary figures have carried a complete textual record. Here the use of descriptive rather than symbolic methods rests on very different and more complicated grounds. Some of the details and patterns customarily reported simply do not lend themselves to symbolic treatment, while the number of textual notes would make it impossible to report these details within the text of a document or even in numbered footnotes, whose profusion would make the text a field of numerals rather than words and phrases. Therefore, the textual record usually had to be presented in unnumbered notes keyed to the line and page of the printed edition, appearing either in a section of notes following the text or in a back-of-book section. In either case, the textual note was at some distance physically from the section of edited text to which it referred. Many textual problems requiring such notes are so complicated that readers need special cues for understanding the significance of emendations or omissions that have occurred, and brief verbal descriptions frequently serve this purpose better than symbols.

Fredson Bowers was the leading exponent of descriptive rather than symbolic textual annotation, and his edition of *Leaves of Grass* is the best example of a diplomatic transcription employing the technique. The notes follow each poem and can be consulted easily. Bowers later argued for the use of descriptive textual annotation for inclusive and clear texts as well, and the practical effect of the method in such an edition was first seen in the *Hawthorne Notebooks*. The system became more highly refined in Bowers' textual notes for the William James edition, and Bowers' exposition of the method appears in his "Transcription of Manuscripts: The Record of Variants." The back-of-book records of emendations and inscriptional details in these series follow the traditional format for literary works. Each line-page reference is followed by the lemma (a word or phrase in the editorial text that indicates the site of editorial activity), followed by a left-opening bracket ( ] ), which divides the lemma from the reading in the source text. The method can be seen at its simplest in the record of the first editorial emendation in Hawthorne's *French and Italian Notebooks:*

"6.3 a little more or less] $\wedge$ little more less" $\overset{\text{a}}{}$

This merely indicates that in line 3 on page 6, the editors have supplied the word *or,* which Hawthorne omitted from this entry in his notebook.

Usually, such textual tables need only three symbols in addition to the left-opening bracket that follows the lemma: the slash (/), which indicates a line break in the source text; the mathematical symbol ~, which represents a repetition of the word that appears after the bracket; and a caret on line ($\wedge$), which can indicate the absence of punctuation in the source text. Thus, in the same Hawthorne volume, "of] of/ of" shows that the editors have omitted the *of* that Hawthorne repeated when he began a new line. And "Liverpool,] l~$\wedge$" shows that the editors have added the comma after Liverpool.

A scheme of descriptive textual annotation should be designed as carefully as one of symbolic representation of emendations and inscriptional detail. The words and phrases that describe more complicated emendations and details in the source can be written out or abbreviated. The *Thoreau Journals* contain descriptive textual notes without abbreviations for the best and most practical of reasons: brevity. The notes seldom run to more than one line with unabbreviated descriptive forms, and using contracted forms would have saved no space while forcing readers to master a table of abbreviations. Still, many editions require abbreviations, to prevent the descriptive textual notes from becoming unmanageable; among the most common are *del.* for *deleted, ab.* for *above the line,* and *interl.* for *interlined.* A descriptive textual record is offered for the clear text version of the sample document in figure 5, below.

## IV. DIPLOMATIC TRANSCRIPTIONS

In modern American editions, a diplomatic transcription is one step removed from the typographic facsimile. The editor uses carefully chosen critical symbols or abbreviations to indicate details of inscription such as interlineations and cancellations instead of reproducing their physical appearance in the original. Editors of diplomatic transcriptions often standardize the placement of such routine elements of the source text as datelines, greetings, salutations, titles, and the indention of paragraphs, and they may also supply missing punctuation, expand ambiguous or archaic abbreviations and contractions, or even supply words unintentionally omitted by the author or destroyed by mutilation of the original source text. But none of these corrections or emendations is made silently: each is given within a form of brackets that indicates such editorial activities. If some emendation or detail of original inscription cannot be described conveniently with symbols or a bracketed interpolation, a footnote immediately adjacent to the text explains the problem at hand.

Examples of exhaustive diplomatic transcriptions are almost as rare as printed facsimiles among editions of modern American materials. Perhaps the best known are Fredson Bowers' *Leaves of Grass,* the Hayford-Sealts genetic text of Melville's *Billy Budd,* and Donald Reiman's edition of *Shelley and His Circle.* In all of these, the reader has immediate access to the details of the original manuscript source text in the diplomatic transcription and to a critically edited reading text, which represents the author's apparent final intentions. In *Leaves of Grass* and *Shelley and His Circle* the reading texts and the diplomatic transcriptions are presented as parallel texts on facing pages. The Hayford-Sealts reading text of *Billy Budd* precedes the genetic text of the author's manuscript. For materials whose diplo-

Figure 3.   Diplomatic Transcription

---

Dear Dick                                   9 April [1982]
   I've begun ⟨nagging⟩ ↑ to nag ↓ members of ye Executive Sub-
Comm. to make up their minds about the date ⟨of⟩ ↑ for ↓ our
planning meeting in Bloomington. Chairman Dave N. has his
summer school teaching schedule to consider. Dave C. may be going
to Italy. Paul S. doubtless has vacation plans.
   Another week in the life of the author of the ADE "Guide ⟨,⟩":
one blizzard (Tuesday) and one lunch with a member of the
"Commee. on ye Manual" (Wednesday).[1]
   I'll state once again that *editing* documents is a ⟨h⟩ lot more fun
than *writing* about editing them. There are only so many ways to say
"the responsible editor should. . . ." More and more frequently I
must restrain myself from typing, "Look fellow editors, this is the
way to do it ↑, and don't give me any [. . .] arguments ↓ !"[2] I realize
that ↑ this ↓ isn't the tone we should strive for.
   I'll let you know when the date for our Bl'ton meeting is set—I
hope that D.C. can be one of our party, but that must be left to
chance. I ⟨co⟩ can hardly blame him for finding an excuse to miss two
days' worth of arguments about the history of the angle bracket as a
symbol for authorial cancellations.
   More seriously, there could be disagreement among members of the
Sub-Comm. ⟨Chesnutt⟩ ↑ One member ↓ will argue that the entire
book should be written in FORSAN. ⟨Nordloh⟩ ↑ Another ↓ may
insist that the book is written too simplistically—that it isn't intended
for those ⟨so⟩ ↑ ⟨too⟩ ↓ ignorant to ↑ that they ↓ confuse a stemma
with a lemma. I wish that you could be there to play peacemaker.[3]
   I'll keep you advised of all developments. Any advice-in-advance
you ∧give∧ will be welcomed ∧—∧ and, perhaps, heeded.
                                        Yours in a quandary—
                                            Mary-Jo

[1]The author has marked this paragraph for insertion at the opening
of the letter's text.
   [2]The phrase ", and don't . . . arguments" added in the margin,
with a guideline for its insertion at this point.
   [3]The author has marked the beginning of this sentence to open a
new paragraph. The following sentence ("I'll keep you advised. . . .")
is marked to "run on" as the second sentence of the new closing
paragraph.

matic transcriptions rival these in complexity, providing a reading text is not only a kindness to the reader but a necessity.

Figure 3 offers a diplomatic transcription using the following textual symbols:

⟨ ⟩         Deleted passages
↑ ↓         Interlined material
∧ ∧         Material interlined with a caret
[roman]     Editorial expansion of abbreviated forms
[. . .]     Unrecoverable canceled matter, with each suspension
            point representing one illegible character

## V. The Middle Ground: Inclusive Texts and Expanded Transcriptions

Most editors compromise to one degree or another between a detailed diplomatic text and a clear reading text. Among editions in the CEAA/CSE tradition, such methods are described as "inclusive." For historian-editors the practice became known as expanded transcription. The difference between the inclusive and expanded methods is not so much the editor's basic conservatism or liberalism in emending and standardizing the text as the degree to which such editorial tinkering is reported to the reader. In both inclusive texts and expanded transcriptions, certain classes of emendations (usually relating to physical format) are performed silently in individual cases although described to the reader as classes of correction and standardization. Editors of inclusive texts that meet CSE guidelines report any emendations in other categories individually in accompanying textual notes. Expanded texts in historical editions offer no such supplementary record of emendations or suppressed details beyond what appears in the text and in footnotes immediately adjacent to the documentary text.

In both techniques, some details of inscription are reported overtly in the editorial text, that is, through the use of textual symbols or numbered footnotes adjacent to the text. And both breeds of editors may standardize certain elements of the format of the source text silently. Datelines and place lines in letters are usually printed above the greetings and text, no matter where they appear in the original. Headings for diary and journal entries are standardized for easy reference. Paragraph indentions and dashes of varying length are made uniform.

Beyond such standardization of the format, inclusive and expansive editors often emend the text without giving any overt indication. Superscript characters are commonly lowered to form an abbreviation or contraction on one line, with a mark of punctuation placed after the resulting form. Archaic holographic symbols are generally rendered in their closest equivalent in print (as *th* or *y* for the thorn, or *per, pre* or *pro* for the tailed *p*). Abbreviations or contractions that editors judge unfamiliar to their readers are not reproduced exactly—they may be expanded silently or overtly, with brackets to indicate that the editorial hand has been at work or a change in typeface to signal supplied words or characters. Erratic punctuation is standardized—silently or overtly—and missing marks of punctuation are supplied.

## A. INCLUSIVE TEXTS

The most cogent description of requirements for an inclusive text appears in the Center for Editions of American Authors' revised *Statement of Editorial Principles* of 1972 (p. 9). First, it states, inclusive methods should be employed for a source text whose audience is "limited mostly to scholars and specialists," and they are specifically recommended to editors whose source texts are "manuscript letters or journals or notebooks" for which no authoritative published version exists. The *Statement* also points out that this method is preferred whenever "reporting the author's process of composition directly is important." Once the editorial text has been established, deletions and revisions may be reported on the same page as the editorial text, as they would have been for a diplomatic transcription, or the editor may supplement that text with accompanying textual footnotes that appear at the bottom of the page or are placed between such "separable" items as letters and entries in a journal. These textual notes should explain the use of symbols in the text and record details of inscription that the editor has been forced to omit from the text itself.

In addition to such notes, the CEAA/CSE inclusive editor was usually required to furnish "in some form" a record of editorial emendations of the source text that were not clearly indicated in that text or its adjacent notes. Thus, an inclusive text might be followed by a back-of-book record of emendations similar to the ones that appear in CEAA/CSE editions of literary works, with their references keyed to the line and page of the edited volume where they occur. An inclusive text of documentary materials, like any CEAA/CSE edition, should also have been accompanied by a report of "editorial decisions in the handling of possible compounds hyphenated at the ends of lines in the copy-text, along with an indication of which end-of-line hyphenations in the newly edited text should be retained in quotations from the text."

In practice, few multivolume CEAA/CSE editions consistently followed these rules for documentary materials. The Washington Irving series was among this small number. Irving's *Journals* and *Letters* used editorial symbols in their texts for most details of inscription. Numbered footnotes at the bottom of the page (*Journals*) or at the close of individual items (*Letters*) reported emendations and details suppressed in the reading text.

Editors have experimented with a variety of methods for documentary source texts. The *Emerson Journals* provide an example of inclusive methods, with editorial symbols within the journal entries for major details of inscription and a further back-of-book record of editorial emendations not apparent in the reading text itself, but the *Emerson Lectures* appear in clear text. Still another series bearing the CSE seal, the *Harold Frederic Correspondence,* imposes different editorial methods on different groups of source texts in the same volume. The 203 letters whose source texts are holographs are offered as inclusive texts, while the 163 letters in the volume that survive as typescripts, transcriptions, or earlier published versions appear in clear text.

One edition adopted inclusive methods midstream in its progress. The first volumes of documentary material in the Mark Twain Papers—*Twain's Letters to His Publishers* and his *Letters to H. H. Rogers*—were heavily emended by the editors, and these volumes contained neither a report of canceled passages nor a record of other details suppressed in the reading text. Ensuing volumes of documentary materials, however, adopted inclusive methods. The volumes of Twain's *Notebooks and Journals* are an example of inclusive textual editing at its best. The reading texts employ conventional editorial symbols to indicate such items as legible canceled passages, revisions, and other significant details of the source texts. A back-of-book record conveniently divides textual notes between "Editorial Emendations and Doubtful Readings" and "Details of Inscription in the Manuscript." The first alerts the reader to elements of the reading text that result from editorial judgment, while the second records elements of Clemens' accidentals and substantives in the source texts that either did not warrant inclusion in the reading text or could not be reproduced symbolically on the printed page.

In the light of experience, the editors of the Twain edition later devised a new form of inclusive textual editing dubbed "plain text" for their author's correspondence. This system is discussed at length in Robert Hirst's "Guide to Editorial Practice" and "Guide to Textual

Commentaries" in *Mark Twain's Letters* (1:xxv–xlvi and 447–63). The Twain editors do not pretend that their reading texts are print facsimiles or even diplomatic transcriptions, but these conservatively emended inclusive texts use typographic equivalents for certain details of the original rather than the editorial symbols customarily used in inclusive texts. Samuel Clemens' use of the conventions of nineteenth-century typography in his personal letter writing and the economies of modern computerized typesetting made this effective, commonsense approach a practical possibility. The letters that appeared in the two earlier volumes, *Letters to His Publishers* and *Letters to H. H. Rogers*, will be reprinted in later volumes of the *Mark Twain's Letters* series, appearing at their appropriate chronological places and reedited in plain text.

None of these inclusive or plain text editions pretends to report all of the details of their sources. Two forms of emendation are made silently within the text, with no record in the textual apparatus: (1) standardization of the manuscript's format, including the placement of such elements as a letter's dateline, salutation, and complimentary close; uniform spacing between lines and uniform indention of paragraphs; and (2) standardization of irregularly formed letters of the alphabet and marks of punctuation. Inclusive editors seeking CSE approval may enlarge this list of silent emendations, listing additional categories in statements of textual method in their volumes.

Certain details of inscription are customarily reported overtly, by using symbols or facsimile printing in the text or by placing footnotes adjacent to the text. Those details include legible canceled passages, especially those that reflect a change in the substance of the author's thought, and legible additions to the original passage, such as interlineations, on-line additions, and marginal insertions. An interlinear spelling correction, for instance, would not fall into this category.

Details of inscription in the following categories are usually omitted from the inclusive text and recorded only in back-of-book textual notes: (1) false starts so brief that they give no sense of the author's preliminary intention; (2) slips of the pen such as dittography (words repeated unintentionally) or minor errors of spelling or punctuation that the author did not correct; (3) authorial corrections of spelling and punctuation (whether as write-overs, interlineations, added characters, or marginal insertions) that do not indicate a change in the desired sense of the passage; (4) illegible canceled passages; (5) catchwords at the bottom of a page that are repeated at the top of the following page; (6) a change in any of the media used in the original manuscript (i.e., variations in paper, ink, or pencil within the same document); (7) symbols that cannot be reproduced in set type in any readable form and must be described rather than represented by visual symbols; and (8) authorial revisions so complicated that not even diplomatic transcription or facsimile printing could represent them clearly.

Similarly, some types of editorial emendation are usually reported within the text rather than in the back-of-book record of an inclusive edition. The following editorial contributions are signaled by a symbol in the text (usually a square bracket) alerting the reader to possible ambiguity: (1) supply of a word, phrase, or a single mark of punctuation omitted by the author; (2) supply of mutilated or obliterated material; (3) any change in the identity of the source text, when two or more sources are conflated to produce the complete text of an item; (4) any editorial expansion of authorial shorthand necessary to make a passage read sensibly, such as completion of dates and expansion of ambiguous contractions and abbreviations or of a set of initials to a full name; (5) any editorial interpolations of factual material; and (6) any editorial omissions of material that the author clearly intended as part of the final letter, diary entry, or essay (e.g., standardized headings).

Finally, some forms of emendation are made silently within the text, with some note of their existence in the back-of-book record: (1) expansion of unambiguous but obsolete contractions or abbreviations; (2) the supply of a missing punctuation mark that is part of a set, such as half of a pair of quotation marks, or one or more commas in a series; (3) the supply of terminal punctuation when the author began a new sentence with a capital letter but omitted the period, question mark, or exclamation point that should have preceded that character; (4) correction of an author's lapse from his or her usual patterns of punctuation or spelling; and (5) the supply of breaks for paragraphs in a lengthy passage.

## B. EXPANDED TRANSCRIPTION

The term *expanded transcription*, describing the textual practices of historical editors, gained currency in the 1954 edition of the *Harvard Guide to American History*. In discussing documentary publication, Samuel Eliot Morison categorized the methods used for American historical materials in three groups: "the *Literal*, the *Expanded*, and the *Modernized*." As an aside, he pointed out, "[I]n addition there is one that we might call the *Garbled* or *Bowdlerized*, which should be avoided" (95). Morison's rules for all three of the recommended methods included providing clues to the provenance of the source text; standardizing the address, dateline, and greeting of letters; marking all editorial interpolations by square brackets; indicating editorial omissions by suspension points ( . . . ); lowering interlineations to the line; and rendering words underscored once in italics and those underscored twice in small capitals. A final instruction to all editors advised them "to prepare a fresh text from the manuscript or photostat" instead of relying on an earlier printed version (97).

Morison spent little time discussing "literal" techniques or "modernized" methods, which he approved for use only for English translations from other tongues and for "an early document, chronicle, or narrative [whose] average reader [might be] put off by obsolete spelling and erratic punctuation." Most of his attention was directed to describing the expanded method of textual presentation that had been used in the first volumes of Boyd's Jefferson edition, then a new and exciting addition to the literature. Unfortunately, Morison confined himself to describing his preferences for expanded transcription and noting his minor differences with Boyd, never explaining the goals or rationale of the method. His six rules for expanded transcription were hardly helpful, for they included advice such as, "Retain the spelling, capitalization, and punctuation of the source text, but always capitalize the first word and put a period at the end of the sentence no matter what the writer does" (98).

Studying Morison's precepts for expanded texts is less illuminating than examining Julian Boyd's reasons for adopting the methods or later editors' motives in modifying the technique in what became known as the "historical" tradition. The patterns of silent emendation cited by Morison were worked out by Boyd and Lyman Butterfield during their fruitful partnership at the Jefferson project in the late 1940s. Acutely aware of the loss suffered by the transfer of any eighteenth-century source text to a twentieth-century printed page, they cast about for some device that would preserve the flavor of the original materials: their solution was to print manuscript materials more or less as they would have been printed at the time of their inscription. While the device itself was not new, an attempt to apply it to American materials was. Consulting products of Benjamin Franklin's press, the two scholars compiled what could be termed a style sheet for compositors of the late eighteenth century. The conventions used in the Jefferson, Rush, and Adams volumes Boyd and Butterfield edited were largely those employed by the printers who were contemporaries of their statesmen-subjects. In printing houses of that day, for instance, the ampersand was retained only when it was part of the name of a business firm or part of the abbreviation *&c* or *&ca* for *etc.*; otherwise the symbol was rendered as "and."

This usage was transferred to the printed texts published in the 1950s and 1960s. Similarly, because the thorn was no longer used in printing by the late eighteenth century, Boyd and Butterfield silently translated it to *th* when it appeared in a manuscript.

Unfortunately, Boyd and Butterfield assumed that their readers and fellow editors would recognize the patterns of silent emendation for what they were—the printing conventions of Revolutionary America. They believed that they were justified in imposing these conventions on the materials at hand, because Jefferson, Rush, and Adams were literate men who would have expected to see such conventions imposed on any holograph materials that they submitted to a printer. In effect, Boyd and Butterfield sought to publish volumes of documents edited as Jefferson, Rush, and Adams themselves would have edited them. And Butterfield recognized the method's limitations for John Adams' own family: letters written by eighteenth-century Adams *women,* often denied conventional education in standard English usage and punctuation, were emended far more conservatively lest nuances of the original be lost by imposing inappropriate conventions. Other scholars, however, missed this central point, assuming that Boyd and Butterfield's patterns of emendation were designed to serve any documentary edition. Some attempted to transfer these methods to manuscript source texts of later periods, in which the reasons for the Boyd-Butterfield printing conventions had no validity. Worse still, some used these methods with documents composed by semiliterate men and women, thus obscuring almost every bit of the original texture and flavor, which Boyd and Butterfield had hoped to preserve.

Not only did editors following this tradition expand certain forms abbreviated in the original, but they also included within the text or its accompanying footnotes elements of the source text that were excluded from the final version of the document. Thus, Boyd and Butterfield and their followers, like inclusive editors in the CEAA mold, reported cancellations and insertions whose existence seemed likely to be of importance to their modern readers. Some editors used textual symbols, others used footnotes adjacent to the text. Unlike inclusive editors of the CEAA/CSE school, however, expansionist editors did not pretend to record every detail of inscription by providing a back-of-book record of such suppressed details or of their emendations of the source text.

Expanded texts can be constructed conservatively or liberally. The text of letters in the *Papers of Ulysses S. Grant,* for instance, is close to a diplomatic transcription of the sources. If the editors provided a back-of-book record of minor emendations, their volumes would easily qualify for the CSE seal. Volumes in the Adams and Jefferson series, however, continue the practices of traditional expansionist emendation. In part, this diversity comes from the traditions of the editions in question, but another factor plays a part. Ulysses S. Grant's letters require fewer silent emendations under the definitions of expanded text, because they are not eighteenth-century materials. Grant and his correspondents used neither the thorn or the tailed *p*. Their style was already a century closer to modern conventions, and the editors of the Grant Papers did not need to bend the rules of expanded methods to create their near-diplomatic transcriptions, for those rules simply did not apply to the textual problems they faced.

The fathers of expanded transcription based their method on another assumption that Morison and their followers ignored. Although Boyd and Butterfield were selective in including details of the source text in their volumes, they did not ignore the requirements of readers who needed access to the contents of the originals. They assumed that microfilm editions of their projects' archives would soon make facsimiles of these source texts available to a wide audience, thus giving readers access to any details of the originals that the printed texts ignored. The Library of Congress did issue an indexed microfilm of Jefferson's surviving personal papers in that institution's Presidential Papers series, but there was no supplementary publication of the tens of thousands of items from other repositories represented by photocopies in the files of the Princeton Jefferson Papers project. Similarly, Butterfield and his staff issued a microfilm edition of the Adams Family Papers at the Massachusetts Historical Society. These reels were not accompanied by any form of index, however, and the project never prepared a similar microform edition of photocopies of Adams materials collected later from other repositories.

Figure 4 presents the text of this chapter's sample document in what might be its inclusive or expanded form, followed by the textual record that might accompany the inclusive text in an edition bearing the CSE emblem. In this expanded form of the document, the abbreviation "D.C." in line 19 has been expanded within brackets, unlike other abbreviations for personal names, because its meaning would otherwise be ambiguous (Don Cook or David Chesnutt?).

## C. TEXTUAL RECORD

The textual record for the inclusive text (see fig. 4) uses the traditional "lemma]" form for locating alterations in the reading text. Line numbers precede the first lemma in each line.

Figure 4. Inclusive Text or Expanded Transcription

1                             9 April [1982]
2  Dear Dick
3     Another week in the life of the author of the ADE
4  "Guide": one blizzard (Tuesday) and one lunch with a
5  member of the "Comm[itt]ee. on the Manual" (Wednesday).[1]
6     I've begun ⟨nagging⟩ to nag members of the Executive Sub-
7  Comm[ittee]. to make up their minds about the date for our
8  planning meeting in Bloomington. Chairman Dave N. has his
9  summer school teaching schedule to consider. Dave C. may be
10  going to Italy. Paul S. doubtless has vacation plans.
11     I'll state once again that *editing* documents is a lot more fun
12  than *writing* about editing them. There are only so many ways
13  to say "the responsible editor should. . . ." More and more
14  frequently I must restrain myself from typing, "Look, fellow
15  editors, this is the way to do it, and don't give me any [. . .]
16  arguments!"[2] I realize that this isn't the tone we should strive
17  for.
18     I'll let you know when the date for our Bl'ton meeting is
19  set—I hope that D[on]. C[ook]. can be one of our party, but
20  that must be left to chance. I can hardly blame him for finding
21  an excuse to miss two days' worth of arguments about the
22  history of the angle bracket as a symbol for authorial
23  cancellations.
24     More seriously, there could be disagreement among
25  members of the Sub-Comm[ittee]. ⟨Chesnutt⟩ One member
26  will argue that the entire book should be written in
27  FORSAN. ⟨Nordloh⟩ Another may insist that the book is
28  written too simplistically—that it isn't intended for those ⟨too⟩
29  so ignorant that they confuse a stemma with a lemma.
30     I wish that you could be there to play peacemaker. I'll keep
31  you advised of all developments. Any advice-in-advance you
32  give will be welcomed—and, perhaps, heeded.
                                  Yours in a quandary—
                                  Mary-Jo

[1]This paragraph was initially the second paragraph in the body of the letter. The author has marked it for insertion at the text's beginning.

[2]The phrase ", and . . . arguments" entered in the margin, with a guideline for its insertion at this point.

1       9 April] entered at the foot of the letter in the MS

3       "Guide"] ~ ⟨,⟩

5       Comm[itt]ee.] Comm$^{ee}$; the] ye

6       the] ye

7       for] ⟨of⟩ ↑ for ↓

11      a lot] a ⟨h⟩ lot

14      Look,] ~ ∧

15–16  lemma. and don't] "and . . . arguments" added in margin, with a guideline directing its insertion after *it*.

16      that this] that ↑ this ↓

20      can] ⟨co⟩ can

28      those so ignorant] those ⟨so⟩ ↑ ⟨too⟩ ↓ ignorant

29      that they confuse] to ↑ that they ↓ confuse

30–31  lemma. I wish] "I wish . . . peacemaker" originally part of the preceding paragraph, with authorial markings for a new paragraph. "I'll keep. . . ." was originally the beginning of a new paragraph, with authorial markings for a "run-on."

31–32  you give] you ↑ give ↓ welcomed—] welcomed ↑—↓

## VI. Clear Text

The term *clear text* has traditionally described the preferred method for presenting the critically edited texts of published works. The texts themselves contain neither critical symbols nor footnote numbers to indicate that an emendation has been made or that some detail has been omitted. All such emendations and alterations are reported in back-of-book tables whose citations are keyed to the page and line numbers of the new printed edition. With the publication of the *Hawthorne Notebooks* in the early 1970s, however, clear text was applied to CEAA-approved volumes of writings not intended for publication—the private writings that had hitherto received more conservative textual treatment, and the decision was soon imitated by editors of the *Howells Letters,* the *Thoreau Journals,* and portions of the *Harold Frederic Correspondence.* Each series won CEAA/CSE endorsement, even though the CEAA and CSE guidelines of the day urged the adoption of more inclusive methods for source texts of this kind.

While there is no official standard for the adoption of clear text in documentary editing, the experience of editors who have used the technique furnishes some useful guidelines. Elizabeth Witherell, editor of the Thoreau edition, provided these words of caution in a conversation with me. She recommended that clear text for manuscript source texts of private writings be used "only when a great deal of editorial emendation is required, or when almost none at all is necessary." This apparent contradiction is easily explained. Thoreau revised many journal passages for use in lectures, essays, and books, so a page of his manuscript may contain two distinct versions of the same passage: Thoreau's original jottings in pen, along with his later revisions of these entries in pen and pencil. Although an ingenious book designer might have improvised a method to present a single typographic facsimile, diplomatic transcription, or inclusive text giving simultaneous access to both stages of composition, the reader would be hard-pressed to make sense of the results. The Thoreau editors chose to present a clear text of the earliest version of the journal entries and to complement each volume with tables of emendations (applying only to that first version), as well as with tables of significant variants between the earlier and later stages of the journals' physical contents. The editors did not pretend that their reading text conveyed all that could be learned from the manuscript journals; they simply provided a legible and reliable text of one of the two versions that exist in the same document.

At the other extreme, Witherell suggested that clear text is a practical option for documents that are themselves close to final versions of the documents that they represent. Neatly inscribed recipients' copies of letters, fair copies of literary manuscripts or of political treatises—each of these is clean enough to serve for clear text. In each instance, the extent of editorial intervention is so slight and of so little substantive importance that the editor can responsibly assign the record of such emendations to a back-of-book table.

The editor who weighs clear text as an option must carefully consider the requirements of the text and its prospective readers, for this treatment can suppress important inscriptional details or distort the documentary value of the resulting editorial text. If a writer customarily sent correspondents copies of letters containing canceled passages, a clear text of such letters would seriously distort the document by omitting such cancellations from the reading text. The edition's readers would be denied immediate access to words, phrases, and paragraphs that were easily read by the letters' recipients. Similarly, if a writer consistently dispatched carelessly proofread letters in which words were inadvertently omitted, a clear text that supplied the missing words silently would be a disservice. In both cases, the editor would have gone too far, and clear text would not be a practical and honest solution.

Before choosing clear text, an editor should analyze the emerging patterns of emendation and details of transcription that would have

Figure 5.   Clear Text

| | |
|---|---|
| 1 | 9 April 1982 |
| 2 | Dear Dick |
| 3 | Another week in the life of the author of the ADE "Guide": |
| 4 | one blizzard (Tuesday) and one lunch with a member of the |
| 5 | "Committee on the Manual" (Wednesday). |
| 6 | I've begun to nag members of the Executive Sub-Committee to |
| 7 | make up their minds about the date for our planning meeting in |
| 8 | Bloomington. Chairman Dave Nordloh has his summer school |
| 9 | teaching schedule to consider. Dave Chesnutt may be going to |
| 10 | Italy. Paul Smith doubtless has vacation plans. |
| 11 | I'll state once again that *editing* documents is a lot more fun |
| 12 | than *writing* about editing them. There are only so many ways to |
| 13 | say "the responsible editor should. . . ." More and more |
| 14 | frequently I must restrain myself from typing, "Look, fellow |
| 15 | editors, this is the way to do it, and don't give me any |
| 16 | arguments!" I realize that this isn't the tone we should strive for. |
| 17 | I'll let you know when the date for our Bloomington meeting |
| 18 | is set. I hope that Don Cook can be one of our party, but that |
| 19 | must be left to chance. I can hardly blame him for finding an |
| 20 | excuse to miss two days' worth of arguments about the history of |
| 21 | the angle bracket as a symbol for authorial cancellations. |
| 22 | More seriously, there could be disagreement among members |
| 23 | of the Sub-Committee. One member will argue that the entire |
| 24 | book should be written in FORSAN. Another may insist that the |
| 25 | book is written too simplistically: that it isn't intended for those |
| 26 | so ignorant that they confuse a stemma with a lemma. |
| 27 | I wish that you could be there to play peacemaker. I'll keep |
| 28 | you advised of all developments. Any advice-in-advance you give |
| 29 | will be welcomed—and, perhaps, heeded. |

Yours in a quandary—
Mary-Jo

to be relegated to back-of-book records in a clear text edition of the source. If these fall into the categories that the inclusive editor would ordinarily report within the text (legible canceled passages with substantive implications, editorially supplied material for a mutilated document, and so on), then the source is not an appropriate candidate for clear text. If the evolving patterns fall into the categories that inclusive editors normally consign to the back-of-book record or emend silently, however, the source is clearly a perfect subject for clear text methods.

And clear text is justifiable in a scholarly edition only when that reading text will be accompanied by a full record of editorial emendations and suppressed inscriptional details or a companion facsimile. Editorial intervention of any degree can be justified only when readers are provided with a complete report of what they have been denied by the editor's decision to be exclusive rather than inclusive.

Figure 5 provides the clear text version of the sample document shown in figure 1. It is followed by samples of the textual record that might accompany it, one using symbolic methods and the other the descriptive approach to such a record.

## A. TEXTUAL RECORDS

### 1. *Symbolic Method*

The textual record for the clear text (see fig. 5) is presented in the symbolic format used by the *Howells Letters*. Editorial emendations are reported in the "lemma] manuscript reading" style, with heavy reliance on traditional textual symbols. Suppressed details of inscription are indicated without the citation of the lemma unless confusion might result from abbreviated treatment.

| | |
|---|---|
| 1 | 9 April 1982] "9 April" entered at the foot of the letter in the MS; "1982" added by the editors. |
| 3 | Guide] ~ ⟨,⟩ |
| 3–5 | This was initially the second paragraph of the body of the letter. The author marked it for insertion at this point. |
| 5 | Comm$^{ee}$ |
| 6 | ⟨nagging⟩ ↑ to nag ↓     the]ye; Sub-Comm. |
| 7 | date ⟨of⟩ ↑ for ↓ |
| 8 | Nordloh] N. |
| 9 | Chesnutt] C. |
| 10 | Smith] S. |
| 11 | a ⟨h⟩ lot |
| 14 | Look,] ~ ∧ |
| 15–16 | "and don't give me any [ . . . ] arguments" added in the margin, with a guideline directing its insertion after "*it*" |
| 17 | Bloomington] Bl'ton |
| 18 | Don Cook] D.C. |
| 19 | I ⟨co⟩ can |
| 23 | Sub-Comm. ⟨Chesnutt⟩ ↑ One member ↓ |
| 24 | ⟨Nordloh⟩ ↑ Another ↓ |
| 26 | ⟨so⟩ ↑ ⟨too⟩ ↓ ignorant to ↑ ⟨that they⟩ ↓ confuse |

27–28  "I wish . . . peacemaker. I'll keep . . . of all developments."
Originally, "I wish . . . peacemaker" was the concluding sentence of the preceding paragraph. The author marked it to
begin the letter's last paragraph and marked the following
sentence to "run on" as part of that paragraph.

28  ↑ give ↓
29  ↑ — ↓

## 2. Descriptive Method

This alternative textual record for the clear text (see fig.5) employs
Bowers' descriptive method of details of inscription (see above, pp.
154–55), which employs the following abbreviations:

*ab.* = above    *del.* = deleted    *interl.* = interlined
*aft.* = after    *insertd.* = inserted

1        9 April 1982] "9 April" entered at the foot of the letter
3        " Guide"] comma *del. aft.* Guide
3–5      This was initially the second paragraph of the body of the
         letter. The author has marked it for insertion at this point.
5        Committee] Comm^ee
6        to nag] *interl. ab. del.* "nagging"; the Executive Sub-Com-
         mittee] ye Executive Sub. Comm.
7        for] *interl. ab. del.* "of"
8        Nordloh] N.
9        Chesnutt] C.
10       Smith] S.
11       lot] *aft. del.* "h"
14       Look,] ~ ∧
15–16    and . . . any arguments] *insertd.* in margin with illegible can-
         cellation *aft.* "any"
17       Bloomington] Bl'ton
18       Don Cook] D.C.
19       can] *aft. del.* "co"
23       Sub-Committee] Sub-Comm.; One member] *interl. ab. del.*
         "Chesnutt"
24       Another] *interl. ab. del.* "Nordloh"
26       so . . . confuse] *del.* "too" *ab. del.* "so"; "that they" *interl.*
         *ab.* "to"
27–28    I wish . . . . of all developments.] Originally, "I wish . . .
         peacemaker" was the concluding sentence of the preceding
         paragraph. The author marked it to begin the letter's last

paragraph and marked the following sentence to "run on"
as part of that paragraph.

28      give] *interl. aft.* "*you*"

29      —] *interl.* with caret


## VII. Conclusion: Electronic Publication and Textual Methods

Electronic publication of facsimiles or editorial transcriptions of source texts broadens the choices open to editors and users of these editions. Digitally scanned images of the sources can conveniently be paired with a variety of parallel texts. Hypertext links, for instance, allow the user access to the image of the source as well as a machine-readable clear text transcription that might serve the needs of a novice, with links to a textual record that notes details of inscription and a diplomatic transcription that might serve an advanced student. Of the samples offered above, for instance, the electronic edition might link versions of figures 1, 3, and 5. An additional step might be required if an editorial transcription is transmitted over the Internet rather than published in the self-contained environment of a CD-ROM. Internet dissemination might require further descriptive tagging, using a standard such as the Standard Generalized Markup Language (SGML) in place of the editor's own textual symbols and any codes imposed by the word-processing software the editor has used (see chapter 9).

Two sessions at the annual meeting of the Association for Documentary Editing in October 1995 focused on electronic editions: "Electronic Editions (I): What Should They Look Like?" and "Electronic Editions (II): Works in Progress." One work in progress described was an electronic archive of approximately 3,000 digitized images of William Blake's illuminated manuscripts, paintings, drawings, and engravings. The editors of the Blake Archive are applying the principles of documentary editing to creating a visual concordance that makes the material available to scholars in new ways. They are also formulating new rules of practice for Internet and CD-ROM publication that other editors working in these media may find useful.

Even with the newest technology, the oldest rules apply. The source text, likely audience, and publishing medium will dictate the choices new editors will make concerning their editions' textual presentation, and there are cautionary lessons to be drawn from earlier enterprises. The sample texts presented here can offer a few lessons.

The fact that in my 1982 letter, I used the thorn as shorthand in drafting correspondence is of some interest, but it could easily be reported in a general statement on my style, without the need to reproduce every such symbol as "ye" or "[th]e" or to supply a textual note every time the thorn appears. The treatment of revisions and substitutions in the clear text, however, conceals not only changes in wording and tone but also factual information, such as the identities of the committee members to whom I referred. In each text, the conventions peculiar to the editorial method used show their own virtues and limitations.

The history of these editorial methods provides even more important lessons. Boyd and Butterfield, for instance, grounded their justification of expanded transcription on the assumption that microform facsimiles of their source texts would be available to the public. However, no such comprehensive facsimile edition of Jefferson's papers or those of the Adamses (beyond the family's personal archive) has been published or is now contemplated, and this accounts for much recent criticism of these editions. Boyd and Butterfield erred, too, in assuming that their readers would understand the reasons for the editorial policies they adopted. No editor is justified in automatically adopting conventions or policies of emendation used by a colleague. The textual methods of an edition must be designed to suit the manuscript or printed materials that provide source texts for that edition. "Generally accepted," "traditional," and "time-honored" are adjectives that should not be used to justify the adoption of any editorial practice. In choosing textual methods, each editor must start afresh, making decisions based on the needs of the edition's audience and on the peculiarities of its source texts.

## SUGGESTED READINGS

The most valuable discussions of editors' choices of one textual method over another appear in the introductions to the editions themselves. Much of this material has now been collected in *Editing Historical Documents: A Handbook of Practice,* edited by Steven B. Burg and Michael E. Stevens (Madison, Wisc., 1997), which is an invaluable complement to *A Guide to Documentary Editing.* An earlier attempt to survey a wide variety of methods is G. Thomas Tanselle's "The Editing of Historical Documents" (*Studies in Bibliography* 31 [1978]: 1–56, reprinted in his *Selected Studies in Bibliography* [Charlottesville, 1979]), an essay that should be read in conjunction with his more recent "Textual Scholarship" (in *Introduction to Scholarship in Modern Languages and Literatures,* edited by Joseph Gibaldi [New York, 1981]). An interesting example of the modern application of different methods to the same source text can be seen in the Franklin Papers edition of *The Auto-biography of Benjamin Franklin* (New Haven, 1964) and in J. A. Leo Lemay and P. M. Zal's genetic text of the same work (Knoxville, Tenn., 1981).

An interesting summary of the arguments concerning the responsibility of editors of private source texts appears in *CEAA Newsletter* 3 (June 1970): 16–21. And Hilary Jenkinson's "The Representation of Manuscripts in Print," *London Mercury* 30 (September 1934), is worth rereading, if only for its reminder to editors: "It is possible to make the path too smooth." Documentary editors have confined their remarks on the use of symbols or descriptive notes for textual problems in unpublished writings largely to the introductions to volumes in which such symbols or notes are employed; many of these are collected in Burg and Stevens' *Handbook of Practice*. For this field, the *Handbook* provides a survey of practices that compares with G. Thomas Tanselle's analysis of methods for published literary works in "Some Principles for Editorial Apparatus," *Studies in Bibliography* 25 (1972): 41–88 (reprinted in his *Selected Studies in Bibliography*).

I. The symbols of classical scholarship were standardized at a conference in Leiden in 1929, and their forms are summarized in the pamphlet *Emploi des signes critiques; disposition dans les éditions savantes de textes grecs et latins: Conseils et recommandations,* by J. Bidez and A. B. Drachmann (Paris, 1932; rev. ed. by A. Delatte and A. Severyns, Brussels, 1938). For examples of textual symbols in the Malone Society's Reprints series, see *John A Kent and John A Cumber* (London, 1923) and *Believe as You List* (London, 1927).

III. In addition to the essays cited in the text, the student of descriptive textual annotation should see Joel Myerson's review essay *"The Autobiography of Benjamin Franklin:* A Genetic Text" in *Newsletter of the Association for Documentary Editing* 4 (May 1982); and Fredson Bowers' comments on Myerson's remarks in a letter to the editor of the newsletter in September 1982.

VII. Readers who wish to anticipate the discussion of SGML tags for documentary sources should consult Peter Robinson's excellent pamphlet, *The Transcription of Primary Textual Sources Using SGML,* Office for Humanities Communications Publications, No. 6 (Oxford, 1994).

# CHAPTER VI

## General Rules and Their Exceptions

Although American documentary editors have worked hard to create guidelines for the creation of documentary editorial texts for almost every form of recorded evidence, situations do arise in which editors must admit defeat. After designing an editorial technique appropriate to the bulk of the sources for an edition, editors follow that technique until they encounter a situation in which the standard documentary formula of "one source equals one editorial text" cannot apply. Whenever the equation proves invalid, they turn to other traditions for appropriate solutions. Yet even here they tend to apply such borrowed techniques conservatively, pointing out to their readers where editorial judgment or guesswork has been employed rather than concealing that fact in the name of elegance or readability.

### I. Conservative Patterns of Emendation

In recent years, a distinct pattern in the choice of editorial method has appeared. As a practical matter, the chosen method should, of course, be the one that best serves the majority of the sources being edited, so that readers will be spared unnecessary announcements of exceptions to the editorial rule. But in the past forty years, American editors have also learned that conservative emendation is more effective than liberal emendation.

Interestingly, a recent survey of veteran editors revealed that nearly all had adopted less intrusive editorial policies than the ones announced in their original statements of editorial methods. It is no longer possible to find editors who endorse without question the practices sanctioning liberal editorial intervention commonly accepted a decade or two ago. G. Thomas Tanselle's 1978 evaluation of the methodology of documentary editions prompted some to reexamine their methods, but most editors who revised their methods did so on the basis of their day-to-day experience. Once again, this underscores the point that no statement of principles is likely to cover all the issues and problems to be encountered in any documentary edition and that the fledgling editor is well advised to examine in detail the practices of a wide range of editions before launching a new documentary project. In particular, the lessons of editors who modified their method in midstream are instructive. The best-known example of evolving editorial methods is probably the Mark Twain project, but the experience of other editors is equally helpful.

Among literary series, the first volume of the *Howells Letters* was emended far more heavily than any other number in the series. In part, this is because Howells himself standardized his own letter writing style as he approached middle age; the later source texts simply needed less emendation. But the frequency of emendation also decreased as the editors themselves grew more accustomed to Howells' usage. Patterns of punctuation or spelling that appeared odd or ambiguous in the early years of the project no longer seemed to need correction or explanation, because they had become familiar to the project's staff. Historical editions, too, are not without their noticeably modified editorial methods. From its inception, the *Ratification of the Constitution* series gave conservative, almost diplomatic treatment to certain documents (such as government records), labeled "LT" to indicate a literal transcription of the source. Other materials in the project, such as private correspondence, diary entries, and the like, were heavily emended in one of the most liberal applications of expanded transcription on record. As the project continued, this dual standard of textual treatment became increasingly unsatisfactory and was abandoned in favor of a single general policy described in volume 13 of the series: "With only a few exceptions all documents are transcribed literally." When the Woodrow Wilson editors reached volume 31, they provided a revised introduction to explain to readers that they had come to follow an increasingly rigorous adherence to the rule of *verbatim et literatim*. The *Henry Laurens Papers*, once an example of expanded transcription, now present text in near diplomatic form. The *Franklin Papers* editors' textual policies, while still far from literal or diplomatic transcription, have become self-consciously more conservative in the past decade.

## A. TEXTS WITH NONSTANDARD ENGLISH

From the beginning, one group of editors ignored the temptation to emend or "improve" their source texts—those who dealt with the records of less-educated people. In recent decades historians and historian-editors have become sensitive to the significance of the evidence available in the writings and records of the poorly educated. Political, social, and economic historians now focus on the less educated as well as on the literate elite in our society, and the documentary records of such groups and individuals are the subject of scholarly editing as well as general scholarly interest.

It should be no surprise that the methods employed in editions such as the papers of black Abolitionists and Southern freedmen differ from those designed to serve the correspondence of Adams and Jefferson. Editors of the traditional statesmen's papers are concerned with documents that fall within the realm of conventional scholarly research. Source texts outside that tradition demand different methods. The methods of emendation and normalization used in the earliest historical papers projects were selected with an eye to illuminating the writings of individuals who were not merely literate but exceptionally well educated. As newer editorial projects confronted the texts of documents that recorded the words and thoughts of the ill-educated, even the wholly illiterate, they discovered that these traditional conventions were unsatisfactory. The documents demanded different methods and even different skills. Randall M. Miller pointed out in his instructive 1985 essay, "Documentary Editing and Black History," that the evaluation of historical documents generated by the African American experience might require expertise in fields as diverse as cultural anthropology, folklore, linguistics, and musicology.

The imposition of normalized punctuation, for instance, is based on the assumption that a source text's author understands the functions of such marks and that he or she would approve such repunctuation if given the chance to be his or her own editor. This assumption was articulated by Julian Boyd: "This expanded text represents the kind of clear and readable form that Jefferson himself would have used for a document intended for formal presentation in print" (*Jefferson Papers*, 1:xxxi). But correction of spelling errors in the writings of an ill-educated writer imposes a false sense of authorial intentions. Worse still, it can destroy much of the special value inherent in documents inscribed by the semiliterate—the phonetic rendering of colloquial language and dialect that make such documents useful to philologists and cultural historians.

In many instances, the records of the less educated suffered nonauthorial normalization long before they became the subjects of scholarly editing. Illiterate individuals had no choice but to dictate letters or memoirs to second parties, who imposed their own notions of correct spelling and punctuation and even syntax upon them. The only way to emend such a dictated source text to bring it closer to authorial intent would be to make it *less* correct syntactically and to introduce phonetic misspellings to match the author's dialect. Luckily, no editor has been tempted to follow such a course. Documents dictated by the illiterate, like documents inscribed laboriously if incorrectly by the semiliterate, must be allowed to stand, even though they may reflect a degree of elegance superimposed by the amanuensis and completely foreign to the authors themselves.

## B. OTHER SPECIAL CASES

A flurry of debate over special requirements for editing the writings of women appears to have ended in agreement that the author's sex in and of itself does not dictate special methods in establishing a text. It is the subject's level of education or habits and patterns of writing and the needs and expectations of the edition's audience that should mold such methods. The author's sex or social class, however, may influence the edition's criteria for selection, the scheme of organization, and the plan for nontextual, informational annotation. For one edition, the sex of a document's author did dictate *who* would do the editing. Donald Reiman, whose *Shelley and His Circle* edition includes correspondence of both men and women, commented: "[A]mong the contexts in which sex affects texts are not only the historical situations of the authors being edited but also the historical context in which modern editors and their readers live." As a result, it became the practice at the *Shelley* project to "assign major essays on the women in the circle to women" ("Gender and Documentary Editing," p. 353).

The sermons and lectures of a popular speaker may bring special problems to later editors' lives not only because of their eventual publication (and translation into another medium) but because their author probably delivered the same sermon or lecture dozens of times to different audiences. This situation faced the editors of Emerson's sermons, whose manuscript versions bear substantial undated authorial revisions. After analyzing the patterns of these emendations, the editors discovered that sermons Emerson delivered only once carried no more signs of authorial second thoughts than those given again and again. They concluded that it was Emerson's pattern to make all revisions prior to the first delivery of any sermon, and their edited texts treat each manuscript sermon as the sum of Emerson's original intentions. Their volumes present these sermons in clear text, with their genetic elements in back-of-book textual apparatus.

## II. DOCUMENTARY PROBLEMS WITH TEXTUAL SOLUTIONS

Even the editor following the most conservative general policies on emendation will encounter situations in which one source text will not provide one editorial text. The summary of methods of inscription and forms of documentary records in chapter 4 hints at some of the occasions on which the documentary editor must borrow the methods of specialists in related fields. Any editor of orally communicated texts, for instance, may have to deal with the theoretical implications of dissonant witnesses to a lost archetype, the central problem of the classicist. Even editors spared this special form of documentary record face the possibility that the best method for editing a specific source text may be one from the tradition of critical and not documentary publication.

### A. GENETIC ELEMENTS IN SOURCE TEXTS

Any document—letter, state paper, literary work, scientific essay, laboratory model—can survive in a form that reflects the development of the author's intentions, preserving not only a final text but also the false starts, preliminary wording, and stylistic evolution of that text. Few editors can escape confronting source texts that carry intrinsic clues to their genesis. These are encountered most commonly when an editor's source text is a manuscript obviously revised during composition. An edition of a draft letter or an author's holograph corrections and additions to galley proofs or the pages of an early edition used to prepare a revised edition will demand identification of original, intermediate, and final versions of the same document.

Genetic editions of texts try to offer the reader access to more than one level of textual creation within a single inclusive page. While the term *genetic text edition* came into usage in German textual studies more than fifty years ago (see Gabler, "The Synchrony and the Diachrony of Texts," and Hay, "Genetic Editing, Past and Future"), it did not become current in American studies until the 1960s. In editing the successive draft versions of *Billy Budd,* Melville's editors adopted the term *genetic text* to describe their diplomatic transcription of the manuscripts of that work, which had been left unpublished at Melville's death. The genetic elements of the transcription were the result of their painstaking efforts to devise a system of symbols and descriptive abbreviations that would allow the reader to understand the order in which the changes were made by the author. In a single set of pages, a densely packed trail of symbols led the reader through two, three, sometimes four versions of the same passage.

The genetic text of *Billy Budd* is one of the most complicated and sophisticated products of modern scholarly editing. Simpler genetic texts have been with us since the first editor presented an inclusive or conservatively expanded text of a handwritten draft. Any editorial method that includes the use of symbols for deletions, insertions, and interlineations can present a genetic text for individual documents. Editors who eschew the use of textual symbols can instead give their readers clear texts of the final version and supply notes that permit the readers to construct their own genetic version.

## 1. Synoptic Genetic Texts

More sophisticated problems of conflation arise when the genetic stages of a document are recorded in not one but several source texts. If the variants between these preliminary versions are wide, the editor may print each document separately in parallel texts or treat each one as a distinct version. But it may be that these separately inscribed evolutionary stages of the text are so directly related that they represent a direct intellectual line of revision. In this case, the editor has the option of creating a "synoptic" text, another term and technique from classical scholarship.

This form of editing is as old as the synoptic Gospels, but the term *synoptic text* was borrowed for modern works by the editors of the James Joyce edition when they described their methods in editing Joyce's *Ulysses*. Joyce's revisions of the novel survived, not in a single draft manuscript, but in manuscript fragments, corrected galleys, and other forms. The Joyce editors combined the information contained in these separate documents to create a synthetic genetic text, a synopsis of information from several source texts combined in one new editorial text. Hans Walter Gabler, director of the *Ulysses* edition, describes their methods in "The Text as Process and the Problem of Intentionality."

The process of textual synopsis is not confined to biblical scholarship and editions of great literary works. The first volume of the *Documentary History of the Ratification of the Constitution* series includes two synoptic texts that trace the evolution of the articles of the American Constitution through the debates of the Philadelphia Convention of 1787 (pp. 271–96). The editors did not have at hand separate copies of the Constitution reflecting its wording at every stage of its consideration. Instead, they worked from four source texts: the draft constitution submitted to the Convention on 6 August 1787; the text of the Constitution as recorded in the Convention journals on 10 September; a printed copy of the report of the Committee on Style, which revised the articles between 10 and 12 September; and the text of the Constitution as adopted on 17 September. To supplement these sources, the editors analyzed James Madison's notes of debates in the Convention, records that indicated the date and nature of each revision of the frame of government.

The successive surviving versions of the Constitution, like those of Joyce's *Ulysses,* qualified as source texts for a synopsis because they were similar enough to allow the editors to draw valid conclusions about the sequence of revisions at each point. The editors reprinted the articles of the Concstitution as adopted by the Convention, thus supplying a reading text of the final stage of the evolution to parallel their synoptic texts.

Synoptic treatment of the records of deliberative political bodies is fairly common among documentary editions dealing with governmental history. The *Documentary History of the First Federal Congress: Legislative Histories* provides three volumes of legislative histories of the bills considered by the U.S. Congress, 1789–1791. They contain a calendar recording every action on a given bill or resolution, as well as transcriptions of surviving manuscript or printed sources of the texts for these measures as introduced to the Congress. Footnotes record amendments to the originals. In a few cases, when the original version of the item has vanished but its final text and a complete record of amendments survive, the editors recreated the original's text by taking the final version and adding or subtracting words or phrases recited in the amendments. In cases of such heavy editorial intervention, the recreated text is accompanied by notes clearly tracing the work involved. In other instances, when a committee report of amendments to a bill has survived, the *Legislative Histories* provide readers with both a literal transcription of the committee report and with the amendments identified in that report, reprinted as footnotes to any previous versions of the bill.

## 2. Collaborative Source Texts

The attentive reader will have noticed that the examples of synoptic genetic texts from the *Ratification* and *First Congress* projects not only draw on multiple source texts but also represent the intellectual contributions of more than one author. Editors of the records of American political and military history have long been concerned with the need to identify not merely the stages of a document's evolution but the separate authors of each revision. In recent years, editors of literary works have come to share this interest.

Source texts that represent collaboration between two or more persons are often more challenging than genetic documents by a single author, and study of such collaborations received close scrutiny and analysis in the decade following Jerome McGann's discussion of the socialization of literary texts (see Stillinger, *Multiple Authorship*). Ideally, both the identity and the specific contributions of each reviser should be recorded. Modern authors often work closely with publishers' editors, and editors employing traditional copy-text theory to construct a single text reflecting final authorial intentions face serious difficulties in such situations, for they must somehow determine which suggestions from an author's contemporary editor were imposed upon the author and which were accepted freely, perhaps with the author's thanks. If authorial intentions are the overriding criteria, the critical editor must then exclude from the new edition passages that were added without the author's full approval while retaining those to which the author gave hearty consent. The pitfalls of this approach are obvious, and attempts to impose it at inappropriate times and places have provided critics of the application of emended copy-text to modern writings with some of their most telling attacks and have led to the notion of "socialized" texts.

Editors of historical documents, especially in legislative and professional affairs, are veterans of dealing with such collaborative documents, for such documents frequently represent action by committee. A manuscript report or public paper may contain passages in the hands of two or more legislators assigned to prepare that document. The rough draft of a state paper may reflect the fact that an executive assigned its preparation to one aide, circulated the draft to other advisers, and then approved or vetoed their suggestions—leaving the record of all these actions on the same scribbled, dog-eared set of pages.

The collaborative aspects of a document's composition can often be represented quite easily if one contributor had primary responsibility for its drafting. This fact can be stated in the document's source note, and the editor can focus on additions, revisions, or deletions in other hands. Such records may be provided by using a special form of symbol enclosing such additions (e.g., "The document was originally inscribed by AB. All revisions by CD appear in the text within square brackets"). But if the collaborators' contributions are fairly equal, or if a third or fourth writer is involved, the editor must consider descriptive notes to supplement the text. Each addition, deletion, or revision might be keyed to a footnote explaining that the words or phrases in question were "added above the line by CD" or "entered by EF in space left in the MS" or "rewritten by GH." This is the method chosen by the editors of the *Eisenhower Papers* in the document discussed in chapter 4.

### 3. The Physical Presentation of Genetic Texts

In principle, electronic editions of any form of genetic text—single-source, synoptic, or collaborative—should solve many problems of presentation gracefully and effectively, but even these new solutions will demand careful thought, planning, and testing of formats. Book editions of such sources are one of the cruelest tests of an editor's ingenuity. Clearly, the choice among a truly genetic text, an inclusive text supplemented by textual notes, and a clear text is both a theoretical and a practical one. The editor will need to find the device that enables the reader to reconstruct inscriptions in the source text with the finest distinctions possible. The use of numbered footnotes with a clear text can serve this purpose, although the multiplication of superscripts necessary to record numerous significant revisions will run counter to the purposes of the editor who wishes to avoid "disfiguring" the documentary text. Obviously, clear text with a back-of-book record cannot serve the reader when the collaborative aspects of the source are central.

Some documents defy efforts to reproduce all the details of their genesis in comprehensible form: the proliferation of symbols or footnote numbers would make the result unreadable. In such cases, it has been traditional to offer the reader parallel texts of the same material. In the classic form, the two texts were truly parallel, printed in two columns on the same page or on facing pages (as in Bowers' edition of *Leaves of Grass*), but modern editors use the term and technique more broadly. The Yale University Press edition of Jonathan Edwards' *History of the Works of Redemption* intends to print a reading version of the manuscript draft of these sermons in a fairly conservative expanded transcription and to provide an accompanying microform of the original manuscripts; the volume's editor freely refers to the printed version as a "pony" that will guide the reader in the use of the microform.

The need to communicate genetic textual elements inspired much of the early investigation of electronic versions of source texts. Hypertext or hyperlink publication was an obvious supplement to or substitute for a printed text in these instances. Any editor who used word processing software with the ability to switch between documents easily saw the potential of electronic methods for linking the editorial transcription to different levels of a document's genesis.

This form of publication is a simple, effective, and logical means to the end of communicating the genetic process to a reader.

## B. MULTIPLE-TEXT DOCUMENTS

Similar treatment can be accorded multiple-text documents, a term coined by David Nordloh to describe sources inscribed in such a way that the reader could reasonably extract the texts of two or more distinct documents from the characters that appear on the same page or set of pages. In multiple-text documents, the entries on the same page are so widely separated in time, intention, and even authority that they must be viewed as separate examples of one author's writing or as examples of the writing of two or more authors. Their textual problems are distinct from those in ordinary drafts, in which authors leave records of their evolving intentions for works prior to their completion.

Notebooks used as literary commonplace books are an obvious example of this type of document. Thoreau first inscribed entries in his journals in ink. Months or even years later, he reworked many of these passages for publication, considerately making his revisions and emendations in pencil and ink that could be distinguished from the original inscriptions. The Thoreau edition provides a clear reading text of Thoreau's original entries. Textual notes in the *Thoreau Journals* reproduce only those revised passages that never achieved print publication, and the same notes can refer the reader to journal entries that served as the basis for works actually published in Thoreau's lifetime and published in other volumes of the edition.

## 1. *"Second Thoughts": Authors Who Try to Rewrite History*

While most authors of letterbooks or diaries are content to leave those documents untouched once their pages have been inscribed, there are others who cannot resist the temptation to go back to improve youthful lapses in style or delete compromising passages. Historical figures who use their years of leisure and retirement to rewrite diary entries and other portions of their personal papers can create a special form of purgatory for their editors. When these revisions were made for a published memoir, the editor can at least refer readers to an authoritative text of the final version of the material in another section of the edition or in the printed source. But when the revised sources remained unpublished in their own day, the modern editor is left with documents whose texts have been deliberately corrupted by their own creators. Providing access to such revised variant passages was a consistent problem for the editors of the Madison, Lafayette, and Washington papers.

When Madison set out to compile autobiographical material, he rewrote his own retained copies of correspondence (or recovered addressees' versions from his correspondents or their heirs), revising the pages to suit his matured notions of style and discretion and adding marginal comments to the documents. Fortunately, Madison's later emendations are usually distinguishable from his original inscriptions. When one of these "corrected" manuscripts has had to be used as a source text, the Madison editors have been able to recover the original words and marks of punctuation, and the later revisions are discussed in footnotes. This method of emendation provides the reader immediate access to the texts of letters and state papers in a form that gives them validity as documents of American political history, while the notes allow the reader to evaluate areas in which Madison felt correction or suppression was necessary to make these materials ready for publication to the world.

The Marquis de Lafayette was a more systematic memoirist. In the early nineteenth century he revised not only personal letters but also his 1779 manuscript "Memoir." These revisions were incorporated into transcribed copies that Lafayette then sent to Jared Sparks, and most of Lafayette's emendations were reflected in the published version, *Mémoires*. The Lafayette editors collated all printed versions of the *Mémoires* against the emended manuscripts to establish the pattern of the author's revisions, disregarding later revisions of the letters and the manuscript "Memoir" that were "purely stylistic." "Significant passages" deleted in the manuscripts or omitted from the printed *Mémoires* appear in the new edition within angle brackets. Any other changes deemed significant by the modern editors are treated in footnotes.

George Washington's motives in revising his early letterbooks are less clear than Madison's and Lafayette's. The volumes contained autograph copies of outgoing correspondence that Washington had laboriously inscribed during the Braddock campaign on the western frontier in 1755. Beginning some thirty years later, he began to emend the letterbooks, directing a clerk to copy these revised texts of the letters into a new set of letterbooks. All but one of the original letterbooks vanished, and few correspondents saved the letters they had received from the young Washington. For those months for which only the emended, later copies of letterbooks survived, the Washington edition had no choice but to use those as source texts. For the summer of 1755, however, they had recourse to the original letterbook, which they used as source text and supplemented with notes reproducing Washington's later notions of "improvement" as extrapolated from the later letterbooks.

One of the most remarkable recent feats in documentary editing was a volume, presenting a previously unpublished manuscript, that combined many of the problems faced by these other projects with a few unique to itself: Rosemarie Zagarri's edition of *David Humphreys' 'Life of General Washington' with George Washington's 'Remarks'.* Humphreys set out to write the earliest and only authorized biography of his former military chief. Washington provided his former aide with source materials, as well as manuscript "remarks" for his guidance. Humphreys never completed his book, although he did incorporate many passages from his draft into shorter pieces about the first president. Questions of synoptic genetic texts, multiple-text sources, and authorial second-guessing arose as Zagarri reconstructed the results from fragments now scattered physically among several repositories and intellectually among other Humphreys writings, incorporating Washington's comments in the text in angle brackets. George Billias, one of the sharpest contemporary reviewers of documentary editions of the Revolutionary era, remarked in wonder: "Incredible as it may seem, this book actually contains new material about George Washington, one of the most thoroughly researched figures in all American history" (248).

## 2. *Other Multiple-Text Documents*

Several forms of multiple-text documents may present problems in transcribing the source but do not pose deep theoretical questions. For example, a writer may have used an existing document as scratch paper for drafting another letter or report. A sheet of paper may carry a letter received by John Smith on one side and Smith's draft of his reply on the other. Some frugal eighteenth-century figures carried this practice to the extreme of drafting replies to a letter over that letter's own lines, inscribing the new draft at right angles to the old lines. Such practices result in two documents that are part of the same physical whole. Although the textual notes that describe the provenance of each item must indicate that it is physically a part of the other, no special textual problems will arise.

A common form of multiple-text document comes into existence when an author becomes a reader, making notes or comments in the margins of the reading matter at hand. While marginalia are more commonly found on printed works, some writers are equally eager to record their own comments on newly received letters or other unprinted documents. Frederick Burkhardt discusses the problem of publishing both the letters sent to Charles Darwin and the naturalist's autograph marginal remarks on these communications in "Editing the Correspondence of Charles Darwin." Here, at least, the editors could easily justify printing the comparatively brief texts to which Darwin's comments referred.

Editors faced with the more conventional form of marginalia, a subject's comments inscribed on the pages of books or articles that he or she was reading, have a greater challenge. Samuel Taylor Coleridge left behind a body of marginalia in copies of his own works as well as in books written by others, and that body of material was so complex and independently significant that his editors treated the *Marginalia* separately, in a special series of five volumes within *The Collected Works*.

### 3. Nonauthorial Emendations and Additions

In many cases, additions to a manuscript made by someone other than the author or the document's recipient may be ignored. These can include dealers' notations, symbols entered by archivists who have cataloged the materials, and notes by collectors through whose hands the manuscripts have passed. To some readers, these may seem no more an intellectual part of the document's text than an owner's signature on the flyleaf of a rare book or pamphlet, but editors should remember that to bibliographers or historians of collecting, such owners' signatures, dealers' notations, and archivists' symbols are important historical evidence. With unprinted documents and rare printed materials, such entries can be helpful in determining the item's provenance, and they should be included in the description of the source text's history. It may not be necessary to reproduce them verbatim in an authoritative edition, but readers should be alerted to their existence by a summary or description in an editorial note.

Still other categories of nonauthorial inscription require more careful notice and on occasion warrant reproduction in the edition itself. Few members of an author's family have resisted the temptation to edit literary memorabilia with pen, pencil, or scissors. Perhaps the worst offender in this category was Sophia Peabody Hawthorne, whose contributions to her husband's posthumous literary image are immortalized in the defaced notebooks and other manuscripts that she prepared for publication in her years of widowhood. Mrs. Hawthorne's activities as editor and censor had such a pervasive influence on her husband's reputation that they could not be ignored by the editors of the Centenary Edition of his works. No physical description of the notebooks would be complete without reference to Sophia's emendations and mutilation, and students of American cultural history would be ill-served by an edition that did not report them. Thus, the textual notes to the clear texts of Hawthorne's writings include detailed descriptions of Sophia's handiwork, as well as notes recording similar revisions by the Hawthornes' son Julian.

It is the degree of historical significance of any nonauthorial additions—their independent documentary value—that determines how fully they should be recorded in a scholarly edition or whether they should be recorded at all. If a writer's spouse marked the deceased's letters and papers for a print edition that was never printed, the nonauthorial emendations clearly have less importance than they would had bowdlerized texts appeared and influenced a wide reading public.

Some examples of posthumous editing by friends, relatives, and publishers can be ignored because the edited or bowdlerized printed texts that resulted have not been as influential as Sophia Hawthorne's. The editors of the *George Washington Papers,* for instance, ignore Jared Sparks' "styling" of punctuation and spelling on the pages of the Washington manuscripts entrusted temporarily to his care while he prepared his selected edition of Washington's writings. Had Sparks' Washington volumes been the only ones available to scholars and laymen in the century and a half before the inauguration of the new George Washington project, an argument could have been made for recording his emendations in the new edition. But in those intervening decades, scholars had access to the original Washington manuscripts on which Sparks based his texts. The source texts were used for several other, and better, editions of Washington's letters and papers, and the public was not left at the mercy of Sparks' version of the documentary record. If the editors of the *George Washington Papers* listed every one of Jared Sparks' "improvements" to Washington's writings, they would have to list, as well, variants in hundreds of other printed transcriptions that followed his. No useful purpose would be served.

In some ways, the treatment of such nonauthorial revisions in manuscripts is comparable to a critical editor's approach to the works of an author whose publisher demanded or imposed changes in a manuscript for the sake of literary style or public acceptance. In such instances, the modern editor must offer readers both the text that the author originally considered final and the revised version that the public actually read. When an author accepted such revisions, they bear directly on his or her sense of craftsmanship and aesthetic convictions. Even if they were imposed over the author's objections, it was they, and not the original words, that were circulated to the world and became known as that author's text. Just as the writer's original intentions form one historically significant document, so does the revised and published version that became a part of literary history through its influence on those who read it.

## C. CONFLATION

Just as a single manuscript can contain many versions of the same document or even the texts of distinct documents, two or more sources may be combined to produce a single editorial text. Few documentary editors will entirely escape the task of conflating, or combining, the elements of two or more sources into one reading text, although some of their methods of presenting the new texts may differ from those traditional to critical textual editing.

### 1. Fragmentary Source Texts

Conflation occurs most frequently when the best source text survives in fragmentary form, while less authoritative versions exist with a more complete text. It is no novelty to catalog a manuscript letter whose last page has been lost but for which a contemporary copy, later transcription, or even printed text will furnish the missing material. David Nordloh and Wayne Cutler discussed the problem of conflating fragmentary sources in the *Newsletter of the Association for Documentary Editing* in 1980 and 1982. Nordloh questioned Cutler's treatment of a letter from Andrew Jackson to James Polk for which two manuscript sources survived. The first was a draft in the hand of Jackson's secretary, revised and signed by Jackson. The second was a copy of the letter made by Polk from the version that he had actually received. Polk's copy contained a postscript added when the fair copy was made from the draft. Three editorial choices were available. Nordloh argued for clear text, in which the postscript would have been printed as part of the letter, with the change in authority indicated in a back-of-book note. An inclusive- or expanded-text editor might have printed the postscript as part of the editorial text, noting the change in authority in a footnote. Cutler chose the most conservative solution to the problem, printing only the contents of the draft as the letter's reading text, with the postscript transcribed verbatim in a note adjacent to the text. Nordloh defended his position with a discussion of the primacy of authorial final intentions. Cutler explained his own decision by analyzing the special reverence of documentary editors for their source texts.

In any documentary edition, conservative methods of conflation better suit the reader. Even if the conflated passages appear in one reading text, notes adjacent to the letter alert the reader to editorial intervention and provide easier and more convenient access to the necessary information. In clear text, without a superscript number to indicate that annotation is present, readers would be ignorant of the crucial textual and evidentiary problem at hand and the need to consult the back-of-book textual record.

When overlapping fragments of the text of the same document survive, and when each version can be considered reliable in terms of substantives if not in terms of accidentals, overt conflation of the sources into one editorial text may be preferable. The fact and location of such conflation can be indicated using numbered notes or other devices. Even here, documentary editors resist the temptation to impose a single pattern of accidentals on the resulting conflated text, although this can produce a text in which one three-paragraph section represents the author's usage in a surviving eighteenth-century manuscript, while another three-paragraph passage shows the style imposed upon the text by a late-nineteenth-century transcriber.

If all the pages of a manuscript source text survive in mutilated form as with documents damaged by fire or water or defaced by descendants or collectors, the editor may have to supply missing words or phrases at regular intervals throughout the editorial text rather than conflate the texts at a single point where one source ends and another continues. If this is a consistent problem in the edition, editors often devise a system of symbols that indicate such routine conflation. To accomplish this purpose with dozens of footnotes indicating the source of words or phrases from the supplementary source text would be needlessly intrusive. The editors of *Mark Twain's Letters* give their readers a chance to evaluate supplied material in mutilated manuscripts by providing photofacsimiles of such pages in their back-of-book textual records.

Frequent conflation may also be required when the author's drafts are routinely copied for transmittal as letters or other communications by a scribe who is less than conscientious. Some editors solve this problem by adopting a special bracket to enclose words in final versions of letters and state papers supplied from the more authoritative draft versions. Such simple devices give the reader simultaneous knowledge of authorial intentions and the text of the document as read by its intended recipient.

A remarkable instance of what might be termed "facsimile conflation" occurred when Dickinson W. Adams prepared a twentieth-century facsimile edition of *Jefferson's Extracts from the Gospels*. Jefferson arranged two compilations of New Testament texts, one known as "The Philosophy of Jesus of Nazareth" and the other "The Life and Morals of Jesus of Nazareth." While "The Life and Morals," a compilation of Greek, Latin, French, and English versions of Gospel verses, survived and was eventually preserved at the Smithsonian Institution, the "Philosophy of Jesus" collection was lost. All that remained were the two mutilated copies of the King James Version of the Gospels at the University of Virginia from which Jefferson had clipped selections and what appears to be a copy of the list Jefferson followed in removing these passages from the New Testaments. Working with photostats of intact copies of the same editions of the Gospels used by Jefferson, Adams created a new body of clipped photocopies; and annotated, indexed versions of the facsimile compilations were published as the first volume of the second series of *The Papers of Thomas Jefferson, Jefferson's Extracts from the Gospels.*

## 2. Reconciling Accounts of Independent Witnesses

In classical scholarship, the surviving witnesses to a lost archetype are usually in the form of scribal copies. Each must be collated with the others to isolate patterns of error that indicate transcriptional descent, to determine whether one or more was a copy made from an earlier and thus more reliable copy. Once this process of textual filiation is complete, variants among the witnesses are used to reconstruct the missing archetype so that the editorial text can represent the best readings provided by the imperfect witnesses.

For editors of modern documentary materials, the problem of reconciling discordant witnesses is most likely to appear when verbatim, even shorthand, accounts survive recording words communicated orally in the form of a speech or conversation. Editors who confront this textual challenge should consult the descriptions of widely differing treatments of such records in the *Woodrow Wilson Papers* (24:viii–xiii) and the *Douglass Speeches* (1:lxxv ff.). Readers who consult these discussions of editorial procedures used in the 1960s and 1970s should remember that computer-assisted collation of machine-readable transcriptions of such accounts now makes their comparison and analysis far easier and more accurate.

In both the Wilson and the Douglass series, the longest surviving verbatim account was chosen as the basic text when the editors needed to conflate variant accounts. (If nothing else, the longest report was usually made by the reporter who stayed alert after rival scribes had lost interest.) Collating each variant version against this basic text often showed that in some cases one variant was based on another. The editors could establish patterns of textual filiation and ignore those reports that were obviously the scribal descendants of another stenographic version. From that point in the editorial process, the two groups of editors followed different courses.

Once the Wilson editors identified those verbatim accounts with claims to authenticity, they isolated and analyzed every crux, or unaccountable variant between the texts. Wilson himself helped his later editors, for he often reviewed transcriptions of the shorthand reports of his speeches prepared by his personal secretary and corrected his aide's inaccurate reporting. The pattern of variants and cruxes determined the final editorial treatment of Wilson's oral texts. Variants were often comparatively minor in length, and many cruxes were easily explained in terms of the mishearing of similar spoken words or the misreading of the reporter's shorthand notes. In such cases, the Wilson editors silently combined the accurate words and phrases from two or more reports into one text. Only when variants were substantial and cruxes inexplicable did they intervene with brackets or numbered footnotes.

While the editors of Wilson's oral communications turned to the techniques of classical and literary scholarship to solve this problem, other documentary editors have performed conflations more overtly. In the *Douglass Speeches,* for instance, the editors could not afford the luxury of conflation and emendation, even with the use of a full textual record. Shorthand-based newspaper reports of Douglass's speeches contained variants that were not only cruxes (in orally transmitted documents, anomalies in reporting the same words) but also reflections of inconsistent reporting of the same passages in the speeches. Such inconsistencies resulted in one newspaper's publishing long passages, which must have taken twenty or thirty minutes to deliver, while another paper ignored this section of an oration completely.

The Douglass editors could not conflate such variant texts as gracefully as editors whose cruxes were largely confined to minor, easily explained anomalies. Whenever it was necessary to add passages to the basic text from a version that had reported a section more fully, the conflated material was added to the basic text in angle brackets, and its source indicated immediately in a note. If the basic text contained a summary of the sentences or paragraphs reported more completely in the second text, a dagger in the editorial text leads the reader to a note where the basic text's summary version is reported verbatim. (For a summary of the Douglass edition's methods, see McKivigan, "Capturing the Oral Event.")

Most editions of nineteenth-century documents follow the patterns used by the Douglass edition. It is rare to find even one complete stenographic report for a speech in this era, and the modern editor is spared the process of collating variants in two independent witnesses of comparable length and detail. Most, like the editors of the papers of Thaddeus Stevens, use the most complete and reliable report of a speech as their basic source text. Footnotes supply significant variants from other reports of the same speech, that is, different versions of text in the source text or passages omitted from the source text but included in other reports.

### III. Basic Rules for Documentary Editing

The format of the texts in the Douglass edition highlights the basic rule for transferring critical textual techniques to documentary source texts. Even when borrowing such methods, the documentary editor will let the seams of editorial tinkering show rather than mislead the reader into assuming that the emended or conflated editorial text is more documentary, more unique and integral, than it is. Editors in the literary tradition of clear texts recognize this rule as well. In the Emerson edition, for instance, clear text was used to present Emerson's *Early Lectures,* which fell within the definition of works with a final authorial intention that could be perceived. For Emerson's *Journals and Miscellaneous Notebooks (JMN)* and *Poetry Notebooks,* however, techniques were adopted that would permit the reader to recover the genetic elements of Emerson's words and phrases. And the editors modified their methods for the different needs of prose and poetry, emending some of Emerson's punctuation in the *JMN* but avoiding even this intrusion in the poetry. Ralph Orth admitted that they made this decision not only because punctuation in poetry is a far more significant editorial intrusion than in prose but because "[t]he passage of the years and the appearance of many textual editions which emended a great deal less than the *JMN* had, showed that readers could easily master a totally unimproved text" (p. 9).

### IV. "Versioning" and Documentary Editing

The current debate among literary scholars over the value of eclectic clear texts versus editorial methods that retain more "documental" elements can be instructive to the editor of historical documents that have little claim to literary merit. These discussions, quite simply, are helpful in determining just when noncritical texts serve the purposes of an audience and when critical methods are more appropriate. Donald Reiman discusses the question in his essay "'Versioning': The Presentation of Multiple Texts." Looking back over decades as an editor of the writings of *Shelley and His Circle,* Reiman remarks: "I have become less and less confident that an eclectic critical edition is the best way to present textual information to scholars." Even for literary works, he argues, the public may be better served by "enough different *primary* textual documents and states of major texts . . . that readers, teachers, and critics can compare for themselves two or more widely circulated basic versions of major texts" (p. 167). Thus he advocates "versioning" rather than "editing": giving the reading public equally convenient access to more than one version of a text rather than a single clear text from which the various prior versions would need to be laboriously reconstructed from textual notes. Electronic publication, of course, offers one form of versioning, as do parallel texts in bound volumes.

Versioning has a long and honorable history among editors of American historical documents. Paradoxically, scholars who often bristled at suggestions that critically achieved, idealized clear texts showing the *final* intentions of the authors of letters or state papers would serve any useful purpose for students of American history showed little reluctance to provide their readers with editorial reconstructions of *preliminary* versions of these same documents, recreating drafts of legislative records to show the genetic levels of their evolution and the specific contributions of collaborators and revisers along the way.

## V. Conclusion

Reconstructions of vanished early versions of historic documents remain exceptions to the general rule of conservative treatment for documentary sources. The important elements of such sources are more likely to survive the flexible application of a conservative editorial approach than more liberal editorial intervention. The reader with a taste for watchwords may be reminded of A. E. Housman's comments on the "science" and the "art" of textual criticism:

> A textual critic engaged upon his business is not at all like Newton investigating the motions of the planets: he is much more like a dog hunting for fleas. If a dog hunted for fleas on mathematical principles, basing his researches on statistics of area and population, he would never catch a flea except by accident. They require to be treated as individuals; and every problem which presents itself to the textual critic must be regarded as possibly unique. . . . If a dog is to hunt for fleas successfully he must be

quick and he must be sensitive. It is no good for a rhinoceros to hunt for fleas: he does not know where they are, and could not catch them if he did. (p. 132–33)

Documentary editors, too, must be knowing and sensitive flea hounds. The fact that their editorial products will be used as documentary evidence imposes a special responsibility. Their imaginations should be directed toward reconstructing inscribed truth, not distracting their readers with uninformed guesses. Liberal policies of editorial emendation and intervention represent the "rhinoceros" approach to documentary editing, for they miss the fleas and crush the source texts under their own weight.

## Suggested Readings

I. For arguments in favor of conservative methods in emending source texts with documentary elements see Hershel Parker's review of two Hawthorne volumes in *Nineteenth-Century Fiction* 33 (1978): 489–92; Ernest W. Sullivan, "The Problem of Text in Familiar Letters," *Papers of the Bibliographical Society of America* 75 (1981): 115–26; and G. Thomas Tanselle's "The Editing of Historical Documents," *Studies in Bibliography* 31 (1978): 1–56, as well as his remarks on the overrated virtues of readability in his essay "Literary Editing" in *Literary and Historical Editing* (ed. George L. Vogt and John Bush Jones [Lawrence, Kans., 1981]).

Excellent discussions of the many facets of the documentary records of the ill-educated can be found in John W. Blassingame's introduction to *Slave Testimony: Two Centuries of Letters, Interviews, and Autobiographies* (Baton Rouge, 1977) and in C. Vann Woodward's review essay in *American Historical Review* 79 (April 1974): 470–81.

II. Examples of clear reading texts without the use of textual symbols can be found in such editions as the *Howells Letters* and the *Franklin Papers*. For remarks on the editorial challenges raised by authorial collaboration with contemporary editors, see Tom Davis, "The CEAA and Modern Textual Editing," *The Library* 32 (1977): 61–74.

The examples of textual method and practice offered in Philip Gaskell, *From Writer to Reader: Studies in Editorial Method* (Oxford, 1978) remain among the most helpful available.

# CHAPTER VII

---

# The Mechanics of Establishing a Text and Text-Related Notes

This chapter examines some mundane but all-important practical aspects of documentary editing: establishing the documentary texts and preparing notes directly related to those texts and their sources. For some editorial projects, all work but final indexing is complete at this point. Some, like the William Henry Harrison Papers, issue nothing more than editorial transcriptions of sources with notes pinpointing the originals' locations and explaining some textual details. Others, like the John Paul Jones microfilm, may produce a series of parallel texts, with images of the originals paired with a series of transcriptions. For other editors, establishing the text and preparing text-related notes and apparatus will be part of a larger process that includes informational annotation and other nontextual apparatus.

Whatever the scope of the project's publication intentions, a sound plan for transcribing and emending documentary sources is only one side of the process by which editors prepare a text to be offered to the public. The mechanical side of that process requires just as much care, demanding relentless attention to detail at every step. The theoretical basis and the practical execution of any editorial plan must both be sound. The most elegantly designed scheme for evaluating textual problems fails if the editor is unable or unwilling to maintain proper control over transcriptions or to proofread those transcriptions accurately, and the best-designed office procedures for transcribing source texts and verifying those transcriptions are useless unless they implement a theoretically valid editorial approach to the source's accidentals and substantives.

## I. TRANSCRIPTION PROCEDURES

In the literature of documentary editing there is often confusion over what is involved in transcription. It is sometimes assumed that an editor's transcription practices—standards for rendering the source text's words, phrases, and other symbols into a typescript or printout that can be used in editing—are reflected precisely in the editorial text that is finally printed. This is seldom the case. The transcription described here is merely the initial conversion of the document's contents to an editorial working copy. This may bear little resemblance to the editorial text that is finally published.

Sources should be transcribed as literally as possible, even when the editorial text will be a heavily emended clear text. Unless that original transcription is literal, the edited transcript cannot provide a clear record of the changes made by the editors—changes that may need to be recorded in the edition's editorial apparatus. Moreover, literal transcription is far easier and more efficient for the transcriber. Translating handwritten or typed pages to typescript is challenge enough without the additional burden of mastering lists of preferred editorial emendations and acceptable corrections. And the availability of word processing equipment eliminates arguments that literal transcriptions demand costly rekeyboarding once emended for publication. Word processing allows the editor to enter such changes when editing is complete and to produce new, clean copy as needed.

If the editor wishes the initial transcripts to reflect some policies of emendation, there must be written instructions that make perfectly clear to the transcriber what forms are to be expanded, which types of misspellings are to be corrected, and so on. At projects where a permanent staff of trained transcribers is available, a considerable amount of emendation can be incorporated into initial transcription. But this is possible only if the editors prepare a carefully planned transcription guide—treating matters such as capitalization, punctuation, and the expansion or retention of contractions and abbreviations. The editor without the time or inclination to prepare such a manual should ask transcribers to type what they see in the sources.

Theory as well as practical considerations argue for a careful record of transcription methods. Even solo editors responsible for their own transcribing are well advised to keep such a log, for transcribing sources is a learning process. As the editor-transcriber moves through the collection, he or she will inevitably learn to recognize meaning in patterns of inscription that earlier seemed meaningless or baffling. Only by keeping track of their hard won knowledge of what matters and how it is to be translated can editors hope to be consistent or accurate. Drawing on her experience as the editor of Mary Shelley's letters, Betty T. Bennett has even suggested that "the transcription of the letters by the editor" be considered a "requisite standard" for all editors of correspondence. She points out that "the act of transcribing the letters may be one of the most valuable tools the editor has for reviewing the subject. In transcribing word after word, one comes as close to the act of writing the letters as possible and can consider words as they unfold into a thought" (p. 217).

Whether functioning as solo scholars or as part of larger teams, documentary editors feel no shame in admitting that they have belatedly solved the mysteries of their subjects' methods of recording sources, only pride in getting to the bottom of puzzles. A fine example of this trait is found in Robert H. Hirst's "Editing Mark Twain, Hand to Hand, 'Like All D—d Fool Printers,'" a description of the Mark Twain project's editors' ceaseless battle to unravel the system of typographical signs and conventions Samuel Clemens used in personal letters.

Perhaps the most persuasive argument for conservative initial transcription is a basic tenet of editorial philosophy: the rule of editorial responsibility. Emendation of the source text is the role of senior editors, not of the junior members of the staff who often bear the brunt of transcriptional keyboarding. Often, certain conventions of documentary publishing are reflected in the initial transcription. Before transcribing begins, the editor usually reaches decisions on retaining or suppressing such details as the position of the date and place lines in letters; the treatment of salutations, closings, signatures, and paragraph indention; the standardization of formal headings in public papers; and the treatment of addresses and endorsements. But more subtle patterns of emendation must be left to the editor who reviews the transcriptions.

When printed source texts are to be transcribed, literal methods are equally essential. The editor should remember that most accepted patterns of correction are merely conventions to make readable in print what was intelligible in an unprinted original. The printed source text already reflects many of these conventions, and any further corrections should be made with the greatest caution; their choice is a serious subject for editorial judgment. Of course, modern computer equipment facilitates later substitution of one system of codes for another, but such "global" changes are effective only if the original codes were used with perfect consistency.

## A. RULES FOR TRANSCRIPTION

"Exact copying," Edith Firth reminded her fellow editors, "involves a fair amount of hack work." There is no way to make transcribing fun, but there are some simple rules that can make the process less painful and will avoid duplication of effort and unnecessary rekeyboarding.

Whenever possible, editors should consult their publishers before transcribing begins. Modern computer typesetting makes the retention of details of inscription like raised letters or archaic symbols much easier, but different programs use different codes for these details. Employing the codes appropriate to the publisher's system from the beginning reduces the number of corrections and changes to be made later in the editorial process.

When the edition is not a single-source project and has created a database to maintain control of cataloged materials, that same tool can aid in regulating and recording the transcription process. Fields in each document's record can be used for the name of the transcriber and the dates on which transcription, emendation, and proofreading have occurred as the new translation of the source moves through the editorial process.

At the risk of insulting the reader's intelligence, I offer these commonsense rules that documentary editors have followed:

1. With manual methods, it was conventional to produce at least two copies of every transcript. The first remained a pristine version that received no emendations or corrections until sent to the printer. The second served as the editor's working copy. With computer equipment, it is still wise to retain a separate file of proofread but unemended transcriptions and to store backup disks carefully. The editor's working copy may be a separate file with a different file name or a printout made from that archival file.

Computer disks have not been tested for longevity, and even mainframe computers have been known to lose stored materials. The truly cautious editor may wish to print out two copies of each computer-created transcript, one for editorial use and the second as insurance should the computerized storage facility fail. As editorial work progresses, of course, backup files should be made for each level of revision, and disks with these files should be stored securely and separately.

2. Transcribers should be instructed to insert a special code in the transcript for material that they cannot read in the source. The editor will need to do a computer search for this code in every transcription.

3. Transcribers should give their work a preliminary review before filing the copy.

4. The physical format of the printout should reflect its intended use as working copy for an editor. Like any such manuscript, it should be double-spaced, with generous margins on all four sides.

5. The word processor's justified right-hand margin function should be turned off for the duration of any editorial project. Tran-

scriptions should introduce no new punctuation in the form of end-of-line hyphenation. Ragged right-hand margins on the typescript are a small price for accuracy.

6. If transcription can wait until the editorial collection is complete, it is often more efficient to assign each transcriber a chronological sequence of source texts or a group of topically related sources. The transcriber can thus become expert in the problems peculiar to the time period or theme in question, as well as with the correspondents involved.

## B. SPECIAL TRANSCRIPTION METHODS

The editor who aspires to the CSE emblem must adopt methods to facilitate the preparation of records of editorial emendations required by that agency. Literal transcription, of course, is a prerequisite, but the transcriber must also transcribe documents in facsimile fashion in certain areas:

1. The transcriber should preserve the end-of-line breaks of the original document so that the editor can create an accurate record of the author's end-of-line hyphenation.

2. In transcribing paginated source materials such as notebooks or journals, it is useful to transcribe not only line for line but also page for page. A new page in the document will call for a new transcription sheet so that the editor will have a convenient record of such breaks.

3. The lines of transcription, as well as their pages, should be numbered so that the editor can prepare textual notes without the use of footnote numbers. Most word processing software offers line numbering as a routine option.

## C. TRANSCRIPTION FORMS AND CONTROL

In past years, specially designed transcription sheets were almost a necessity for projects that aimed for CEAA/CSE approval. Those sheets carried line numbers along one margin, and their standardized headings included spaces in which to record the completion of special procedures demanded by the CSE: verification, or perfection of the transcript against the original document, completion of requisite proofreadings, and so on. Computer-assisted systems are a special boon here, for such details of format can be entered automatically.

Even projects without expectations of CSE approval learned the value of establishing appropriate formats for their transcriptions, and computer equipment makes the generation of special headings simple. The transcription's heading should indicate the document's title, preferably in the form that will appear in the printed edition. The transcription should also bear the project's code for the location of the original of the source text, as well as the identifying number assigned to that version. Each succeeding page of the printout should repeat the document's date and identifying source information as well as the new page number. Word processing equipment makes creation of such headers easy and routine.

Each transcription will require its own unique identifying number. For a project that has collected materials, this can be based on the accession number assigned the photocopy. When an edition is based on an archival collection, and no identifying numbers have been assigned to the sources at the beginning, the word processor can be programmed to assign sequential numbers to each transcription. Sequentially assigned transcription numbers may also be called for when source texts are transcribed from microfilm reels.

Use of automated equipment for logging transcriptions has many advantages. A system that links data in the control file allows easy and accurate transfer of that information to the transcription record for the same document. Editors can design in advance any forms they or the transcribers will need and can store these formatted headings. When needed they can be called up by a word-processing macro command. It will be easy to match transcriptions of variant versions of a text with their sources, and if several transcribers are at work simultaneously, each can access the central database to determine which sources need attention and which are already being keyboarded. Later reviews of the transcription can be indicated in fields for the initials of the editors and the duties performed, such as verification, annotation, final proofreading, rekeyboarding, and so on. Database logs of transcription and other editorial processes eliminate the need for hundreds of file drawers and notebooks in editorial projects.

Linking transcription files to the project's control file system may be the point at which many editors rethink early decisions to use flat-file databases or still less sophisticated computer methods. An edition with a few hundred transcriptions may be able to manage without a relational database, but larger ones may have to investigate one. And projects in which a number of editors and transcribers work simultaneously on transcriptions and notes may need to investigate networking equipment so that each member of the staff can access information when necessary. While access should be open to all, there should be strict control over the entry of information in the record of a document's progress through publication, to ensure consistency and currency of recordkeeping.

### D. FILING TRANSCRIPTIONS

Nonarchival editorial projects with large staffs and no facilities for networking their computer work stations often find it convenient to file a copy of each transcription's printout in the file that holds the photocopied source. This provides all concerned with easy, logical access to the transcriptions in progress. This is impossible, of course, when the source texts are original manuscripts that could be damaged by chemical reactions to the transcriptions' paper or inks or when the source texts are on microfilm. Other projects simply store hard-copy printouts of transcriptions in notebooks, file drawers, or boxes in the chronological or topical order in which they will appear in the projected publication.

## II. SOURCE OR PROVENANCE NOTES

Often the first words of their own that editors contribute to their editions are those that describe the physical realities of the sources that they edit. While a junior member of the staff may transcribe the words of a letter's address leaf or a government document's endorsement, it is the senior editor's responsibility to design the format in which such information will appear. This source note or provenance note is the one form of annotation required of every documentary edition. If the edition uses textual symbols, there may be no notes that describe details in the manuscript sources. If the edition forgoes explanations of allusions in the source, there may be no historical (or informational) footnotes. But the editor of every documentary edition, scholarly or "general," must tell readers the location of the originals of the sources used for the edition and must describe the physical form of those sources.

An edition of diaries or letterbooks may be drawn from comparatively few physically distinct sources, and the location and physical details of such sources are often detailed in an introductory note to the volume or in the back-of-book textual apparatus. Additional notes within the text cue the reader when the editorial text progresses from one source to the next. But the editor whose source texts are many and varied (such as letters recovered from a hundred manuscript repositories) must devote time to designing source notes. Customarily, such notes first state the physical form of the source.

For letters, the editor must indicate both the means of inscription (author's autograph, handwritten copy, typewriting, printing) and the version of the letter inscribed in this manner (recipient's copy, retained copy, draft, transcription). Many editors find it unnecessary to give both of these facts explicitly for each item. Instead, the introductory statement of editorial method can explain that all source texts for letters are addressees' copies unless otherwise indicated, or it may announce that all letters described as recipients' copies are in their authors' hand unless otherwise noted.

It is often necessary to adopt a series of codes indicating methods of inscription. In such systems, "A" usually represents autograph inscription, "L" letter, and "S" signed by its author. Thus, "ALS" would stand for a letter written and signed by its author. Items inscribed after the mid-nineteenth century demand a new series of symbols to indicate typewritten (usually "T"), carbon copy, and even telegram. Variations on these symbols are countless. For helpful samples, would-be editors should consult the lists of such codes in editions whose sources resemble their own both in time of inscription and archival nature. An authoritative description of these codes may be found in "Appendix: Abbreviations used by Manuscript Collectors, Curators, and Dealers," in Lewis J. and Lynn Lady Bellardo's *A Glossary for Archivists, Manuscript Curators, and Records Managers.*

The descriptive symbol for the source's documentary version is usually followed immediately by the name of the owner-institution of the original source text or by an alphabetical symbol for the repository. Most projects rely on modifications of the Library of Congress's *National Union Catalog* symbols for repositories, the same ones used in cataloging materials for the project. Many documents will require identification of the source text's collection, not merely the name of its source repository. Not only does this aid the reader in locating the original for comparison, but it can also furnish valuable information as to the document's provenance. When the collection is arranged in a single consistent order (chronologically or alphabetically by author), no further details are needed. If the collection's arrangement is in various series or is otherwise erratic, it may be necessary to provide numbers for the documents' volumes, boxes, folios, or record groups. With a computerized editorial system, this information can be imported from fields in the control file when the transcription is prepared.

The source's version and location are usually followed by certain details of inscription that are not part of the body of the document. These should be carefully described or printed verbatim in the order of their inscription. Thus, for a letter, the editor first indicates its address, then its postal markings, then any endorsement by its recipient, and finally any significant dockets by clerks or later owners of the original manuscript. The editors of the *Mark Twain Letters* took advantage of the capabilities of computer composition by using the easily recognized icon for an envelope (empty parentheses) to introduce any text drawn from such a source.

Formats and even locations of source notes vary widely. Literary editors who use extensive back-of-book records sometimes choose this area for the location of source information and even nontextual annotation, as well as for the conventional reports of editorial emendations and hyphenation lists. In the *Howells Letters* and the *Frederic Correspondence*, the source note is defined as part of the textual apparatus to be consigned to the back of the book, although informational footnotes follow each document. The *Mark Twain Letters* edition presents an abbreviated source note immediately preceding the text of each letter, giving nothing more than a code for the owner-institution of a manuscript or a short title for a letter's printed source. The back-of-book textual record for each letter carries fuller information: precise location of the source, details of physical appearance, history of the item's earlier publication, etc.

Some editors find the source note a convenient place to list enclosures in the original document when these are not printed in the edition. Other editors describe enclosures in footnotes keyed to references to the items in the body of the documentary text. The latter method fails, however, if the edition's central figure or his or her associates frequently enclosed newspaper clippings, promissory notes, or the like, without commenting on their transmittal in the covering letter or report. In such cases, the editor has no choice but to expand the source note to list these items. When the enclosures in a given document can be identified but have not survived with their covering letter or report, the editor should refer readers to a convenient and reliable source for another copy of these vanished items and summarize their contents when pertinent. The editorial comment "enclosure not identified" is a perfectly honorable form that spares readers the trouble of hunting for information the edition does not give.

Whatever the form of the source note or its location in the volume, its function, like that of all editorial apparatus, must be consistent throughout the edition. Readers must know that they will always find information on the source's manuscript version and location in (a) an unnumbered source note preceding the document or its historical annotation, (b) the first numbered footnote appended to the document, or (c) the first element of information in a back-of-book textual apparatus for the item. The information in these notes must be presented uniformly, using the same codes and the same sequence of information each time. There is no room for creativity in this part of the editorial apparatus, as variation will only confuse the reader.

## III. Transcriptions as Working Copy

When the time approaches for a group of transcriptions to receive editorial attention, it is necessary to provide hard-copy printouts rather than expect that proofreading and annotation can be conducted on an on-screen image. Normally mild-mannered editors have been known to come nearly to blows over whether these transcriptions should be placed in notebooks or kept in file drawers. In truth, the best method is the one that suits the individual editor and edition. Some find it convenient to separate each transcript from its neighbors by a sheet of tinted paper, this leaf to be used by the editor in drafting annotation. Whatever the method chosen, each transcription should be accompanied by some sort of separate annotation sheet or other convenient place for special queries or cautions concerning the source texts to which they refer. On this sheet the transcriber can remind the editor that the source text was an enclosure in another item or indicate special reasons for any apparent novelties in treatment. Again, word processing makes the design of special headings for such annotation sheets a simple matter.

### A. ESTABLISHING THE EDITORIAL TEXTS

The initial transcriptions must be reviewed and reviewed again to ensure that they meet the standards of a documentary series. Mastery of the following terms and techniques is essential:

1. *Proofreading* traditionally indicates oral proofreading involving two or more people, in which one member of the editorial staff "holds" the newer version of the text while the second member of the team reads aloud, word for word, or letter for letter in an old-spelling edition, and every punctuation mark from the earlier textual version on which the later transcription, galley proof, or page proof is based. Thus, when proofreading a source text's initial transcription, one editor reads aloud from the source text while the second follows the characters on the typescript.

2. *Visual collation* occurs when a single editor compares two versions of the text visually. To increase accuracy, it is customary to place a ruler or other straight-edged device under each line in both

versions so that one's eye will not accidentally skip an inscribed, typed, or printed line in either copy.

3. *Mechanical collation* requires a mechanical collating device that can detect variants between two printed texts presumed to be identical. The earliest machine of this kind, the Hinman Collator, made possible the convenient collation of sample copies from each printing of a published work. CSE editors later expanded the use of machine collation to check corrected page proof against unbound gatherings for their editions. Hinman collators are no longer manufactured, and their only successor is Randall McLeod's Portable Collator. Mechanical collation today is more likely to take the form of the more accurate electronic collation, in which two machine-readable versions of an edition's text or notes are compared by computer.

4. *Verification* means checking the accuracy of editorial transcriptions made from photocopied source texts against the originals for each text or checking the accuracy of the contents of informational annotation. Verification of texts may have to consist of a visual collation, although team proofreading is preferable. Verification of quotations in such notes follows the edition's general policies for proofreading or visual collation of documents printed in their entirety. The verification of other elements in the notes should always be performed by someone other than the original annotator.

Some of the terms and practices described above refer to processes employed by editors in the CEAA/CSE tradition. Editors without such aspirations can ignore some of these stipulations, but they should not ignore the reasons for their existence or the lessons of the experience of editors outside the CSE tradition who have employed other methods.

1. No one denies that team proofreading is a more effective insurance against error than visual collation. It is especially useful in the transcription of nonprinted source texts, for oral proofreading ensures that the person who reads aloud (preferably the senior editor responsible for the edition's consistency) will not be influenced by the interpretation of the transcriber, even when a solo editor was the transcriber. Whenever the oral reading produces a character, word, or phrase at variance with the transcription, the editor will naturally pause to reevaluate his or her interpretation; but that reassessment should come with a fresh eye, uninfluenced by what someone else has seen in the source text.

For printed source texts, the differences in accuracy between proofreading and visual collation may be less marked, for fewer instances of subjective interpretation will arise. But any veteran of the process can attest that the visual collation of printed sources easily leads to skipping lines in either the source or its transcription. And those who have experimented with both methods report that oral proofreading is far less tiring to the eye (although not, obviously, to the voice) than visual collation, where editors must continuously switch their field of vision from primary to secondary textual version while remembering what they have just seen.

Considerations of time and staff size often make impossible the number of independent proofreadings the editor might wish for projects that have externally produced galley proofs and page proofs. For projects that must compromise on the matter of independent, team proofreadings, the use of cassette tape recorders offers a useful supplement. The member of the team reading from the source can record that part of the proofreading process at his or her convenience, while the second team member can check those recorded, spoken words against the transcription or galley version later. Two or more staff members may do such checking against the same tape, thus producing semi-independent proofreading sessions. Tape-recorded proofreading has an advantage beyond that of easing scheduling problems. Any member of the team can interrupt proofreading when voice or eyes begin to falter and return to the task later without inconveniencing a colleague.

2. Even when the editorial text will not receive a number of multiple formal proofreadings, the editor should perform at least one proofreading against the source text. This should be done as late as possible in the editorial process, preferably immediately before copy is formatted for printing. This rule merely recognizes the fact that editors become progressively more familiar with the peculiarities of their source texts, and in many cases the preparation of informational annotation will make the source more intelligible. Proofreading against the source text immediately after transcription will be markedly less accurate than proofreading performed weeks or months later.

3. Ideally, all transcriptions should be perfected against the originals of their source texts, not merely against photocopied versions, but this is often impractical. When it is not feasible, the edition's introduction should make this omission clear. Whenever verification of a given document or group of documents is performed by someone other than one of the editors, this fact should also be noted. Verification of transcriptions against originals is required of editions aspiring to CSE approval.

4. Traditionally, some editors have preferred to proofread or collate galley proofs of documentary texts against the source texts in-

stead of against transcriptions. This practice offers the editor a last chance to catch errors of interpretation or mistranscription. Editors who adopt this method usually do so only if the same kind of proofreading has been applied to the printer's copy before it was sent to the compositor. Publishers do not look kindly on the long lists of author's alterations to galley proofs that could otherwise arise from the technique. Computer systems have so revolutionized American publishing, however, that many editors would be hard pressed to define "galley proofs," and some editorial projects are themselves the producers of the page proofs that go to the press's production department.

5. Proofreading should be supplemented by visual collation and simple "reading for sense" of both documentary texts and annotation. Transcriptions, printer's copy, galleys, and page proof should be read (not only proofread) by as many people as possible. If a project's staff is a small one, it is wise to enlist professional colleagues as reviewers of the edition.

## B. BACK-OF-BOOK TEXTUAL NOTES

For many editors, textual responsibility does not end with proofreading and perfecting the editorial reading text. Whenever an edition relegates all or part of its record of emendations or details of inscription to the back of the book, the editor must establish an accurate reporting system for that apparatus as early as possible. Even though these records will be checked again and again, the possibility of error is reduced substantially if their format is established in advance.

The process of such reporting may begin with the transcriber. If instructed to keyboard only final authorial intentions in letters, journals, or draft works, the transcriber must also initiate a record of what is omitted—authorial deletions or interlineations or nonauthorial contributions in the source text. Word-processing equipment provides the luxury of keying the deleted or interlineated material within a set of tags reserved for each detail of inscription, for instance "<int>" and "</int>" for the beginning and end of interlined material instead of creating some physically separate file of notes or cards. When an edition has already established the method by which such details will be reported (that is, through symbols, narrative description, descriptive abbreviations, or a combination of these methods), the transcriber can enter remarks in their proper predetermined form.

When the editor reviews the transcriptions, the process of correcting minor authorial errors or slips of the pen begins. Once, changes such as suppressed inscriptional details had to be recorded on index cards with references to the transcription's page and line number. Editions that provided separate records of inscriptional details and editorial emendations had to distinguish between the two groups from the moment record keeping began. Word processing equipment eliminates such dual record keeping, for the editor can designate separate codes for each sort of textual record in advance, and the appropriate codes can be entered for each note.

No matter what their policies in reporting emendations and inscriptional details, all CSE editors traditionally have supplied one kind of textual record in the back of the book—the report of ambiguous end-of-line hyphenations. This report lists all such ambiguous authorial hyphenations (possible compound words whose end-of-line division coincides with the position of the hyphen) in the source as well as any new ambiguous hyphenations introduced in a modern printed edition. Such a record allows scholars to quote accurately from the new text. To identify such ambiguities in the source, the editor can refer both to dictionaries contemporary to the document's inscription and to the author's customary usage. Most projects create an in-house record of their author's preferences in hyphenating specific compounds. Complete consistency is too much to expect, but useful patterns emerge. Obviously, keeping such a lexicon in a computer file expedites processing of the entries, and patterns can be recognized earlier.

Once the editor has established that line-end hyphenation occurs at a point where the author would ordinarily have hyphenated a compound, that hyphen is marked in the transcription for retention in the print edition should typesetting place the word in the middle of the line. The Thoreau edition streamlined the scope of its hyphenations by forgoing a justified, or consistently even, right-hand margin in printed volumes of Thoreau's private writings. Thus, no new hyphens were added when the documentary texts were typeset, and the Thoreau editors needed to report only the retention or omission of ambiguous line-end hyphens that appeared in the source texts themselves. Editors whose editions employ justified right-hand margins in their editions will still need to check galley proofs and page proofs (or their electronic equivalents) for new and potentially misleading hyphens.

Since all such back-of-book textual records are keyed to typeset lines, not to footnote numbers within the texts, the final preparation of their contents must await page proofs from the compositor or the project's own desktop publishing system. Work on these lists will have begun far earlier, and records of emendations and inscriptional details can be keyboarded and proofread well ahead of time. The editor should first devise a format for such reports, generally one in which the first column for each entry in a list bears a reference to the line and page of the transcription or printer's copy. After page proofs are reviewed, new page-line references to the print edition can be substituted.

Editors should remember, too, that they are responsible for making their textual records easier for readers to use, not only easier for editors to compile. When an edition is a documentary one, readers are best served by having as much pertinent textual information as possible easily available, either within the text or in adjacent footnotes. When back-of-book records are required, they should demand no more of the reader than necessary. Instead of asking their readers to consult a separate section for records of ambiguous hyphenations, for instance, the editors of Mark Twain's *Notebooks and Journals* categorized these problems as a special form of editorial emendation and included them in the general emendations lists for each section of the *Notebooks*. In the *Howells Letters*, where textual issues are far simpler than in the Twain texts, a combined record of both emendations and "details" serves the reader equally well.

## IV. COMPUTERS AND TEXTS

Establishing texts for scholarly editions at the turn of the twenty-first century is a mixture of old wisdom and new technology. Ongoing projects begun before the computer era strive to ensure that the procedures they follow with computerized equipment maintain the same standards of accuracy established with manual methods of checking and proofreading. Projects that rely on visual collation of copy should either perform collation against computer printout or convert to team proofreading: collation against a video screen for any length of time is physically impossible. Even in team proofreading, most editors find it easier to use hard-copy printout from a computer than to check the same images on a video terminal. Thus, computerization introduces a new step—ensuring the accurate transfer of corrections from the printout to the electronic system's memory. As more and more projects in scholarly editing become their own desktop publishers, there will be new shortcuts and new pitfalls. More than ever, novice editors should consult veterans.

## Suggested Readings

For a discussion of the nature of an established text see Fredson Bowers, "Established Texts and Definitive Editions," *Philological Quarterly* 41 (1962): 1–17. Anecdotal but useful accounts of the lessons to be learned in establishing texts are found in Ronald Gottesman and David Nordloh, "The Quest for Perfection: or Surprises in the Consummation of *Their Wedding Journey*," and Frederick Anderson, "Hazards of Photographic Sources," both in the first number of the *CEAA Newsletter*, March 1968. As for the textual record required in an edition of private writings, see Nordloh's comments in *CEAA Newsletter* 3 (June 1970). G. Thomas Tanselle addresses the problems of editorial records for literary works in "Some Principles for Editorial Apparatus," *Studies in Bibliography* 25 (1972): 41–88, but there are no comparable studies of the special problems arising in creating such an apparatus for documentary sources.

For cautionary words on an edition's failure to recognize the limitations of a microfilm as a source text without verification of a transcription against the original, see Jo Zuppan's review of the recent John Bartram edition in *Virginia Magazine* 101 (1993): 302–3.

# CHAPTER VIII

---

# Nontextual Elements
## *Informational Annotation and*
## *Its Supplements*

Most modern documentary editors offer more than accurate transcriptions and notes describing the location and provenance of their source texts. They supply, as well, editorial notes and other devices that clarify wording, references to historic figures and events, or images whose meaning might otherwise elude the modern reader. Even while establishing the documentary texts that form the core of any edition, editors must consider the documents' need for editorial explanatory or informational annotation, glossaries and gazetteers, back-of-book records, and even the form of the index that provides the ultimate access to the contents of texts and notes alike. While struggling to maintain the integrity of the editorial texts, they must weigh the advantages of adding editorial comments on context, fact, and allusions to elucidate those texts. This chapter discusses the options for an edition's nontextual, informational contributions.

Often the texts themselves, the textual apparatus, and the notes on provenance supply a substantial amount of historical information. Providing legible versions of faded manuscripts, deciphering inscriptions the author tried to obliterate, tracing the history of a manuscript's or pamphlet's physical location—all these are scholarly functions that add to the human store of factual knowledge. But documentary editors are usually obliged to go further. Here they venture into one of scholarly editing's most controversial realms.

In providing information of this kind, editors strive to keep in mind both the author's meaning and the needs of two audiences: (1) the group or individual to whom the document was originally directed and (2) the readers who will use the new annotated edition. Part of this responsibility is discharged by providing readable texts of illegible manuscripts or obscure, hard-to-locate pamphlets that give modern readers much the same physical access to these documents' verbal contents as was enjoyed by their original readers. But this is often not enough. Modern readers almost invariably need additional facts or explanations to understand those words or images as they were intended by their creators and as comprehended by their original readers.

## I. Theories and Rationales of Annotation

Many editors have attempted theoretical statements of the goals of annotated editions, hoping that general guidelines would protect future editors from repeating past errors. In 1963, Lester Cappon claimed that proper informational annotation was part of the very "rationale" of modern documentary editions, but that rationale is still not sharply defined.

Among literary scholars, Arthur Friedman suggested his useful "Principles of Historical Annotation in Critical Editions of Modern Texts" more than five decades ago (1941), but he focused on the needs of editions of published works, not of the private writings of literary figures, concentrating on "notes of explanation" that "attempt to make a work more intelligible by showing its relationship to earlier works," not those "notes of recovery" that would "supply information that would presumably have been known to the author's contemporaries, but that has been lost by the passage of time" (p. 118). More than thirty years later, another literary scholar, Martin Battestin, raised points of more general relevance in "A Rationale of Literary Annotation: The Examples of Fielding's Novels." Battestin conceded that "no single rationale of literary annotation" would find acceptance, but he suggested three variables that affected the extent and methods of annotation: first, "the character of the audience which the annotator supposes he is addressing"; second, "the nature of the text he is annotating"; and third, and admittedly the most unpredictable, "the peculiar interests, competences, and assumptions of the annotator himself" (p. 60).

The specific problems of historical documentary editing were addressed by Charles Cullen in "Principles of Annotation in Editing Historical Documents; or, How to Avoid Breaking the Butterfly on the Wheel of Scholarship." Cullen held that the "proper scope" for annotation is determined "first, last, and always [by] the subject of the volume or series." By subject he meant both the form of the source text and the identity of the person or group that provides the series' focus. Annotation to a group of diaries can be confined to supplying information that would have been known to their author—no other contemporary audience need be considered. Considerably more information on public events might be provided in an edition of correspondence between political leaders, for readers would need the facts that would enable them to gauge the response of each letter's recipient, as well as the motives of its author. The correspondence between a writer and contemporary readers with expert knowledge in a given field demands fairly technical annotation to present accurately the facts and data that would have influenced both.

Much-needed humor was introduced to the debate in Nathan Reingold's 1987 review essay of the Darwin edition. Reingold offered a charming, half-serious analysis of the three schools of annotation adopted by modern American scholars. These were "the Unwinding Scroll in which bits of the past are disclosed in chronological order while the editors pretend (not always successfully) not to know what the scroll will later contain"; second, "the Omniscient Eye," whose followers "see all, know all, and often cannot resist telling all"; and, last, "the Electron Microscope school" which comes into play "when literary and historical editors minutely scrutinize physical objects and the signs affixed to them for levels of meanings mere reading of a manuscript cannot disclose (nor sustain in some cases)" ("The Darwin Industry Encounters Tanselle and Bowers," p. 17).

## II. SPECIAL SOURCES, SPECIAL NEEDS

Many of American documentary editing's traditional conventions of informational annotation assume that an edition will contain the written words of well-educated, politically or socially prominent men. Policies of informational annotation, like textual methods and criteria for selection and organization can be skewed by such assumptions. In providing informational comment, the editor should attend to the needs of the writers and sources being edited instead of relying on guidelines appropriate to the kind of sources commonly edited forty years ago. As an example, editors should ask whether their authors' sex affects the clarification their texts may demand. Drawing on her own experience in "Gender Consciousness in Editing: The Diary of Elizabeth Drinker," Elaine Forman Crane pointed out that what was significant in the life of an eighteenth-century woman differed markedly from what would have been important in the life of her male contemporaries. An early (and masculine) editor of Drinker's diary abridged its entries by excluding "strictly private matters," precisely what historians of women and the family nowadays consider matters of importance. Crane's edition of Drinker's diary had to include not only a faithful transcription of the complete journals but also informational apparatus that identified the people who figured in Drinker's life, whether or not they met the criteria of political or social "importance" in their own day. Beyond this, the editors had to clarify Drinker's ladylike euphemisms for physical functions, references of special significance in the life of a mother who, "like most eighteenth-century women, was a primary caregiver, and [for whom] health was a constant concern." Questions of pregnancy, availability of medicines, and rumors of epidemics may have been of passing concern to Philadelphia businessmen of the day, but they were matters of central concern for wives and mothers like Elizabeth Drinker.

The assumption that source texts will contain words and words alone should also be reexamined. Historians of science were the first to confront the problems presented by images as documents that demanded analysis and annotation as urgently as verbal sources. Reese Jenkins discussed this issue in "Words, Images, Artifacts and Sound: Documents for the History of Technology." Documents generated by architects and artists have now joined volumes of edited sources. While other series of the Latrobe edition could treat pertinent drawings as "embellishments" or illustrations, images themselves were the documents published in the three volumes of his *Engineering Drawings, Architectural Drawings: Latrobe's View of America.* For an analysis of that series' editorial methods see John C. Van Horne, "Drawing to a Close: The Papers of Benjamin Henry Latrobe."

## III. THE NEEDS OF THE MODERN AUDIENCE

Any scheme of informational annotation or commentary should be designed with the interests of its specific audience in mind. The most basic question in this regard is whether the edition will address scholars or laypeople. Scholars who consult documentary editions are more likely to bring a knowledge of the people, topic, or historical era on which the documents focus. But the editor must bear in mind the *kind* of knowledge each group of expert readers will possess. Military historians are more likely to read the *Papers of Nathanael Greene* than the *William Dean Howells Letters.* Thus, they would need few reminders of the significance of major battles or minor skirmishes of the American Revolution, whereas literary critics reading the *Howells Letters* might appreciate an additional sentence or two from the editor pointing out the date and outcome of a specific Spanish-American War engagement mentioned by Howells.

In addition, scholars are more likely than general readers to have access to pertinent reference works, and the amount of information they need from the editor may be comparatively small. An edition designed for a general audience often provides notes and comments that create a more independent, self-contained body of knowledge. The editors cannot expect an audience of laypeople to consult dozens of hard-to-find supplementary reference tools any more than they would leave these laypeople to puzzle over an obsolete term that would be easily understood by an expert in the field. And offering too little informational annotation can limit an edition's audience. By assuming that only experts in a certain field will consult a volume and offering light annotation, an editor may fail to open the edited documents to a wider audience. (See Lillian Miller's discussion of this problem in her review of *The Correspondence and Miscellaneous Papers of Benjamin Henry Latrobe*.)

## IV. A Practical Framework for Informational Commentary: What Editorial Apparatus Should Explain

Veterans of the process of supplying informational annotation and its supplements are more reluctant than mere observers of the process to suggest what any other editor should explain. Still, they agree that two immutable laws can help narrow the range of what requires annotation: (1) Never explain what the documentary text itself makes clear. (2) Never forget that your edition will have some form of index. This device is the most effective tool known for clarifying and streamlining editorial commentary. Self-evident as these rules seem, they, like all the others that follow, have been broken on many occasions.

Editors may provide informational commentary in a variety of formats: footnotes, headnotes, bracketed interpolations in the text, back-of-book notes keyed to page-line references, and nonannotational supplements such as glossaries, genealogies, and biographical directories. Whatever combination is chosen from the ones described in this chapter or invented on the spot, the sum of their parts, together with the facts imparted by the documents themselves, is usually aimed at providing the reader with some basic level of information. And that information usually falls into the following categories:

### A. INFORMATION KNOWN TO THE DOCUMENT'S AUTHOR OR CREATOR

1. Identity of persons mentioned in the documents when some form of biographical knowledge is required to understand the text.

Identification should focus on the person's role at the time of the document's creation.

2. The substance of documents not printed in the edition which are essential to approximating authorial knowledge. Editions of letters written *by* famous authors, for instance should, whenever possible, provide synopses of the communication to which each is a reply. If enclosures are not routinely printed in an edition, they should be listed and, when necessary to understanding the source, summarized for the reader's convenience.

3. Information about places or historical events referred to in obscure or obsolete language or necessary to a modern reader's understanding of the document. The editor should, however, resist the temptation either to write lengthy accounts of such events or to translate into modern terms every archaic phrase used by an author. Readers of seventeenth-century materials, for instance, usually have some knowledge of seventeenth-century history and usage. The document's context will dictate whether the editor need go beyond a one-phrase clarification of a term to a paragraph of narrative prose.

4. Bibliographical data on published works mentioned prominently in the document, especially when these have influenced the author or are cited by the writer as sources. If the author has provided a comprehensible citation, nothing more is required of the editor.

B. INFORMATION AVAILABLE TO THE DOCUMENT'S
ORIGINAL AUDIENCE

In many cases, the facts presented to enable the reader to share the author's knowledge will satisfy this requirement as well. Still there are instances when more editorial comment is needed.

1. Whether or not a letter or other transmitted document arrived at its intended destination. When endorsements or dockets on the source provide this information, and their texts appear in the provenance note, nothing more need be done. If the facts of transmission are not self-evident, editorial notes should provide what is known from other sources.

2. The immediate response to the document: action prompted by a public communication of a government official; reaction to a lecture or professional paper; reply to a personal letter. Selective editions that focus on the writings of a specific figure generally provide more of these summaries and synopses than editions that publish both sides of a correspondence or the broadly defined "papers" of a statesman.

3. Any other *contemporary* result of the document or its transmission. Even the source's present location may be significant here. For example, most editors become suspicious when a document is found in a collection where it does not logically belong. This often indicates that the document served a purpose other than the one its author originally intended and that it was forwarded or even re-forwarded to another individual or group for action or review.

The reader will have noticed that these two categories focus on factual knowledge. There is a third category that goes beyond the factual and must be approached with caution.

## C. MODERN KNOWLEDGE OF THE DOCUMENT'S MEANING AND SIGNIFICANCE

By and large, this area of comment and analysis is better left to users of the documentary edition. Responsible editors avoid this category of notes whenever possible, although special circumstances demand the modification of the most cautious policies. The editor's annotational responsibility generally ends with making clear what the document meant when it became part of the historical record, and documentary editions are seldom the place for a lengthy analysis of later misconceptions of a document's meaning. Daniel Feller reminded his fellow editors: "Documents endure; historical scholarship does not" ("'What Good Are They Anyway?': A User Looks at Documentary Editions").

There are some generally accepted exceptions to this rule. One is a letter of recommendation for an office-seeker—it is only fair to let the reader know whether the applicant succeeded. Correcting a misattribution or establishing a new attribution of authorship may also demand editorial attention to the history of a document after its creation and original dissemination. For instance, when the editors of the Adams Papers printed three documents written by John Adams as part of "The Constitutional Debate between Thomas Hutchinson and the House of Representatives" (*Papers of John Adams* 1:309–46), the editorial comment on the first two documents was confined to their historical backgrounds. For the third, however, the editors also presented comments made by later writers on the essay's place in the history of American Revolutionary political thought. The document required such special attention because the Adams editors were the first modern scholars to recognize that it was, in fact, the work of John Adams. Thus, they needed to place it in the broader context of Adams' work and of the role his writings played in the development of eighteenth-century political theory and practice.

## V. Consistency and Clarity:
### The Annotator's Watchwords

While it is difficult to tell someone exactly how to annotate documents, it is somewhat easier to refer them to examples of first-rate annotation. Thirty years after the publication of Lyman Butterfield's *Letters of Benjamin Rush,* editors such as Harold Syrett still pointed to the volumes as a model for others to imitate, and readers of the edition seconded this view. In 1952, J. H. Powell remarked of the Rush volumes that their notes were an essential part of the presentation of the manuscripts; and Henry Graff, also writing in 1952, remarked, on picking up the volumes three decades later, "I still found that the texts and their notes took me into Benjamin Rush's world." Unfortunately, students cannot read Butterfield himself on the subject of annotation, for he never published any guidelines to his own practice. Butterfield and other exemplary annotators achieve their ends through consistency and clarity. That consistency entails establishing a recognizable pattern of annotation that readers can grasp quickly. If the editor's introduction promises readers that persons mentioned in the text will be identified at their first appearance, that promise must be kept, and readers can reasonably assume that if there is no footnote identification for an unfamiliar personal name, they need only refer to the index for the location of the earlier note.

Clarity is a more elusive goal than consistency, since it cannot be ensured by the most detailed style sheets or the most explicit statement of editorial method. Informational annotation should be as brief and as clear as possible. Many scholars have discovered to their chagrin and surprise that drafting such notes places the greatest strain imaginable on their literary craftsmanship. And the ordeal has few rewards, for if notes are well written, they do not impress readers with their brilliance or wit; they merely supply a name or fact or date so that readers can get on with the business of mastering the documentary texts.

As in all aspects of documentary editing, the editor's most effective weapon is a firm sense of the edition's source, medium of publication, and audience. At the most practical level, this means that, while preparing informational notes, the editor will constantly refer to the passage in the source. Staying focused in this way can eliminate hours of hunting for information that is not germane to the words or phrases in question or of drafting paragraphs irrelevant to understanding the troublesome passage.

Bearing in mind the edition's planned publication format saves similar hours of wasted effort. Knowing that the final edition will contain glossaries or genealogies liberates the editor from working into the footnotes definitions or lengthy descriptions of family relationships. An editor with a firm sense of the edition's opportunities for maps or other illustrations can also streamline footnote texts. And electronic publication can sharply reduce the need for verbal cues for cross references—a standard symbol like an asterisk can cue users to links to needed information elsewhere in the edition.

Of course, a clear sense of the edition's audience is the most important key to fulfilling the mission of consistency and clarity. Readers who consult edited documents—whether in printed volumes, in microforms, or electronic editions—do so because they are motivated by some preexisting interest in the subject. These readers are remarkably adaptable creatures who soon detect annotational patterns for themselves. After a few pages, for instance, the reader will sense that the editor has chosen to identify names mentioned in a series in a single footnote following that series rather than in several footnotes keyed to each item in the group. If this pattern is maintained throughout the edition, readers will adjust their rhythm of reading accordingly. If the pattern changes without warning or reason, readers will be distracted from the text while vainly attempting to figure out just what has happened to the scheme to which they had become accustomed.

## VI. OVERANNOTATION: THE EDITOR'S NEMESIS

Some of the most acute and witty contributions to the literature of scholarly editing concern the dangers of self-indulgent overannotation. Documentary editions should be the beginning of research, not its culmination. Informally, many editors have come to the conclusion that their duties are often discharged by showing their readers where to pursue further research on a given point rather than by pursuing every lead themselves in the footnotes of their editions. And there is no shame in an editor's resorting to what Martin Battestin termed "those most pitiable of adverbs, 'probably,' and 'possibly'; or declaring his utter helplessness in that still more humiliating phrase—'Not identified'" (p. 78). Excessive informational annotation is the "occupational disease of editors," said James Thorpe (*Principles of Textual Criticism*, 201), and Battestin warned editors to fight off this contagious "impulse to tell all that they have learned rather than what readers need to know" (p. 69).

Symptoms of the disease usually appear in one of two forms. In one, the editor simply furnishes too many footnotes, explaining matters that require no clarification or whose explication goes beyond the needs of any reader or any documentary text. Overly detailed factual annotation prompted criticism of the *Jefferson Davis Papers* and early numbers in the *Madison Papers* series. The other form of the plague was ascribed to Julian Boyd, the father of the modern tradition of historical editing. In later volumes of the *Jefferson Papers,* readers saw increasingly frequent uses of a technique in which Boyd gathered together topically related documents, prefacing them with long editorial introductions, monographs that had little to do with the texts at hand. Valuable as these essays were, some critics suggested that they might better have been published as separate works unrelated to the Jefferson edition, and Boyd's successors at the *Jefferson Papers* openly disavowed the practice. The introduction to volume 22 of the Jefferson edition explained that Charles Cullen and his associates had largely abandoned Boyd's "file folder" method of topical organization and its corollary of lengthy editorial notes introducing each such segment. "When a file folder system is frequently employed," Cullen wrote tactfully, "the reader must understand the Editor's organizational logic in order to make full use of the edition. If editorial staffs change, so does the logic, and readers are increasingly ill-served" (*Jefferson Papers,* 22:vii).

Automated methods give editors quantitative assistance in diagnosing their own self-indulgence in annotation. The editors of the *The Papers of George Catlett Marshall* routinely monitor themselves by running a program that anticipates the amount of space that will be occupied by documentary texts and notes in volumes they are preparing. When they find that the ratio of notes to documents has passed an acceptable level, they know that they must review their own work and cut accordingly.

## VII. ANNOTATIONAL FORMS

Choosing occasions for editorial comment and setting the length of such explanations are not the only annotational parameters the editor must consider. The virtues and vices displayed in editorial annotation and explanation can appear in a wide variety of physical designs, and even the format of such notes on the printed page can impose interpretation on the documents or mystify readers rather than enlighten them. The wide choice of annotational designs available for inspection and comparison in American documentary editions sometimes seems a testimonial to their editors' and designers' artistic impulses. Informational notes appear in the following guises:

A. SOURCE NOTES

Data on source location and provenance may appear in numbered or unnumbered notes adjacent to the document to which they refer or in a back-of-book textual record (see chapter 7). The function of these notes can be as varied as their locations. Some editors exploit the source note as a convenient site for any historical annotation that refers to the document as a whole. For instance, if an individual's name first appears in the edition as a letter's author or recipient, the source note for that letter may be a convenient place to identify that person. Similarly, source notes sometimes include explanations of editorial decisions that affect the document as a whole: assignment of a date to an undated source, attribution of authorship to an unsigned document or identification of the unnamed recipient of a letter. Other editors prefer to keep source notes free of such editorial comment. In their editions, a numbered footnote keyed to the heading's date might explain the reasons for assigning a day, month, or year to the document, while a footnote keyed to the document's title might explain the methods used to determine the item's author or recipient.

B. FOOTNOTES

American documentary editions feature a number of formats for informational footnotes. Here are some of the most common methods that have been used for editorial annotation that appears immediately adjacent to the documentary texts (as opposed to in a back-of-book record):

1. A format that distinguishes between textual and informational notes. Julian Boyd introduced this convention in the *Jefferson Papers,* but the example has not been widely imitated. Each documentary text is followed by an unnumbered source note that indicates the source's provenance, variant versions, and so on. This note is set in a typeface that distinguishes it from the double-columned notes that follow. The only numbered footnotes are those related to textual details. Informational annotation appears in a single, unnumbered note. For the reader's convenience, the key words and phrases to which portions of this note refer are printed in small capitals.

This device works well only for short documents that require little editorial explanation; it is less satisfactory for longer ones that demand lengthy explication. As a purely practical matter, the reader of a fifteen-page printed text will be hard put to find references to specific words or phrases in five pages of double-columned notes at the close of that document. There are also philosophical objections to combining information that might have appeared in a dozen separate notes. Arranging such data in one note, printed in paragraphs with topic sentences, imposes an interpretive order on the information, and the editor is also more likely to go too far in telling the reader what the editor believes the document means.

2. A combination of an unnumbered source note with bottom-of-page numbered notes covering both textual and contextual details. This format can be seen in the John Marshall and Franklin editions. In the Marshall volumes, the unnumbered source note follows the document's text; in the Franklin volumes, it precedes the text. Although the source note may contain comments on general textual problems, such as the existence of mutilated passages, specific textual matters appear in the notes keyed to the text by superscript numbers.

Bottom-of-page footnotes are generally more expensive in terms of production costs than end-of-item methods, but they are the format of choice for any edition in which the individual documentary texts consistently run more than ten or twelve pages and require frequent annotation. Clearly, it is inconvenient for a reader to flip back and forth across several pages of text to locate an end-of-item note.

3. End-of-item numbered footnotes. This is the most common convention among historical editions. It appears in the Cooper edition, the *Irving Letters,* and the *Mark Twain Letters.* The source note or provenance note appears first, either as footnote number 1 or as an unnumbered note preceding the numbered footnotes. The source note provides general textual information, but explanations of specific textual problems are mingled with informational footnotes in one sequence of notes for each document. In such editions, it is customary to break the end-of-item rule for footnote location when annotating the text of an exceptionally long source. Bottom-of-page footnotes are provided then, although the sequence of such numbered notes still begins and ends with each document.

4. Headnotes for provenance combined with numbered footnotes. Such formats place provenance information in an unnumbered note that precedes the documentary text. Numbered footnotes provide further textual details, as well as historical explication. This format was modified in the eighth volume of the Madison edition, where the source note was moved to the end of each documentary text as an unnumbered note preceding the numbered series. This was required by the changing nature of the edition's source texts. More and more sources were located in variant versions or were found to require lengthy lists of enclosures or discussions of complicated patterns of transmittal or referral. These factors inflated the unnum-

bered headnote from a few lines to several unwieldy paragraphs. The Henry and Franklin editions, which still use the headnote device, have thus far avoided such textual problems, and the format continues to serve their projects well. When special considerations demand a detailed editorial explanation of some detail in the source, a numbered footnote is inserted within the headnote.

## C. BACK-OF-BOOK ANNOTATION

Some editions of the writings of literary figures consign source notes to their back-of-book records (see chapter 7), and the *Hawthorne Notebooks* and the *Emerson Works* place informational notes there as well, using page and line references instead of superscript numbers in the texts. The relegation of any of this information to the back of the book has serious consequences. Whenever the editorial texts' primary function is to provide historical evidence, the provenance of the original must be readily available to every reader.

Back-of-book records of informational annotation serve the reader only when such notes are infrequent and inconsequential to grasping the meaning of most of the source text's contents. This distinction was recognized by the Thoreau editors. Thoreau's manuscript journals, for instance, are literary daybooks, not diaries of the author's life. The informational notes in the printed edition are therefore few in number and supply little beyond the sources of scattered literary allusions. Thoreau's letters, however, are filled with references to friends, casual acquaintances, and the events of his daily life, and the volumes of his correspondence carry informational notes immediately after each letter.

## D. INTRODUCTORY EDITORIAL NOTES

Any format for footnotes or back-of-book notes can be supplemented or even replaced by editorial introductory passages or headnotes. Some editions, especially those directed toward a general readership or those that are the products of substantial selection and topical organization, rely solely on these notes, eschewing footnotes altogether (see, for instance, the series *Freedom: A Documentary History of Emancipation*). In near-comprehensive editions, however, such notes customarily refer to the specific document or group of documents that they introduce. Compilers of topically arranged volumes or of highly selective editions may ignore this rule. Whenever all or part of a series is organized by topic, each group of documents should be preceded by an editorial introduction that explains the criteria for selection, as well as the scheme of organization of the texts that follow, and it should provide whatever information the reader will need to understand the texts in that section.

In selective editions organized in a single chronological series, editors often find it necessary to insert paragraphs of editorial comment as transitional bridges between sections of documents. Such notes provide a context for the materials they introduce, summarizing the events not documented by the texts and offering the reader the information required to comprehend the texts that follow. In the *Webster Correspondence,* such notes are printed at regular intervals between the texts of letters. In the *Jay Papers,* whose volumes are organized by chapters, such notes open each unit. Chapter organization is also common to selective editions of nineteenth- and twentieth-century materials such as the Edison, Eisenhower, and George Marshall papers. Such notes should be terse, and their authors must guard against the temptation to summarize and quote the documents themselves. Even in a selective edition, the documents must tell the story. If the texts and their footnotes do not present a coherent narrative, the editor may need to reconsider the justification for publishing these sources in printed volumes as a documentary edition.

## VIII. CITATION OF SOURCES

The length of footnotes and introductory notes can be affected not only by the editor's skill in writing clearly and concisely but also by the devices employed to give sources for these statements. All documentary editors concede that sources must be given for any direct quotations that appear in their historical notes, and they generally omit sources for information that can be verified in any conventional reference book or textbook. On other points there is little agreement. The care with which citations are offered in editorial notes seems to depend on the editor's assumption that a source is obvious or obscure and the degree to which footnote length would be inflated by offering a full list of citations for a given sequence of facts.

The more recent the date of the documents involved, the more likely editors are to leave readers to their own devices in retrieving sources for historical annotation. Editions of late nineteenth- and early twentieth-century materials, no matter how light or heavy their annotation, seldom give detailed citations for the sources of these notes. Excepted from this rule are editions of documents dealing with the history of groups of ill-educated people. Here, editors are acutely aware that they are part of a new historiographical movement and that the sources of their notes will not be obvious even to fellow specialists. As an example, the *Marcus Garvey Papers* provide not only more informational annotation than the *Woodrow Wilson Papers* but also more detailed citation of sources for each fact.

At times, the cumbersome nature of the research process required to produce a given set of notes makes specific source citation impractical. The biographies of delegates to federal and state ratifying conventions in the *Ratification of the Constitution* series carry no source citations. For many of these delegates, the editors functioned as primary biographers, drawing on dozens of original sources for even the briefest sketches. A list of all these sources, complete with full details of publication, would have been five times as long as the note produced by consulting these books, manuscripts, and newspapers.


A. IMPLIED SOURCES OF INFORMATION

The need to repeat full citations can be eliminated if certain facts are presented in ways that imply their source. The editors of the *Booker T. Washington Papers* found that the voluminous records of the Tuskegee Institute provided invaluable data on students, faculty, and supporting personnel at the school. While the editors' biographical sketches for an individual who figured prominently and consistently in Washington's life provide full citations of references, another method was used for persons merely mentioned in passing. These notes give little beyond each man's or woman's full name and dates of association with the institute, the editors having already made readers aware of the existence of the institute's records.

When the content of a note is assumed to indicate its source, the volume's introduction should make this policy clear. The editor of the papers of a Revolutionary general can responsibly inform readers that all casualty figures for battles come from Mark M. Boatner's *Encyclopedia of the American Revolution* unless otherwise indicated. The editor of a volume of political correspondence can note that sketches of persons identified as members of the U.S. House or Senate are based on their entries in the *Biographical Directory of the United States Congress* unless another source is cited. It is fairly common for editors to omit the *Dictionary of American Biography* as a source for biographical information, and the editors of the Webster *Legal Papers* used their volumes' indexes to indicate sources of biographical data, with an asterisk for individuals with entries in the *Dictionary of American Biography* and a dagger for those whose sketches appear in the *Biographical Directory of the American Congress*.

Generally there should be no more than three or four categories of such implied sources, and the device should be used only for sources whose omission from footnote citations will save considerable space in the edition. Readers who must remember the meaning of angle brackets, Library of Congress symbols for manuscript repositories, and lists of short titles should not be expected as well to master an array of implied citations unless some useful purpose is thereby served.

Changes in the nature of reference works and secondary literature relating to an edition's subject may force a change in policies in citing sources. For documents relating to Dwight Eisenhower's army command during World War II, his editors could responsibly omit citations for almost every matter but direct quotations in their informational notes. The monographic literature on the war years is so full that readers could reasonably be expected to find sources for confirmation and further research. But with Eisenhower's transition to peacetime commander of NATO, the historiographical riches end. For the volumes covering this portion of Eisenhower's military career, the editors' notes carry full and detailed citations, as they represent original research whose sources cannot be anticipated by readers of the edition.

## B. THE FORM OF CITATIONS IN EDITORIAL NOTES

The length and kind of information supplied in editorial notes can also determine the format of the source citations. The longer and more complicated the note, the more pains the editor must take to make clear which facts come from which source. In lightly annotated series like the *Andrew Johnson Papers,* all sources for a given footnote follow the note's text, separated only by a period. This method fails in selective editions or any other series whose notes frequently carry several direct quotations. Here it may be necessary to insert source citations within the body of the note, enclosed in parentheses following each quoted passage. Parenthetical citation of sources is also more effective for lengthy footnotes dealing with two or more topics. Parentheses enable the editor to insert the source for each factual category as it arises, rather than producing a confusing list of a dozen sources at the note's end.

New problems of citation arise in editions that employ introductory editorial notes as well as footnotes. Since headnotes may be several pages in length, it will be more convenient for the reader to have the source citations immediately available while reading the headnote. The source citations can be supplied periodically within parentheses or in numbered footnotes at the bottom of each page. Editors should remember that because headnotes immediately precede the documents they introduce, readers will become impatient with summaries or quotations from documents whose complete texts follow within a few pages. And an editor needs to give a set of facts only once: data presented in a headnote should not be repeated in footnotes.

### *1. Bibliographical Economies*

Editors can save space not only by reducing the frequency with which they cite sources but also by the efficiency with which they recite the necessary bibliographical information. Many of these shortcuts are part of the standard practice of historians, literary critics, or other scholars.

*Short titles.* Documentary editors must keep a running bibliographical record of every printed work or manuscript collection cited in their notes. These sources should be presented as clearly and concisely as possible, and the editor may place an arbitrary limit on the number of times a source may be cited before it warrants short-title treatment in the notes. Once a book or article meets this standard, the editor chooses an appropriate abbreviated form to use throughout the edition. All earlier references are then changed to reflect the new short title, and all later references should employ the shortened form. This will entail a separate file of short titles for the edition. These contractions, with complete bibliographical data for the works they represent, will form part of the editorial apparatus in the published volume. Word-processing equipment makes it easy to check references to a specific source for consistency and to convert any full citations to a shortened form when a volume or collection qualifies for short-title treatment.

A documentary edition's bibliographical file should have a separate section for repositories cited in notes. If the edition uses Library of Congress symbols or some other scheme of abbreviated forms to indicate the location of the originals of its source texts, the same system can be used for manuscripts cited or quoted in notes. Maintaining a bibliographical file for manuscripts as well as printed works will ensure consistency of citation, and the file can serve as the basis for any list of location symbols that appears in the published edition.

*Abbreviations.* Like any other authors of a work of nonfiction, documentary editors use abbreviations for words that appear frequently in their citations. These include "Jour." for "Journal," "Procs." for "Proceedings," and other common forms. Again, a record must be kept of these abbreviations; they should be used consistently; and a complete list of abbreviated terms should form part of the final editorial apparatus.

*Alternate citation methods.* The Einstein and Edison editions take advantage of a form of citation common to scientific and technical works that obviates the need for short titles and abbreviations: the author-date method, in which textual citations to a work give only the author's last name and the work's date of publication. The back matter then includes a list of full references for every work cited, in which entries begin with the author's name and the date of publication. The first edition of the *Guide,* for instance, would be cited as "(Kline 1987)." The system can easily be modified to include codes for manuscript collections or other nonprint sources. This system streamlines editorial annotation by removing all full bibliographical citations from notes and eliminating the need to keep track of citations for short-title lists.

Documentary editors are denied one method of citation. Their notes may not carry the formula "This book will henceforth be cited as . . ." when a title first appears. Any abbreviated form of citation used consistently throughout the edition must be linked to some short-title compilation or full bibliography, not disposed of in a footnote explanation. Annotation in such series is too complicated to expect readers to leaf back through hundreds of pages to discover the meaning of a short title in an earlier footnote.

## IX. PREPARATION OF INFORMATIONAL NOTES

Even if veteran editors have difficulty explaining to others exactly how or when to insert footnotes or when to use headnotes, they can offer some helpful practical advice for any scheme of annotation, be it light or heavy.

1. As editors prepare notes, they maintain a rough running index of the contents of those notes and the documents they explain. This annotation index facilitates cross-referencing related notes and texts and helps guard against repetition of information. Most word-processing programs can perform enough indexing functions to serve this need nicely for a solo editor or a small team. At projects where several editors work on a single volume, one editor usually has the responsibility of periodically entering colleagues' individual annotational index entries in a cumulative index available to the staff as a whole.

2. All editors should establish and maintain a record of broad editorial decisions on matters of informational annotation as well as textual treatment. During the volume's preparation, this helps the editor remain procedurally consistent, and it is invaluable in training new members of the editorial staff. Such a record will also be the basis of that section of the edition's introduction that explains the conventions of annotation or source citations. In preparing such a statement, however, the editor should remember the advice of Wilmarth Lewis: "Resist the temptation to invent ingenious devices for presenting your notes. . . . Do not on any account be clever. References should be made in as concise a manner as possible, but compression can be carried too far; the edition should not be turned into a private language intelligible only to those initiated into it" (32–33). A recent edition, *Frank Norris: Collected Letters,* appeared without an index or any statements of editorial policies; this example should not be imitated (see Cook, "Precise Editing in a Book Club Format").

3. When working in an electronic file, editors find it useful to be able to distinguish easily between documentary texts and editorial annotation, both for purposes of retrieval and when determining the final design. With computerized typesetting and book production methods, one set of codes can be inserted at the beginning and end of sections of documentary text and another set inserted for notes. An editor's word-processing program can be directed to show each element in a different type face, so that editors can scan the copy quickly on screen or off. When design of the edition is complete, appropriate typesetting codes can be substituted.

4. Ideally, the person who prepares a footnote or introductory note should not be the one to verify his or her own handiwork. When one has misread a source once it is easy to do so a second time. Independent verification also ensures that the footnote's wording makes sense not only to its author but also to the first of many readers. Even a solo editor should consider retaining a temporary assistant for this task.

5. Before copy is submitted to the printer, editors should enlist colleagues to read over the documentary texts and their notes. The unbiased reaction of potential members of the edition's audience is the best insurance against the unintelligible edition against which Lewis warned his peers.

6. When the editor suspects that a footnote is unnecessary, it should be omitted. In imposing annotation on a documentary text, the best rule is "When in doubt, leave it out."

## X. Supplements to Informational Annotation

Editorial notes, numbered or unnumbered, are only one device that makes documentary volumes useful. American editors have experimented with several supplements to these notes, and some are so commonplace that their informational function has been forgotten.

A well-designed table of contents assists the reader who must follow cross-references that give a document's date or number in the series but not its page in the volume. The Woodrow Wilson project used an analytical table of contents that did not list documents in their page order or chronological sequence but was, instead, a quasi index that located specific documents through subject listings. This method can be used only in a nearly comprehensive edition, for when editorial selection has been at work, the reader needs a convenient list of documents in chronological order to determine quickly whether a specific item was chosen for publication. The highly selective edition of Charles Sumner's correspondence features a front-of-book alphabetical index of the recipients of letters featured in the volumes.

Most volumes of edited texts will contain some form of editorial introduction that provides background information on the edition's central figure or subject and places the documents in historical context. Even documentary editions that do not aspire to be "scholarly" usually require such historical introductions. At the very least, the volume that prints the letters or writings of a single person or family should give basic facts about these authors. Bruce Dierenfield's glowing review of an edition of letters exchanged by Charles and Barbara Taylor, a World War II soldier and his wife, closed with this gentle reproof: "[T]he editors regrettably ignore the family backgrounds of both letter writers, making it difficult to understand fully the values, expectations, and fears that they took into wartime. Finally, there is little in this collection to suggest that the Taylors were southerners besides Barbara's return address."

Other editors have streamlined documentary annotation by providing a special biographical directory, a section of sketches of individuals who figure prominently in their volumes. This may appear in either the front or the back of the book. Editors who choose such a device should include these sketches in the material covered by the volume's index. Otherwise, the reader will continually have to check two alphabetically arranged units (the biographical sketches and the index entries) to locate the needed information. Editions of the records of a family or of family-focused correspondence often profit from genealogical tables. These provide readers with a convenient tabular display of complicated relationships by blood and marriage as well as easy access to full names and birth and death dates for dozens of individuals mentioned in the letters or documents that have been edited.

Whenever documents in an edition consistently use unfamiliar foreign words or technical phrases, the editor should consider a glossary for these terms. Otherwise, the edition will have to translate the terms each time they appear or translate them only once, leaving the reader to flip back through hundreds of pages in search of the initial explanation. When the subject of an edition has left behind an inventory or catalogue of his or her personal library, it is often useful to reprint this list, so that modern readers can easily determine which editions of specific works were available to the subject-author.

Any group of documents that continually presents unfamiliar place names may also require a gazetteer that provides appropriate geographical or topographical information. Specially designed maps can supplement or replace such a gazetteer in many instances. Editors must remember that commissioning maps can be an expensive proposition that may have to be reserved for special purposes. Editors of the *George Washington Papers,* for instance, provided no modern maps of Washington's military campaigns for early volumes of their "Revolutionary" series, because such aids were easily available in standard sources. The editors found that there were no comparable maps or battle plans of later campaigns, however, so subsequent volumes provide custom-designed maps. Editors who wish to include customized maps should take special care in choosing the preparer, however. Cartography and drafting are refined skills; people who can produce pie charts and presentation graphics often cannot produce a map that is accurate and attractive enough to supplement a documentary edition. No map is preferable to a poor one.

Often, a selective book edition not accompanied by a microform or other facsimile supplement will list documents in the larger collection that have been omitted from the volumes. Such formal lists are common in CSE series, and their presence eases citations to documents not printed in full in the edition. Other editions provide calendars, listings of unpublished materials that include brief abstracts of the documents' contents.

Editions of a public figure's papers often provide a chronology of the significant events in his or her career for the period covered by each volume. Such a chronology should be part of the volume's introductory section so that the reader can master its contents before reading the documentary texts. An otherwise favorable review of volume 8 of *The Papers of Andrew Johnson* commented wistfully of one such guide: "A chronological appendix on presidential reconstruction is so helpful that it deserves placement in the front of the next volume" (Cimprich, p. 153).

## XI. CONCLUSION

All of the above warnings against the dire consequences of overannotation and indictments of editorial self-indulgence should not discourage novice editors from learning everything they can about the documents they edit, and none of these rules or guidelines excuses editors from trying to explain every element of the document to themselves, if not to their reader. Charles Cullen pointed out that "the adoption of a casual attitude toward annotation inevitably results in a casual questioning of the documents" (p. 86). Editors must understand the texts they publish before deciding which elements require annotation, and Cullen provided this useful motto: "The editor is under no obligation to explain every subject or identify every person mentioned in a document he is printing. He is, however, obliged to consider doing so" (p. 89).

To be sure, standards are high in the fellowship of documentary editorial annotators, and their standards of accuracy can place still another burden on prospective members. It is a tribute to these scholars that the editorial annotation in their volumes has gained a reputation for unassailability. In a protracted controversy with the editors of the *Woodrow Wilson Papers* over questions of Wilson's health, Juliette and Alexander George and Michael Marmor explained that they felt an urgent need to correct possible errors because "the *Papers of Woodrow Wilson* is widely regarded as an unimpeachable source of data" (849).

As an incentive, I remind would-be editors that even the most prosaic research can uncover exciting historical evidence. Routine annotation of Martin Luther King's academic papers at Crozer Theological Seminary and Boston University demanded that King edition staff members investigate the historical and intellectual context of those early writings. In the process they discovered that King's borrowings from several sources crossed the line into plagiarism. Discussion of the implications of these findings filled a special issue of the *Journal of American History* (June 1991) titled "Becoming Martin Luther King, Jr."

## SUGGESTED READINGS

Robert N. Hudspeth, "Hawthorne's Letters and the 'Darksome Veil of Mystery,'" *Documentary Editing* (September 1986): 7–11, offers an interesting discussion of the interplay of textual and informational apparatus, while Nathan Reingold's witty "Reflections of an Unrepentant Editor," *American Archivist* 46 (1983): 14–21, are a refreshing tonic.

I. For the justification of annotation as part of the editorial process, consult Lester Cappon's "A Rationale for Historical Editing Past and Present," *William and Mary Quarterly*, 3d ser. (January 1996): 526–75, along with George C. Rogers, Jr., "The Sacred Text: An Impossible Dream," in Vogt and Jones, eds., *Literary and Historical Editing* (Lawrence, Kans., 1981), 23–33. Two provocative discussions of the dilemma of the editor-annotator are: Anne Middleton, "Life in the Margins; or, What's an Annotator to Do?" *Library Chronicle of the University of Texas at Austin* 20 (1990): 167–83, and Betty Bennett, "The Editor of Letters as Critic: A Denial of Blameless Neutrality," *TEXT* 6 (1994): 213–23.

An excellent example of a scholar's amplification of the raw material provided by a documentary edition is Bernhard Fabian, "Jefferson's Notes on Virginia: The Genesis of Query xvii, The different religions received into that State," *William and Mary Quarterly*, 3d ser., 12 (January 1955): 124–38.

V. The scholar in search of models for annotation procedures should consult Steven B. Burg and Michael E. Stevens, *Editing Historical Documents: A Handbook of Practice* (Madison, Wisc., 1997). Attempts to define the proper model for annotation in correspondence can be found in Wilmarth S. Lewis's "Editing Familiar Letters," in Dainar, ed., *Editing Correspondence* (New York, 1979), and Robert Halsband's "Editing the Letters of Letter-Writers," *Studies in Bibliography* 11 (1958): 25–37.

VI. Perhaps the most widely criticized edition in terms of overannotation is the *Jefferson Papers*, particularly in respect to the lengthy editorial notes provided in volumes 17 and 18. A useful history of the project, with special attention to the evolution of annotation practices, appears in Noble E. Cunningham, Jr., "The Legacy of Julian Boyd," *South Atlantic Quarterly* 83 (1984): 340–44.

Editors themselves have offered some of the most telling critiques of their colleagues' annotation procedures. See, for instance, Lyman Butterfield's "New Light on the North Atlantic Triangle in the 1780s," *William and Mary Quarterly* 21 (October 1964): 596–606, and George C. Rogers' review of the *Mason Papers*, ibid. 28 (October 1971): 676–79.

Other worthwhile reviews take various editions to task: the *Adams Legal Papers* in *Journal of American History* 53 (December 1966): 590–91; the *Calhoun Papers* in the *American Historical Review* 73 (December 1968): 1637; the *Jefferson Davis Papers* in ibid. 82 (December 1977): 1329–30, *Journal of American History* 62 (1976): 950–52, and *American Archivist* 39 (1976):

210–11; the *Franklin Papers* in *Journal of American History* 60 (March 1974): 1071–73; the *Hamilton Papers* in ibid. 60 (September 1973): 409–11; the *Henry Papers* in *American Historical Review* 84 (April 1979): 547–48; the Lafayette series in *William and Mary Quarterly* 36 (July 1979): 484–86; the *Madison Papers* in *Mississippi Valley Historical Review* 49 (December 1962): 504–6, *Journal of American History* 51 (September 1964): 299–300 and 59 (June 1972): 115–17, *William and Mary Quarterly* 20 (1963): 146–50 and 35 (April 1978): 147–55, and *Papers of the Bibliographical Society of America* 62 (1968): 149–50; the *Robert Morris Papers* in *American Historical Review* 83 (December 1978): 340–41; the *Letters of Benjamin Rush* in *Mississippi Valley Historical Review* 39 (September 1952): 325–27; and the *Woodrow Wilson Papers* in *American Historical Review* 83 (December 1978): 1356–57. Gaspare Saladino's review essay of two editions of Founding Fathers' papers includes a rare comparative analysis of nontextual apparatus: "Charmed Beginnings and Democratic Murmurings," *Documentary Editing* 6 (March 1984): 1–7. Daniel Feller's review of volume 8 of the Clay papers, "Compromising Clay," *Documentary Editing* 8 (September 1986): 1–6, is a perceptive analysis of the changes in this series during its long career.

VII. Differing forms for source notes can be compared in the Adams and Henry papers. The Jefferson and Adams papers use introductory editorial notes in a traditional fashion, while the *Freedom* and *Ratification* series employ the technique in a different way for volumes that are selective and topically organized.

X. For examples of special biographical supplements to annotation see the *Howells Letters* and the Livingston, Mason, and *Ratification* series. Introductory chronologies are furnished in volumes of the *Webster Correspondence*, the *Jefferson Papers*, and the *Johnson Papers*.

Although reviewers have not given as much attention to such supplementary tools as to editorial annotation, many have addressed the subject intelligently. See especially the reviews and review essays dealing with documentary editions in American Philosophical Society *Memoirs* 35 (1953), *Journal of American History* 68 (September 1981): 366–67, *Mississippi Valley Historical Review* 48 (December 1961): 510–11, *William and Mary Quarterly* 12 (April 1955): 358–60 and 22 (October 1965): 660–63, and *American Historical Review* 68 (April 1963): 762–65 and 77 (June 1972): 831.

# CHAPTER IX

---

# Publishing the Edition
## *Options for the*
## *Twenty-first Century*

The documentary transcriptions and notes so lovingly prepared by editors must sooner or later be shared with a wider public. In the past, "publication" meant a choice between printed books or microform facsimiles. Today, electronic data storage and word processing have not only revolutionized the production of these formats but also added new options for publication and distribution. Still, not all editors have equal access to the new technology. For many years to come, while some editors will be able to maintain complete control over the production of printed volumes through desktop publishing techniques, themselves creating the camera-ready copy that will be reproduced for printed pages, others will continue to hand over manuscript in the form of a word-processed printout to a publisher who may even insist on having the copy rekeyboarded, thus subjecting the editor to the traditional sequence of proofreading galley proofs and page proofs.

Having such a diversity of publishing procedures in use simultaneously complicates the task of this chapter of the *Guide*. I apologize to editors who will never need to master some of the traditional techniques discussed here. The steps by which documentary transcriptions and notes have traditionally been converted to printed pages in a bound volume add up to a process that requires the editor's relentless attention to tasks that can be challenging or frustrating, even dull. But even the editor with access to newer methods should not ignore the lessons of the old, for they are marvels of meticulousness and qualitative review. For all editors, whatever their sources or publishing media, the act of publication will continue to require the cooperation of numerous technicians who know nothing of the rationale for any editorial decisions and who sometimes do not share the editor's passionate concern for every mark of punctuation. This kind of intellectual stamina is demanded of editors who publish in any format. While executing a program of proofreading or collation of copy to ensure an accurate edition, editors must also prepare or revise the front and back matter or their equivalents, complete indexing, and maintain their own sanity.

## I. Book Editions: From Hot Type to No Type

Much of the terminology of modern print publishing, and many practices of documentary editing are based on methods of book production that have already become obsolete. Modern technology, of course, introduced a new set of questions that every editor must ask of a press, but some practices of proofreading and collation still in use were developed in the days when printer's copy was set by hand or by "hot metal" methods in which a compositor produced lines of metal type which were placed in metal trays and onto a proof press, in which sheets of paper were pressed onto the inked type to produce galley proofs. The galley proofs were checked for errors before the corrected type was locked into page frames that produced page proofs, which showed how each page in the published book would appear. Once corrections to the page proof had been made, large sheets were printed out that usually contained eight pages to a side, and these were folded and trimmed to form signatures of successive pages, which could then be sewn together to form the book.

By the late 1970s, few publishers still printed pages for published books from inked type. Instead, photo-offset printing used corrected page proof sheets to produce negative photographic images on thin metal plates that transferred the page images to rollers on the offset press. Paper run through the inked rollers emerged as sheets to be trimmed and bound into a book. The simplest photo-offset editions were done from typewritten pages rather than page proof.

Computer technology, of course, provides more options. Machine-readable forms of an edition, appropriately coded for changes of typeface and spacing, will be run through computers that can use one of a variety of methods of computerized typesetting (also referred to as computer-assisted composition). The computer will make certain typographic decisions like line endings and justifications, and the record that results is then used to drive the typesetter itself. These typesetters, in turn, respond to the computer record by summoning up the appropriate images for letters, numbers, and marks of punctuation and projecting these images onto photographic paper or film, which produces the twentieth-century equivalent of the first sheets once printed from inked metal type in galleys. In computer composition, as with manual methods, these sheets, the first that can be checked for accuracy in print, are still called galley proofs. An increasing number of computerized composition systems create page images at the outset, thus allowing authors or editors to skip the galley proof stage and go straight to pages.

The most convenient and reliable introduction to changes in book production and the accepted methods of dealing with modern and traditional techniques is *The Chicago Manual of Style*, 14th edition (1993). While most students are used to turning to this reference work for advice on annotational forms and punctuation, too few venture as far as Chapter 19, "Composition, Printing, Binding, and Papermaking." This section provides not only an excellent survey of traditional bookmaking but also a sound discussion of modern computerized technology. The *Manual*'s back-of-book "Glossary of Technical Terms" is a godsend in an area of constantly evolving vocabulary.

While the various methods of computer-composition offer great economies in production costs, they have also created new problems for the documentary editor. With hot type, the editor could assume that the compositor who corrected galleys would tinker only with those sections where errors had occurred. Because of the labor costs involved, the compositor seldom reset more material than was absolutely necessary. Collation or proofreading of the corrected material could be confined to lines where corrections had been demanded and to the lines above and below those passages. Even with hot type, however, compositors were known to introduce new and inexplicable errors after page proof had been checked and approved: decades ago, CEAA editors learned to employ mechanical collators to compare corrected page proofs against pages pulled from the first print run of their volumes.

Computer-assisted methods have introduced new opportunities for error during proof correction. In some early computerized systems, when the compositor corrected errors in electronically generated galleys, computer systems produced an entirely new tape or disk instead of entering corrections on the original one. If the system had received new design instructions in the weeks or months since creating the first tape, these modifications were reflected in the new tape, which was the basis for the printout that reflected the final page design to be used in photo-offset printing. Such design modifications occurred most often in the spacing used in the chosen typeface. Thus, the line breaks in computer-generated page proof could be entirely different from those in the galley proof. Editors preparing a record of ambiguous line-end hyphenations in the new edition learned to wait for page proof.

For all editors, computer-assisted composition means that page proof must be checked far more scrupulously than formerly. The practice of using collating machines to compare galleys, page proof, and gatherings was once a common solution. As these machines became scarcer, documentary editors and their publishers became more ingenious in coping with the idiosyncrasies of computer methods, and new rules for proofreading and collation emerged. Today, for instance, many editions use equivalents of the "compare" function in word-processing software to check the machine-readable versions of galleys and page proofs against each other (see Saatkamp, "The Editor and Technology"). Computer proofreading of this sort far outstrips manual records in terms of speed and accuracy.

Whatever the methods used to produce a volume, wise editors still demand advance sample pages from their publishers' designers. And the wisest ones submit copy for truly representative samples of documentary texts, footnotes, textual apparatus, glossaries, and any other special features planned for the edition. Inappropriate design and format can be corrected easily at this point. Even with more easily modified computer systems of typesetting, an editor is ill advised to demand a new typeface for footnotes or a revised pattern of paragraph indention after receiving galley proofs.

No new editor now looking for a book publisher should accept a press that refuses to accept machine-readable text and notes instead of hard copy that would have to be rekeyboarded. But editors who accept the responsibility of providing those electronic disks must be sure, in advance, that their word-processing system will produce something compatible with that used by the press's compositor. If this proves impossible, the editor should allow for the costs of converting these disks into a form that can be read by the printing system.

Editors at older projects who still do not furnish the press with machine-readable copy for a computerized system must be especially effective at communicating their own wishes. They will, for instance, learn to place a check mark or an "OK" above odd usages in the documentary texts so that no publisher's editor will "correct" such authorial errors. They must furnish publishers with legible typed copy, double-spaced, with generous margins for questions from the press or for instructions to the compositor.

Details that seem obvious to the editor after years of experience with the documentary edition may demand explanation to those who will publish those volumes. The designer cannot project the patterns of the printed book until she or he knows which elements of the texts or notes require visual emphasis and which can be left to speak for themselves. The editor who submits machine-readable copy that includes in-house codes must supply the compositor with a key to those codes.

A volume's size can have an influence on its usefulness. While publishers will understandably argue the economics of issuing one large volume instead of two smaller ones for the same texts, the editor should remember that a volume running to a thousand pages will itself be extraordinarily expensive, and, because of its bulk, as Charles Hobson pointed out, it will "serve a strictly utilitarian function as a reference or research tool." Such a tome "is better designed for use at the library table than for holding comfortably on one's lap while sitting in an easy chair" (230).

An editor's questions cannot stop with broad considerations of design or electronic systems. If copy will be rekeyboarded by a compositor, the editor must be sure that the printer's copy is marked appropriately. Most major university presses and commercial publishers claim to follow the methods described in the *Chicago Manual of Style*, but all have their peculiar house rules for certain matters. Close and early communication with the publisher's staff will minimize mark-up problems.

A. DESKTOP PUBLISHING

More and more editors now produce their own camera-ready copy. Commercial software usually described as "desktop publishing" allows an author or editor to create machine-readable files that will generate images of pages of the final print edition in final form, complete with appropriate typefaces and page numbers. In truth, of course, this is not desktop *publishing* but merely desktop *page makeup*. The official publisher still discharges the roles of contracting with printer and binder, marketing, and sales.

At first glance, this might seem a dream come true for editors desperate to prevent typesetters and publishers' copy editors from tinkering with editorial texts and notes, but there is a dark side. Commercial and university presses are not unaware of the savings realized by accepting machine-readable files or camera-ready files. In response to these technological changes some have reduced or eliminated their own staffs of compositors, proofreaders, and editors, who once could be counted on to review successive volumes of documentary series for style and sense. While documentary editors may welcome their role as desktop publishers, they know that the volumes still need prepublication review from scholars and laypeople who have had nothing to do with their preparation. Thus, computer technology makes the editor's need to enlist friends and colleagues in such prepublication review more urgent than ever.

## II. Microforms

Final preparation of texts and notes for a microform publication is largely a process of physical arrangement of the items to be photographed and quality control of the resulting product. Editor and microform publisher should agree on the form of target or introductory note that precedes each item in the microform, and camera-ready copies of these notes can be generated by word processing equipment once proofreading and verification are completed.

Even with the most sophisticated microfilm or microfiche cameras, materials should be photographed in the order in which they will appear on the published reels, to take advantage of automatic frame-numbering devices. This means that the editor must not only complete but execute the plan for chronological or topical sorting in time to meet the microphotographer's schedule. Although items can later be stripped into the master negatives used to generate the film or fiche copies, splicing can produce an uneven surface that compromises quality of reproduction.

Microform facsimiles must be proofread, not for errors in a compositor's resetting of characters, but for standard quality of images. Again, reshooting frames and splicing them into the negative can lower quality levels. Prudent microform editors ask their publishers' production staff for an advance review of samples of the original or photocopied materials that will appear in the film or fiche. These technical experts can often predict which sources will not reproduce satisfactorily, and the troublesome items can be transcribed well in advance. Such microforms will include images of the source's target, the source itself, and the editorial transcription.

Most scholarly microforms will be accompanied by a separate finding aid that contains not only an index to the documents but statements of editorial method and historical introductions analogous to those required of book editions. Microform indexes are usually generated by the edition's control files, and even if they are seldom as elaborate and polished as book indexes, they should be as accurate and clear as the edition's budget and schedule will permit. Although the general rules for indexing that appear later in the chapter are geared to book editions, their principles apply to microform finding aids as well.

## III. Electronic Editions

As yet, there are no completed scholarly documentary editions in electronic form to which we can point as models. Several projects are in progress, though, and their tentative findings and the related experience of nondocumentary electronic editions justify some general statements here. I remind readers that these bits of advice and wisdom are recorded early in the year 1996, with full knowledge that much of what follows will be out of date before this book receives another revision.

Electronic publication in the next decade seems likely to fall into two distinct categories: self-contained electronic editions in media such as CD-ROMs, in which the editor is limited by proprietary textual and retrieval software used by a given commercial publisher, and editions designed for distribution over the Internet or some other electronic network in which the end-users' software will determine the appearance of the electronic texts and the ways in which those texts may be accessed.

### A. CD-ROM Editions

The *Lincoln Legal Papers* edition is one of the first to work in this format. The project's experience and methods are ably discussed in Martha Benner's paper, "The Abraham Lincoln Legal Papers: The Development of the Complete Facsimile Edition on CD-ROM." Digitally scanned images of collected photocopies were linked to their records in a relational database for publication on CD-ROMs, and the Lincoln Legal editors followed a four-step process in designing and producing this edition: (1) converting documents to electronic form, (2) developing a search program and user interface for retrieval, (3) constructing a prototype disc for testing, and (4) pressing the master copy for the product. Every step but the last was performed by the project staff.

Unlike microforms, the images for a CD-ROM can be recorded in any sequence. The user's search commands will reorder them later. This consideration was central for an edition of legal papers, where records for the same case may be accessioned from dozens of sources over a period of months or years. The unpredictability of the needs of users of legal papers also dictated an electronic medium. In microforms, orderly physical arrangement is a key to usability. When an editor can be sure that most readers will be served by a single sequence of images, film is comparatively easy to use. But researchers approach legal records with a variety of interests, ranging from the law itself to social or demographic history. Electronic editions enable each scholar to retrieve and reorder documents at a single workstation.

But ease of access in an electronic facsimile edition depends on appropriate editorial machine-readable indexing: the images of the sources are not open to full-text searching as are transcriptions. With a CD-ROM, the editor may be limited by the proprietary software used by the chosen publisher, and preliminary discussions must concern the number and form of searchable fields as well as the quality of the images to be scanned in for the new publication. Although there will be no separate index in the traditional sense, a CD-ROM edition should include the thesaurus of indexing terms or descriptors used in its creation. CD-ROM editions, like microforms, also demand statements of editorial method appropriate to their format.

Certain problems of a physical rather than an intellectual nature remain to plague editors of CD-ROMs. There are as yet no recognized standards for archival quality in this format, and the proprietary nature of the software that provides user interface may make some editions intellectually obsolete if the original publisher goes out of business—no other publisher may be able to provide support for the use of the discs.

B. INTERNET DISTRIBUTION OF ELECTRONIC TEXTS

Literary scholars have been at work for several years producing machine-readable texts suitable for transmission to colleagues around the world. Most of these undertakings have been informal, directed toward fellow scholars collaborating in a textual venture. Only recently have scholars in the humanities turned their attention to more formal publication and distribution over the "Net." Perhaps the best known is Jerome McGann's "Rosetti Archive" at the University of Virginia, which its creator describes in "The Complete Writings and Pictures of Dante Gabriel Rosetti: A Hypermedia Research Archive." Most texts transmitted in this fashion have been machine-readable transcriptions rather than scanned images, although the Rosetti project will provide images of manuscripts and printed works as well as machine-readable texts. For the moment, facsimile publication is limited both by the time necessary to transmit the information needed to record the visual information on a page and by the fact that accurate reproduction of some of these images demands hardware and software unavailable to a wide number of users. And for documents of recent origin, copyright considerations and restrictions in permissions to use the material may limit the use of electronic transmission.

The unpredictability of the reader's work station creates unique challenges in this form of electronic publication. The codes used by one piece of word-processing software to produce italic type, superscript characters, and the like bear little resemblance to those used by another manufacturer's product. Thus, documentary texts distributed in this fashion must receive some standard coding if their details are to be understood by readers around the world. It seems likely that this standard will be Standard Generalized Markup Language (SGML), a comprehensive system of sets of tags (paired sets of symbols denoting the beginning and end of a command) and codes.

Fortunately, commercial word-processing products now include options that will convert these proprietary codes to SGML's tags for details of physical appearance and inscription. Additional tags can be added to indicate analytical aspects of the text such as proper names or parts of speech, and SGML-encoded texts can accommodate hypertext links as well. Peter Robinson's *The Transcription of Primary Textual Sources Using SGML* is presently an editor's best introduction to the system's ability to meet the needs of documentary texts. The experience of scholars like those at the Brown University Women Writers' Project and the Library of Congress's National Digital Library will continue to be invaluable.

### C. STANDARDS FOR ELECTRONIC EDITIONS

The basic rule for any electronic edition is that it must work at least as well as a print or microform series. The added expense entailed by some formats can be justified only by improved service to the edition's audience. A well-designed electronic edition may offer users any or all of these bonuses: (1) access to several versions or views of the same text (image, diplomatic transcription, clear text); (2) options for organizing and reorganizing the edition's texts in more than one way; (3) annotation that serves more than one document without cross-references or back-of-book index citations; (4) easy and immediate access to a cumulative index for an ongoing series; or (5) inexpensive and easy incorporation of maps, drawings, and other related images.

### IV. THE DOCUMENTARY EDITOR AND THE DOCUMENTARY PUBLISHER

Whether editors choose book or microform or electronic publication, they are seldom responsible for every aspect of production unless their projects are of limited size and their aspirations for distribution modest enough that they control all of the manufacture and distribution themselves. For projects of larger scope, some organization or firm will be found to act as publisher and may assume responsibility for various aspects of manufacture and distribution. The most important factor in making the final publication process as painless as possible is the degree to which the editor and publisher view this as a cooperative venture, not a war between competing factions. The best defense against such friction is an exchange of ideas. Misunderstandings usually arise from mutual ignorance. A press that has survived one documentary series is more likely to be prepared for the special problems presented by a second, while the veteran of one documentary edition is more likely than a novice to understand the limitations and capabilities of publishing design and technology.

Editors are responsible for making their needs known to the publisher—and doing so as early as possible. They must not assume that anyone else will understand the special problems of their texts, notes, and apparatus, and if they fail to explain them adequately, they risk an edition that will be a source to be avoided rather than one to be consulted eagerly and conveniently. A convenient guide to editorial responsibility toward publication issues appears in Beth Luey's "Publishing the Edition."

At this point in the history of documentary editing, the majority of editors and publishers with experience in documentary editions are those who have produced microform or book editions. Their advice will serve, as well, those who will publish edited documents in an age of electronic dissemination. Confer with the publisher's editors and designers as soon as a publisher has been chosen. Never be afraid to betray ignorance by asking questions. And never hesitate to volunteer information or ideas to the publishing staff.

Documentary editors unfamiliar with the principles of book or microform design or electronic formats must brief themselves on their chosen medium of publication, formally or informally. By consulting other editions, they can get an idea of which methods are visually and intellectually effective for certain kinds of texts and annotation. Steven Burg and Michael Stevens' *Editing Historical Documents: A Handbook of Practice* makes such comparisons far easier. When tentative decisions are reached concerning publishing format and design, the editor should consult an expert in the chosen medium to learn whether this plan is economically practical and technically feasible. Ideally, editors choose publishers early in their project's career, so that they can direct questions to the designer or production director who will be responsible for their own texts and notes. If this is impossible, they will need to recruit their own advisers.

## V. FRONT AND BACK MATTER

Every format—print, microform, or electronic—demands editorial contributions equivalent to a book's front and back matter. Because of the special production problems created by documentary editions, their book publishers prefer to be given copy for the documentary texts and editorial notes as early as possible. Thus, many editors have adopted the custom of preparing front and back matter only after these transcriptions and typed notes have gone to the compositor. Even editors who are their own desktop publishers or who issue nonbook editions may prefer to postpone drafting some of these auxiliary sections until work on the text and notes is complete: it is far easier to explain what you've done after you've done it.

In any documentary book edition, such prefatory sections and appendixes are far more significant than in scholarly monographs or narrative histories, and the rule carries over to other media. If readers are to make full use of any documentary edition, they must know the project's standards for establishing texts and furnishing annotation, as well as textual records and tables that may be necessary to recover details of the original sources. "Full disclosure" should be the motto of all editors in preparing these sections. The users' need to know is paramount. The various files and memoranda compiled during the editing process serve a vital function when the editor prepares the explanatory statements and apparatus that allow readers to make use of the final product, whether it be printed volumes, microforms, or electronic texts. Specific groups of documents may require special editorial discussions, but each group published simultaneously should contain the following elements:

1. Statements of editorial method, covering textual matters, informational annotation, and other editorial policies
2. A list of all textual symbols used in the editorial texts and a list of any abbreviations used, such as "ALS," "D," and "Dft"
3. A list of short titles for published works and abbreviated forms designating repositories used in the edition or their appropriate equivalents
4. When the source text's provenance so demands, the editor must inform readers that permission to cite or to quote certain items should come from their private or institutional owners. In some cases, the sources' provenance may also require formal statements that the editor has received permission to reproduce these texts or been granted permission to reprint material in copyright.

Editions that employ clear text in printed volumes often place the first and second of these elements in the back of the book, immediately preceding the record of emendations and inscriptional details. In other editions, all four elements precede the first documentary text. Even in electronic editions, it is prudent to design the initial on-screen menu, or choice of commands and search options, so that readers will be encouraged—or even instructed—to read these statements in a logical order before using the texts themselves.

## A. STATEMENTS OF EDITORIAL POLICIES

Once documentary texts and annotation have been proofread, collated, and verified, the editor must polish for publication the editorial statements on textual policies, methods of factual annotation, and indexing. These statements not only explain the standards set for the edition but also describe the methods employed to ensure that those standards are achieved. In all of this, the editor must check and check again.

### *1. The Statement of Textual Method*

The statement of textual method indicates which of the broad options the editor has chosen for textual treatment of the sources. In an edition employing anything but facsimiles or diplomatic transcriptions, the editor will probably need to expand on this general statement and elaborate on the treatment of specific textual problems in the source materials.

Whatever textual method is chosen, the editor should also make clear the implications of that method for the documents at hand. Even with a back-of-book textual record, the reader deserves fair warning if clear text produces edited versions of letters that are at substantial variance with the texts read by their recipients. Editorial decisions on what is included in inclusive texts may consistently mask categories of details significant to a group of readers. Of course, the responsibility of the editor who does not supply such a textual record is even greater. If certain items in the edition demanded textual treatment different from the norm, the editor should warn the reader of such exceptions. If the textual notes to these exceptional items do not indicate that special liberties have been taken with them, the editorial introduction should list such documents for the reader's guidance.

CSE guidelines suggest that the editor also describe the methods followed by the editorial staff in proofreading, collating, and verifying the editorial texts of documents. Among historical editions, only the Woodrow Wilson Papers offers the readers a similar exposition of editorial practices. Ideally, all documentary editions should provide this information.

### 2. The Statement of the Pattern of Annotation

The statement of the pattern of annotation presents the editor's general policies on providing identification or explication of matters mentioned in the documentary texts. It also points out any supplementary devices such as biographical directories, glossaries, or gazetteers. The editor should never hesitate to be honest about the limitations of the edition's informational annotation. The preface in each of the twenty-six volumes of the *Hamilton Papers* closed with the forthright statement, "Finally, the editors on some occasions were unable to find the desired information, and on other occasions the editors were remiss." Such admissions of human fallibility do not prevent scholars from benefiting from the edition's documentary texts and editorial notes.

### 3. Special Statements of Editorial Policy

The circumstances that most commonly require additional explanatory sections arise from the edition's scope or its organization. Selective editions demand a clear statement of the editor's criteria for choice. Editions arranged by some topical logic rather than chronology require statements of these organizing principles. The absence of such statements remains the cause of the sharpest criticism of selective series.

In addition, many editions' source texts demand statements concerning the searches that uncovered these original materials. Models of these accounts are the "Primary Sources" sections of the Eisenhower edition's "Bibliographical" statements for each chronological subseries. These describe the project's search for materials as well as any peculiarities of arrangement in government records or other repositories (see, for example, vols. 9:2259–73, 11:1521–23, and 13: 1507–11).

### B. TEXTUAL SYMBOLS AND OTHER SOURCE-RELATED TABLES

The editor can never assume that any symbol or abbreviation used for textual details or the forms of source texts will be self-evident in its meaning. No reader can be expected to guess about such matters. Although few editors would be rash enough to omit a list of their textual barbed wire, some have been careless, offering inadequate definitions of the meanings adopted for the inscriptional forms represented in their editions. Indicating that "L" stands for letter is not enough. The editor must indicate if *letter* means the final version of that source, the recipient's copy. Such definitions may vary according to the peculiarities of the source texts involved, and readers deserve every clue they can be given.

### C. SHORT TITLES AND SYMBOLS FOR REPOSITORIES

Most editors find it desirable to separate the list of short titles and symbols for repositories from the list that explains alphabetical symbols for the forms of source texts. If many printed sources and repositories have been cited in abbreviated form, it is best to provide a separate list for each category.

The three sections described above should appear in every volume or other unit of a continuing series. Some editors have assumed that they need be discussed fully only in the first number of such an edition, but this places an unreasonable burden on the reader, for few individuals can afford to purchase every number in a series, and no library can guarantee its patrons that volume 1 in each set will remain on its shelves. Further, continuing multipart series may create a need for modified statements of editorial method. Editorial practices may change over the years in which the volumes are published. Whenever this occurs, the editor is obliged to explain modifications of textual treatment, informational or textual annotation, and format. And successive numbers in a chronologically arranged series may take the editor into new categories of documents that require fresh textual or annotational methods. Whenever this occurs, the introduction to the volume in which the problem first occurs should carry an explanation of the problem and of the solution the editors adopted. In some cases, succeeding volumes in a series adopt devices that will allow the reader to consult the edition as a whole. The clearest example of such a technique is the Madison editors' use of their indexes to provide cross-references to pertinent annotation in earlier volumes. Whenever the index to a specific volume becomes part of a broader information-retrieval system, the editorial note introducing the index entries should be expanded to explain the method involved. If basic statements of textual method are not republished in succeeding numbers, readers of later units will find only amendments to earlier editorial laws, not comprehensible recitations of current practice. Because these sections should be as concise as possible, their repetition in each volume involves the addition of comparatively few pages, and their inclusion makes succeeding volumes appreciably more useful.

## D. OPTIONAL EDITORIAL APPARATUS

Any edition's design may demand special features: informational annotation supplemented by glossaries, gazetteers, or discrete sections of biographical sketches or clear reading texts accompanied by textual records, historical collations, and hyphenation lists. Any selective edition not supplemented by a comprehensive facsimile edition of the larger collection from which it draws usually provides some sort of calendar or checklist that provides access to the documents that are not part of the printed volumes. And any selective edition—as well as editions organized by topic rather than by chronology—must provide the reader with a table of contents.

## E. PERMISSIONS FOR USE AND COPYRIGHT CONSIDERATIONS

Lucky indeed is the editor of an archival edition whose source text is owned by the agency sponsoring the publication project and for which no conflicting claims of intellectual property rights exist. All others must obtain, at the very least, permission of the individuals or institutions that own the source texts to print the editorial texts based on those documents. And editors dealing with sources of the modern era must become familiar with modern U.S. statutes on copyright and intellectual property.

Computer-based control files ease the task of identifying the dozens or hundreds of owners of letters in an edition of correspondence. Word-processing software expedites preparation of a form letter seeking permission to publish and integrating the addresses of the owners who must receive the request.

Advice from a publisher's legal staff, not computer hardware or software, is the most effective aid in avoiding claims of copyright infringement by authors (or their heirs) of the private or public source texts on which the edition is based. Such claimants should be identified earlier rather than later in the edition's career so that their wishes can be determined while time remains for any necessary negotiations—or for revision of the edition's scope if agreement cannot be reached. Useful summaries of copyright-related problems appear in Michael L. Benedict's "Historians and the Continuing Controversy over Fair Use of Unpublished Manuscript Materials" and James Thorpe's MLA pamphlet, *The Use of Manuscripts in Literary Research: Problems of Access and Literary Property Rights.*

## VI. CSE INSPECTIONS

In decades past, inspections by a team of scholars delegated by the Council for Scholarly Editions followed a carefully prescribed and rigorous pattern. Editors submitted not only documentary texts and informational notes but also draft introductory statements and textual apparatus. CSE guidelines once suggested that editorial texts be given no fewer than five independent proofreadings at the "most appropriate" points in the process of creating printed volumes. At least one (and preferably two) of these proofreadings were to precede submission of copy to the "printer."

Today, the "Guidelines for Scholarly Editions," issued by the Modern Language Association of America's Committee on Scholarly Editions, are far more practical—and less explicit. Recognizing the variety of methods now used to produce machine-readable versions of texts and notes that appear in print, the 1992 guidelines say: "Proofing at every stage to safeguard accuracy is of the highest importance."

In the days of generous NEH support, CEAA/CSE inspections were generally conducted at the offices of the project that had produced the edition, and costs of the inspection were subsidized by the NEH. Today, budgetary considerations make it impossible to maintain the practice of on-site inspection for all volumes, and there are comparatively limited funds for subventions of the costs of inspections. While the CSE prefers to conduct the inspection of the first volume in a continuing series at the project's offices, the review of later volumes is customarily performed long-distance, with the editor submitting materials to the inspector by mail and answering pertinent questions by e-mail, letter, or telephone.

Today the editors and the inspectors named by the CSE are left to work out the methods most appropriate to the unique problems presented by the texts in question and the technical methods to be used in their publication. While this might seem less daunting than the older, more detailed standards, the newer policy in fact places greater responsibility on the editors and inspectors, for they must repeatedly design their system of inspection and approval afresh rather than relying on a preexisting rulebook. Editors following these guidelines today often confer with inspectors even before their initial volumes are ready for inspection, so that problems can be anticipated and resolved. Once the manuscript for that first volume has reached the status of printer's copy, with initial proofreading and verification of documentary texts and textual apparatus completed and final versions of nontextual annotation ready for review, the inspectors begin their official work. If the inspector raises points that require clarification or correction of textual method, the editor can make these adjustments before the editorial texts enter page composition, where corrections and revisions are more difficult and expensive.

Inspectors still read the statements of editorial method carefully and make comparisons of a representative sample of editorial texts and textual apparatus against photocopied source texts provided by the editor or against originals of those sources located at repositories that the inspector can visit conveniently. And editors still must be prepared to answer any questions about textual matters and informational annotation. When a volume is recommended by its inspector and approved by the CSE, the editor may move the corrected, machine-readable version of text and notes forward in the composition process and inform the publisher that the verso of the book's title page may bear the emblem "An Approved Text."

## VII. FINAL ESTABLISHMENT OF THE DOCUMENTARY TEXT

Even though CSE inspections usually occur before copy proceeds to the composition of galleys, no responsible scholarly editor pretends that responsibility for guarding the text's integrity ends at this point. All the painstaking work of an editor can be undone if there is a failure to monitor the progress of the texts through the ensuing stages of production. Editors need to establish policies for proofreading or collating proofs long before receiving them. Publishers do not take kindly to delays in production schedules caused by an editor's agonizing over the best methods for checking these materials. Whatever combination of proofreading or collation is chosen, there must be a system of clearly assigned responsibility.

In addition to proofreadings and visual collations, editors, like any responsible authors, must read transcriptions and galleys and page proofs or their equivalents for sense. Oral team-proofreading can conceal errors of transcription in homophonic words, and human fallibility is always at work. Completely illogical words and inexplicable omissions have been known to survive the most rigorous series of independent proofreading sessions.

## A. TEXTUAL NOTES AND APPARATUS

Only with a printed facsimile edition will proofreading, collation, and verification of the documentary transcription end with checking the body of that transcript. With all other methods, there will be editorial notes that point to specific details in the source that have been emended or suppressed in the version that the new edition presents.

Editors working within the CSE tradition may not be able to complete their textual apparatus until galleys—or even page proofs—are available. It is only then that the editor whose textual apparatus will refer to printed lines can begin the work of calculating the line numbers. In projects whose editions use justified right-hand margins, editors will need to check galleys for the introduction of new ambiguous line-end hyphenations and list each one. These lists remain tentative until page proof arrives and the final hyphenation list can be created.

After page proofs have been checked to ensure that errors marked in the galleys have been corrected and that no new errors have been introduced, the CSE editor can prepare the final version of the back-of-book textual apparatus and hyphenation lists. And the subsequent galleys or page proofs of the editorial appartus must be proofread.

## B. NONTEXTUAL ANNOTATION

Even though there are no published standards for verifying and proofreading nontextual annotation, an editor must maintain the integrity of these editorial contributions as well as that of the documentary texts. Quotations in notes deserve the same high standards of proofreading and perfection applied to the documentary transcriptions. And these standards must be maintained when the editor reviews galley proofs, page proofs, and gatherings or their equivalents so that no new errors are introduced.

## VIII. THE INDEX

Paradoxically, any documentary edition's most important tool for access to its texts and notes—the index—will be the last to be prepared in final form. No reader who has tried to make sense of a badly indexed or unindexed collection of texts will quarrel with the editorial law that no edition of documents is any better than the index that serves it. Because the design of the index is central to an edition's success, editors find themselves planning that finding aid long before the documentary texts and their notes are ready for publication—perhaps before the first text is transcribed or the first note written. For the editor of an electronic edition, indexing may mean the entry of appropriate subject headings for a self-contained edition like a CD-ROM or appropriate SGML-tagging of proper nouns in texts bound for the Internet—or it may mean using the computer's facility for word indexing of texts for full-text searching.

Here I will limit myself to indexing in its more traditional meaning, the creation of some separately typed or printed list of alphabetically arranged subject entries that must be consulted independently of the printed pages or microform frames to which it refers. Before automated systems became common, the preparation of index slips began only when page proof was available. A senior editor might mark the words or phrases in the proof that deserved index entries, while a junior staff member then wrote out a slip for each entry. Slips were sorted manually. The editor could make corrections and changes once the slips had been sorted. A typist then transcribed the slips onto sheets of paper for the printer. The typed index, its galleys, and its page proofs had to be proofread individually. Documentary editors tried nearly every conceivable device to speed the task of indexing: some even prepared a preliminary form of the index slips from printer's copy, entering handwritten page numbers on these slips once page proof became available.

Grueling as the process was, editors ignored it at their peril. Julian Boyd's edited volumes of the *Jefferson Papers* appeared without individual indexes. Installments in a cumulative index appeared in paperbound format for every six volumes. The first task of Boyd's successor at the edition was to create a reliable cumulative index for the volumes prepared under Boyd's supervision. All future Jefferson volumes would carry their own indexes. (For a fascinating description of the process, see the introduction to vol. 21 of the series, the cumulative master index for the twenty volumes that preceded it.) Microforms demanded equivalent finding aids, and Richard Ryerson, the current editor of the Adams Papers, suggests that underutilization of the microfilm edition of Adams Family Papers "may be as much a result of the film's lack of an index as it is of any inconvenience or actual difficulty in reading the text" ("Documenting the Presidency of John Adams: The Adams Papers Project").

By far the most effective aid now available to the indexer is the computer. The human brain and eye remain the best instruments for designing index entries and pinpointing references that the index should carry, but the human hand cannot compete with the computer's speed and accuracy in sorting, arranging, and printing out entries. Computerized recording of index entries has special advantages

beyond its speed. With an indexing system like CINDEX, an indexing system for documentary editions developed by David Chesnutt
of the Laurens Papers, the indexer need enter the number for each
page only once on the computer terminal. This is followed by the
subject headings for that page. A quick review of these entries ensures accuracy of page references, and there is no danger that the indexer will err while preparing two dozen separate entries for page 119
or 536. More important, computer indexing allows the editor to begin indexing as soon as copy is ready for the publisher. The CINDEX
system, devised for a mainframe and later adapted to desktop word
processors, is now widely used, and its programs allow the editor to
begin not only the planning but the execution of the index months
earlier than would otherwise be possible. Quite simply, the index entries can be made from typescript or its equivalent, using the sequential page numbers assigned there. The computer then sorts the entries,
and the editor can refine and correct all of the entries, subentries, and
sub-subentries at this point. When page proofs are available, the
computer can display the corrected entries in their old page order,
corresponding to the pages of printer's copy. In a matter of hours,
any member of the staff can manually change these page numbers to
correspond with the page numbers and page breaks in page proofs.

A. DESIGNING THE INDEX

Documentary editors who have never before prepared an index
should not try to pick up the skill on the job. Reliable introductory
books on the mechanics of indexing abound. Good choices might
be: Chapter 9 of Beth Luey's *Handbook for Academic Authors*, Judith Butcher's *Typescripts, Proofs, and Indexes*, or Sina Spiker's *Indexing Your Book: A Practical Guide for Authors*. After mastering
elementary rules, novices should examine indexes in documentary
editions whose contents resemble those of their own and should
compare those indexes with one another and with the entries under
"Indexing" in Luey's *Editing Documents and Texts* as well as with
samples in *Editing Historical Documents: A Handbook of Practice*.
Next comes a careful analysis of the materials to be indexed and the
audience that will rely on that guide.

Many editors have traditionally regarded the indexing system of
the Adams Papers as a model. In preparing the index to the edition's
first unit, *The Diary and Autobiography of John Adams*, Lyman Butterfield in effect created a thesaurus that established a pattern of entries and subentries that proved adaptable to the succeeding thirty
volumes of Adams diaries, letters, and public papers. Butterfield be-

lieved in the serendipitous value of documentary editions, and his indexes reflect a determination to make the unexpected in the Adams Papers volumes available to readers. The specific subject entries in the Adams series cannot meet the needs of other editions, but they demonstrate an intelligent planning and anticipation of readers' needs that form a standard against which others can measure their own efforts.

Admirable as the Adams Papers indexes are, editions that have used them as models are now criticized for their treatment of subject entries. The Adams model places many topics as subentries under the name of the individual who is the subject of the volume in question. Thus, readers interested in a topic like suffrage would need to remember to look under both "Suffrage" and "Adams, John: views on suffrage." In fact, the most consistent criticism of indexing in documentary editions, whether the records of an individual or a movement, of a politician or a novelist, centers on their emphasis on indexing proper names. As any indexer can testify, these are the easiest things to recognize and organize in an index. But David Nordloh has pointed out that an index of an edition of letters confined to personal-name entries "not only suggests but enforces the notion that an author wrote *to* people but not *about* anything" ("Supplying What's Missing in Editions of Selected Letters," p. 42).

Accurate and helpful subject indexing demands the knowledge and experience of the scholar or scholars who compiled the edition; it cannot be delegated to a junior staff member, much less to an outside indexer. Only someone intimately familiar with the materials to be indexed and with the needs of the people who will use the edition can design an effective system of subject entries, and only someone with that same knowledge can match the terms that appear in the documents with the appropriate index entries. The indexes to volumes of the *Letters of Delegates to Congress* series, for instance, routinely contain entries like "Delaware River, defense." No outside indexer could be expected to know that the names of posts like Fort Mifflin and Fort Mercer should be included under "Delaware River."

The index of a documentary edition of a work compiled or written for publication often includes the sources cited by the author. The absence of index entries for those sources in *Jefferson's Parliamentary Writings: "Parliamentary Pocket-Book and A Manual of Parliamentary Practice"* challenged readers who tried to determine when and how Jefferson employed his own primary sources (see Constance B. Schulz's review of that work in *Virginia Magazine of History and Biography*).

The thought and hard work demanded by good subject indexing serve the editor as well as readers. A properly designed index reduces the number and length of editorial notes. The most obvious example of this is the elimination of "see above" references to earlier identifications of individuals when the index provides a key to such sketches. Most commonly, the index entry for such a note will carry a key word such as "sketch," be introduced by an asterisk, or be printed in boldface or italic type. The index can also give the reader access to pertinent information in other volumes in a continuing series, eliminating the need for another category of cross-references in the notes. In the index to the *Madison Papers,* for instance, such cross-references to earlier volumes are shown within parentheses. Most important, an index with complete subject entries enables readers to gather facts or trace ideas for themselves, tasks that might otherwise demand editorial summaries of one kind or another.

While computers eliminate the physical work of manual indexing with 3-by-5 cards, they do not eliminate the need for careful thought and planning. Even though the rules for indexing one series cannot be transferred wholesale to any other edition, a few guidelines can be drawn from the experience of American editors:

1. The index should cover all the materials in the unit it professes to index. If a selective edition of correspondence includes a checklist or calendar of letters omitted from the printed volume, this list's entries should be indexed. If the editor uses devices such as a biographical directory or gazetteer to streamline annotation, then data recorded there should be indexed. A volume's introduction and its appendixes deserve index entries, as do any lengthy descriptive notes on illustrations. There is no excuse for a partial index. Even if some of an edition's elements, such as biographies, are already in alphabetical order, the reader deserves an index that presents a guide to every page in the volume with the exception of elements like the title page, table of contents, acknowledgments, and bibliography.

A few modern documentary editions have broken this rule where informational annotation is concerned. Beginning with volume 8, the *Andrew Johnson Papers* provide no index references for persons, places, or events mentioned in footnotes unless that reference is an identification note for an individual; otherwise, index entries cite only pages within documentary texts. And the index to volumes of *Nathaniel Hawthorne: The Letters* does not cover any editorial notes. The Johnson editors justify their decision as an economy of space in volumes with sparse and infrequent informational annotation. The rationale for the Hawthorne index is less clear. Neither system has found imitators.

2. The editor should generally provide one index and one index only for each unit or group of units published simultaneously. This general rule was often ignored in some early editions of the papers of famous American lawyers, with a separate index for legal terms and yet another index for names of legal cases. Both the recent Daniel Webster *Legal Papers* and the John Marshall *Selected Law Cases* volumes have a single index.

3. Index entries and subentries should reflect the nature of the documents in the edition. With an edition of letters, for instance, it is usually wise to indicate which page numbers in a personal-name entry pinpoint the pages where that individual's correspondence appears: a string of undifferentiated page numbers would not suffice. A volume of legislative papers, for example, might require an index that breaks entries down into subentries that allow the reader to trace the evolution of specific pieces of legislation or of committee action on bills or resolutions. The editors of *The Correspondence of John Bartram,* the pioneering American botanist, were roundly criticized for an index that identified Bartram's human associates but omitted plant names and collecting locations, matters of considerable interest to botanists and historians of science (see Robert McCracken Peck's review in *William and Mary Quarterly*).

4. Index entries should be phrased to serve the needs of the readers of the specific edition in question. The index to a volume of legal papers, for example, can use technical phrases drawn from the law, although such subject entries would be pretentious and baffling in the index to the personal correspondence of a poet. Editors of the *Journals* of South Carolina's legislature in the *State Records of South Carolina* series modeled their indexes on those of the existing Easterby and Green edition of the *Journals of the Commons House of Assembly*, so that scholars would not have to master a new scheme of retrieval.

5. Whenever a documentary edition focuses on a central figure or organization, index entries under that name need to be broken down into intelligible subentries. The reader can assume that every entry in the index is in some way related to that central figure. Certain topics, however, can be located best under the entry for the edition's subject. Efforts to avoid this approach have been embarrassingly unsuccessful, as have experiments in limiting index entries for the central figure to "mentions," which result in useless columns of undifferentiated page numbers.

Editors are divided over the proper arrangement of such subentries. Some impose a strict alphabetical arrangement on subentries. When the index entry and its subentries stretch on for a page or more, this may be cumbersome. Others, whose texts are chronologically arranged, present the subentries in the order in which the topics or events to which they refer arise in the edition. Readers with some knowledge of the subject's career often find this a more convenient device.

6. Even though the final form of the index may not be prepared until page proof or its electronically generated equivalent is available, editors should keep the index's design in mind while preparing the edition itself. Unnecessary cross-references can be eliminated from the notes if the index will provide easy access to such material.

7. A properly maintained running annotational index expedites final indexing immeasurably. When such a preliminary index shows that the "John Smith" mentioned in the text of a letter of 4 March 1866 is "Smith, John C. (1820–1895)" while the "Jack Smith" in a letter a week later is "Smith, Jackson F. (1833–1903)," the person entering data for the final index has no need to hesitate or to key in an erroneous entry.

The most basic rule is that editor-indexers must put themselves in their readers' places. Their goal is to anticipate the entries and subentries users will expect to find for the specific information they seek as well as to supply cross-references for the unexpected facts and ideas the editors have uncovered in their work.


## IX. After Publication

When the last bit of corrected page proof for the index or textual apparatus has been proofread or mechanically collated, editors can do little but wait for the reviews of the printed volumes. While some reactions from readers are fair and helpful, others are ill-informed and illogical. Angus Easson identified three kinds of reviews inspired by scholarly editions: the "occasioned" variety, in which the reviewer produces an essay on the author represented in the edition; the "literary-critical" essay, which predicts the ways in which the world of literature and criticism will be changed by the new edition; and last, and rarest, the "bibliographical" review, which actually discusses "the principles and practices of the edition." Ideally, Easson, commented, "The reviewer should be capable or have experience of being an editor, though yet not be a bitter or frustrated one" ("Reviewing Editions: Letters, Journals, Diaries," p. 51).

Editors of microform and electronic editions will probably face a similar postpublication situation. The only difference may be that creators of textual archives distributed over the Internet can expect to be assailed by a never-ending series of reviews as the nature of those archives are expanded and improved. Still, editors must consider all these criticisms. The elegance of the annotation and the scrupulous accuracy of the editorial texts mean nothing if they have not served their audience's purposes.

The most frequent criticism of documentary editions in the past was that their editors produced printed volumes too slowly. Consumers of microforms and electronic texts will be just as impatient. More realistically, observers might wonder that any editorial staff survives to produce a single tome, microfilm reel, or SGML-encoded text, much less to publish ten or twenty or a hundred. Yet, somehow, dozens of editors have done so, and this guide has attempted to share the lessons drawn from both their mistakes and their inspired decisions.

What this book cannot share is the paradoxical satisfaction of documentary editing. If editors do their jobs well, they inspire work that will supersede much of their own. The documents that they publish will lead other scholars to search for sources that escaped their attention, and their notes will encourage others to dig a bit deeper for the historical truth that evaded them. What seemed comprehensive or definitive in their volumes will later prove to be only a landmark step toward that ultimate goal. The honest editor is, if anything, pleased by such results. Documentary editions are properly regarded not as the end of scholarly research but as its beginning. The scholar who finds documentary editing a congenial discipline must be a pioneer at heart, ready to establish a foundation of evidence on which others will build.

## SUGGESTED READINGS

Beth Luey's *Editing Documents and Texts: An Annotated Bibliography* (Madison, Wisc., 1990) is especially useful on the topic of publishing editions, for her entries offer a broad historical and methodological sample of debate and technique. Aside from examining her entries for individual editions, the reader may wish to consult those for the following: CEAA, CSE, collation, compositorial studies, computers, copyright, indexing, microfilm, microforms, proofreading, publishing, reviewing, and typesetting.

A useful aid prepared by a publisher for documentary editors whose series it will print was the *Guide for Authors and Editors Compiled by Historical Publications Editors*, first published by the North Carolina Division of Archives and History, Department of Cultural Resources, Raleigh, North Carolina, in 1979, and now available in an equally helpful revised second edition. Philip Gaskell, *From Writer to Reader: Studies in Editorial Method* (Oxford, 1978), provides useful comparisons of the methods employed by twelve different literary editions in presenting their series. An interesting presentation of comparative design is found in a book by the Association of American University Presses, *One Book/Five Ways: The Publishing Procedures of Five University Presses* (Chicago, 1994).

The earlier experiences of university presses with scholarly editions are presented in Herbert S. Bailey, Jr., "Thoreau and Us," *Scholarly Publishing* 2 (July 1971): 327–28; Harry Clark, *A Venture in History: The Production, Publication, and Sale of the Works of Hubert Howe Bancroft*, University of California Publications, Librarianship, no. 19 (Los Angeles, 1973); Chester Kerr, "Publishing Historical Sources: A Prejudicial View of the Problem of Finance," *Proceedings of the American Philosophical Society* 98 (August 1954): 773–78; and Henry H. Wiggins, "Publisher to Alexander Hamilton, Esqr.," *Scholarly Publishing* 9 (April 1978): 195–206 and (July 1978): 347–60. More up-to-date accounts appear in Sharon Butler and William P. Stoneman, eds., *Editing, Publishing and Computer Technology. Papers given at the 20th Annual Conference on Editorial Problems. University of Toronto 2–3 November 1984* (New York, 1988).

V. Interesting examples of statements of revised editorial methods in continuing series can be found in the succeeding volumes of the *Einstein* editions and *Mark Twain's Letters*. Models for elements of front matter can be found in the explanations of symbols for textual sources in the *Franklin Papers* volumes, and models for explanations of changing editorial methods in the *Wilson Papers*, vol. 3, and the *Madison Papers*, vol. 8.

VI. New editors may develop more sympathy and understanding for the trials of editors of CEAA editions before the era of computer composition from Frederick Anderson, "Team Proofreading: Some Problems," *CEAA Newsletter* 2 (July 1969): 15; Michael De Battista, "Tape Proofreading: An Adaptation for Part-Time Staff," *Scholarly Publishing* 7 (January 1975): 147–50; Eleanor Harman, "Hints on Proofreading," ibid., 151–57; and James B. Meriwether, "Some Proofreading Precautions," *CEAA Newsletter* 2 (July 1969): 17–18.

VIII. The only printed exposition of the methods of the CINDEX program for indexing documentary volumes is David R. Chesnutt, "Comprehensive Text Processing and the Papers of Henry Laurens," but that presentation is already out of date, for the CINDEX program now offers provisions for sub-subentries, refinements in "sort first" and "sort last" procedures, programs for single or multivolume indexes, and other refinements not mentioned in Chesnutt's article. CINDEX has now been modified for use with desktop equipment as well as with mainframe computers.

# APPENDIX I

# Form Letters

These form letters represent the communications that might be issued by editors undertaking an edition of the papers of Margaret DeWitt as they begin their search for DeWitt records.

## I. A "Blind" Search Letter to Libraries

The first is a letter prepared for libraries not known to be repositories of DeWitt manuscripts:

> return address
> telephone number
> e-mail address if available

Dear _____:

This project is sponsored by the National Endowment for the Humanities, the National Historical Publications and Records Commission, and the East Utopia University Department of American Studies. We plan to publish an edition of the papers of Margaret DeWitt (1841–1913), and these volumes will be issued by the East Utopia University Press. We wish to obtain photocopies of all surviving letters to and from DeWitt, as well as any other papers written by DeWitt or addressed to her.

If your collections include any such manuscript or printed materials, we wish to order positive photocopies (preferably Xerox or similar paper prints) at this time. Should your institution's policy require advance payment for such photoduplication orders, please advise us, and we shall be happy to oblige. Otherwise, we shall send payment promptly upon receipt of the photocopies.

Thank you for your attention to this request.

## II. A Letter to Libraries Owning Pertinent Documents

When the editors of the DeWitt Papers write to an institution where DeWitt materials are known to exist, the second paragraph of the form letter would begin as follows:

RLIN records and *American Literary Manuscripts* indicate that your collections include correspondence between DeWitt and Teresa Snyder and Mertie Maria Pedrick. Alfonse Gaston's biography of DeWitt includes a reference to a draft essay by DeWitt of 7 October 1879 in the Aikman collection at your library. We would like photocopies of these items as well as of any other DeWitt material in your collections.

## III. LETTERS TO AUTOGRAPH DEALERS AND AUCTIONEERS

The DeWitt project's form letter to dealers and auction houses that have listed DeWitt manuscripts for sale should open with the paragraph describing the project's scope and sponsorship. It might then continue:

> We noted with interest the listing for a DeWitt letter to Susan Aikman of 12 April 1877 in your recent catalog #124. While we realize that you cannot disclose the identity of the purchaser of this item, we ask your cooperation in forwarding the enclosed letter to the client who has made this purchase.
>
> Thank you for your attention to this request. Should any other DeWitt materials come to your attention in the future, we would appreciate advance notice of their sale. If you could furnish our staff with a photocopy or detailed abstract of such manuscripts, we, in turn, could provide you with historical background for the item, as well as comments on its significance for DeWitt's career, which might expedite preparation of your catalog entries. This would only increase the value of the document to its eventual purchaser, and it would ensure a complete record of DeWitt material for our files.

The "To whom it may concern" letter enclosed to dealers and auctioneers for transmittal to the purchaser of a DeWitt letter would be in this style:

> Mr. X, the proprietor of X Manuscripts, Inc., has kindly agreed to forward this request to you as the purchaser of the DeWitt letter of 12 April 1877 offered for sale by his firm.
>
> [Here insert the description of the project's scope and sponsorship.]
>
> We would be most grateful if you could furnish our project with a photocopy of this item for our files. No further use of the photocopy will be made without your permission, and, of course, the photocopy will not be made available to scholars outside our staff.
>
> Should the letter be considered for inclusion in our edition, we will honor your wishes in regard to any further publication of the manuscript and to the protection of your privacy as the item's owner.
>
> We hope that you will agree to cooperate in our work. For our part, we will be delighted to inform you of any new light that our research sheds on the DeWitt letter in your collection.

# APPENDIX II

## Sample Control File
## Database Records

Martha Benner of the Lincoln Legal Papers devised samples of entry screens in three kinds of databases that might be used to enter control file data for the letter that was used in chapter 5, to illustrate various methods of textual treatment.

Sample 1 shows a "flat-file" entry screen. A flat-file database is very straightforward, and editors accustomed to using 3-by-5 cards can easily move to this system. The disadvantages of this database become apparent when editors begin to use it as something other than an electronic file cabinet. This form of database "holds" data very well, but it does not surrender them easily. (1) To see all the documents in the collection that pertain to David Chesnutt, the user must search separately in each field in which Chesnutt's name might appear (author, recipient, and mention). (2) Only fields that contain a single item can be properly indexed. An editor usually needs to be able to arrange data in a variety of ways. In this flat-file example, one cannot print a comprehensive list of names followed by all the documents each individual authored, received, or was mentioned in. Nor can an index of subjects be printed out. (3) Fields that hold more than one named item (author, recipient, mention, place, subjects) are never long enough. There will always be that one document that has many names or subjects or demands just ten more spaces. When fields that hold multiple items are expanded to a size that will hold the data in that one document, the same amount of space is automatically reserved in every record, quickly increasing the file's size to astronomical proportions.

Sample 2 shows the entry form for the same letter in a relational database. This database avoids most of the problems of the flat-file database. All of the fields from Sample 1 that might need to hold multiple items (author, recipient, etc.) are now handled in separate files. The names that could appear in the author, recipient, and mentioned fields are handled as separate records in the name file, and their function in the document is identified. While our sample letter needs only one entry (New York City) in the place field, it will not be unusual to need to identify two or more places in the same document. In this relational database, locations that appear in the place field in Sample

1 are now handled as separate records in the place file, and their relevance to the document can be indicated. Multiple subject entries are handled in the subject file. Notice that all the records for the name, place, and subject files contain the field "ACCNO" for the accession number of the document concerned. Here the accession number is 59442, the number of the letter to Richard Showman, and this links the files together.

In Sample 2, users can search the name field for "David Chesnutt" and see all the documents Chesnutt wrote or received as well as those that mention him. In addition, a list can be printed that includes as much of the document information as desired, including Chesnutt's role. A list of subject headings can be produced, as well as a list of all the documents assigned a given heading. Combining the lists produced by these extra files, name, place, and subject, will give a comprehensive index for the collection.

Sample 3 goes a bit further and, through the use of reference table files, reduces both the time spent in data entry and redundancy in the database. This can result in savings of storage space for the data and can improve the reliability of those data. All of the critical data are contained in the reference tables, and names, places, and subjects are keyed in only once. There is only one place to go to check or change the spelling of a name used throughout the database; there is only one place in which to see a list of all the subjects used. File "keys"—"NAMEID," "PLACEID," and "MAINID"—then identify the data record. Data are broken down into their smallest parts, which gives complete flexibility in extracting and manipulating information for a variety of reports, including a complete printed index.

While Sample 3 theoretically represents the best option, a fully relational database can be awkward and intimidating for novices. And it requires constant referral to keys and codes. Perhaps most important, a completely relational database like this one demands a thorough knowledge of database management software, and it may create a more elaborate control file than many smaller projects need or their editors may want.

## Data Entry Forms

### SAMPLE 1
### Flat-File Model

**First screen, Document File.** Enter one record per document.

| | | ACCNO: | 59442 |
|---|---|---|---|
| DOCNAME: | letter | DATE: | 04/09/1982 |

AUTHOR: Mary-Jo Kline     RECIPIENT: Richard K. Showman

MENTION: Nordloh, David; Chesnutt, David; Smith, Paul; Cook, Don

PLACE: New York City, New York; Bloomington, IN; Italy

ORIGLOC: ICarbS     COLL: ADE Archives     CYPLOC: drawer 2

PTDCITE: A Guide to Documentary Editing     Pgs: 2     TYPE: ADftLS

SUBJECTS: Association for Documentary Editing: Guide to Documentary Editing; Editing

FIRSTLN: I've begun to nag members of ye Executive

COMMENT: This letter is the basis of demonstrations of textual methods in the guide.

# Data Entry Forms

## SAMPLE 2
### Relational Model

**First screen, Document File.**  Enter one record per document.

| | |
|---|---|
| ACCNO: | 59442 |
| DOCNAME: letter | DATE: 04/09/1982 |
| ORIGLOC: ICarbS    COLL: ADE Archives | CYPLOC: drawer 2 |
| PTDCITE: A Guide to Documentary Editing    Pgs: 2 | TYPE: ADftLS |
| FIRSTLN: I've begun to nag members of ye Executive | |
| COMMENT: This letter is the basis of demonstrations of textual methods in the guide. | |

**Second screen, Name File.**  Enter as many records as are necessary to include all names. Six records are viewed here in table form.

| ACCNO | NAME | FUNCTION |
|---|---|---|
| 59442 | Showman, Richard K. | recipient |
| 59442 | Kline, Mary-Jo | author |
| 59442 | Nordloh, David | mentioned |
| 59442 | Chesnutt, David | mentioned |
| 59442 | Smith, Paul | mentioned |
| 59442 | Cook, Don | mentioned |

**Third screen, Place File.**  Enter as many records as are necessary to include all places associated with the document. Three records are viewed here in table form.

| ACCNO | PLACE | RELEVANCE |
|---|---|---|
| 59442 | New York, New York | authored in |
| 59442 | Bloomington, Indiana | mentioned |
| 59442 | Italy | mentioned |

**Fourth screen, Subject File.**  Enter as many records as are necessary to include all subjects. Three records are viewed here in table form.

| ACCNO | SUBJECT |
|---|---|
| 59442 | Association for Documentary Editing |
| 59442 | Guide to Documentary Editing |
| 59442 | Editing |

**First screen, Document File.**   Enter one record per document.

|  |  |  |  |
|---|---|---|---|
|  |  | ACCNO: | 59442 |
| DOCNAME: | letter | DATE: | 04/09/1982 |
| ORIGLOC: | ICarbS     COLL:   ADE Archives | CYPLOC: | drawer 2 |
| PTDCITE: | A Guide to Documentary Editing     Pgs:     2 | TYPE: | ADftLS |
| FIRSTLN: | I've begun to nag members of ye Executive |  |  |
| COMMENT: | This letter is the basis of demonstrations of textual methods in the guide. |  |  |

**Second screen, Name File.**   Enter as many records as are necessary to include all names. Six records are viewed here in table form. It is also possible to streamline the content of the FUNCTION field by using codes: 01 for author, 02 for recipient, 03 for mentioned, etc.

| ACCNO | NAMEID | FUNCTION |
|---|---|---|
| 59442 | SH00501 | recipient |
| 59442 | KL00502 | author |
| 59442 | NO00503 | mentioned |
| 59442 | CH00504 | mentioned |
| 59442 | SM00505 | mentioned |
| 59442 | CO00506 | mentioned |

**Third screen, Place File.**   Enter as many records as are necessary to include all places associated with the document. Three records are viewed here in table form. Codes (as explained in the paragraph above) could also be used here in the RELEVANCE field.

| ACCNO | PLACEID | RELEVANCE |
|---|---|---|
| 59442 | USNY001 | authored in |
| 59442 | USIN001 | mentioned |
| 59442 | IT00001 | mentioned |

**Fourth screen, Subject File.**   Enter as many records as are necessary to include all subjects. Three records are viewed here in table form.

| ACCNO | MAINID |
|---|---|
| 59442 | M00001 |
| 59442 | M00002 |
| 59442 | M00003 |

# Data Entry Forms

## SAMPLE 3
## Full Relational Model

### Reference Tables

**Name File.** This file will contain one record for each person that is included anywhere in the document collection. Other fields can be added, if needed, to give more information about the person.

| NAMEID | LASTNAME | FIRST-MID |
|--------|----------|-----------|
| SH00501 | Showman | Richard |
| KL00502 | Kline | Mary-Jo |
| NO00503 | Nordloh | David |
| CH00504 | Chesnutt | David |
| SM00505 | Smith | Paul |
| CO00506 | Cook | Don |

**Place File.** This file will contain one record for each place that is included anywhere in the document collection.

| PLACEID | COUNTRY | STATE | CITY |
|---------|---------|-------|------|
| USNY001 | United States | NY | New York City |
| USIL001 | United States | IN | Bloomington |
| IT00001 | Italy | | |

**Subject File.** This file will contain all general subject topics that apply to your collection.

| MAINID | MAINTOPIC |
|--------|-----------|
| M00001 | Association for Documentary Editing |
| M00002 | Guide to Documentary Editing |
| M00003 | Editing |

# GLOSSARY

**Accession number.**   The number assigned a document or its facsimile when it is added to editorial files, usually reflecting the sequence of processing.

**Accidentals.**   Elements of a verbal text such as spelling or marks of punctuation which affect primarily the text's formal presentation.

**Archetype.**   The original from which variant copies of a text have evolved. Typically it is lost and must be reconstructed from surviving witnesses.

**Archival collection edition.**   Edition whose source texts are limited to a specific group of manuscripts or printed works owned by a particular institution, which may also sponsor the editorial project.

**Archival medium.**   A medium that can provide safe storage of the data it contains for a substantial length of time. Microforms are one example.

**Authoritative edition.**   A qualitative term referring to the level of rigor reflected in an edition. Such an edition is a collection of accurate and reliable transcribed versions of those elements of the sources that can be either translated into printed symbols or adequately described in editorial notes.

**Back matter.**   Portions of a book or other publication that follow the body of the texts. These may include commentary, textual notes, index, bibliography, appendixes, or any other supplements so located.

**Biographical directory.**   The section of an edition containing sketches of individuals who figure prominently in the documents therein.

**Calendar.**   Chronologically arranged list of documents with brief summaries of their contents and notes of their owner-repositories; commonly used as a supplement in modern documentary editions.

**CD-ROM** (Compact disk, read-only memory).   A computer disk with especially large storage capacity, for material intended to be read on a computer. Some CD-ROMs can only be read by the user, not written to; others will receive additional data.

**Clear text.**   An editorial reading text for a document that is presented uncluttered with textual or informational footnotes of any kind.

**Collation.**   Character-by-character comparison of two or more texts. Traditionally, the process by which editors isolate patterns of error that indicate transcriptional descent, to determine whether one or more texts is a copy made from an earlier and thus more reliable copy. Some twentieth-century editors have used the term to describe the process of visual comparison by which transcriptions, galleys, etc., are checked for error. With modern technology, the "compare" function in word-processing software performs this function by comparing the machine-readable versions of galleys and page proofs against each other.

**Comprehensive edition.**   Edition that includes all the materials defined in the project's rubric. Unlike the descriptions "authoritative" and "definitive," this one is strictly quantitative.

**Control.**   Inclusive term for the filing procedures and access tools that enable editors to locate materials collected for their edition.

**Copy-text.**   The term popularized by W. W. Greg to designate the version of a text that can be considered authoritative in matters of accidentals (e.g., spelling, marks of punctuation) for the editorial reading text. When only one edition reflects the author's personal scrutiny and later editions were "reprints," that early copy-text's authority extends to substantive readings as well.

**Critical or textual methods.**   Editorial practices employed when an editor plans to establish an authoritative text that does not reflect every element of any single surviving documentary source but, instead, embodies the editor's critical judgment of what an author's true intentions were.

**Crux.**   An unexplained and unaccountable variant.

**Definitive edition.**   Once defined as an edition of an individual's writings that was not only all-inclusive in scope but also so rigorous in textual methods that the reader would never have reason to consult the original materials on which those texts are based. Modern documentary editors are more realistic about the chances of achieving such perfection and usually use *definitive* as a synonym for *authoritative*.

**Diplomatics.**   The systematic study of the record-keeping methods of particular groups of clerks or administrators.

**Diplomatic transcription.**   A style of source transcription in which all details of inscription are recorded, either symbolically in the reading text or in adjacent descriptive footnotes.

**Dittography.** Unintentional repetition of words by a copyist or writer.

**Documentary editing.** A term that became current in the later 1970s to describe the process of creating reading texts intended to capture the substance and quality of the source texts so that the editorial texts would have substantially the same evidentiary value as their sources.

**Emended text.** Text in which the editor has corrected errors that appeared in the source text.

**Endorsement.** A notation made on a letter or other inscribed document, its envelope, or its address leaf after its receipt.

**Enumerative bibliography.** Reliable and comprehensive listing of printed works, their various editions, and comments on those works.

**Expanded transcription.** A style of source transcription that includes silent (unrecorded) emendation, or correction, of original details deemed insignificant and standardization of formats. The practice gained currency after it was described in the 1954 edition of the *Harvard Guide to American History.*

**Facsimile edition.** An edition that aims at reproducing precisely all of the details of the source text. This may be in the form of a duplicate image (photographic, microform, or digitally scanned) or, rarely, a typographic facsimile.

**Flat-file database.** Computerized database whose unit of construction is a single file. When several files are linked in a database, it is said to be relational.

**Front matter.** Portions of a book or electronically published equivalent that precede the text of the work, such as the table of contents, preface, and introduction.

**Galley proofs.** The first printed sheets available for proofreading or collation after a manuscript has been set in type. Even though recent book production methods do not require that a typographer rekeyboard an author's text, unpaginated proof sheets of that text are still referred to as galleys. Because electronic copy does not need to be rekeyboarded, the galley proof stage is now often omitted.

**Genetic-text edition.** Textual edition that tries to offer the reader access to more than one level of textual creation within a single page.

**Historical editing.** The techniques developed in the 1940s and 1950s by American editors who focused on the papers of figures significant in American political and military history, such as John Adams, Thomas Jefferson, and Benjamin Franklin.

**Holographic.** Handwritten by the author.

**Hot type.** Individual letters or lines of letters that are cast from hot metal then placed in metal trays to create "pages" of type.

**Hypertext.** System for computerized storage and manipulation of text and graphic elements; characterized by "links," by which parts of a document can be connected to different parts of the same or other documents.

**Inclusive texts.** In the CEAA/CSE tradition of documentary editing, texts that fall between diplomatic transcriptions and clear reading texts. While often similar to expanded transcriptions, inclusive texts generally contain more punctilious reporting of emendations and standardizations.

**Lemma.** A word or phrase in the editorial text indicating the site of editorial activity.

**Letterpress.** Among scholarly editors, a term used to describe an eighteenth- and early-nineteenth-century method for creating facsimile copies of outgoing correspondence, in which a thin, nearly transparent sheet of paper was moistened and pressed against the inscribed surface of handwritten material. Ideally, enough ink was transferred from the original to the back of the blank sheet so that the handwritten words showed through, giving a legible and complete copy. In the mid-nineteenth century, chemically treated paper replaced moistening agents. Also used to describe printing technologies in which printed pages are produced by pressing sheets of paper against inked type.

**Literary editing.** The term coined in the 1960s and 1970s to designate the methods of literary scholars working under MLA guidelines to establish texts of the writings of major authors.

**Mediated search.** A search of computer-based information sources that requires the assistance of a librarian or other information specialist.

**Multiple-text documents.** The term coined by David Nordloh to describe sources inscribed in such a way that a reader could reasonably extract the texts of two or more distinct documents from the characters that appear on the same page or set of pages.

**OCLC (Online Computer Library Center).** A nationwide bibliographic utility.

**Overt emendation.** Corrections or other changes indicated within the editorial text itself (usually enclosed in some form of bracket) or in notes immediately adjacent to the text.

**Page proofs.** Printed sheets showing typeset material laid out and numbered as the pages should appear in the published version. Traditionally, the next step beyond galley proofs in the production of a printed work. Even with computerized methods, the term is still applied to the first hard-copy version showing page breaks and page numbers.

**Papers.** In documentary editing, records that cannot be defined as any form of letter or diary.

**Parallel text.** Variant versions of the same text presented so that they can be viewed simultaneously. In books they appear on facing pages; in computer media they are joined by hypertext links.

**Private writings.** Materials such as personal diaries and family correspondence written with no intention of publication.

**Relational databases.** Computerized databases that allow the user to link information in several different files.

**Report capability.** The ease with which data from a database can be formatted and reformatted in printouts organized in a variety of modes.

**Resolution.** The degree of sharpness of focus in a reproduction of a visual image.

**RLIN (Research Libraries Information Network).** A nationwide bibliographic utility.

**Scholarly edition.** An edition with texts established and verified according to the standards of the academic community. Such editions are also often referred to as authoritative.

**Selective editions.** Those that represent some portion but not all of the materials uncovered by the search for documents for an edition.

**Shelf list.** A term, borrowed from library science, referring to a list in which the sequence of records matches the physical arrangement of the books, folders, or photocopied documents represented by each record.

**Silent emendation.** Changes made in an edited text that are not enumerated or made evident individually, although they may be acknowledged as a group somewhere in the edition.

**Socialization of texts.** A term popularized in the 1980s by Jerome McGann and others to describe how, in the course of commercial book production, authorial intentions become enmeshed in the complex interaction of publishers, editors, and production staff.

**Source text.** The handwritten, typed, printed, or otherwise recorded document that is the basis for the editorial text.

**Standard Generalized Markup Language (SGML).** A standardized set of tags that may be used in the transcription of textual documents for computer-based use. "SGML markup" is commonly used to describe any group of tag sets that adheres to this standard.

**Substantives.** In copy-text editing, the elements in a source text with substantial intellectual meaning, for example, the choice of words as contrasted with such "accidentals" as marks of punctuation.

**Synoptic texts.**   Editorial texts that provide a synopsis of the evolution of the text.

**Targets.**   Editorially supplied labels for each item reproduced in a microform.

**Textual editing.**   Critical editing. (See *Critical or textual methods.*)

**Thesaurus.**   In indexing, the list of terms or headings approved by the editors for use in the index.

**Transcription.**   In textual or scholarly editing, translation of a source text into typescript or machine-readable form. More generally, transcriptions are copies made substantially later than a document's composition.

**Typographic facsimile.**   An exact duplicate, insofar as this is possible within the limits of modern typesetting technology, of the appearance of the original source text.

**Variorum edition.**   Edition in which the locations of all extant copies of each document are cited and variants among the versions noted; also, an edition that summarizes all available commentary on a given text.

**Verification.**   Checking the accuracy of the contents of informational annotation or the accuracy of texts in a documentary edition.

**Versioning.**   A method of editing whose goal is to give the reader equally convenient access to more than one version of a text rather than to a single clear text from which the variant versions must be laboriously reconstructed from textual notes.

**Visual collation.**   Comparison of two versions of a text by a single editor who must look at first one version and then the other to determine variants or accuracy of transcription.

**Witnesses to an archetype.**   Copies made directly from the archetype or even later transcriptions based on earlier scribal versions.

# REFERENCES

*Listed here are books and articles that relate directly to documentary and textual editing and are cited in the text or listed in the suggested readings sections at the end of each chapter. Routine reference works and primary source editions are omitted.*

Abbot, W. W. "An Uncommon Wareness of Self: The Papers of George Washington." *Prologue* 21 (Spring 1989): 7–19.

Abbott, Craig S. "A Response to Nordloh's 'Socialization, Authority, and Evidence.'" *Analytical and Enumerative Bibliography* 1 (1987): 13–16.

Anderson, Frederick. "Hazards of Photographic Sources." *CEAA Newsletter* 1 (March 1968): 5.

———. "Team Proofreading: Some Problems." *CEAA Newsletter* 2 (July 1969): 15.

Arksey, Laura, et al., eds. *American Diaries: An Annotated Bibliography of Published American Diaries and Journals,* 2 vols. Detroit, 1982, 1987.

Association of American University Presses. *One Book/Five Ways: The Publishing Procedures of Five University Presses.* Chicago, 1994.

Bailey, Herbert S., Jr. "Einstein's Collected Papers: Planning and Development." *Scholarly Publishing* 20 (July 1989): 202–17.

———. "Thoreau and Us." *Scholarly Publishing* 2 (July 1971): 327–28.

Battestin, Martin. "A Rationale of Literary Annotation: The Example of Fielding's Novels." *Studies in Bibliography* 34 (1981): 1–22. Reprinted from *Literary and Historical Editing,* edited by George L. Vogt and John Bush Jones, 57–79.

Beales, Ross, Jr., and Randall K. Burkett. *Historical Editing for Undergraduates.* Worcester, Mass., 1977.

Beard, William D. "American Justinian or Prairie Pettifogger? Lincoln's Legal Legacy: Documenting the Law Practice of Abraham Lincoln." *Documentary Editing* 14 (December 1992): 61–64.

Bebb, Bruce, and Herschel Parker. "Freehafer on Greg and the CEAA: Secure Footing and 'Substantial Shortfalls.'" *Studies in the Novel* 7 (1975): 391–94.

Becker, Robert Stephen. "Challenges in Editing Modern Literary Correspondence: Transcription." *TEXT* 1 (1984): 257–70.

Bedini, Silvio A. *Thomas Jefferson and His Copying Machines.* Charlottesville, 1984.

Bell, Alan. "The Letters of Sir Walter Scott: Problems and Opportunities." In *Editing Correspondence,* edited by J. A. Dainard, 63–80.

Bell, Whitfield. "Franklin's Papers and the Papers of Benjamin Franklin." *Pennsylvania History* 22 (1955): 1–17.

Bellardo, Lewis J., and Lynn Lady Bellardo. *A Glossary for Archivists, Manuscript Curators, and Records Managers.* Chicago, 1992.

Benedict, Michael L. "Historians and the Continuing Controversy over Fair Use of Unpublished Manuscript Materials." *American Historical Review* 91 (1986): 859–81.

Benjamin, Mary A. *Autographs: A Key to Collecting.* New York, 1963.

Benn, Tony. "The Diary as Historical Source." *Archives* 20 (April 1993): 4–17.

Benner, Martha L. "The Abraham Lincoln Legal Papers: The Development of the Complete Facsimile Edition on CD-ROM." *Documentary Editing* 16 (1994): 100–107.

Bennett, Betty T. "The Editor of Letters as Critic: A Denial of Blameless Neutrality." *TEXT* 6 (1994): 213–23.

Bentley, G. E., Jr. "Blake's Works as Performances: Intentions and Inattentions." *TEXT* 4 (1988): 319–30.

Berkeley, Francis L., Jr. "History and the Problem of the Control of Manuscripts in the United States." *Proceedings of the American Philosophical Society* 98 (June 1954): 171–78.

Berlin, Ira, Joseph P. Reidy, Barbara J. Fields, and Leslie Rowland. "Writing *Freedom's* History." *Prologue* 14 (Fall 1982): 129–39.

Berlin, Jean V. "Selecting the Essential Webster." *Documentary Editing* 13 (June 1991): 25–29.

Bidez, J., and A. B. Drachmann. *Emploi des signes critiques; disposition dans les éditions savantes de textes grecs et latins: Conseils et recommandations.* Paris, 1932; rev. ed. by A. Delatte and A. Severyns. Brussels, 1938.

Billias, George Athan. Reviews of *Naval Documents of the American Revolution,* vol. 2. *American Historical Review* 73 (October 1967): 216–17, vol. 5. Ibid. 77 (June 1972): 831.

———. Review of Rosemarie Zagarri, ed., *David Humphreys' 'Life of General Washington' with George Washington's 'Remarks'. Journal of American History* 79 (1992): 248–49.

Blegen, Theodore C. "Our Widening Province." *Mississippi Valley Historical Review* 31 (June 1944): 3–20.

Bowers, Fredson. *Essays in Bibliography, Text, and Editing.* Charlottesville, 1975.

———. "Established Texts and Definitive Editions." *Philological Quarterly* 41 (1962): 1–17. Reprinted in his *Essays in Bibliography, Text, and Editing,* 359–74.

———. "Four Faces of Bibliography." *Papers of the Bibliographical Society of Canada* 10 (1971): 33–45. Reprinted in his *Essays in Bibliography, Text, and Editing*, 94–108.

———. "The Function of Bibliography." *Library Trends* 7 (April 1959): 497–510.

———. "Multiple Authority: New Problems and Concepts of Copy-Text." *The Library* 27 (June 1972): 81–115. Reprinted in his *Essays in Bibliography, Text, and Editing*, 447–87.

———. *Principles of Bibliographical Description*. Princeton, N.J., 1949.

———. "Some Relations of Bibliography to Editorial Problems." *Studies in Bibliography* 3 (1950–51): 37–62. Reprinted in his *Essays in Bibliography, Text, and Editing*, 15–36.

———. "Transcription of Manuscripts: The Record of Variants." *Studies in Bibliography* 29 (1976): 212–64.

Boyd, Julian P. "'God's Altar Needs Not Our Pollishings.'" *New York History* 39 (January 1958): 3–21.

Boydston, Jo Ann. "The Collected Works of John Dewey." *Papers of the Bibliographical Society of America* 85 (1991): 119–44.

———. "The Press and the Project: A Study in Cooperation." *Scholarly Publishing* 15 (1983–84): 301–12.

Brilliant, Ira. "The Manuscript Society Information Exchange Database Opens at Arizona State University." *Manuscripts* 42 (1990): 5–12.

Broeker, Galen. "Jared Sparks, Robert Peel, and the State Papers Office." *American Quarterly* 13 (1961): 140–52.

Brooke, Christopher N. L. "The Teaching of Diplomatic." *Journal of the Society of Archivists* 4 (April 1970): 1–9.

Burg, B. Richard. "The Autograph Trade and Documentary Editing." *Manuscripts* 22 (Fall 1970): 247–54.

Burg, Steven B., and Michael E. Stevens. *Editing Historical Documents: A Handbook of Practice*. Madison, Wisc., 1997.

Burke, Frank. "Automation and Documentary Editing." *British Journal for the History of Science* 20 (January 1987): 73–79.

———. "The Historian as Editor: Progress and Problems." *Public Historian* 4 (1982): 5–19.

Burkhardt, Frederick. "Editing the Correspondence of Charles Darwin." *Studies in Bibliography* 41 (1988): 49–159.

Butcher, Judith. *Typescripts, Proofs, and Indexes*. New York, 1980.

Butler, Sharon, and William P. Stoneman, eds. *Editing, Publishing and Computer Technology. Papers Given at the 20th Annual Conference on Editorial Problems. University of Toronto 2–3 November 1984*. New York, 1988.

Butterfield, Lyman H. "Archival and Editorial Enterprise in 1850 and 1950: Some Comparisons and Contrasts." *Proceedings of the American Philosophical Society* 98 (1954): 159–70.

———.*Butterfield in Holland: A Record of L. H. Butterfield's Pursuit of the Adamses Abroad in 1959*. Cambridge, Mass., 1961.

———. "New Light on the North Atlantic Triangle in the 1780s." *William and Mary Quarterly*, 3d ser., 21 (October 1964): 596–606.

———. "The Papers of Thomas Jefferson: Progress and Procedures in the Enterprise at Princeton." *American Archivist* 12 (1949): 131–45.

———. "The Scholar's One World." *American Archivist* 29 (1966): 343–61.

Byrne, Sherry. "Guidelines for Contracting Microfilming Services." *Microform Review* 15 (Fall 1986): 253–64.

Cappon, Lester J. "American Historical Editors before Jared Sparks: 'they will plant a forest. . . .'" *William and Mary Quarterly*, 3d ser., 30 (July 1973): 375–400.

———. "The Historian as Editor." In *In Support of Clio: Essays in Memory of Herbert A. Kellar,* edited by William B. Hesseltine and Donald R. McNeil, 173–93. Madison, Wis., 1958.

———. "'The Historian's Day'—From Archives to History." In *The Reinterpretation of Early American History: Essays in Honor of John Edwin Pomfret,* edited by Ray Allen Billington, 233–49. San Marino, Calif., 1966.

———. "A Rationale for Historical Editing Past and Present." *William and Mary Quarterly*, 3d ser., 23 (January 1966): 56–75.

Cardwell, Guy. "Author, Intention, Text: The California Mark Twain." *Review* 11 (1989): 255–88.

Carter, Clarence E. *Historical Editing.* Bulletin No. 7. Washington, D.C., 1952.

———. "The United States and Documentary Historical Publication." *Mississippi Valley Historical Review* 25 (June 1938): 3–24.

Cayton, Mary Kupiec. "A Transcendentalist in Transition: Emerson and His Sermons, from Sacred to Secular." *Documentary Editing* 13 (March 1991): 9–12.

Center for Editions of American Authors. *Statement of Editorial Principles and Procedures: A Working Manual for Editing Nineteenth-Century Texts,* rev. ed. New York, 1972.

Chesnutt, David R. "Comprehensive Text Processing and the Papers of Henry Laurens. " *Newsletter of the Association for Documentary Editing* 2 (May 1980): 12–14.

———. "Historical Editions in the Digital Age." *d-lib magazine,* November 1995, http://www.diblib.org.

———. "Historical Editions in the States." *Computers and the Humanities* 25 (1991): 377–80.

———. "Optical Scanning and CINDEX: Tools for Creating a Cumulative Index to the Laurens Papers." *Newsletter of the Association for Documentary Editing* 5 (May 1983): 8–11.

———. "Presidential Editions: The Promise and Problems of Technology." *Documentary Editing* 16 (1994): 70–77.

Cimprich, John. Review of *The Papers of Andrew Johnson,* vol. 8. *Journal of Southern History* 58 (1992): 152–53.

Clark, Harry. *A Venture in History: The Production, Publication, and Sale of the Works of Hubert Howe Bancroft.* University of California Publications, Librarianship, no. 19. Los Angeles, 1973.

Claussen, Martin. "Revisiting America's State Papers, 1789–1861: A Clinical Examination and Prognosis." *American Archivist* 36 (1973): 523–36.

Cohen, Philip, ed. *Devils and Angels: Textual Editing and Literary Theory.* Charlottesville, 1991.

———. "Textual Instability, Literary Studies, and Recent Developments in Textual Scholarship." *Resources for American Literary Study* 20 (1994): 133–48.

Cook, Don L. "Precise Editing in a Book Club Format." *Documentary Editing* 10 (September 1988): 6–10.

———. "The Short Happy Thesis of G. Thomas Tanselle." *Newsletter of the Association for Documentary Editing* 3 (February 1981): 1–4.

Cox, H. Bartholomew. "Publication of Manuscripts: Devaluation or Enhancement?" *American Archivist* 32 (1969): 25–32.

Crane, Elaine Forman. "Gender Consciousness in Editing: The Diary of Elizabeth Drinker." *TEXT* 4 (1988): 375–83.

Creasy, William C. "A Microcomputer Editorial Procedure." In William C. Creasy and Vinton A. Dearing, *Microcomputers & Literary Scholarship*, 1–22. Los Angeles, 1986.

Cullen, Charles T. "Principles of Annotation in Editing Historical Documents; or, How to Avoid Breaking the Butterfly on the Wheel of Scholarship." In *Literary and Historical Editing*, edited by George L. Vogt and John Bush Jones, 81–95.

Cunningham, Noble E., Jr. "The Legacy of Julian Boyd." *South Atlantic Quarterly* 83 (1984): 340–44.

Cutler, Wayne. "The 'Authentic' Witness: The Editor Speaks for the Document." *Newsletter of the Association for Documentary Editing* 4 (February 1982): 8–9.

Dainard, J. A., ed. *Editing Correspondence: Papers Given at the Fourteenth Annual Conference on Editorial Problems, University of Toronto, 3–4 November 1978.* New York, 1979.

Daniels, Maygene. "The Ingenious Pen: American Writing Implements from the Eighteenth Century to the Twentieth Century." *American Archivist* 43 (1980): 312–24.

Davis, Tom. "The CEAA and Modern Textual Editing." *The Library* 32 (1977): 61–74.

De Battista, Michael. "Tape Proofreading: An Adaptation for Part-Time Staff." *Scholarly Publishing* 7 (January 1975): 147–50.

Dearing, Vinton. "Textual Criticism Today: A Brief Survey." *Studies in the Novel* 7 (1975): 394–98.

Dierenfield, Bruce. Review of Judy Barrett Litoff and David C. Smith, eds., *Miss You: The World War II Letters of Barbara Wooddall Taylor and Charles E. Taylor. Journal of Southern History* 58 (1992): 386–87.

Dunlap, Leslie W., and Fred Shelley, eds. *The Publication of American Historical Manuscripts.* Iowa City, 1976.

Easson, Angus. "Reviewing Editions: Letters, Journal, Dairies." In *Literary Reviewing*, edited by James O. Hoge, 44–67. Charlottesville, 1987.

"The Editor's Craft: Looking Back to Look Ahead." *Documentary Editing* 17 (March 1995): 22–24.

Edwards, Mary Jane. "CEECT: Progress, Procedures, and Problems." *Papers of the Bibliographical Society of Canada* 26 (1987): 13–26.

"Electronic Editions (I): What Should They Look Like?"; "Electronic Editions (II): Works in Progress." *Documentary Editing* 18 (March 1996): 13–14.

Eppard, Philip B. "The Archivist's Perspective: Implications for Documentary Editing." *Documentary Editing* 16 (June 1994): 47–50.

Evans, Frank B., et al., "A Basic Glossary for Archivists, Manuscript Curators, and Records Managers." *American Archivist* 37 (July 1974): 415–31.

Fabian, Bernhard. "Jefferson's Notes on Virginia: The Genesis of Query xvii, The different religions received into that State." *William and Mary Quarterly*, 3d ser., 12 (January 1955): 124–38.

Feller, Daniel. "Compromising Clay." *Documentary Editing* 8 (September 1986): 1–6.

———. "'What Good Are They Anyway?': A User Looks at Documentary Editions." *Documentary Editing* 8 (September 1986): 1–6.

Filby, P. W. *Calligraphy and Handwriting in America, 1710–1967.* New York, 1963.

Finkenbine, Roy E. "Garveyism and the 'New Documentary Editing.'" *Documentary Editing* 7 (March 1985): 7–11.

Fishbein, Morris. "The Evidential Value of Nontextual Records: An Early Precedent." *American Archivist:* 45 (Spring 1982): 189–90.

Fones-Wolf, Ken. "Human Frailties and Editorial Rigidities: *The Letters of Eugene V. Debs.*" *Documentary Editing* 15 (September 1993): 61–64.

Ford, Worthington C. "The Editorial Function in United States History." *American Historical Review* 23 (1917–18): 273–86.

Franklin, Wayne. "The 'Library of America' and the Welter of American Books." *Iowa Review* 15 (Spring-Summer 1985): 176–94.

Friedman, Arthur. "Principles of Historical Annotation in Critical Editions of Modern Texts." *English Institute Annual* 1941: 115–28.

Gabler, Hans Walter. Review of *James Joyce, Ulysses: A Facsimile of the Manuscript. The Library* 32 (1977): 177–82.

———. "The Synchrony and the Diachrony of Texts: Practice and Theory of the Critical Edition of James Joyce's *Ulysses.*" *TEXT* 1 (1984): 305–26.

———. "The Text as Process and the Problem of Intentionality." *TEXT* 3 (1987): 107–15.

Gaskell, Philip. *From Writer to Reader: Studies in Editorial Method.* Oxford, 1978.

Geckle, George L. Review of Christopher Marlowe, *Dr. Faustus. TEXT* 7 (1994): 492–511.

George, Juliette, Alexander George, and Michael Marmor. "Research Note: Issues in Wilson Scholarship: References to Early 'Strokes' in the *Pa-*

*pers of Woodrow Wilson." Journal of American History* 70 (March 1984): 845–53.

Gibson, William M. "The Center for Editions of American Authors." *Professional Standards and American Editions: A Response to Edmund Wilson*, 1–6. New York, 1969.

Gilman, William H. "How Should Journals Be Edited?" *Early American Literature* 6 (Spring 1971): 73–83.

Gilmore, William J. Review of *The Letters of John Greenleaf Whittier*, edited by John P. Pickard. *Journal of American History* 63 (1976): 672–73.

Gordon, Ann. "A Future for Documentary Editions: The Historical Documents Study." *Documentary Editing* 14 (March 1992): 6–10.

Gottesman, Ronald, and Scott Bennett, eds., *Art and Error: Modern Textual Editing*. Bloomington, Ind., 1970.

Gottesman, Ronald, and David Nordloh. "The Quest for Perfection: or Surprises in the Consummation of *Their Wedding Journey*." *CEAA Newsletter* 1 (March 1968): 12–13.

Greetham, D. C., ed. *The Marquis of the Text*. Ann Arbor, 1996.

———, ed. *Scholarly Editing: A Guide to Research*. New York, 1995.

———. "Textual and Literary Theory: Redrawing the Matrix." *Studies in Bibliography* 42 (1989): 1–24.

———. *Textual Scholarship: An Introduction*. New York, 1992.

———. *Textual Transgressions: Essays toward the Construction of a Bibliography*. New York, 1996.

———. *Theories of the Text*. Oxford, 1996.

Greg, W. W. "The Rationale of Copy-text." *Studies in Bibliography* 3 (1950–51): 19–36. Reprinted in *Bibliography and Textual Criticism*, edited by O. M. Brack, Jr., and Warner Barnes, 41–58. Chicago, 1969; and in *Art and Error: Modern Textual Editing*, edited by Ronald Gottesman and Scott Bennett, 17–36.

Grele, Ronald, J. "Movement Without Aim: Methodological and Theoretical Problems in Oral History." In *Envelopes of Sound: Six Practitioners Discuss the Method, Theory, and Practice of Oral Testimony and Oral History*, edited by Ronald J. Grele, 33–34. Chicago, 1975.

Gruber, Ira D. Review of *Naval Documents of the American Revolution*, vol. 1. *William and Mary Quarterly* 22 (1965): 660–63.

Hajo, Cathy Moran. "Computerizing Control over Authority Names at the Margaret Sanger Papers." *Documentary Editing* 13 (June 1991): 35–39.

Halsband, Robert. "Editing the Letters of Letter-Writers." *Studies in Bibliography* 11 (1958): 25–37. Reprinted in *Art and Error: Modern Textual Editing*, edited by Ronald Gottesman and Scott Bennett, 124–39.

Hamer, Philip M. "'. . . authentic Documents tending to elucidate our History.'" *American Archivist* 25 (1962): 3–13.

Hamilton, Charles. *Collecting Autographs and Manuscripts*. Norman, Okla. 1961.

Harman, Eleanor. "Hints on Proofreading." *Scholarly Publishing* 7 (January 1975): 151–57.

Harrison, Teresa M., and Timothy Stephen. "On-Line Disciplines: Computer-Mediated Scholarship in the Humanities and Social Sciences." *Computers and the Humanities* 26 (1992): 181–93.

*Harvard Guide to American History*, edited by Frank Burt Freidel, with Richard K. Showman. Cambridge, 1974.

*Harvard Guide to American History*, edited by Oscar Handlin et al. Cambridge, 1954.

Hattaway, Herman. Review of William C. David, *Jefferson Davis: The Man and His Hour. Journal of American History* 79 (1992): 1178–79.

Hay, Louis. "Genetic Editing, Past and Future: A Few Reflections by a User." *TEXT* 3 (1987): 117–33.

Henige, David. Review of *The Juan Pardo Expeditions. Documentary Editing* 13 (June 1991): 30–34.

Herst, Herman, Jr. "Philatelists Are the Luckiest People." *Manuscripts* 32 (Summer 1980): 187–90.

Hesseltine, William B., and Larry Gara. "The Archives of Pennsylvania: A Glimpse at an Editor's Problem." *Pennsylvania Magazine* 77 (1953): 328–31.

Hill, W. Speed. "The Case for Standards in Scholarly Editing." *Literary Research* 13 (1988): 203–12.

———. "Theory and Practice of Transcription." In *New Ways of Looking at Old Texts,* edited by Hill. Binghamton, N.Y., 1993.

Hirst, Robert H. "Editing Mark Twain, Hand to Hand, 'Like All D—d Fool Printers.'" *Papers of the Bibliographical Society of America,* 88 (June 1994): 157–88.

Hobson, Charles. Review of *The Correspondence and Miscellaneous Papers of Benjamin Henry Latrobe,* vol. 3. *Virginia Magazine of History and Biography* 97 (1989): 228–30.

Hodge, M. J. S. "Darwin: The Voyage, London, and Down." *Annals of Science* 50 (1993): 179.

Holloran, Peter. "Rediscovering Lost Values: Transcribing an African-American Sermon." *Documentary Editing* 13 (September 1991): 49–53.

Holmes, Oliver W. "Documentary Publication in the Western Hemisphere." *Archivum* 16 (1966): 79–96.

Hornberger, Theodore. Review of *The Papers of Thomas Jefferson,* vols. 1 and 2. *American Quarterly* 3 (1951): 87–90.

Housman, A. E. "The Application of Thought to Textual Criticism." 1921. Reprint in *A. E. Housman: Selected Prose,* edited by John Carter, 131–50. (Cambridge, England, 1962). Also in Gottesman and Bennett, 1–16.

Howard, Ronald W. "Lewis Morris, in Eighteenth-Century New Jersey and New York: A Review." *Documentary Editing* 17 (March 1995): 11–15.

Howard-Hill, T. H. "Enumerative and Descriptive Bibliography." In *The Book Encompassed: Studies in Twentieth-Century Bibliography,* edited by Peter Davison, 122–29. Cambridge, 1992.

————. "Shakespeare Edited, Restored, Domesticated, Verbatim and Modernized." *Review* 15 (1993): 115–225.

Hudspeth, Robert N. "Hawthorne's Letters and the 'Darksome Veil of Mystery.'" *Documentary Editing* (September 1986): 7–11.

Hurlebusch, Klaus. "'Relic' and 'Tradition': Some Aspects of Editing Diaries." *TEXT* 3 (1987): 143–53.

Hutson, James H. Review of *The Papers of Benjamin Franklin,* vol. 27. *Pennsylvania Magazine* 114 (1990): 295–96.

Jackson, Donald. "What I Did for Love—of Editing." *Western Historical Quarterly* 13 (1982): 291–97.

James, Judith Giblin. "'I Know my Worth': Lillian Smith's Letters from the Modern South." *Documentary Editing* 16 (December 1994): 85–87.

Jameson, J. Franklin. "Gaps in the Published Records of United States History." *American Historical Review* 11 (1905–6): 817–31.

Jenkins, Reese V. "Words, Images, Artifacts and Sound: Documents for the History of Technology." *British Journal for the History of Science* 20 (1987): 1–8.

Jenkins, Reese V., and Thomas E. Jeffrey. "Worth a Thousand Words: Nonverbal Documents in Editing," *Documentary Editing* 6 (September 1984): 1–8.

Jenkinson, Hilary. "The Representation of Manuscripts in Print." *London Mercury* 30 (September 1934): 429–38.

Johnson, Thomas H. "Establishing a Text: The Emily Dickinson Papers." *Studies in Bibliography* 5 (1952–53): 21–32.

Kerr, Chester. "Publishing Historical Sources: A Prejudicial View of the Problem of Finance." *Proceedings of the American Philosophical Society* 98 (August 1954): 273–78.

Ketcham, Ralph L. "The Madison Family Papers: Case Study in a Search for Historical Manuscripts." *Manuscripts* 11 (Summer 1959): 49–55.

Kimnach, Wilson H. "Realities of the Sermon: Some Considerations for Editors." *Documentary Editing* 5 (February 1983): 5–10.

Kirkham, E. Kay. *How to Read the Handwriting and Records of Early America.* Salt Lake City, 1964.

Kitching, Christopher. "Record Publication in England and Wales, 1957–1982." *Archives* 17 (April 1985): 38–46.

————. "The Status of Documentary Editing in the United Kingdom." *Documentary Editing* 11 (June 1989): 29–31.

Kline, Mary Jo. *A Guide to Documentary Editing.* Baltimore, 1987.

Knight, David. "Background and Foreground: Getting Things in Context." *British Journal for the History of Science* 20 (1987): 3–12.

Kohn, Richard H., and George M. Curtis III. "The Government, the Historical Profession, and Historical Editing." *Reviews in American History* 9 (June 1981): 145–55.

Kraditor, Aileen S. Review of *The Letters of William Lloyd Garrison*, vols. 1 and 2. *Reviews in American History* 1 (1973): 519–23.

Krattenmaker, Tom. "Reading Jefferson's Mail." *Princeton Alumni Weekly,* 10 November, 1993, 10–15.

Kristeller, Paul Oskar. "The Lachmann Method: Merits and Limitations." *TEXT* 1 (1984): 11–20.

Labaree, Leonard W. "In Search of 'B Franklin.'" *William and Mary Quarterly,* 3d ser., 16 (April 1959): 188–97.

———. "350 Were Approached, Only Three Said 'No'." *Williams Alumni Review,* February 1967, 11–12.

Landon, Richard, ed. *Editing and Editors: A Retrospect: Papers Given at the Twenty-First Annual Conference on Editorial Problems, University of Toronto, 1–2 November 1985.* New York, 1988.

Landow, George P. "Hypertext in Literary Education, Criticism, and Scholarship." *Computers and the Humanities* 23 (1989): 173–98.

Leland, Waldo Gifford. "The Prehistory and Origins of the National Historical Publications Commission." *American Archivist* 27 (1964): 187–94.

Lemisch, Jesse. "The American Revolution Bicentennial and the Papers of Great White Men: A Preliminary Critique of Current Documentary Publication Programs and Some Alternative Proposals." *American Historical Association Newsletter* 9 (November 1971): 7–21.

Lennox, John, and Janet M. Paterson, eds. *Challenges, Projects, Texts: Canadian Editing. 25th Annual Conference on Editorial Problems, University of Toronto, November 17–18, 1989.* New York, 1993.

Lewis, Wilmarth S. "Editing Familiar Letters." In *Editing Correspondence,* edited by J. A. Dainard, 25–37.

Library of Congress. *Symbols of American Libraries.* Washington, D.C., 1992.

Link, Arthur S. "Where We Stand Now and Where We Might Go." *Newsletter of the Association for Documentary Editing* 2 (February 1980): 1–4.

Luey, Beth. *Editing Documents and Texts: An Annotated Bibliography.* Madison, Wisc., 1990.

———. *Handbook for Academic Authors.* New York, 1987.

———. "Publishing the Edition." *Documentary Editing* 13 (June 1991): 40–45.

Maas, Paul. *Textual Criticism.* Translated by Barbara Flower. Oxford, 1958.

Madden, Dennis D. "Historical Editing and the Practical Application of Archival Skills: Surveying Common Ground." *Documentary Editing* 16 (March 1994): 10–12.

Mailloux, Stephen. *Interpretive Conventions: The Reader in the Study of American Fiction.* Ithaca, 1991.

Mancher, Michael. "The Text of the Fruits of the MLA." *Papers of the Bibliographical Society of America* 68 (1974): 411–12.

Matthews, John. "The Hunt for the Disraeli Letters." In *Editing Correspondence,* edited by J. A. Dainard, 81–92.

McClure, James P. "The Neglected Calendar." *Documentary Editing* 10 (September 1988): 18–21.

McElrath, Joseph R., Jr. "Tradition and Innovation: Recent Developments in Literary Editing." *Documentary Editing* 10 (December 1988): 5–10.

McGann, Jerome J. "The Complete Writings and Pictures of Dante Gabriel Rosetti: A Hypermedia Research Archive." *TEXT* 7 (1994): 95–105.

———. *A Critique of Modern Textual Criticism.* Chicago, 1983.

McGirr, Newman F. "The Adventures of Peter Force." *Records of the Columbia Historical Society* 42 (1942): 35–82.

McHaney, Thomas L. "The Important Questions Are Seldom Raised." *Studies in the Novel* 7 (1975): 399–402.

McKivigan, John R. "Capturing the Oral Event: Editing the Speeches of Frederick Douglass." *Documentary Editing* 10 (March 1988): 1–5.

Meadows, A. J. "Changing Records and Changing Realities." *British Journal for the History of Science* 20 (January 1987): 67–71.

Meats, Steven. "The Editing of Harold Frederic's Correspondence." *Review* 2 (1980): 31–39.

Meriwether, James B. "Some Proofreading Precautions." *CEAA Newsletter* 2 (July 1969): 17–18.

Merriam, Thomas. "An Experiment with the Federalist Papers." *Computers and the Humanities* 23 (1989): 252–54.

Middleton, Anne. "Life in the Margins; or, What's an Annotator to Do?" *The Library Chronicle of the University of Texas at Austin* 20 (1990): 167–83.

Middleton, Arthur Pierce, and Douglass Adair. "The Mystery of the Horn Papers." *William and Mary Quarterly,* 3d ser., 4 (October 1947): 409–45.

Miller, F. Thornton. Review of *John Marshall Papers,* vol. 6. *Virginia Magazine* 101 (1993): 172–73.

Miller, Lillian B. Review of *The Correspondence and Miscellaneous Papers of Benjamin Henry Latrobe. Virginia Magazine of History and Biography* 94 (1986): 227–29.

Miller, Randall M. "Documentary Editing and Black History: A Few Observations and Suggestions." *Maryland Historian* 16 (1985): 3–9.

Modern Language Association. *Professional Standards and American Editions: A Response to Edmund Wilson.* New York, 1969.

Moggridge, D. E., ed. *Editing Modern Economists: Papers Given at the Twenty-Second Annual Conference on Editorial Problems, University of Toronto, 7–8 November 1989.* New York, 1988.

Moore, Alexander. "Present at the Creation: John Franklin Jameson and the Development of Humanistic Scholarship in America." *Documentary Editing* 16 (September 1994): 57–60.

Morris, Richard B. "The Current Statesmen's Papers Publication Program: An Appraisal from the Point of View of the Legal Historian." *American Journal of Legal History* 11 (1967): 95–106.

Mumford, Lewis. "Emerson Behind Barbed Wire." *New York Review of Books,* 18 January 1968, pp. 3–5.

Myerson, Joel. "*The Autobiography of Benjamin Franklin:* A Genetic Text." *Newsletter of the Association for Documentary Editing* 4 (May 1982): 9–10.

Myerson, Joel, and Daniel Shealy. "Editing Louisa May Alcott's Journals." *Manuscripts* 42 (1990): 19–33.

National Historical Publications and Records Commission. *Historical Documentary Editions.* Washington, D.C., 1993.

———. *Historical Editions, 1988: A List of Documentary Publications Supported by the National Historical Publications and Records Commission,* Washington, D.C., 1988.

Neufeldt, Leonard N. "Neopragmatism and Convention in Textual Editing, with Examples from the Editing of Thoreau's Autograph Journal." *Analytical and Enumerative Bibliography,* n.s., 1 (1987): 227–36.

Newcomer, Lee N. "Manasseh Cutler's Writings: A Note on Editorial Practice." *Mississippi Valley Historical Review* 47 (June 1960): 88–101.

Newman, Debra. Review of *The Marcus Garvey and Universal Negro Improvement Papers,* vols. 1 and 2. *American Archivist* 47 (1984): 308–10.

Nickell, Joe. *Pen, Ink, and Evidence: A Study of Writing and Writing Materials for the Penman, Collector, and Document Detective.* Lexington, Ky., 1990.

Nida, Eugene A. "Editing Translated Texts." *TEXT* 4 (1988): 13–27.

Noble, Richard A. "The NHPRC Data Base Project: Building the 'Interstate Highway System.'" *American Archivist* 51 (1988): 98–105.

Nordloh, David J. "The 'Perfect' Text: The Editor Speaks for the Author." *Newsletter of the Association for Documentary Editing* 2 (May 1980): 1–3.

———. "Socialization, Authority, and Evidence: Reflections on McGann's *A Critique of Modern Textual Criticism.*" *Analytical and Enumerative Bibliography,* n.s., 1 (1987): 3–12.

———. "Substantives and Accidentals vs. New Evidence: Another Strike in the Game of Distinctions." *CEAA Newsletter* 3 (June 1970): 12–13.

———. "Supplying What's Missing in Editions of Selected Letters." *Scholarly Publishing* 17 (1985–86): 37–47.

———. "Theory, Funding, and Coincidence in the Editing of American Literature." In *Editing and Editors: A Retrospect,* edited by Richard Landon, 137–55.

North Carolina Division of Archives and History. *Guide for Authors and Editors,* compiled by Joe A. Mobley and Kathleen B. Wyche. Raleigh, 1992.

Oberbeck, Lois More. "Researching Literary Manuscripts: A Scholar's Perspective." *American Archivist* 56 (1993): 62–69.

Oberg, Barbara. "Documentary Editing as a Collaborative Enterprise: Theirs, Mine, or Ours?" *Documentary Editing* 17 (March 1995): 1–5.

Oetting, Edward. "The Information Exchange Database: 'The Future is Now.'" *Manuscripts* 42 (1990): 13–17.

O'Neill, James E. "Copies of French Manuscripts for American History in the Library of Congress." *Journal of American History* 51 (December 1965): 674–91.

Orth, Ralph. "An Edition of Emerson's Poetry Notebooks." *Documentary Editing* 6 (March 1984): 8–11.

Parker, Hershel. *Flawed Texts and Verbal Icons: Literary Authority in American Fiction.* Evanston, Ill., 1984.

———. Review of the centenary edition of *Works of Nathaniel Hawthorne,* vols. 12 and 13. *Nineteenth-Century Fiction* 33 (1979): 489–92.

Parker, Hershel, and Bruce Bebb. "The CEAA: An Interim Assessment." *Papers of the Bibliographical Society of America* 68 (1974): 129–48.

Peck, Robert McCracken. Review of *The Correspondence of John Bartram. William and Mary Quarterly* 50 (1993): 356–58.

Peckham, Morse. "Notes on Freehafer and the CEAA." *Studies in the Novel* 7 (1975): 402–4.

Powell, J. H. *The Books of a New Nation.* Philadelphia, 1957.

———. Review of *The Letters of Benjamin Rush. Mississippi Valley Historical Review* 39 (September 1952): 325–27.

Prögler, J. A. "Choices in Editing Oral History." *Oral History Review* 19 (1991): 1–16.

Rapport, Leonard. "Dumped from a Wharf into Casco Bay: The Historical Records Survey Revisited." *American Archivist* 37 (1974): 201–10.

———. "Fakes and Facsimiles: Problems of Identification." *American Archivist* 42 (1979): 13–58.

Reagor, Simone. "Historical Editing: The Federal Role." *Newsletter of the Association for Documentary Editing* 4 (May 1982): 1–4.

Reeve, Thomas C. "The Search for the Chester Alan Arthur Papers." *Manuscripts* 25 (Summer 1973): 171–85.

Reiff, Janice L. *Structuring the Past: The Use of Computers in History.* Washington, D.C., 1991.

Reiman, Donald H. "Gender and Documentary Editing: A Diachronic Perspective." *TEXT* 4 (1988): 351–59.

———. "Gentlemen Authors and Professional Writers: Notes on the History of Editing Texts of the 18th and 19th Centuries." In *Editing and Editors: A Retrospect,* edited by Richard Landon, 99–136.

———. *Romantic Texts and Context.* Columbia, Mo., 1987.

———. *The Study of Modern Manuscripts: Public, Confidential, and Private.* Baltimore, 1993.

———. "'Versioning': The Presentation of Multiple Texts." In his *Romantic Texts and Contexts,* 109–29.

Reingold, Nathan. "The Darwin Industry Encounters Tanselle and Bowers." *Documentary Editing* 10 (June 1988): 16–19.

———. "Reflections of an Unrepentant Editor." *American Archivist* 46 (1983): 14–21.

Rice, Howard C. "Jefferson in Europe." *Princeton University Library Chronicle* 12 (Autumn 1950): 19–35.

Robinson, David. "The Legacy of Emerson's Journals." *Resources for American Literary Study* 13 (1983): 1–9.

Robinson, Peter. *The Transcription of Primary Textual Sources Using SGML.* Office for Humanities Communications Publications, No. 6. Oxford, 1994.

Robson, John M. "Practice, Not Theory: Editing J. S. Mill's Newspaper Writings." *Studies in Bibliography* 41 (1988): 160–76.

Roelevink, Johanna, and Augustus J. Veenendaal, Jr. "Undeleting the Dutch

Past: The Netherlands Government Commission on National History." *Documentary Editing* 12 (June 1990): 45–48.

Rogers, George C., Jr. Review of *The Papers of George Mason*, vols. 1–3. *William and Mary Quarterly*, 3d ser., 28 (October 1971): 676–79.

———. "The Sacred Text: An Impossible Dream." In *Literary and Historical Editing*, edited by George L. Vogt and John Bush Jones, 23–33.

Rosenberg, Robert. "Technological Artifacts as Historical Documents." *TEXT* 3 (1987): 393–407.

Rothenberg, Marc. "Documenting Technology: The Selective Microfilm Edition of the Thomas A. Edison Papers." *Documentary Editing* 12 (September 1990): 53–55.

Rowland, Buford. "Recordkeeping Practices of the House of Representatives." *National Archives Accessions* 53. Washington, D.C., 1957.

Rutland, Robert. "Recycling Early National History through the Papers of the Founding Fathers." *American Quarterly* 28 (Summer 1976): 250–61.

Ryerson, Richard A. "Documenting the Presidency of John Adams: The Adams Papers Project." *Prologue* 21 (Spring 1989): 21–37.

———. "Editing a Family Legacy: The Adamses and Their Papers." *Documentary Editing* 11 (September 1989): 57–62.

———. "The Other Historians: Archivists, Editors, and Collective Biographers." *Pennsylvania History* 57 (1990): 3–12.

Ryjes, T. K. "Keynes's Lectures, 1932–1935: Notes of a Representative Student. Problems in Construction of a Synthesis." In *Editing Modern Economists*, edited by D. E. Moggridge, 91–127.

Saatkamp, Herman J., Jr. "The Editor and Technology." *Documentary Editing* 12 (March 1990): 9–12.

———. "Private Rights vs. Public Needs." *Documentary Editing* 13 (December 1991): 77–84.

Saladino, Gaspare. "Charmed Beginnings and Democratic Murmurings." *Documentary Editing* 6 (March 1984): 1–7.

Samore, Ted. Review of *The New American State Papers, 1789–1860. Government Publications Review* 7A (1980): 101–3.

Schneider, Stewart P. Review of *National State Papers of the United States*, parts 1 and 2. *Government Publications Review* 8A (1981): 443–44.

Schulz, Constance B. "Do Archivists Need to Know How to be Editors? A Proposal for the Role of Documentary Editing in Graduate Archival Education." *Documentary Editing* 16 (March 1994): 5–9.

———. "'From Generation unto Generation': Transitions in Modern Documentary Historical Editing." *Reviews in American History* 16 (1988): 337–50.

———. Review of *Jefferson's Parliamentary Writings: "Parliamentary Pocket-Book and A Manual of Parliamentary Practice. Virginia Magazine of History and Biography* 97 (1989): 224–26.

Scott, Patrick G., and William B. Thesing. "Conversations with Victorian Writers: Some Editorial Questions." *Documentary Editing* 11 (June 1989): 37–42.

Shaw, Peter. "The American Heritage and Its Guardians." *American Scholar* 45 (1976): 733–51.

Sheldon, Richard N. "Editing a Historical Manuscript: Jared Sparks, Douglas Southall Freeman, and the Battle of Brandywine." *William and Mary Quarterly,* 3d ser., 36 (April 1979): 255–63.

Shelley, Fred. "Ebenezer Hazard: America's First Historical Editor." *William and Mary Quarterly,* 3d ser., 12 (January 1955): 44–73.

———. "The Interest of J. Franklin Jameson in the National Archives: 1908–1934." *American Archivist* 12 (1949): 99–130.

Sherrill, E. Grace. "'The Daily Crucifixion of the Post': Editing and Theorizing the Lowry Letters." In *Challenges, Projects, Texts,* edited by John Lennox and Janet M. Paterson, 25–53.

Shillingsburg, Peter L. "The Autonomous Author, the Sociology of Texts, and the Polemics of Textual Criticism." In *Devils and Angels,* edited by Philip Cohen, 22–43.

———. "Critical Editing and the Center for Scholarly Editions." *Scholarly Publishing* 9 (October 1977): 31–40.

———. "An Inquiry into the Social Status of Texts and Modes of Textual Criticism." *Studies in Bibliography* 42 (1989): 55–77.

———. *Scholarly Editing in the Computer Age: Lectures in Theory and Practice,* 3d ed. Ann Arbor, 1996.

Sifton, Paul G. "The Provenance of the Thomas Jefferson Papers." *American Archivist* 40 (1977): 17–30.

Simon, John Y. "The Canons of Selection." *Documentary Editing* 6 (December 1984): 8–12.

———. "Editors and Critics." *Newsletter of the Association for Documentary Editing* 3 (December 1981): 1–4.

Simpson, Brook D. "Blacks in Blue and The Fight for Freedom." *Documentary Editing* 7 (September 1985): 6–10.

Simpson, Claude M., William Goetzmann, and Matthew J. Bruccoli. "The Interdependence of Rare Books and Manuscripts: The Scholar's View." *Serif* 9 (Spring 1972): 3–22.

Spiker, Sina. *Indexing Your Book: A Practical Guide for Authors.* Madison, Wisc., 1988.

Stachel, John. "'A Man of My Type'—Editing the Einstein Papers." *British Journal for the History of Science* 20 (January 1987): 57–66.

Stewart, James B. Review of *The Letters of William Lloyd Garrison,* vols. 3 and 4. *Reviews in American History* 4 (1976): 539–46.

Stewart, Kate. "James Madison as an Archivist." *American Archivist* 21 (1958): 243–57.

Stillinger, Jack. *Multiple Authorship and the Myth of Solitary Genius.* New York, 1991.

Sullivan, Ernest W. "The Problem of Text in Familiar Letters." *Papers of the Bibliographical Society of America* 75 (1981): 115–26.

Tanselle, G. Thomas. "Bibliographical Problems in Melville." *Studies in American Fiction* 2 (Spring 1974): 57–74.

———. "The Editing of Historical Documents." *Studies in Bibliography* 31

(1978): 1–56. Reprinted in his *Selected Studies in Bibliography*, 451–506.

———. "Editorial Apparatus for Radiating Texts." *The Library* 29 (September 1974): 330–37.

———. "Historicism and Critical Editing." *Studies in Bibliography* 39 (1986): 1–46. Reprinted in his *Textual Criticism Since Greg*, 109–54.

———. "Literary Editing." In *Literary and Historical Editing*, edited by George L. Vogt and John Bush Jones, 35–56.

———. *Selected Studies in Bibliography*. Charlottesville, 1979.

———. "Some Principles for Editorial Apparatus." *Studies in Bibliography* 25 (1972): 41–88. Reprinted in his *Selected Studies in Bibliography*, 403–50.

———. "Textual Criticism and Literary Sociology." *Studies in Bibliography* 44 (1991): 83–143.

———. *Textual Criticism and Scholarly Editing*. Charlottesville, 1990.

———. *Textual Criticism Since Greg*. Charlottesville, 1987.

———. "Textual Scholarship." In *Introduction to Scholarship in Modern Languages and Literatures*, edited by Joseph Gibaldi, 29–52. New York, 1981.

———. "Two Basic Distinctions: Theory and Practice, Text and Apparatus." *Studies in the Novel* 7 (1975): 404–6.

Taylor, Robert J. "Editorial Practices—An Historian's View." *Newsletter of the Association for Documentary Editing* 3 (February 1981): 4–8.

———. "One Historian's Education." *William and Mary Quarterly*, 3d ser., 41 (1984): 478–86.

Tebbe, Jennifer. "Print and American Culture." *American Quarterly* 32 (1980): 259–79.

Teute, Fredrika J. "Views in Review: A Historiographical Perspective on Historical Editing." *American Archivist* 43 (Winter 1980): 43–56.

Thorpe, James. *Principles of Textual Criticism*. San Marino, Calif., 1972; reprint, 1995.

———. *The Use of Manuscripts in Literary Research: Problems of Access and Literary Property Rights*. New York, 1979.

"Using Databases in Editorial Projects: A Workshop." *Documentary Editing*, 15 (March 1993): 15.

Van Dusen, Albert E. "In Quest of That 'Arch Rebel' Jonathan Trumbull, Sr." In *Publication of American Historical Manuscripts*, edited by Leslie W. Dunlap and Fred Shelley, 31–46.

Van Horne, John C. "Drawing to a Close: The Papers of Benjamin Henry Latrobe." *Documentary Editing* 11 (September 1989): 63–69.

Vogt, George L., and John Bush Jones, eds., *Literary and Historical Editing*. Lawrence, Kans., 1981.

Walker, John A. "Editing Zola's Correspondence: When Is a Letter Not a Letter?" In *Editing Correspondence*, edited by J. A. Dainard, 93–116.

Warren, Jack D. "The Counter-Revolutionary Career of Peter Porcupine." *Documentary Editing* 16 (December 1994): 88–93.

Weber, Ralph E. *United States Diplomatic Codes and Ciphers, 1775–1938.* Chicago, 1979.

Wiberley, Stephen E., Jr. "Editing Maps: A Method for Historical Cartography." *Journal of Interdisciplinary History* 10 (Winter 1980): 499–510.

Wiggins, Henry H. "Publisher to Alexander Hamilton, Esqr." *Scholarly Publishing* 9 (April 1978): 195–206 and (July 1978): 347–60.

Williams, T. Harry. "Abraham Lincoln—Principle and Pragmatism in Politics: A Review Article." *Mississippi Valley Historical Review* 40 (June 1953): 89–106.

Wilson, Edmund. "The Fruits of the MLA." *New York Review of Books,* 26 September 1968, pp. 10ff. Reprinted and expanded in his *The Devils and Canon Barham: Ten Essays on Poets, Novelists and Monsters,* 154–202. New York, 1973.

Wolf, Edwin, II. "Evidence Indicating the Need for Some Bibliographical Analysis of American Printed Historical Works." *Papers of the Bibliographical Society of America* 63 (1969): 261–77.

———. "The Reconstruction of Benjamin Franklin's Library: An Unorthodox Jigsaw Puzzle." *Papers of the Bibliographical Society of America* 56 (1962): 1–16.

Wood, Gordon S. "Historians and Documentary Editing." *Journal of American History* 67 (March 1981): 871–77.

Woodward, C. Vann. "History from Slave Sources." *American Historical Review* 79 (April 1974): 470–81.

———. "Mary Chesnutt in Search of Her Genre." *Yale Review* 73 (Winter 1984): 199–209.

Wright, Conrad E. "Multiplying the Copies: New England Historical Societies and Documentary Publishing's Alternative Tradition." *Documentary Editing* 11 (June 1989): 32–36.

Yeandle, Laetitia. "The Evolution of Handwriting in the English-Speaking Colonies of America." *American Archivist* 43 (1980): 294–311.

Zboray, Ronald J. "Computerized Document Control and Indexing at the Emma Goldman Papers." *Studies in Bibliography* 43 (1990): 34–49.

Zuppan, Jo. Review of *The Correspondence of John Bartram. Virginia Magazine of History and Biography* 101 (1993): 302–03.

Zweig, Ronald W. "Electronically Generated Records and Twentieth Century History." *Computers and the Humanities* 27 (1993): 73–83.

# INDEX

Abbreviations, 142, 155, 158, 161
Accessioning documents, 57–58
Adams, Charles Francis, 4
Adams, John, 176, 217
Adams, John, edition, 4, 6, 17, 162, 163;
   and attribution of works, 95; compre-
   hensiveness, 73; and diaries, 89; and
   document control, 56; and expanded
   transcription, 164; organization, 85,
   87–88
Adams Family edition, 6; and annota-
   tion, 217; and diaries, 127; index, 253,
   254–55; microfilm edition, 164; organization, 87–88
Additions, authorial, 149, 160, 163.
   See also Interlineations
Additions, editorial, 151–52, 161–62.
   See also Emendation
Alcott, Louisa May, edition, 80
Alternative readings, 151
*American State Papers* series, 4
Annotation: and audience's needs, 82,
   214–15; back-of-book, 223; citation of
   sources for, 224–28; differs in literary
   and historical editions, 11; explained
   in statement of editorial policy, 247;
   final proofreading of, 252; footnotes,
   221–23; forms, 220–24; in inclusive
   texts and expanded transcription, 157;
   and indexing, 256; informational,
   211–32; information in, 215–17; introductory editorial notes, 223–24; preparation of, 228–29; provenance notes,
   124–25, 161–62, 201–4, 221; and selective editions, 23; source notes, 124–25,
201–4, 221, 222; supplements to,
   230–32; textual, 144, 147–55, 207–9;
   theories and rationales, 212–13
Arrangement of documents, 58–60
Association for Documentary Editing
   (ADE), 18, 21, 23
Attribution of documents, 94–96
Audience, 82, 158, 212–13, 214–15
Audio recordings, transcribing, 131–32
Authentication of documents, 94–96
Authorial symbols, 108–10, 149–50, 161

Back matter, 245–50
Bartram, John, edition, 257
Berger, Victor and Meta, edition, 115
*Billy Budd* (Herman Melville), 7, 152,
   155, 178–79
Biographical directories, 230, 249
Blake, William, edition, 108, 171
Book editions. *See* Print editions
Bowers, Fredson: and annotation, 154;
   and choice of copy-text, 21; and genetic texts, 182; and *Leaves of Grass*,
   7, 155; *Principles of Bibliographical
   Description*, 45, 108; on problems of
   multiple copies, 98
Boyd, Julian P., 15, 18; and annotation,
   220, 221; and arrangement of documents, 84; and coded text, 119; on
   correction of Jefferson's spelling, 176;
   criticism of, 12; database used by, 34;
   and editorial symbols, 147; and expanded transcription, 172; and facsimiles, 142; and indexes, 253; and manuscript cataloging, 5–6; and nonverbal

Boyd, Julian P. (*continued*)
documents, 109; plan for comprehensive publication, 72–73; and shorthand, 116; and silent emendation, 162–63, 164
Burr, Aaron, edition, 78, 79, 85, 95
Business records, transcribing, 125
Butterfield, Lyman, 15, 18, 218; on document control, 35; and editorial symbols, 147; and expanded transcription, 172; and indexes, 254–55; on integration of diaries and journals within other papers, 89; and manuscript cataloging, 5–6; and silent emendation, 162–63, 164

Calendars, 249; and audience's needs, 82; facsimile supplements and, 75; historical editions and, 73–74; in Jefferson Papers, 72–73; literary editions and, 73, 74, 80; and possible distortion of collections, 81; selective editions and, 23; in Webster edition, 86
Calhoun, John C., edition, 6, 73, 81, 153
Cancellations: in clear text, 167; conventions of treating, 148; in diplomatic transcription, 155; in expanded transcription, 163; in facsimiles, 142; in inclusive texts, 160; and standardization, 140
Capitalization, 104, 120
Carbon copies, 98, 106
Cataloging of documents, 56–62
CD-ROMs, 76, 79, 171, 241–42
Center for Editions of American Authors (CEAA), 17, 19, 163; and clear text, 166; and distinction between literary and historical editing, 10; editing principles attacked, 12–14; editions given seal of, 19–20; and facsimile supplements, 80; and inclusive texts, 157, 158–59; list of authors to be published, 7–8; and mechanical collation, 237; and organization of editions, 87; and proofreading, 205; and selective editions, 23; and silent emendation, 140; standards for editions, 9–10, 15; *Statement of Editorial Principles and Procedures*, 17, 158. *See also* Committee for Scholarly Editions
Child, Lydia Maria, edition, 76
Chronologies, 231–32

CINDEX (indexing system), 24, 254
Ciphers, 118–20
Citation of sources, 225–28
Clay, Henry, edition, 6, 73, 81
Clear text, 166–71; CSE/CEAA and, 9, 123, 166; and evolution of documentary editing, 22; and fragmentary source texts, 188–89; and front and back matter, 246; and genetic texts, 182; and literary editions, 11
Clemens, Samuel. *See* Twain, Mark
Coded communications, 118–20
Coleridge, Samuel Taylor, edition, 186
Collaborative source texts, 180–82
Collation, machine, 205, 237, 238
Collation, visual, 204–7
Collection, document, 38–56
Committee for Scholarly Editions (CSE), 101, 107, 108, 164; and back-of-book textual record, 208; and clear text, 9, 123, 166; creation of, 19–20; and facsimile supplements, 80; "Guidelines for Scholarly Editions," 250; and inclusive texts, 157, 158–59, 160; inspections, 250–51; and lists of omitted documents, 231; and machine collation, 205; and organization of editions, 87; and proofreading, 205, 206, 252; and publication of diaries and journals, 128; rules for documentary editions, 15–16; and selective editions, 23; and silent emendation, 140; and statement of textual method, 246–47; and transcription of nonverbal documents, 108; transcription requirements, 199. *See also* Center for Editions of American Authors
Complimentary closes, 124, 160
Comprehensive editions, 71–84
Computers: and annotation, 228, 229; and copyright, 249; and creation of facsimiles, 142; and documentary editing, 24–26, 33–34, 90–91; and document control, 35–38, 62–65, 200; and indexing, 253–54; and mechanical collation, 205; and production of print editions, 236–40; and proofreading, 209; and supplements, 80; and texts, 209; and transcription, 198, 207. *See also* Electronic editions; Internet
Conflation, 188–92
Contents, table of, 230, 249

Contractions, 104, 142, 151, 155, 158, 161

Control, documentary, 34–38, 56–65

Control files, 60–62, 63–65, 90

Conventions of textual treatment, 136–72

Cooper, James Fenimore, edition, 89, 222

Copyright, 249–50

Correspondence: CEAA requirements for editions of, 9–10; choosing source text for, 97–100; missing or no longer extant, 72–73; transcribing, 122–25

Darwin, Charles, edition, 126, 186, 213

Databases: and document control, 34–38, 90; and transcription, 198

Datelines, 124, 142, 155, 157, 160, 161–62

*David Humphreys' 'Life of General Washington' with George Washington's 'Remarks,'* 185

Davis, Jefferson, edition, 74, 220

Davy, Sir Humphry, edition, 124

Deletions. *See* Cancellations

Desktop publishing, 239–40

Dewey, John, edition, 19, 20, 87

DIALOG, 39

Diaries and journals: CEAA requirements for editions of, 9–10; in inclusive texts and expanded transcription, 157; publication of, 89–90; transcribing, 127–29

*Diplomatic Correspondence of the American Revolution* (Jared Sparks), 4

Diplomatic transcription, 15, 155–57

Directories, biographical, 230, 249

Documentary editions: computers and, 24–26, 90–91; defining and organizing, 70–91; history of, 1–26; initiating a project, 33–65; literary vs. historical, 10–11; selective vs. comprehensive, 71–84. *See also* Electronic editions; Microforms; Print editions

Documentary history, 85

*Documentary History of the First Federal Congress,* 85, 180

*Documentary History of the First Federal Elections,* 85

*Documentary History of the Ratification of the Constitution,* 76, 85, 175, 179–80, 225

*Documentary History of the Supreme Court,* 143–44

Documents: accessioning, 57–58; authentication and attribution, 94–96; cataloging, 56–62; collecting, 38–56; controlling, 34–38, 56–62, 62–65; conventions of treatment, 136–72; labeling and arranging, 58–60; with multiple authors, 180–82; multiple-text, 183–88; mutilated, 189; nonverbal, 108–11, 214; omitted, lists of, 231, 249; printed, 44–46, 99, 100–102, 107–8, 143; privately held, 46–48, 54–56; searching for, 41–48. *See also* Handwritten documents; Oral documents; Typewritten documents

*Documents Relative to the Slave Trade in America,* 5

Douglass, Frederick, edition, 45–46, 129–30, 190–92

Drawings, 108–10, 214

Drinker, Elizabeth, edition, 213–14

Edison, Thomas A., edition: and annotation, 224, 228; and computers, 36, 38, 90–91; and document control, 56; microform index, 78; and nonverbal documents, 110; organization, 86

*Editing Documents and Texts: An Annotated Bibliography* (Beth Luey), 21, 26–27, 254

*Editing Historical Documents: A Handbook of Practice* (Steven Burg and Michael E. Stevens), 21, 244, 254

"Editing of Historical Documents" (G. Thomas Tanselle), 17–19

Editorial insertions. *See* Additions, editorial

Editorial notes, 223–24

Editorial policy, statement of, 246–47

Editorial symbols. *See* Symbols, editorial

Editorial texts, 204–7

Edwards, Jonathan, edition, 130, 182

Einstein, Albert, edition: and annotation, 228; and facsimiles, 141; and foreign-language sources, 112–13; and journals, 90; and nonverbal documents, 110; organization, 86, 87

Eisenhower, Dwight D., edition: and annotation, 224, 226; and attribution of works, 95–96; and carbon copies, 106; and multiauthor works, 182; and selectivity, 81; statement of editorial policy, 247; and telegrams, 121–22

Electronic editions: as supplements to print editions, 75–76, 78–79; and facsimiles, 23; and front and back matter, 246; and genetic texts, 182–83; production of, 241–43; standards for, 243; and textual treatment, 171–72. *See also* Computers; Documentary editions; Internet

Electronic records, transcribing, 132–33

Emendation: CEAA/CSE rules for, 15; in clear text, 166, 169; conservative patterns of, 174–77; in diplomatic transcription, 155; of editions of correspondence, 123; in expanded transcription, 157–58; in inclusive texts, 157–58, 160–61; nonauthorial, 186–88; and nonstandard English, 175–77; principles of, 140; of sermons, 177; of shorthand, 117. *See also* Overt emendation; Silent emendation

Emerson, Ralph Waldo, edition, 7, 8; and annotation, 223; and editorial symbols, 12–13, 16, 108, 147; as inclusive text, 159; and nonverbal documents, 109; and sermons, 177; techniques used by, 192

Enclosures, 203

Endorsements, 124, 139

English, nonstandard, 175–77

Expanded transcription, 18, 123, 157–58, 161–64, 172

*Extracts from the Gospels* (Thomas Jefferson), 141, 189–90

Facsimile editions, 23, 75–79, 79–80, 141–44

Files, control, 60–62, 63–65, 90

Financial records, transcribing, 125

Finding aids, microform, 240

Footnotes, 221–23. *See also* Annotation

Foreign-language sources, 112–16

Forgeries, 94

Fragmentary source texts, 188–90

Franklin, Benjamin, 162

Franklin, Benjamin, edition, 6; and annotation, 153, 222, 223; and attribution of works, 95; changing editorial policy, 74, 175; comprehensiveness, 73, 74; and document control, 56; and nonverbal documents, 109

Frederic, Harold, edition, 143, 159, 166, 203

Freedom: A Documentary History of Emancipation, 85, 223

Front matter, 245–50

Gaps, in source text, 148–49

Garrison, William Lloyd, edition, 81

Garvey, Marcus, edition, 39, 225

Gazetteers, 231, 249

Genealogical tables, 230–31

Genetic texts, 178–83

Glossaries, 231, 249

Gompers, Samuel, edition, 36–37

Government records, transcribing, 126–27

Grant, Ulysses S., edition, 74, 163–64

Greene, Nathanael, edition, 214

Greg, Walter W., 2, 8–9, 15, 21, 147

Hamilton, Alexander, edition, 4, 6, 73, 85, 143, 247

Handwritten documents, 96–100, 104–5, 139–40

Harrison, William Henry, edition, 71, 195

Hawthorne, Julian, 187

Hawthorne, Nathaniel, edition, 7, 8; and annotation, 154, 223; and authorial symbols, 108; censorship, 186–87; and clear text, 17, 166; index, 256

Hawthorne, Sophia Peabody, 186–87

Headings within documents, 142, 155, 157

Headnotes, 222–23, 226–27

Henry, Joseph, edition, 35–36, 63, 86, 109–10, 223

Historical editions: compared with literary editions, 10–11, 17–20, 21; comprehensiveness, 72–73; and computers, 24; and conventions of textual treatment, 137; critical reception, 11–12; organization, 73–74

*History of the Works of Redemption* (Jonathan Edwards), 130, 182

Howells, William Dean, edition, 8, 214; changing editorial policy, 175; and clear text, 20, 166; and source notes, 203; and textual records, 209

Humphreys, David, 185

Hyphenation, 158–59, 208, 238, 249, 252

Inclusive texts, 157–61

Indexes, 252–58; and annotation, 256; computers and, 90–91; of control files, 63–65; designing, 254–58; electronic, 78; Madison edition and, 248; microform, 77–78, 240

Insertions. *See* Additions, authorial; Interlineations

Inspections, CSE, 250–51

Interlineations, 115, 142, 148, 149, 152, 155, 160, 161–62, 163

Internet, 76, 78, 171, 242–43. *See also* Computers; Electronic editions

Interpolations, editorial. *See* Additions, editorial

Interviews, transcribing, 131

Introduction, editorial, 230

Introductory editorial notes, 223–24, 226–27

Irving, Washington, edition, 8, 15, 159, 222

Jackson, Andrew, edition, 188

James, William, edition, 20, 154

Jay, John, edition, 4, 119–20, 224

Jefferson, Thomas, 176

Jefferson, Thomas, edition, 8, 11, 12, 17, 162, 163; and annotation, 220, 221–22; and coded text, 119; and conflation of texts, 189–90; and copying of letters, 98; and editorial symbols, 147; and expanded transcription, 164; and facsimiles, 141, 142; index, 253, 255; manuscript collection and cataloging, 5–6; microfilm supplement, 164; and nonverbal documents, 109; plan for comprehensive publication, 72–73; and shorthand, 116; and topical arrangement of documents, 84

Johnson, Andrew, edition, 80, 226, 231–32, 256

Jones, John Paul, edition, 79, 195

Journals. *See* Diaries and journals

Joyce, James, edition, 22, 179, 180

King, Martin Luther, Jr., edition, 131, 232

Labeling of documents, 58–60

Lafayette, Marquis de, edition, 112, 114, 130, 184

Latrobe, Benjamin Henry, edition, 76, 77, 78, 109, 214

Laurens, Henry, edition, 74, 107, 175

*Leaves of Grass* (Walt Whitman), 7, 154, 155, 182

Leisler, Jacob, edition, 113

Letterbooks, 97–98

Letterpress copies, 98

Letters. *See* Correspondence

*Letters of Delegates of Congress,* 255

*Letters of Members of the Continental Congress, The,* 5

Lewis and Clark edition, 111

Libraries, location symbols for, 40

Lincoln, Abraham, edition, 38, 79, 85, 241

Line breaks in source text, 142, 151

Lists of omitted documents, 231, 249

Literal transcription, 18, 109

Literary editions: and annotation, 203, 223; and calendars, 73, 74, 80; and choice of source text, 100–102; compared with historical editions, 10–11, 17–20, 21; comprehensiveness, 73; and computers, 24; conventions of textual treatment, 136–37; and inclusive texts, 158–61; lack of facsimile supplements, 79–80; Shaw's evaluation of, 17

Machine collation, 205, 237, 238

Madison, James, 180

Madison, James, edition, 6, 17; and annotation, 220, 222; and coded text, 119; comprehensiveness, 73; index, 248, 256; and Madison's changes to his documents, 184; organization, 89; and statements mistakenly attributed to Madison, 95

Manuscripts. *See* Documents; Handwritten documents

Maps, 110–11, 231

Marginalia, 142, 185–86

Marshall, George C., edition, 81, 95–96, 121–22, 220, 224

Marshall, John C., edition, 73, 85–86, 222, 257

Mechanical collation, 205, 237, 238

Melville, Herman, edition, 7, 8, 152, 155, 178–79

Microforms: for Adams and Jefferson editions, 164; encouraged by NHPRC, 6–7; and expanded transcription, 172; and facsimiles, 23, 141; and genetic texts, 182; indexes to, 77–78, 253; publication of, 240; as supplements to print editions, 10, 75–78; for Webster edition, 86. *See also* Documentary editions

Missing documents, 111
Modern Language Association, 7, 13, 15–17. *See also* Center for Editions of American Authors; Committee for Scholarly Editions
Morris, Gouverneur, edition, 94
Morris, Robert, edition, 74, 89
Multiauthor documents, 180–82
Multiple-text documents, 183–88
Mumford, Lewis, 12–14, 15, 147
Mutilated documents, 189

National Endowment for the Humanities (NEH), 7–8, 10, 13, 18, 23, 250
National Historical Publications and Records Commission (NHPRC), 6, 8, 17, 23, 42, 141; and electronic editions, 24; and literary and historical editing, 10, 18; and microform editions, 6–7, 76; surveys users of documentary editions, 72; and transcription of nonverbal documents, 108. *See also* National Historical Publications Commission
National Historical Publications Commission (NHPC), 5, 6, 14–15. *See also* National Historical Publications and Records Commission

Newspapers, 45, 102
Nonauthorial emendation, 186–88
Noncritical editing. *See* Documentary editing
Nonstandard English, 175–77
Nonverbal elements and documents, 108–11, 214
Norris, Frank, edition, 229
Notes. *See* Annotation
Omissions of text, 151, 161
Oral documents, 129–32, 177, 190–92
Organization of documentary editions, 70–91
Overt emendation, 140, 160. *See also* Emendation

Page breaks, 142
Pamphlets, 107–8
Paragraphing, 139, 155, 157, 160, 161
Peale, Charles Willson, edition, 76, 109
Periodicals, 45
Photocopies, 5, 48–51

Photographic facsimiles. *See* Facsimile editions
Pictures, 108–11, 214
Presidential Papers series (Library of Congress), 77, 164
Print editions: and facsimiles, 142; organization of, 58–60, 84–90; publication of, 236–40; supplements to, 75–80. *See also* Documentary editions
Printed sources, 44–46, 99, 100–102, 107–8, 143
Private writings, 15–17, 166–67. *See also* Correspondence; Diaries and journals
Professional records, transcribing, 125–26
Proofreading: computers and, 24, 209; CSE and, 250; during production of edition, 251–52; methods of, 204, 205–7; of microform editions, 240; of print editions, 237–38
Provenance notes, 124–25, 161–62, 201–4, 221, 222
Published sources, 127, 166. *See also* Literary editions; Printed sources
Publishers, 243–44
Publishing, desktop, 239–40
Punctuation: and coded text, 120; in diplomatic transcription, 155; and documents by poorly educated people, 176; in expanded transcription, 158; and facsimiles, 142; in handwritten sources, 104; in inclusive texts, 158, 160, 161; in transcription of journals, 127; in transcription of unlocated originals, 111

Recordings, sound, transcribing, 131–32
Records, transcribing: business and financial, 125; electronic, 132–33; government, 126–27; oral, 129–32; professional and technical, 125–26
Rush, Benjamin, edition, 5, 6, 11, 162, 163; and annotation, 218; and editorial symbols, 147

Salutations, 124, 142, 155, 160, 161–62
Scope of documentary editions, 71–84
Selective editions, 23, 71–84
Sermons, 129–32, 177
Shelley, Mary, edition, 196–97

*Shelley and His Circle,* 22, 142, 155, 177, 193
Shorthand, 107, 116–17, 127–28, 161
Silent emendation: Boyd and Butterfield's patterns of, 162–63; in CEAA/CSE editions, 15, 140; and editions of correspondence, 123; in expanded transcription, 157–58; in inclusive texts, 157–58, 160–61. *See also* Emendation
Sound recordings, 131–32
Source notes, 124–25, 161–62, 201–4, 221, 222
Source texts: collaborative, 180–82; fragmentary, 188–90; gaps in, 148–49; handwritten, 104–5; in inclusive texts, 161; nonverbal, 108–11; printed, 107–8; selecting, 93, 96–102; transcribing, 102–11, 122–33; transcriptions as, 111; translating, 111–22; typewritten, 105–6
Sparks, Jared, 4, 94, 184, 187
Speeches, 129–32, 190–92
Spelling, 104, 127, 142, 176
Standardization: in diplomatic transcription, 155; in editions of correspondence, 123–24; in expanded transcription, 157–58, 161–62; of handwriting, 104–5; in inclusive texts, 157–58, 160; principles of, 139–40; in transcription of journals, 127–28
Statement of editorial policy, 246–47
*State Records of South Carolina,* 126, 257
Stevens, Thaddeus, edition, 192
Subscripts, 105
Sumner, Charles, edition, 230
Superscripts, 105, 158
Supplements, 75–80
Symbols, authorial, 108–10, 149–50, 161
Symbols, editorial: in expanded transcription, 157; explained in front matter, 247–49; history of use of, 6, 144, 147; in inclusive texts, 157, 161; rules for using, 152–53; texts requiring, 144, 147–55
Synoptic genetic texts, 179–80

Table of contents, 230, 249
Tables, genealogical, 230–31
Tables, transcribing, 125

Tanselle, G. Thomas, 17–19, 22, 44, 45, 132, 174–75
Tapes, transcribing, 131–32
Targets (for microform editions), 77
Taylor, Charles and Barbara, edition, 230
Technical records, transcribing, 125–26
Telegrams, 120–22
*Territorial Papers, The,* 5
Text, clear. *See* Clear text
Texts: and computers, 209; editorial, 204–7; final establishment of, 251–52; genetic, 178–83; inclusive, 157–61; requiring symbols or annotation, 144, 147–55
Textual notes, 207–9
Thoreau, Henry David, edition, 8; and annotation, 155, 223; and clear text, 166–67; and hyphenation, 208; and multiple-text documents, 183
Transcription: of business and financial records, 125; clear text, 166–71; conventions of, 136–72; of correspondence, 122–25; diplomatic, 15, 155–57; of electronic records, 132–33; expanded, 157–58, 161–64; explained in statement of editorial policy, 246–47; of foreign-language sources, 113–14; forms and control, 199–201; of government records, 126–27; of handwritten materials, 104–5; of journals and diaries, 127–29; literal, 18, 109; of printed materials, 107–8; procedures, 102–11, 122–33, 195–201; of professional and technical records, 125–26; of published works, 127; of records of oral communications, 129–32; of shorthand, 116–17; of sound recordings, 131–32; of typewritten documents, 105–6
Transcriptions: filing, 201; as source texts, 99, 111; as working copy, 204–9
Translation, 111–22; of codes and ciphers, 118–20; of foreign-language sources, 112–16; policies for, 114–15; of shorthand, 116–17; of telegrams, 120–22
Twain, Mark, edition, 7, 8; and annotation, 222; and catalog of Clemens correspondence, 80; changing editorial policy, 175; as inclusive text, 159–60; and mutilated manuscripts, 189;

Twain, Mark, edition (*continued*)
organization, 84; selection criteria, 74;
and source notes, 203; and textual
records, 17, 209; and Twain's conventions, 108, 197
Typewritten documents, 96–100, 105–6
Typographic facsimiles. *See* Facsimile
editions

*Ulysses* (James Joyce), 22, 179, 180
Underlining, 149, 161–62

Variorum editions, 5, 12
Verification, 205
Versioning, 192–93
Visual collation, 204–7

Walpole, Horace, edition, 84
Washington, Booker T., edition, 225
Washington, George, 98
Washington, George, edition: comprehensiveness, 73; and foreign-language
sources, 115–16; and maps, 231; organization, 88–89; Sparks' edition, 4, 5,
94, 187; and Washington's changes to
his documents, 184–85
Webster, Daniel, edition: and annotation, 224, 225; index, 257; organization, 86; and selectivity, 83; and topical arrangement of documents, 84, 85
Whitman, Walt, edition, 7, 8, 154,
155, 182
Whittier, John Greenleaf, edition, 82–83
Wilson, Woodrow, edition: and annotation, 225, 232; and carbon copies, 106;
changing editorial policy, 175; and
facsimiles, 143; and foreign-language
sources, 112; and oral communications,
190–91; and selectivity, 82; and shorthand, 107, 116–17; statement of editorial policy, 247; table of contents, 230
Women, writings of, 177, 213–14
Wordsworth, William, edition, 142
Writings, private, 15–17, 166–67. *See
also* Correspondence; Diaries and
journals